What Shall We Wear to This Party?

Also by Sloan Wilson

Voyage to Somewhere
The Man in the Gray Flannel Suit
A Summer Place
A Sense of Values
Georgie Winthrop
Janus Island
Away From It All
All the Best People

What
Shall We Wear
to This Party?

The Man in the Gray Flannel Suit
Twenty Years Before & After

Sloan Wilson

ARBOR HOUSE

New York

To Betty, my wife, and Jessica Ruth
The start, the end, and the middle of truth.
                              S.W.

Contents

Prologue

There are at least two good reasons for writing about one's life and times: (1) because, like a former President of the United States or a famous general, one has led a life which almost everyone wants to hear about; and (2) because one belongs to a group of people, such as doctors, astronauts or prostitutes, which in itself has some interest.

Seeing that I am neither a general nor a former President, I am writing my story because I am a member of that great fraternity of the men in gray flannel suits. This ununionized body of men, of course, existed long before I wrote a novel about them in that long-ago year, 1955. My book both publicized them and made them into a running joke which occupied comedians for years. Perhaps because of that, many a man shucked his gray flannel and bought worsted, silk, double-knit or even blue denim instead. I myself turned traitor the moment the book was published and donned brown flannel.

I was not surprised to note, however, that men in gray flannel suits retained their identity, no matter what they wore. There is a snobbish old navy saying which maintains that you can take the man out of the forecastle but you cannot take the forecastle out of the man. So it is with gray flannel. Leave him naked or put him in a suit of armor, the man in the gray flannel suit tends to remain triumphantly his gray flannel self. Recently I have been told that after a hiatus of some twenty years, the gray flannel suits themselves are coming back in fashion. To my astonishment, I find that a few college boys are wearing them. What college boys wear, of course, is no business of mine, but in my heart I know that a sophomore or even a senior in a gray flannel suit is impersonating an officer as much as he would be if he donned an admiral's uniform. To be a *real* man in a gray flannel suit, you have to start a long while back, long before this crop of college boys was born.

Most men in gray flannel suits, as I understand them, were born long enough ago to retain some memory of the Depression. I was nine years old when the great Wall Street crash occurred, and, though I was surrounded by the cotton batting of fairly prosperous parents, I heard them talking in the night then and all through the Thirties about the possibility of banks failing and all the rest. It is possible that I think of money differently than younger people do. For example, I can remember a truck driver who gave me a lift telling me, and meaning it, that there was going to be a new American Revolution soon, and that he was going to help lead it because his family was starving. He was *working* at the time.

College was a different experience for men in gray flannel suits than it is for youngsters today. For one thing, we did not have girls living in our dormitories. Girls had to be *sneaked* into dormitories. That may seem like a superficial change, but almost everything about sex in the youth of the gray flannel men was sneaky, and that's a fact which left many of us feeling guilty. As a result we read a great many books about giving our children a proper sex education and we did not lecture our sons as sternly as our fathers had lectured us. I think my son is proud of having taken part in the sexual revolution. Until now I have not admitted that I think that I and a few loyal battalions of gray flannel men fought at least the earliest skirmishes for him.

Then, of course, there was the war, World War II. Although that great struggle sometimes seems almost forgotten now, I think it fair to say that it had the most massive effect on my whole generation, an impact which dwarfs any other educational experience to which we might have been subjected. I myself was only half aware of this until I started to write this present book. To my astonishment I found that the war, which filled only four of my fifty-five years, threatened to usurp my whole remembrance. I am no militarist and in a way was miserable from May of 1942, when I entered the service, to February of 1946, when I got out. Still, the war burned itself into my memory. Why?

I think that one reason is that I and many other young men accepted World War II as an authentic struggle between good and evil. I, for one, felt it was therefore a test of myself which had to be passed for the survival of my self-respect. Would I be brave enough to stand up under gunfire? Regardless of that, could I endure being seasick for months at a time? And even if one proved brave, could one learn all the new military skills fast enough to prove competent in battle? Or would one forever know oneself as a bumbling coward?

Maybe the youth today would reply, "I'm a lover, not a fighter," but in those old days of World War II, a guy with the medals got the girls, or at least we thought he did. And the guy with the rank really did get the girls—the phenomenon was known as RHIP (Rank Has Its Privileges). What man who styled himself a lover, not a fighter, would have had a chance in 1943 against a twenty-six-year-old air force colonel with a rainbow of campaign ribbons on his chest?

I and most of the men I knew tried to get ahead in the service. When the war was over and we were all mustered out, we were glad to get back to the long dreamed of delights of civilian life, even though it meant that whatever honors or rank we had won were shucked along with our old uniforms. The only thing we kept was our own judgment of whether we passed the great test of the war. Those who figured that they passed it rescued something of unparalleled value from the war which can never be put into words. Those who knew that they had failed soon were able to deny, I think, that any meaningful test had ever occurred, and for them, that may be right. The test was only there for those who saw it.

Once they got into civilian life, the gray flannel men did not take long vacations. The war left them, I think, with a lust for security, permanence, even luxury and prestige, though those are supposed to be bad words. They wanted everything which they had been missing for four years. They wanted to catch up to the men who for one reason or another had not gone to war. Many of these men flocked to big corporations. There their military experiences served them well. If big companies of that day insisted on a kind of uniform-of-the-day, be it gray flannel or blue pin stripe, the eager veterans donned it cheerfully. The structure of large corporations, with chains of command, assistants and assistants to assistants, was not unlike the armed forces.

Many of the men in gray flannel suits progressed fast in business life. It took them some time to learn that corporate endeavor is unlike a war in at least one important respect: there is no great cause, no titanic struggle between good and evil, nothing but a scramble for the buck.

For almost all of us the scramble for the buck, if not morally uplifting, was pressingly necessary, for there were never enough dollars to raise a family, to build the kind of house which filled our dreams—or at least those of our wives—to join the country club which declared its members first-class citizens of the suburb. Instead of being as peaceful as the men at war had dreamed, civilian life turned out to be hectic enough to spur the development of tranquilizers. As soon as one house was built, more children arrived, or a raise large enough to demand the planning of a grander house was earned. And sometimes, when that ultimately grand house was finished, the gray flannel man was transferred to another city. It wasn't always easy, even for the prosperous. And, for those who could not climb with the leaders, there often was a cruel sense of failure not unlike that suffered by men who failed the great test of the war and found their bunkmates or tentmates looking at them with condescension or contempt.

Under all this stress a lot of marriages failed. Sometimes when a man was miserable he could not get out of his head the idea that somewhere, somehow he could someday find a woman who would adore him uncritically and make him happy. Often the woman turned out to be a secretary in his office, and occasionally she actually did adore him uncritically and make him happy. The women in the suburbs had a poorer selection of men to rebuild their lives. Ditched husbands and unhappy wives conducted themselves in a way that made some writers think the suburbs were full of wildly exuberant people.

A lot of us settled down in our second marriages, finding respectability a great relief. The children grew up somehow, usually better than any psychologist could have predicted. And the men in gray flannel suits, now in their fifties, still look pretty good when you see them on the commuting trains. Some of them will still stand up to give a lady a seat, if she's pretty enough, and they will open doors for ladies when they are walking from one car to another. When called a male chauvinist pig, a man in a gray flannel suit looks confused. He is supporting a wife, a former wife, maybe a mistress and three daughters in college, in addition to his mother in a nursing home. On weekends he also does the dinner dishes. What more do women expect of him?

When I planned this book, I intended to write some sort of sociological treatise on men in gray flannel suits, but I soon discovered that my tolerance for generalizations is scant, and since I've never written a sociological treatise in my life, I'm not notably good at it. So instead of trying to tell the story of all men in gray flannel suits, I have settled for the only one I know well, my own. Since no one is really typical of anything, I make no claim to universality. Like most men, I am a universe of one, but I do have a gray flannel suit hanging in my closet, where one has hung for more than twenty years, and I shall be glad to show it to anyone who doubts my credentials.

I would like to add a few notes of warning. This is not my past as God may have recorded it, with complete objectivity, but the fifty-five years of my life as I have remembered them. I think Freud said, "Memory is art." I think he means that memory is selective and molded, sometimes twisted, by emotion. Unless one has kept a tape recorder going for a half century, however, one has nothing but memory as a guide to the past.

I'm not sure whether I remember a lot of the dialogue or made it up. Anyway, it's what I *think* we all said.

When I place a person in an unfavorable light, I change his or her name unless the person is a public figure whose fame makes the point of the story.

Like many accounts which feature one's self, this one leaves its author feeling naked—a condition which most writers learn to endure, but which is difficult for a man who is used to wearing a gray flannel suit. Now that the last pages have been typed, I intend to button up tightly.

—SLOAN WILSON
Ticonderoga, N.Y.

Part 1
"Beware of All Enterprises That Require New Clothes"

—THOREAU

1

In the summer of 1947, when I was twenty-seven years old, an old friend telephoned me with an interesting piece of information.

"I think you could get a job at *Time*," he said. "They're hiring writers and as far as I can see, you have all the qualifications."

For about two years, I knew, my friend had been working at *Time*, and ought to know what was going on there.

"How much are they paying?" I asked.

"About five grand a year to start. It won't take you long to double that if you measure up, and you can double it again if you're really any good."

At that time I was making fifty dollars a week as a reporter for the Providence *Journal* in Rhode Island, and my wife was pregnant with our second child. I had written several short pieces for *The New Yorker* and a slender novel which had sold only sixteen hundred copies. The idea of a job in New York was attractive despite the fact that among newspaper people it was considered fashionable to make fun of *Time* magazine. My father, who had been an editor of the old *Literary Digest* and a professor of journalism at New York University, had refused to have *Time* in the house. Still, no other publication I knew was offering five thousand dollars a year to beginning writers and the promise of much more.

In those days I was still young enough to think in melodramatic terms. The question obviously was whether I would sell my soul to the devil. The answer came to me unhesitatingly: yes! The devil would undoubtedly prove to be a difficult employer, but no problem he could offer would be worse than trying to raise two children on fifty dollars a week. The obstetrician's bill for our first child had not yet been paid.

"If you're interested," my friend said, "come down here Wednesday. Beth and I are giving sort of a cocktail party that night. Quite a few of the guys from the shop will be there. You can get a feel of the outfit. Bring your wife if you can. I'll try to set up some appointments for interviews Thursday."

Elise, my wife, also experienced mixed emotions when I told her about the possibility of a job with *Time*. Born in Boston, she viewed any trip outside of New England as a journey into enemy territory.

"I guess you better look into all this," she said, pausing with the scissors over her dress pattern. "But why do I have to go?"

"I hate to go to cocktail parties alone, and I think the general idea is that we are trying to impress people. I'll be the poor talented writer with his beautiful wife, who obviously would grace all company events."

"Ha! And me big as a house?"

She was four months pregnant, but did not show it much.

"You look fine," I said.

"What shall we wear to this party? We might as well be going to a whole new world."

"It doesn't matter what we wear! I'm supposed to be a writer, not a model."

"We can't go down there looking like country cousins. What kind of person is this friend of yours? Will the women wear formal cocktail dresses to his party, or is he sort of bohemian?"

"I have no idea. He said a lot of *Time* people would be there. I doubt if *Time* writers are really bohemians. I don't know what they wear."

"How about your friend? I didn't even know you had a friend at *Time*."

"Actually he's not a very close friend. I met him in Stillman Infirmary when I had pneumonia during my freshman year. He had some kind of disease that made him cough a lot, and he wanted to write. Bad lungs and literary ambitions were the only bonds we had."

"But he's kept in touch with you all these years? Is he married?"

"Yes, but I never met his wife."

"Look, do you mind if I don't go? We'll save a lot of money if I stay here—not only the rail fare, but also the price of a new dress and a sitter. We're going to need every cent we can save, because I can tell that for a project like this there's no doubt that you need a new suit."

"You can stay here if you want, but I don't need any new clothes," I replied, and was surprised by the strength of my desire to go looking for a job in my usual attire, a perfectly decent blue serge suit which had been created by snipping the lieutenant's stripes and the gold buttons from my coast guard uniform. In 1947, I had been home from the war for only about a year. My blue uniforms were almost new because I had spent the last half of the war in the Southwest Pacific, where we wore khaki and gray lightweight stuff. My altered blue uniforms felt comfortable and I was still proud enough of my military service to enjoy clinging to the garb of a line officer, even though in real life I was often treated as an apprentice seaman. A man's clothing should speak for him, I thought, and those old uniforms could represent me better than could some fancy new worsted or tweed.... I had worn some of those blue uniforms on the Greenland Patrol. If they had protected me there, maybe I could count on them in New York.

"You can't go to see the *Time* people looking like a bum," Elise said with considerable exasperation.

"I think that Thoreau wrote, 'Beware of all enterprises that require new clothes.'"

"Didn't the war require new clothes?"

"Thoreau was right. People should have been wary of it."

Her exasperation increased, but she took the best of my blue serge suits from the closet and began snipping away the frayed parts.

In New York I stayed in my mother's apartment on West 11th Street, where she had lived since the death of my father shortly before the war. My mother was sixty years old. In her younger days she had done a good deal of writing for magazines and she shared my father's less than enthusiastic opinion of *Time*.

"Why on earth do you want to work for those smart alecks?" she asked when I explained my mission.

"They pay more than anybody else and I need the money."

She made a wry face, as she often did when I mentioned money, or sex. Because of inheritances from her mother and grandmother, she had never faced real financial need. Ever since I had started to make my own way in the world she had found it difficult to understand my exaggerated concern for paying bills. The ethic of our family, however, was such that grown sons were supposed to be self-supporting. It was enforced.

"Why don't you get a job with *The New Yorker*?" my mother asked.

To me that was like asking why I didn't fly to heaven. All my life I had dreamed of working for *The New Yorker*, and my hopes had soared when I'd sold them several short pieces on a freelance basis. To my dismay I had discovered that the magazine did not hire the writers of fiction. Mostly they hired editors, and they were wise enough to know that would-be novelists were not necessarily the best candidates for that kind of job.

Because mother thought I could get *any* kind of job, it was difficult to explain all this.

"If you're going to be interviewed for a job," she said finally, "you at least ought to get yourself a new suit. I'll give you the money, or make it a loan if you want."

"No, this suit is fine," I said with stubborn pride. "Damn it, I want to be myself when I meet these people. If they're the kind of editors who turn a writer down because he shows up in an old naval uniform, I'd rather learn that early than late."

"Are you sure you don't *want* to get turned down?" mother asked.

❂   ❂   ❂

At a little after six that afternoon I took a taxi to the apartment where my friend was giving a party. I do not name my friend here because some of this story might embarrass him, and it was—after all—kind of him to call me about the possibility of a job at *Time* and help me to explore it. Inside the door of his apartment, which was a rather lavish suite on East 53rd Street, he greeted me effusively. In Harvard's Stillman Infirmary, where we had lain coughing together for more than a month, I had been at ease with him. Now I felt that somehow we came from different planets. A tall slender man, he was dressed in elegant gray flannels, a pink Brooks Brothers shirt and highly shined English cordovans. It wasn't his dress so much that seemed to set him apart, it was also his accent, which was more Harvard than it had been while we both had been at Harvard. His apartment with Persian rugs and delicate antiques made me think wryly of my house, which was furnished mainly with early American basinettes and diaper pails. His wife also made me realize that we were leading our post-Harvard lives in very different ways. To my astonishment I found that my friend had married a woman who looked old enough to be his mother. She was attractive, with a vivacious, intelligent face over a birdlike body, which made her black cocktail dress look too big. Perhaps the reason that she startled me so was that her gray hair was done in a style almost precisely like that of my mother, and like my mother, she seemed to like to take charge of me, pulling me here and there for introductions. Most of the women she introduced me to were much younger than she. They struck me as intellectual types, running to short hair, hornrimmed glasses and dresses which were in such aggressively good taste that, to me, they were not in the least sexy. My wife certainly would have had no need to worry about what to wear to this party, I thought with pride. Even in an old maternity dress, my rather regal Elise would have outshone this competition.

As at many suburban get togethers, the women at this urban party gathered near the kitchen, while the men sat in a circle of chairs at the other end of the living room. At first glance they looked like a seminar of seniors in my day, when Harvard students still dressed well. The young *Time* men looked as scholarly as if they worked for *The New York Times* or *The New Republic*. No one used *Time* jargon or spoke in the reversed sentences which I still associated with the magazine. No balding tycoons were present.

"I hear that you're thinking of joining us," a young man with a middle-aged figure said after draining his martini glass.

"I don't really know enough about *Time* to make any decisions about it."

"I've been around here for five years and I *still* don't know enough about *Time* to make decisions. If I did, I would have quit years ago."

"You don't like it?"

"Only a few writers like to work for *Time*. I was going to say that nobody does, but there are a few natural-born masochists who thrill at the very thought of the Luce whip."

"Just how is that whip used?"

Several of the *Time* men sitting nearby hastened to help the middle-aged-appearing writer answer this. To me the chorus of their complaints made surprisingly little sense. They were asked to rewrite a lot, but wasn't every writer? The senior editors were sons of bitches, but aren't all editors? Instead of expressing their own views and the truth as they saw it, they had to express the views of their superiors and the truth as *they* saw it, but wasn't that the fate of almost any newspaper reporter?

The trouble with these *Time* men, it seemed to me, was that despite their high pay, they had never really reconciled themselves to being employees. A cut above most reporters, they were almost novelists, almost playwrights, almost freelance writers, but they had not been able to cut the cord that tied them to the mother company. Like adolescents, they yearned for liberty without having the capacity for independence. And, like some adolescents, they had nothing but abuse for the parent who fed them. Although they talked eagerly about plans to leave the company, they reacted with alarm to a report that a friend had just been fired and endlessly discussed all possible reasons for that event.

When these men finally got off the subject of Time Inc., they discussed politics. There was no debate because each of these *Time* writers was a flaming liberal. They were also experts on poetry, economics and history. How could *Time* be so different from its writers?

To me it was all very confusing. Part of the evening might have been funny if the *Time* men had not been so obviously miserable. Incessantly mixing their complaints about their work and their fears of getting fired, they seemed even more troubled than men I had known during the war who were stuck for the duration aboard uncomfortable, dangerous ships.

A good many of the men, including our host, drank heavily and I had enough of the martinis to make me want to get out before I had more.

"Don't let those guys bother you," my host said as I said good-by. "We're all unwinding. Tuesdays and Wednesdays are our weekend. We've just put the magazine to bed."

"Sure."

"*Time* is the greatest company in the world if you can measure up," he continued, slurring the last few words. "Millions read *Time*. How many read your book . . . I'm sorry, what was the name of it ? . . ."

"Not quite that many. And, *Voyage to Somewhere*."

"Well, *Time* is money, as they say. Any writer who is tired of being raggedy-ass poor should come to us."

"If need is a qualification, I'm sure I'll get the job."

"I bet you will, but will you get sore if I say something personal?"

"Go ahead."

"Buy yourself a decent suit before the interview. There are stores that can fit you right away. *Time* is one place where it doesn't pay to look poor."

The next morning I determinedly ironed my trusty old navy-blue coast guard uniform in my mother's apartment and walked to 9 Rockefeller Plaza where the Time and Life Building then stood. Since I was a little early for my appointments, I walked slowly around Rockefeller Plaza. It would be fatal, I thought, to be overcome by preconceived views of *Time* while applying for a job there. Even my father's attitude toward the publication should not affect me too much. As a former editor of the *Literary Digest*—which had died by predicting that Alf Landon would beat F.D.R. in 1936—he of course had resented the lusty, brawling new infant which had proved to be the magazine of the future. The sour views of the *Time* people I had heard the previous evening were, after all, not much different from the complaints often voiced by the employees of the Providence *Journal*, but the bitterness of those at the *Journal* did not prevent them from putting out one of the best newspapers in the world. Naturally, I would be a fool to expect *Time* to be everything I wanted it to be, but if I were man enough to say what I thought at the office, instead of saving it for cocktail parties, I might eventually find some niche in which I could be myself.

Despite these thoughts, I felt frightened as the time for my first appointment neared and I headed toward the revolving doors at 9 Rockefeller Plaza. Suddenly I was aware that the building I was to enter was extremely tall, maybe seven or eight hundred feet. Time Inc. was a giant about to swallow me. The revolving doors and the doors of the elevator inside were colored gold. The lobby looked more like that of a bank than of a publishing company. The women I saw in the elevator and in the personnel department were all glossily beautiful and fashionably dressed, like, as I imagined them, expensive call-girls. The halls were thickly carpeted, and the men who strode them looked to me like field generals hurrying to battle, despite their suits of somber grays.

My first appointment, as I remember it, was with a personnel man named Dudley Darling—the last name was Darling, anyway. I wondered what they would call him if he were an enlisted man in the coast guard. . . . Get out that bow line, Darling! Oh, come on, I told myself, this is no time to be a smart ass.

He was a tall, handsome man with the professional charm of an undertaker. As I filled out the forms he gave me, it occurred to me that on paper I looked like a better candidate for a job than I did in person. On paper I offered Mr. Luce: Harvard, a fairly good military record, two years on a good newspaper, a novel published to fair reviews, if poor sales; a half dozen pieces run by *The New Yorker* and other magazines.

When Darling looked up from the forms, however, he saw a bulky man in a rather strange looking blue serge suit who was so unaccountably tense that he couldn't sit still and who kept scratching his face nervously.

"Do you have any of the letters of recommendation I mentioned over the telephone?" Darling asked.

At my friend's request, he had telephoned me in Rhode Island. The business of letters of recommendation had always embarrassed me. Immediately after the war few people in civilian life knew me, and I did not yet want to tell my superiors on the Providence *Journal* that I was looking for a new job. The important thing, I felt, was to get letters from people with some sort of prestige. The only men of this sort whom I knew were Harvard professors whom I had met as an undergraduate. One of them, Paul J. Sachs, whose daughter had married my wife's older brother, had responded nobly, mostly because he believed that all young writers or artists of any sort deserved all the help they could get. Paul Sachs, who was the head of the Harvard Fine Arts Department, a famous art collector and a member of the family which founded the banking firm of Goldman Sachs, was a big name if there ever was one, and I saw Mr. Darling's face light up as he read the letter I handed to him. A note from Paul Sachs, I figured, was worth more at Time Inc. than my entire military career.

"That's a very fine letter," Mr. Darling said, glancing at his watch. "Mr. Fixx will see you now. He's in charge of hiring writers."

Mr. Fixx! To go to Mr. Fixx's office, Mr. Darling led me through more lushly carpeted corridors. Perhaps because I was so tense, my mind kept playing tricks with the odd names of the men I was meeting.

Calvin Fixx inspected one of the forms I had filled out for Mr. Darling. For what seemed a long while he studied it. He was a lean man with a pale, narrow face, a friend of Whittaker Chambers—the man who was to accuse Alger Hiss of espionage—I later learned, and a student of the murky depths of Communism. And, even before knowing this, I thought he looked a little like a character from a Russian novel.

"You seem to have good qualifications," he said in a soft voice.

"Thank you."

He stared at me with large, luminous eyes.

"My job is to hire writers," he almost whispered. "It's an odd sort of job. How would you go about it?"

"I think I'd look at their fingers," I said, feeling quite clever.

"Their fingers?"

"I have calluses on my fingers. From typing a lot. I wouldn't hire a man without calluses."

"With that test I'm afraid we'd end up with an awful lot of secretaries."

I gave an uneasy laugh.

"Why do you want to work here?"

It somehow seemed inappropriate to blurt out that I just wanted to make a lot of money. I heard myself stammering something about liking the company, which somehow seemed less of a lie than saying I liked their magazines. "I want to write," I concluded. "I think that the training here might do me good."

"Let's see how you write," he replied. "In the next room a girl will give you some paper and a typewriter. I want to see what kind of an auto-biographical sketch you can write for me in an hour."

The room in which the girl with the paper was waiting for me was a small cubicle, entirely empty except for a table, a chair and a typewriter, all made of gray metal. The girl, who handed me the paper as solemnly as though it were a gun with which to shoot myself, did not answer my smile. She turned and walked out the door, shutting it quickly behind her as though she were afraid I might escape.

An autobiographical sketch! What kind of nonsense was this?

Obviously I should cough up a fast piece of self-promotion, closely geared to Time Inc. . . .

"My first memory is of the mailman delivering our eagerly awaited copy of *Time* magazine, and the whole family gathering to read it aloud.

"In 1943, I was given command of the United States Coast Guard Cutter *Nogak*, which then was on the Greenland Patrol. The best part of this new responsibility was that I could make sure that the entire crew got the overseas editions of *Time*.

"My father was one of the men who founded the School of Journalism at New York University. He was also a poet and a novelist, not a great success, but a working lover of the English language. He would not allow a copy of *Time* in the house. The only other magazine he would not let me read was *Captain Billy's Whiz Bang*, which specialized in dirty jokes. I've been curious about both magazines ever since. . . ."

Why not just write that and take the train back to Providence?

Money, unpaid bills, the hope of entering the "big time," however confusing, came the honest if less than inspiring answer.

Years later I used this scene in fiction. In *The Man in the Gray Flannel Suit* I had the protagonist write that he would be glad to give any information relevant to his application for work but that he did not feel it appropriate to attempt an autobiography as part of the process of getting a job.

This, however, as I'd already admonished myself, was real-life. Glancing at my watch, I saw that ten minutes had already vanished.

"I was born on May 8, 1920, in a remodeled farmhouse which, I was told, straddled the town line dividing New Canaan and Norwalk, Connecticut," I began.

2

Before long I learned that it was a handy circumstance to be straddling such diverse communities as New Canaan and Norwalk. At that time New Canaan was, as it is now, a fashionable suburb, while Norwalk was a small industrial city with a good harbor much used by commercial fishermen. Some of the tough street kids from Norwalk made fun of the effete youths from New Canaan, while some of the New Canaan boys looked down their noses at Norwalk and everybody in it. I soon formed the habit of saying I came from Norwalk when I was with the Norwalk boys, but when my parents took me to the New Canaan Country Club, I told the children there that I came from New Canaan. The happy geographical accident of my birthplace allowed me to lie and tell the truth at the same time, a great asset for anyone who hopes to grow up to be a writer.

The reason I assumed I would be a writer as soon as I could think at all was not any great sense of hidden talent, nor any desire to rebel against conservative parents. The fact was that both my parents were writers and talked about writing all the time. Of course I had no idea of what it really meant to be a writer, but just as the puppies of our cocker spaniel turned out to be dogs, it seemed natural for me to expect to be a writer, even though most of the writers who came to parties at our house frankly seemed kind of dull.

My early youth was happy in an unconventional way, partly because both my parents were too busy to bother much with me. My mother, Ruth Danenhower Wilson, was a strong advocate of women's liberation almost half a century before the phrase was invented and spent most of her time during my infancy writing articles for *Scribner's Magazine* and a book entitled *Giving Your Child the Best Chance*. My father, Albert F. Wilson, commuted to the city, where he was a professor of journalism at New York University, and spent much of his time at home writing poetry, some of which was published in good magazines. I was brought up mostly by a Scottish nursemaid named Annie, whose last name I forget but whose smiling face and warm hugs I remember with gratitude. Most of my time was spent in the kitchen with Annie and a variety of Irish servants who came and went. When I began to talk, my mother was shocked to find that I had a pronounced Scottish burr which lapsed sometimes into Irish brogue, but never into Connecticut English.

I always respected my mother because she obviously was more authoritative than other ladies, but she was difficult to love in those early years because I rarely saw her—except when her duties as a mother required her to do something unpleasant to me. In those days most experts on child care recommended strict discipline and a precise schedule for feeding and everything else. Frequent doses of castor oil were regarded as a natural part of childhood. I screamed and fought so when a spoon of this dreadful liquid neared my lips that gentle Annie refused to give it to me. Mother was called from her desk, and in the sincere belief that she was helping my character as well as my body, would brook no nonsense from me. If I did not swallow the castor oil as soon as it was offered, she held my nose with her left hand, and jammed the hated stuff down my throat when I gasped for breath. Sometimes I succeeded in knocking the spoon from her hand several times before she accomplished this difficult feat and covered both of us with the nauseous substance, but Mother never gave up when a question of doing something-for-my-own-good was at stake.

When I was about five years old, Mother's devotion to duty resulted in an accident which gave me severe pain for a few minutes and a chance to boast the rest of my life about having had a traumatic experience on which all my weaknesses could forever be blamed. The family doctor had ordered that I take a brown tonic called rhubarb of soda. I did not like the stuff, and Mother had to resort to her usual heroic measures to make me swallow it. One morning she took a bottle of iodine from the medicine closet by mistake. The poison burned my lips and throat, but when I thrashed around Mother did not see anything particularly unusual in my behavior and forced two tablespoons of the fiery liquid down my throat. Noticing that the liquid left an odd brown stain around my lips, she finally looked at the label on the bottle and screamed. Fortunately my father was at home. He came running from his study. I can still remember everyone screaming while he poured raw eggs and a bottle of heavy cream down my throat to make me vomit. By the time the doctor arrived, the pain had gone and I was asleep in Annie's arms. Afterward my family treated this episode as a joke because it was the only mistake anyone had ever seen my mother make; but neither she nor I ever really saw anything funny in it. That accident left her feeling guilty and me feeling more than a little wary of her for a long time.

In that era many families thought it best to protect children from worry by keeping any problems concerning health or money secret. As did a great many youngsters, I grew up like a prisoner of war, trying to peer through veils of censorship by piecing together hints and parts of conversations I was not supposed to hear. Like experienced prisoners, children soon get very good at this sort of thing. No one ever told me that my father suffered several heart attacks during the first years of my life and that he lived in fear of sudden death. My older sister and I somehow always knew it and also agreed that it was too terrible a fact ever to be discussed, even between us children, until we were much older. It also did not take us long to deduce the fact that we were mysteriously rich, that the money somehow came from our mother, not our father, and that it was the subject of a great deal of concern.

"I think you should take some of your money out of bonds and put it into stocks," I once heard my father say to my mother. I of course had no idea of the nature of either stocks or bonds, but the phrase "your money" hit me hard. The only explanation I could figure out was that Mother was somehow better at her work than Dad was, and this made me feel sorry for my father. They talked about money quite a lot as the stock market went up and down, and there was never any question about whose money it was.

When I was about five or six years old, my father's health deteriorated to the point where doctors advised him to retire and spend his winters in Florida. He was only about forty years old, a handsome man whose appearance and manner gave no hint of ill health. My sister and I were told nothing about the reason for moving to Florida, except that it never got cold there and we could eat oranges from our own trees. Our mother had recently presented us with a new brother, and she seemed very tired and worried. She kept saying that in Florida Dad would get time to write the novel he had long planned, but neither of them seemed to look forward to this prospect much.

I do not remember whether it was the first time we went to Florida or one of the times soon after that when my mother's grandmother, who was then in her eighties, decided to accompany us. My great-grandmother Sloan's husband had long been dead, but he had been a successful businessman in the small city of Oswego, N.Y., where he had had a lot to do with building railroads. She retained some of his prerogatives, and usually traveled in a private railroad car. My family shared this conveyance with her. The trip to Florida then took two days and a night. When I got bored I saw nothing wrong in asking the Pullman porter to make up some extra bunks for my teddy bears and my sister's dolls. He looked at me rather oddly, but did the job. After tucking our toys under clean sheets, my sister and I followed our parents to the diner, which was several cars ahead. We had to walk through some day coaches aboard which people were trying to sleep sitting up. My sister, who was three years older than I, asked my mother why we didn't invite a few of these weary men and women, some of whom had children with them, to share the extra bunks in our private car.

"Then it wouldn't be a private car," my mother replied. "It's a nice thought, dear, but your grandmother needs privacy. At her age I think she deserves it, don't you?"

Frankly I didn't think the old lady deserved any such thing. Everyone kept telling me what a wonderful old lady she was and what a beautiful, gracious woman she had been, but great-grandmother Sloan looked to me like a witch, and she called me "Bobbie" all the time. My mother had explained this by telling me the old lady thought I was her son, who had long been dead. The fact that my great-grandmother thought I was a dead boy seemed fairly spooky to me, and I stayed away from her as much as possible.

"God, the old bitch must be rich," I heard one Pullman porter say to another while explaining that ours was a private car.

A lot of things suddenly came together in my mind. Because of money, not just because of courtesy toward the aged, everyone obeyed this old, old lady's orders—despite the fact that she was barely strong enough to wave her cane, and so far from intelligent that she couldn't distinguish me from her dead son. Money must be a strange and mysterious thing. Among other things, it was invisible, for little could be hidden on the old lady's frail body, and she hardly ever carried a purse with her. Yet how quickly her strong young chauffeur leapt to his feet at her mumbled commands!

"Is great-grandmother Sloan really very rich?" I finally asked my father.

"Compared to most people she certainly is," he replied.

"Where does she keep her money?"

"In banks. Now what's got you thinking so much about money?"

"I don't know."

"The main thing for you to understand is that money isn't really very important. My father and mother hardly ever had a nickel when I was growing up, but it didn't hurt me any. In some ways it helped. At least I know better than to think it's impossible to live without money. I want you to learn that. You'll never need a nickel more than you can make by yourself."

It was a well meant lesson, but I failed to understand it. Somehow the fact that my father and many other people kept insisting that money wasn't important when its effect on railroad travel, at least, was so immediately clear just increased the mystery of the stuff. Why did some people have it and other people not have it? Why, in my experience at least, did only women have it? And why was it somehow wrong to talk or even think about it?

A lot of people appear to think that children think only about childish things, but as far back as I can remember, I was obsessed by worries and questions about money. Once I studied a dollar bill with a magnifying glass, trying to make sense out of the image of George Washington, the assortment of strange symbols, and the words, "In God We Trust." What a strange, potent piece of paper it was!

When a few years later the stock market crashed and I heard Mother talking to my father about "losing so much money," I recognized the chill of fear in her voice. It was the same tone that was there when she talked to the doctor behind closed doors about the state of my father's health.

"Don't worry," my father's calm voice replied over and over again. "Don't worry, don't worry. Everything's going to be all right."

And for a long while everything was all right. After my great-grandmother died, my parents bought a relatively modest house from Mr. John D. Rockefeller himself, on the fringe of whose winter estate in Ormond Beach, Florida, it stood. Old Mr. Rockefeller, who was then in his nineties, wore a tweed cap with ear flaps even in the warmest weather. He often took strolls along River Road in front of our place. Sometimes he stopped in to chat with my father and to drink a cup of hot water with a little salt, his favorite beverage at the time. Everyone said that he was the richest man in the world, but he looked like a mummy, and it was impossible to imagine how he had ever earned such wealth. What was the secret of it all?

At that time Mr. Rockefeller was in the habit of giving dimes to the public, and he gave me many of them, often touching me on the head and saying, "God bless you, child."

Almost every Sunday he went to a Baptist church on the other side of the river, which was frequented mostly by black people, and when he gave parties for children, as he did in his own house every Christmas, he sang hymns and talked about God a lot. Like him, and unlike my father, my mother went to church every Sunday and talked about God a good deal. Thinking about this and the words "In God We Trust" on the dollar bills, I more or less concluded that there must be some fairly strong connection between money and religion. It seemed reasonable to assume that God rewarded the faithful more than the unfaithful, but why did the black people who also went to the Baptist church every Sunday wear such tattered clothes?

3

Of course I soon found that there was more in life than money to wonder and worry about. One was fighting. I never thought about fighting much until we moved to Ormond Beach, Florida, which at that time was a small hamlet of winter people surrounded by many native Floridians, both black and white. A white family who lived near us had gone broke in the recent Florida land boom, and was trying to eke out a living by turning its home into a tourist house. This family had a son about my age, then about eleven, a lanky youth whom I envied because he possessed a .22 rifle, a weapon which my father said I was too young to own. Often he hunted squirrels and rabbits in the orange grove behind our house and in the jungle area which separated his family's property from ours. One day while I was fooling around with a basketball in our back yard, he appeared, parting a row of bamboo trees as though they were a curtain. Resting his gun against an orange tree, he watched me, arms folded. His approach was direct.

"I bet I can lick you," he said.

In the genteel private day-schools I had attended, few fights were permitted to last long, and I didn't have much experience. To tell the truth, I was terrified, both of this young intruder and of the idea that maybe I couldn't fight or was too scared to try. I stared at him and said nothing.

"You couldn't fight a damn flea," he said.

My heart was beating so fast and my throat was constricting so much that my voice came out as a squeak.

"Fuck you," I piped. It was a phrase that our chauffeur used quite often when he argued with other men, and it had always sounded effective.

Now it certainly had an effect. My young neighbor put his head down and charged, fists flailing. He was a little taller than I, but not quite as heavily built. I grabbed him around the waist and soon we were both scrambling in the dust, landing blows where we could. One of his fists hit my nose, causing me to bleed, scream with rage and gush tears at the same time. I got my hands around his throat and rolled on top of him. When our gardener came running, we were both screaming while I was pounding his head on a rock. The black gardener hauled me off, and jumping to his feet, my enemy disappeared through the curtain of bamboo trees, forgetting even his gun.

"What's the matter with you?" the gardener asked. "Was you trying to kill that boy?"

As I wiped the blood from my nose with my sleeve, I was too confused to think much. The gardener obviously had been shocked by my actions, but I had *won*, unbelievable as it seemed. I had been challenged and I had *won*.

"You split that boy's head, and you be in for a peck of trouble," the gardener said.

"Don't tell my folks," I said.

"I won't tell nobody, but you better be careful. If you gonna fight, you better learn to fight fair."

I didn't really know what that meant. Fighting was fighting, and I had won. Never had I felt such soaring self-confidence. Not only had I won, I reflected; I had enjoyed it. I could hardly wait to fight again.

Opportunities were plentiful, both at school, where I found I was bigger than most of the other boys and didn't really have to do much more than threaten, and in the surrounding orange groves, woods and beaches, where boys of many different backgrounds roamed. As long as I had enough sense to avoid boys much bigger or older than I, I rarely had trouble and began to dream of growing up to be not a writer, but heavyweight champion of the world. This fantasy came to a sudden end when I met a boy about my own size whose name after more than forty years, I still remember: Bill Cochran. He had blond, almost invisible eyebrows and cold blue eyes. In almost no time at all he had me flat on my back, and was twisting my arm so painfully that I screamed.

"Say 'Uncle,'" he almost whispered.

"Uncle!" I gasped.

With a laugh he let me up.

"You can't fight worth a damn," he said.

Without comment I ran home. The next day I went to the public library in Daytona and took out all the books on wrestling and boxing I could find. Nothing in the world seemed more important than beating Bill Cochran.

"Boxing is a science," one book emphasized, and I certainly studied it harder than I had any other form of discipline. At my request and somewhat astonished, my father gave me a punching bag and I worked out for hours every afternoon alone. After about six weeks of this, I went looking for Bill Cochran. I was half relieved and half frustrated when I couldn't find him anywhere. Some of the other boys said that Bill's family had moved away.

None of the other boys I knew wanted to fight with me. The truth apparently was that I had got a reputation for going crazy when I fought, and sensible youngsters stayed away. Feeling like a miniature Alexander the Great who had no more worlds to conquer, I began thinking about the black boys. The black boys and the white boys rarely mixed much at that time in that part of Florida, but some people said the blacks could fight better than anyone. At the age of eleven, I ached to find out, and the direct approach seemed best. Going to a place on the local golf course where the black caddies waited for jobs, I selected one about my age and size.

"Hey you," I said, "want to fight?"

"Hell no," he replied. "I ain't going to fight no white boy. My daddy would beat my ass."

"I'll give you a quarter," I said. "Win or lose, I'll give you a quarter if you try."

That was in the year 1931, and quarters were not easy for children to get. The black boy got to his feet and we walked to a spot under a big live oak tree. Rather half-heartedly he swung a light right at me. I hit him hard with a left hook I had been practicing, and the next thing I knew, I was flat on my back. He was sitting astride me and was hitting me on the face, first with his left, then with his right. There was no way I could avoid his punches and when I yelled "uncle," he didn't stop. Suddenly a big black man came running from the golf course and grabbed the black boy by the scruff of the neck, flinging him into the grass a few feet away from me.

"Don't you know better than to fight with no white boys?" he roared. "You got any idea of the trouble that makes?"

"He asked me," the black boy said, getting up.

"That's right," I admitted. "I said I'd give him a quarter."

Feeling in my pocket, I found the coin and held it out in my hand. The black man grabbed it and handed it back to me.

"You take your damn quarter and get out of here," he said. "You learn to leave black boys alone!"

I had a black eye and my nose was bleeding, but the injuries were not what hurt most. As I watched, the black man kicked the black boy hard on the bottom and said, "Now you run on home!"

The black boy ran toward the river and I ran toward the sea. When I got to the beach I stopped, my breath coming hot and hard. With all my strength I hurled the quarter into the surf which thundered at my feet.

4

The discovery that at least two boys of my own size could beat me easily put an abrupt end to my career as a bully and would-be heavyweight champion of the world. It was better to be a writer after all, I decided, and this opinion was reinforced by two dramatic events: My father had a novel published, and we met H. G. Wells—who appeared to be nothing but a little fat man, but who was treated almost like God by everyone, including my mother, simply because he wrote so many books.

My father's novel was a light fantasy entitled *Poko'Moonshine,* which hardly anyone reviewed and almost no one bought, but that made no difference to our family. Dad had, after all, written a real book which looked beautiful in its silvery cover with his name on it. I can still remember the pride on his face when he opened the box of advance copies sent by the publisher, Dodd, Mead, and the intense satisfaction which mother took in telling people about her husband's triumph.

To celebrate this success the whole family, including my father's mother, a cousin of mine and our tutor, went abroad. I assumed that the money earned by my father's book paid for this expedition, and my respect for literary endeavor increased. We took fifty-six pieces of baggage with us, a guitar I was learning to play and my English bulldog, Punch, which I refused to leave behind. Aboard the Italian liner *Vulcania* we had a string of staterooms with private sections of deck. Almost as soon as the ship left New York, I became desperately seasick. The bulldog also was miserable and began howling like a wolf at the moon. That's the way we met H. G. Wells. The famed author had the next stateroom to me and complained to my father about the noise. Identifying himself as a fellow writer, my father hustled me into other quarters and invited H. G. Wells to have a drink with him and my mother at the bar. Never had I seen my regal mother turn so nervous and deferential. H. G. Wells was traveling with a beautiful woman who was reputed not to be his wife, but mother forgave him even that. She put on her best dress and for years afterward she and dad talked about the time they had a drink with H. G. Wells, who gradually began to seem to be a close family friend, though none of us ever saw him again. Every time Wells had a book published, dad bought it for mother, and though thousands of miles from England, they shared the distant sounds of applause.

During most of the months we spent in Europe I had a severe cold, and—in an attempt to toughen me up—my parents put me under the instruction of a German gymnast who gave lessons on the beach in front of the Grand Hotel in Cannes. The gymnast knew no English and tried to communicate with me in deep guttural grunts as he taught me intricate exercises. The only result of this was that I strained a neck muscle in such a way that my head rested on my left shoulder, and the chilly winds on the beach made my cold worse. Bundled in a heavy sweater, I spent most of my time huddled behind a beach umbrella watching the muscular instructor doing giant swings before an admiring audience of beautiful girls. As he twirled around a bar he had suspended from two poles on the beach, he sweated profusely and kept grunting as though in pain. The beautiful girls rarely stopped to chat with him for long after his performance, and—for all his beefy beauty—he never was treated with the awed respect which everyone aboard the *Vulcania* had accorded fat little Mr. Wells. I had no idea how hard it was to write books, but I figured it must be easier than doing giant swings, and it certainly was more effective when it came to earning affection and money. Despite my aching neck and strangling cough, I began to spend much of my spare time with a notebook and pencil, trying to write a story. It was about two English bulldogs in love and it was called *Just Nip*. Both my mother and father said it was great and, when we got home, it was included in a mimeographed "literary magazine" put out by my school. One of the prettiest girls in my class congratulated me on it, and after that, I never had a moment's doubt about my future. It always seemed a little odd to me that other people wanted to play football, fly airplanes, become bankers or do anything else but master the mysteries of a trade which could make a fat little man like Wells stand as a giant in the eyes of most people, even when compared to a muscular German Apollo.

The trouble was that *Just Nip* drained my creative resources, and between the ages of about twelve and sixteen, I suffered a bad case of writer's block. Ambitious as I was, there was nothing I could do but dream and read of the exploits of Hemingway, Fitzgerald and Faulkner, who—along with H. G. Wells—were my father's household gods. We never got a chance to meet them, but one does not expect to come into actual contact with divinities very often, and we followed their successes eagerly in the magazines which came in the mail from New York.

Not even a child can sustain himself on fantasies alone, of course, and —while I dreamed of capturing the imagination of beautiful women, as Wells had—I had to cope with the reality of dealing with the girls I met at school in Florida and at the Rogers Rock Club on the northern end of Lake George, New York, where my family spent the summers. Like most adults nowadays, I tend to take the passions of young boys lightly, and to see something intrinsically humorous in calf love. But the dumb adoration I felt for girls from the earliest time I can remember never seemed funny to me at the time. It is a curious fact that after all these decades I can still remember the names of the many girls who fascinated me and the exact way they looked. My family often ridiculed me for being "girl crazy," and my mother said that even at the age of five, before we left New Canaan, I was obsessed by a little blonde girl who lived nearby named Barbara Foote.

"You came in one day all upset because your swing was broken," mother reported. "You said you were very angry at whomever did it unless it was Barbara Foote, and you couldn't be angry at her for anything."

I'm not sure I remember Barbara Foote, though I seem to sense a dim daffodil-like presence, but I do remember Betsy, Merlin, Susan, Anne, Judy, Inez and a whole host of names that followed. None of these girls did I ever touch—other than accidentally—but, one after the other, they seemed to combine everything desirable and forever out of reach. Although I hated classes of all kinds, they made school an exciting business, for there were always those beautiful girls in the corridors or sitting next to me in class. I was perfectly well aware that my excessive emotions would appear ridiculous to anyone, most of all the girls themselves, and went to great efforts to hide them. I couldn't just look at a girl in those days; I had to sneak peeks, often between the fingers of a hand with which I pretended to cover my eyes.

In my era, I am grateful to remember, the girls did not wear blue jeans to school. They wore cotton or linen dresses in bright shades of pink, yellow and green, and usually their hair was brushed to a glossy sheen. On the beach they wore colorful bathing suits which covered them from neck to thigh, but nothing could hide the marvelous grace of their young bodies as they dove into the surf. Merlin had brown hair and a bathing suit with blue and white stripes. Inez had long exotic black hair and sported a scarlet halter considered very daring in those days with shorts to match. Both girls were about three years older than I and both developed beautiful figures when they were only about thirteen. I can still see them leaping in the waves with the sun shining on their tanned shoulders. I followed them carefully at a polite distance, trying to impress them with my skill as a swimmer, but they never glanced my way except to laugh, as though they knew the secrets of my heart and could not get over my absurdity.

There was a boy at my school about three years older than I who excelled in every sport as well as in the classroom. He won silver cups playing golf and tennis, and most of the girls looked at him with almost the awe with which my mother regarded H. G. Wells. It was partly this boy whose name I have forgotten, who convinced me that girls, like loving cups, were trophies who always went to the victor of some strenuous event, and who would forever be denied to the losers in life. As I entered my teens it seemed to me that I just was not good enough at anything to deserve the attention of any of the dazzling young women I admired so much. Since I couldn't think of anything to write and was too awkward for success at most sports, I decided to become the best sailor in the world.

Both in Florida and on Lake George, sailing was regarded by most of my contemporaries as serious business. At the local yacht clubs fleets of catboats and sloops skimmed over the blue waters in pursuit of victories which were rewarded with loving cups as big and shiny as those which are given to winners at golf and tennis.

At the age of nine I had been taught to sail a dory by an older cousin. The rushing water and the angry sound of a luffing sail in a gust of wind had scared me; and, though I never really got over an instinctive fear of the sea, I found it was possible and even pleasurable to control it. My father bought me an eleven-foot catboat in Florida a year or so later and allowed me to sail it alone on the Halifax River. When I was about thirteen, I started spending almost all my spare time on the boat, and began entering regattas. Before long I found I could win a race once in a while, and, with my appetite whetted, I took every available book on sailing from the local library and studied each one more avidly than I had all the books on boxing. The fact that I could sail all winter in Florida gave me an edge over the youngsters who raced on Lake George, and soon I found myself a local champion of the catboats. To my surprise I discovered that this seemed to give unusual pleasure to my parents, and they eagerly offered me the very best in boats, sails and equipment.

Always I had been vaguely aware that my mother's father had been a naval officer and an arctic explorer and that her brother was also a naval officer. She herself had been born at the Naval Academy, but her father had died young in circumstances that were never discussed. And in other circumstances that were never discussed, her brother and she had had some sort of falling out, and she seemed to disapprove of him to the point that he rarely visited us. Mother had seemed so hellbent on her literary aspirations that I never realized she considered herself a sort of daughter of the sea who admired sailors almost as much as she did literary men. As soon as I showed a marked interest in sailing, she started talking about sending me to the Naval Academy and making an admiral out of me. Her maiden name, Danenhower, she explained to me, meant "hewer of Danes," and signified that we were probably the descendants of a long line of Vikings and should take naturally to the sea. To my surprise I found that during the years she had lived at Annapolis, while her brother was studying there, she had picked up an extensive nautical vocabulary and even could read some of the signal flags on naval vessels. She said she welcomed my interest in writing, but it did not have to preclude a naval career. My grandfather Danenhower had not only been a hero of the *Jeanette* Expedition—which had made a disastrous attempt to reach the North Pole—but had also written a book about it. Many other naval officers also wrote books, she said, and so bought me a whole shelf of volumes by commanders, captains and admirals.

My father's pleasure in my new interest in sailing was more immediate and practical. In his own youth he had been a champion oarsman on Lake George and a long distance runner at the University of Virginia. His bad heart had long made any exercise or competition impossible for him, but he liked to attend regattas with me and watch me try to win. Soon he became active in organizing and running regattas. At our place on Lake George he organized a little yacht club, became commodore of it and patrolled the races in a Chris-Craft launch which he was skillful at handling as a rescue boat. No youngster ever had more backing from his family than I, for my parents' nautical ambitions soon outran even my own. In a few years we went from an eleven-foot catboat to a twenty-two-foot Star boat, to a twenty-eight-foot inland scow which was supposed to be one of the fastest types of sailing craft in the world, to a forty-three-foot schooner and finally a sixty-foot ketch. These larger craft were run by a professional captain but allowed my parents to take a more active role in the sport.

All this was a little bewildering to me, but I continued to work as hard at learning everything possible about boats as a professional athlete might strive to master his profession. One thing I had guessed perfectly correctly about boats: they were a wonderful mechanism for winning the attention of beautiful girls. On a Star boat I could even ask my favorite girl of the moment to crew for me, and often as not she would say yes. Most girls were not very good at handling the jib or backstays, but I learned to do those chores fairly well myself, and a regatta meant a good three hours of being able to show off and to have a beautiful girl all to myself.

It was harder to impress girls on the schooner and ketch, because our Nova Scotian captain kept hogging the limelight by doing all the difficult work himself. But after managing to control my abject fear of height, I learned to climb the rigging and swing around up there indefinitely, providing I had an appreciative audience on deck or on a nearby wharf. I got myself a yachting cap and a blue turtleneck sweater, and though they failed to make me look like an authentic naval hero, they filled me with self-confidence. Ashore, the girls still did not pay much attention to me; but when I got them out on the water they had no one else to occupy them, and I basked in the warmth of their smiles as we skimmed around the red buoys in pursuit of loving cups.

So went my early youth.

5

There was once an editor of the old *Saturday Evening Post* who gave writers a sage bit of advice: "Never try to make the readers feel sorry for a man on a yacht."

Like much advice from editors, this did not apply to me at all. I have never in my life felt more sorry for any man than I did for my father, who would never ask for pity, even if he had wanted it. It's true that he spent much of his time during the Great Depression aboard yachts, but he had a problem that no riches could solve: he was dying and he knew it. Every year his heart attacks grew worse. His agony always remained too terrible to be discussed by anyone in the family, but it was always evident because this old athlete, whose body preserved the semblance of power even when he got fat, could not raise a hand to pull a line aboard our boat or to put a fender over the side, even in small emergencies. He just had to sit quietly in the cockpit while I climbed the rigging. When even my mother admired the view from the top of the mast by having herself hauled up in a boatswain's chair, Dad just smiled and said, "I must admit that I feel sort of sorry for you people with sea-going ancestors. My forefathers at least had enough sense to stay on the ground."

He was always a cheerful man, no matter what was happening. It is possible that his love of life was increased by his knowledge that it would be short for him. His books failed and his breath often came short, but all he had to do was enter a room to make people brighten up. In his youth he had longed to be a physician, and—after working his way through the University of Virginia by serving as an assistant to a doctor— he became an editor on the old *Literary Digest* simply because he could not raise the money to go to medical school. A great healer missed his trade, but even without medical knowledge, he went through life making everybody who knew him feel better.

As a boy I grew up worshipping my father. He never said much to me, but he also never came near me without touching my head or caressing my face. Much of his advice was terrible. As I reached my mid-teens he tried to talk me into being a physician—even though I hated high-school chemistry so much that I quit the course, and despite the fact that I had inherited none of his ability to express warmth for people simply by touching them or talking to them. This son of generations of New England schoolmasters, parsons and farmers had the strictest moral code of anyone I ever met. To him sex outside of marriage was literally unspeakable. He refused to talk about it at all, and when I mustered the courage to ask him direct questions, he referred me to books. The rigidity of his morality was softened by the fact that he applied it only to himself and to abstract situations in literature. When actual sinners turned up in the shape of pregnant servant girls or erring friends, no one was kinder than my father, and he often backed up kindness with money, sound practical advice about where to find good lawyers or doctors, and that smile of his with the twinkle in the eye which said that no sinner was bad even though every sin was unbearable.

For a while I was troubled by the contrast between my father and the Nova Scotian yacht captain, whom my father had hired, I believe, to help make up for the fact that he himself could not help his sons in active sports. Over the years the captain became not a second father to me, but an example of the opposite side of the coin of virility which my father represented. While my father could hardly get out of his chair, the young captain was as muscular as a professional boxer, and he often picked fights in bars for the sheer joy of showing that it was not much trouble for him to knock much bigger men to the floor. My father said he had never hit anyone in his life, and he quietly boasted to me once that he had never in his whole life gone to bed with any woman but my mother. The young captain brought a different girl down to the boat almost every night when the family was not aboard. I have no memory of my father ever raising his voice in anger. The young captain shouted and roared at the slightest provocation. He had such a terrible temper that he had been fired from several jobs aboard fishing and merchant vessels for attacking his superiors, yet before my father he was always quiet and respectful. One reason, I realized, was that my father had money and the captain didn't, and jobs for yacht captains during the depression were hard to find, but the admiration the captain felt for my father went beyond the servility of an employee.

"Your father," the captain used to say to me, "he's really *some man.*"

I of course agreed, but it was impossible for me at that time to define what the peculiar quality of virility in my stout ailing father was. It took me a long time to understand that he enjoyed either a peculiar freedom from fear, even in the face of death, or a marvelous ability to control any sign of anxiety. One reason he was able to make people feel good simply by entering the room was that his self-confidence and courage were just as catching as depression and fear can be. His self-assurance also made it unnecessary for him ever to be petty. When I told him that our yacht captain, like almost all yacht captains, was taking ten percent kickbacks on shipyard bills, dad smiled and said, "I know. That's why I don't give him a raise. I don't like the system, but if I called him on it, he'd have to get mad and quit because of his own self-respect. As things are he doesn't really get much money, and I think he works very hard, don't you?"

My father's worldliness and his strict moral code for himself sometimes seemed to me to be only one of many self-contradictions in an extremely complex man. He told me once that the only lasting joy in life was personal achievement, but when his books failed to attract attention and he went for years without thinking of anything to write, he cheerfully busied himself by arranging regattas for his children and dabbling in local politics. I never knew until after his death that he wrote several plays and tried for years to get them produced without success. Disappointment was something he did not share with anyone, but when every once in a while he had a short poem published in a magazine, the whole family celebrated.

With his nautical wife and would-be nautical children, my father prided himself on being the product of generations of landsmen and flatly refused to learn nautical terms. He liked to call the bow of a boat "the sharp end" and the stern "the blunt end." Yet he never got seasick, even when mother and I took to our bunks and the captain himself said he didn't want any dinner. Once, when a severe storm broke late at night on Lake George, he woke up everyone in our cottage, which was near the water, and said he thought he heard people screaming. I told him I thought it was the wind, but he insisted on hurrying to his launch and speeding to the middle of the lake, where he found two people clinging to a capsized sailboat. One of these survivors insisted on putting him up for a Carnegie lifesaving medal. My father wrote a letter to decline the honor.

"It's true that I found two people in the water," he wrote, "but they climbed aboard my boat by themselves, and I didn't even have to take my cigar out of my mouth. How can a man smoking a cigar be classed as a life-saving hero?"

Often my father told me with pride that he had worked his way through college without a nickel's help from anyone, but he dressed like a millionaire and liked to boast to an English friend that in eight generations, his family had never been in trade.

"The truth is we never had anything to trade and had to teach school," he said to me, "but the English really go for this stuff of never having been in trade. That's one claim your mother's people can't make. They were *all* in trade at one time or another."

My father's bad heart had prevented him from serving in World War I, but somehow he knew more about war than the heads of most departments of state. As soon as Hitler came into power in Germany—back in the very early Thirties—dad told me that there was going to be a second world war, and that after a year or two the United States would get in it. He said that the United States would win without much trouble, not because we were braver than Germans, but because we had much more oil and steel. Germans had always been kind of crazy, he said. For years they had been going around picking fights they couldn't win.

Astonishingly enough, he told me in 1934 that the second world war would start in a few more years, and that our part of it would last about four years.

"That's about the length of most big wars," he said. "It will take us a long while to get started, but no one will be able to stand up against us in the end."

He advised me to try to skip the whole war by becoming a medical student even if I had to seek out a fourth-rate university.

"There is nothing heroic about being killed in a war," he said. "Anyone can do it. They treat young men like natural-born cannon fodder. I once saw a monument to two million British dead."

"I don't think it's right to tell your son he should be a draft-dodger," mother said with all her Annapolis indignation.

"An intelligent man should never allow himself to be ordered to charge machine guns and barbed wire," he replied mildly. "If you insist on being a hero, stick with your mother's naval tradition. Somehow the navy never gets hurt as bad as the infantry."

"That's not true!" mother retorted.

"And do your best to be an officer," dad continued imperturbably. "Enlisted men always get the dirty end of the stick. It's an unfair system, but you can't beat it and it's best to be on the right side of it."

"I think you are a perfect cynic," mother said to him.

"Ah, well," he concluded, "it's good to achieve perfection at anything."

Although my father had helped to found the School of Journalism at New York University, he always claimed that writing could not be taught, and was embarrassed by the gratitude of some of his successful students. One of these was Dale Carnegie, who wrote dad an effusive letter when *How To Win Friends and Influence People* became a great popular success. I had never seen dad so disgusted.

"The worst damn thing I ever did was to teach that man to write," he exploded. "Now he's got everybody slapping backs and flattering strangers the way he always did. I cannot imagine a more terrible end to my career as a teacher."

Although he said he couldn't teach anyone to write, he was great at encouraging anyone who set pen to paper.

"Don't worry about spelling," he said. "Don't worry about grammar. Let form take care of itself. Meaning and feeling are all!"

"But the boy has to learn to spell," mother objected.

"If he learns how to write he can hire a secretary to do that for about forty dollars a week," dad observed.

One of my father's proudest hours came shortly after I had been sent to Exeter Academy, when I was fifteen years old. I was not there to witness the incident, but everyone involved except Dad told me a great deal about it.

In the fall of 1935, my parents, my brother, who was only ten years old, and the yacht captain sailed the family's sixty-foot ketch from New York with the intention of entering the intracoastal water route to Florida at Cape May, New Jersey. To make up for my absence as a deckhand they had hired a nineteen-year-old boy who had proved himself good with small boats on Lake George. While they waited for good weather, they anchored behind Sandy Hook in New York Harbor. There was a schooner about the size of our ketch lying there, and her captain bet our captain a hundred dollars that he could beat him to Cape May. Our captain was not a man to refuse such a challenge, though he did not at the time tell my father about it. When the schooner put out to sea before a fall gale had abated, our captain upped anchor and followed—assuring my parents that our big ketch would experience no trouble. The ketch was apparently all right, but everyone aboard except dad and the captain soon got helplessly seasick, and dad was not supposed to lift a hand in any physical effort. All day the wind got worse, and daughter of the Vikings or not my mother begged to be put ashore. There was no good port before Cape May, the captain pointed out. When night fell the gale increased and dad suggested that the captain take in the mainsail, but the big ketch was running neck-and-neck with the schooner, and the captain said he saw no immediate reason for such caution. About this time dad noticed that the captain was drinking whiskey, which the man usually did not do at sea. After about an hour, during which the wind continued to rise, dad ordered the captain to take in the mainsail. The captain replied that in such a storm he could not do the job himself. The nineteen-year-old boy was called from his bunk but proved to be so weak and frightened that he was useless. Dad took the wheel of the ketch, which required a great deal of strenuous spinning in those weather conditions, and rounded the vessel into the wind while the captain wrestled with the huge gaff-rigged mainsail. Before the sail was half-way down, the captain lost control of the halyards. The big gaff jammed in the shrouds and everything got all tangled up.

"I can't do no more," the captain said, coming aft with bloody hands. "We'll just have to run before it."

For several hours they ran while the seas got worse and the big shoal-draft ketch yawed dangerously. The captain kept sneaking drinks from a bottle of whiskey in the chart table, and soon dad perceived that he was too drunk to do anything well. Suddenly the vessel broached, and lay on her beam ends with the seas crashing over her decks.

"Jesus, I think we're lost," the captain said.

Mother heard this as she stuck her head up the hatch in alarm, and the words did not do much to soothe her nerves.

"Nonsense!" dad shouted. It was one of his favorite words, the one he used instead of curses.

"The bitch won't steer," the captain said.

"Maybe not, but she'll float," dad observed, and went down to look at the chart himself.

"I think I see some lights ashore," he said when he came back. "Is that Atlantic City?"

"Yes," the captain said.

"Let's try to take her in there."

"Can't. You'd never get her across the bar in weather like this."

"I think I'll try," dad said. "Let me take the wheel."

No one ever knew how he did it, but my father, bad heart and all, straightened that heavy vessel out on a course for Atlantic City. With the mainsail a lashing tangle and no one to help him but a drunken captain who kept muttering "impossible, impossible," my father sailed that clumsy vessel through the surf pounding on the bar which stretched across the harbor of Atlantic City at that time. He managed to control the vessel as she careened through a narrow channel between concrete breakwaters in the dead of night. Suddenly coasting into the quiet of the inner harbor, he said, "Captain, do you think you'll be able to get the anchor down?"

Some of this story I heard from my mother and brother, but most of it I heard from the captain himself, who was honest enough to make no effort to look good himself.

"I just damn well got drunk," he said to me weeks later, "and I didn't think anybody could get across that damn bar at Atlantic City."

"They say it's a terrible bar," I said.

"You know something?" the captain replied. "I thought your old man was going to kill us. Then, when he got over the bar like he was the greatest goddamn surfman of all time, I thought sure he'd fire me, but he never said a damn word—just put the anchor down. When he took your mother ashore the next day he told me not to worry because any man can have a bad night."

6

Almost everyone I knew, except the boys who were there, told me that Exeter Academy was a wonderful school. A cousin of mine who had graduated from it said that frankly he thought I was too spoiled and too lazy a student to survive at Exeter, but that if I could learn to meet the school's high standards it would be the making of me.

It came as a great shock to realize that my cousin's judgment of me was apparently right. When my first report card was issued, I found I had failed all subjects except one, English. Part of this was my own fault, I knew, and part of my failure perhaps could be blamed on the small Florida schools and tutors which until then had been responsible for my education. The only remedy was hard work, and I began studying at night with a flashlight under a blanket long after the lights were supposed to be out.

"How do you like Exeter?" my father asked when I went home to Ormond Beach for the Christmas vacation.

"I hate it," I blurted out. "I know I'm supposed to love it, but I hate it."

"Why?"

My emotions were too incoherent to enable me to give him a good explanation. I missed my family and I missed the pretty girls in the day school I had attended. I missed Florida, the regattas, and the long after noons of lazing on the deck of a sailboat. I hated Exeter's dreary New Hampshire climate. I hated studying Latin because it was dull, and I saw no real reason to learn it. What was worse, I hated almost all sports, an admission which was a real blasphemy for any Exeter boy and maybe for any American. I hated the fact that the masters (some of them, at least) threw chalk and blackboard erasers at boys who could not solve algebra problems or translate Latin quickly. The teachers also terrorized us by reminding us frequently that boys who could not "keep their work up" were expelled from the school, and probably would find it difficult or impossible to get into a good college. The general idea seemed to be that if a boy couldn't get into a good college, there was no future at all for him, except maybe as a private in the French Foreign Legion.

My hatred of the school even extended to many of the students. Without knowing it, I had absorbed a little of my father's Puritanism. When a roommate of mine wanted to decorate our room with various bits of women's underwear which he claimed were trophies of conquest, I was genuinely shocked.

I had never known that masturbation was such a big deal until I went to Exeter Academy. It seemed fairly obvious that everybody did it, but unlike the students at Exeter, most people didn't keep talking about it all the time and predicting the most grotesque results of it. Like me, the boys I knew at Exeter had learned little or nothing about sex at home except the business about the birds and the bees and some blunt warnings about venereal diseases. The result was that they speculated about it constantly and worried about it like young soldiers preparing to go into their first battle. I too worried and speculated, but I was too prudish to exchange my thoughts on the subject with other students. Most of them made the subject sound ugly. The books to which my father had referred me had all emphasized the beauty of sexual relationships, but the mechanics of the flesh which the authors tried to explain did not seem very attractive. How could the beautiful girls I knew in Florida ever be expected even to think of such things?

I don't remember how much of this I was able to discuss with my father, but he got the general drift of the fact that I was not unduly delighted by Exeter Academy.

"Do you want to drop out?" he asked me.

"Yes," I replied.

Dad thought a moment while he stuffed his pipe with tobacco and lit it.

"If you possibly can, I think you should try to stick the year out," he said at last. "You'll feel better if you can beat the system before you quit it. If at the end of the year you pass all your subjects, I'll send you to any school you want."

There was no possible way he could have given me a better incentive. When I returned to Exeter I worked almost around the clock, and well before June I lifted my marks from the bottom to the middle range. I think my father hoped that I would want to stay at Exeter once I "beat the system," as he put it, but he held to his promise when I reminded him of it, and asked me what school I wanted to try next.

I had a ready answer. A boy I knew at Lake George had told me of the existence of a small school that had two campuses, one near Saranac Lake in the Adirondacks, and one in Coconut Grove, Florida. The students spent their fall and spring terms in the mountains, but went south for the winters, just as my family did. The main sport at this "Adirondack-Florida School" was sailing, the one sport I really enjoyed, and I would be close enough to my parents to permit weekend visits.

"It sounds pretty fancy," dad said. "Do you think you could get into a decent college from it?"

"I don't know," I replied, for college seemed too far in the future to worry about.

"I've heard of the Adirondack-Florida School," my mother said. "It's got a fairly good reputation. It would be nice to have Sloan close to home. Why not try it for a year?"

So it happened that instead of going to Exeter again the following September, I went to the Adirondack end of the school's operation and sailed boats on small mountain lakes. After Christmas vacation at home, I went to the school's Florida campus, where they had a fleet of small sloops and a fairly large schooner for cruises to the keys. It also happened that my father's big ketch was moored in Miami, not far from my school. Since their disastrous cruise south, mother had refused to go aboard anything less than an ocean liner. Dad was trying to sell the boat, a transaction which, in those depression years, was not easy.

"Since nobody is using the ketch, why don't you have the captain anchor her off my school?" I asked.

My parents saw nothing wrong with this and agreed. So to the glee of the cousin who had called me too spoiled for Exeter, I became possibly the only schoolboy in the United States who had a yacht with a captain ready for his pleasure on weekends.

"My God, you'll ruin the boy!" one of my aunts said. "Whoever heard of such a thing?"

My good fortune lasted only a few months before the boat was sold, but it became a legend among my family and friends. My parents had sent me off to school with a yacht, and neither they nor I were ever allowed to forget it.

During the short period I had the ketch at school, I found that many of my classmates liked to dream with me about taking long voyages aboard her. Why not sail her to Maine or Nova Scotia during the next summer vacation and share the expenses?

That idea stuck with me even when dad announced that he had sold the boat. There already were two men, I knew, who owned fairly large sailing vessels and voyaged around the world with a crew which both worked the ship and paid expenses. One of these men, Irving Johnson, wrote books and magazine articles about his cruises. What better career could be imagined for someone like me, who loved boats and felt almost a family obligation to write?

When I told my father of this dream, he did not discourage it immediately, perhaps because he thought I would forget about it long before I could try to turn it into reality. Somewhat to my surprise, my mother discussed the idea with some enthusiasm.

"It would be great training if you ever decided to go into the navy," she said, "and it would be good business training too, if you had to handle the money. I think that most parents don't give their children enough responsibility when they're young. After all, some of your forefathers commanded clipper ships out of Salem and Portsmouth when they were barely out of their teens. People used to grow up quickly in those days."

With this support my dream grew brighter. If I could find the proper vessel, I might take college students on summer cruises which could serve as preparation for a great cruise around the world after graduation.

"I don't think we can make plans for so distant a future," my father said, and I knew that he was thinking of the probability of war, a subject which had begun to obsess him.

"If I'm going to do anything, I have to make plans," I replied.

"How about making some immediate ones?" he asked. "What college do you want to go to?"

"I don't know," I said. "I don't think the Naval Academy is the place for me. Maybe I'm some kind of a throwback. I just like sailing ships."

That sounded better than the truth, which was that a yacht seemed to me to spell freedom, while a naval vessel represented discipline with a lot of yelling and stiff punishments.

"I'd recommend the University of Virginia, but I don't think it's as good as it was in my day. How about Harvard?"

"Why Harvard?" I asked.

"Because it's supposed to be the best. If you aim for that and miss, there will still be plenty of places for you to go."

After that I began to assume that I was going to Harvard, though I had never seen the place nor heard a great deal about it. The name had a rather nice ring to it, and I figured it would be a good place to find students who could help me take a big schooner around the world.

In my youth, it was much easier to get into Harvard than it is in this day when almost everyone wants to go to college. Although I was never a brilliant student, Harvard accepted me, and in the fall of 1938, my parents drove me from Lake George to Cambridge, Massachusetts. Dad's green Lincoln was followed by a pick-up truck carrying antique furniture for my room. In those days it was not thought odd for a Harvard freshman to fix up his room elaborately.

In Cambridge my father and mother stayed at the Commander Hotel while I got settled in Massachusetts Hall. Before she went home, mother insisted that I buy clothes from a long list which she had prepared. In Florida and at Lake George, there had been no need for formal wear. To make myself ready for Boston society, mother decreed that I buy both black- and white-tie evening outfits, three handsome sports jackets and a gray flannel suit.

After I hung these new clothes in my closet in Massachusetts Hall, I felt ready for Boston society, but Boston society gave no sign of being ready for me. I knew not a single soul in the entire state of Massachusetts. The boy who lived across the hall from me got a mail box full of invitations to parties, but all I got was advertisements and notice of social events which the college had arranged for newcomers.

"Are you having a good time?" mother asked over the telephone two weeks after my arrival in Cambridge.

"Good enough," I said.

"Are you getting asked to a lot of parties?"

"Not really."

"They have a list of students to be asked to coming out parties," mother said. "I have an old Vassar friend in Boston. I think she could get your name on it."

Sure enough, in a few days my mail box was full of engraved invitations asking me to parties being given by strangers. The first time I went to one I wore my white-tie outfit with its top hat, only to find that all the other young men wore simple dinner jackets with plain white shirts. I wore my black-tie outfit to the first dinner I was asked to, only to find that the other men were wearing white ties. I never did get the hang of Boston society. If it hadn't been for the free champagne and all the beautiful girls, I would have said to hell with it.

The trouble with the pretty girls was that they seemed almost impossible for me to meet. Too shy and too conscious of my inability to dance well, I never had the courage to cut in on a stranger. The male equivalent of a wallflower, I just stood with a glass of champagne in my hand and watched the beautiful girls twirling in a circle of friends.

After signing up for courses in naval science which were part of the Reserve Officers Training program at Harvard, I met a good many young men who, like me, found some romantic satisfaction in being in love with the sea. I talked up the idea of chartering a schooner and sharing the expenses for a cruise from Florida to Nova Scotia the following summer. To my great satisfaction I found that almost everyone I talked to in the naval science course was interested in the idea. Before long I had a list of fifteen men who said they would put money down the moment I found a suitable vessel.

When I went to my parents' home in Florida for the spring vacation,

I asked my father for permission to charter a sailing vessel big enough for fifteen students for the following summer.

"Chartering for the whole summer would be too expensive," he said. "You'd be better off buying a boat. These days big yachts are going for almost nothing. After a year or so we might sell at a profit."

"Where would I get the money?" I asked.

"I'll ask your mother. Maybe we can help."

The result of this conversation was the purchase of an enormous schooner which was lying at the Royal Palm docks in Miami. From the tip of her imposing bowsprit to her taffrail she measured eighty-seven feet. Because the owner's bride got seasick on their honeymoon aboard the *Aigrette*, as she was called, the vessel was for sale cheap.

Even at the time I wondered why my father made such an extraordinary purchase for the sake of his elder son. He said he thought that the experience of running a charter boat would give me a better education than even Harvard could. He had a dread of his sons' "going soft," because we had never experienced the hardships of poverty which he had suffered in his youth. He also brooded about the onset of war and the state of his own health, which was getting worse. Whatever his reasons, he was enthusiastic about my plan for sailing the coast with a paying crew of college boys and seemed to enjoy overseeing the job of getting the vessel ready.

In June of the year 1939, fifteen college boys came aboard the *Aigrette* in Miami. Dad, who said he did not want to go, stood at the end of the wharf waving farewell. As soon as we got out of the harbor, we raised sail, cut off the engine and chartered a course for Havana, which we had decided to visit before heading north. Before land was out of sight, my friends from the naval science course broke out sextants to see if we could actually use the navigation we had been taught. I doubt if any vessel our size had more navigators aboard than the *Aigrette* did during that sweet month of June as gentle wind eased us toward Havana.

Cuba offered so many delights that it was difficult to get my crew out of the place. The members of the Havana Yacht Club almost adopted us and there were parties aboard our boat or in their bar almost every night. When we finally sailed, we caught a hard fair wind all the way to Charleston, South Carolina, where some of the crew had friends, and there was another round of parties. Falling behind schedule, we charted a course for Halifax, Nova Scotia, where the girls seemed even prettier than the belles of Havana and Charleston. Almost all of us fell in love with a Halifax girl. The summer of 1939 was a long rollicking one for all of us, the best summer most of us had ever spent.

I remember that summer of '39 with the strangest emotions. It was of course idyllic—a beautiful eighty-seven-foot schooner manned by fifteen college boys looking for nothing but a good time. Guiltily I realize that I did not experience the bliss that the circumstances seemed to warrant. At the age of nineteen I had neither the experience nor the knowledge necessary for captaining such a ship and I lived in constant fear of disaster.

In ways which young people of today probably could not understand, I was also troubled by the many beautiful girls I admired so much. My beloved father, I knew, genuinely believed that men should remain chaste until marriage. His devotion to me was such that he assumed I shared his opinion that decent men remain above the base ruttings of lesser beings. In Puritanism there can be a certain snobbery, and I longed to remain with my father amongst the aristocrats of purity. The only trouble was that whenever I found myself alone with a really pretty girl, I was transported into another world which my father apparently had never glimpsed. There was nothing base about the pretty girls in this special world, where all perceptions were heightened, all music beautiful, all food delightful. After a few kisses I found that all my father's elaborate warnings against sexuality meant absolutely nothing to me. It was possible, I admitted to myself, that, as he said, my moral fiber would be sapped, I would get diseases which would turn me into a sideshow freak . . . but once a girl started to unbutton her blouse, I didn't care. I was a believer in love at any price. This of course made me fundamentally different from my father. Since I loved him, this disturbed me almost, if not quite, enough to give up the girls.

That summer of 1939 we were all too busy to think much about the news that interrupted the music on our radio. We were at sea heading back toward Boston when we heard on the radio that Hitler had just invaded Poland and that England was about to declare war. At sunset that night the sky was tinged with a strange glow of green, with clouds like bonfires all around the western horizon. Below decks everyone but the helmsman gathered around the radio while the oddly calm voice of the announcer chatted about the onset of doom.

"I wonder how long it will be before we get into it?" Fred Queen, whose father was a master mariner, asked.

Late that night on a radio broadcast from England, I heard for the first time Big Ben, the great voice of London, toll its solemn notes. Remembering my father's forecasts, I thought the bell was tolling the end of many things. For my generation the first casualty it mourned was the end of youth.

7

In August of 1940, my father died in his sleep at our house on Lake George. I had known of his heart condition, but somehow I had never expected him really to die. I felt as though the keystone had been pulled from the whole arch of my life.

Everything changed. The house in Florida was put on the market because mother thought she could carve out a new life for herself better in New York City. The big schooner was put on the market because Dad was really her motivating force, despite the fact that he was rarely aboard her. Without his encouragement to bolster me, I lost interest in running a charter vessel. The job now appeared impossible anyway because most of my friends in the Naval Reserve spent the summer taking training cruises on a battleship. The time for yachting had passed.

I survived the only way I knew how: I fell profoundly in love. The girl's name was Elise Pickhardt. She seemed to me to be the most beautiful girl I had ever seen, and a good many young men in Boston shared that opinion. At the coming-out parties she whirled about like a comet with a long tail of boys waiting to cut in.

One of the young men who had cruised with me aboard the *Aigrette* introduced me to her at a cocktail party about three months before my father died.

"Oh, you're the guy with the big boat," she said.

I allowed as how I was. She was a terrifying girl to meet, I thought. Recently I had read Maugham's *Of Human Bondage*, and I could see how a man could easily be obsessed with this young woman, Elise Pickhardt. For some reason I had always been afraid of unrequited love, bondage of the sort Maugham had written about. Since this Elise Pickhardt was one of the most popular girls at the dances, I didn't think I had much of a chance with her. The day after I met her I thought a long while before looking through the telephone book for the Pickhardts. When I called her up I had a strange sense of starting an extremely important chain of events.

A maid answered the telephone. There was a long wait before Elise came to the phone. Yes, she remembered me. Yes, she would like to have dinner and go to a movie with me, but Thursday? No. Friday? No. We finally arranged a date two weeks in the future.

Obviously it would be absurd to allow myself to fall in love with a girl who was almost as hard to see as the President of the United States. Love, like fear, can be controlled, I thought. None of that human bondage stuff for me.

All through the spring of 1940, I managed to keep my friendship with Elise light. Before my father died I drove up to her family's summer place in New Hampshire almost every week, but so did lots of other young men. Toward the end of July, I invited Elise to visit my parents at Lake George. My mother went through the business of writing her mother. In early August I proudly drove Elise to our summer home. Both of us were still trying to keep our relationship light. I installed Elise in our guest house. She was there only a few hours before my father died. I ran directly from my father's deathbed to her arms, and there was no pretense of lightness anymore.

Love is such a surprisingly simple, short word. I told Elise I loved her when it might have been more exact to say that I needed her and assumed that need was a part of love. No matter how strong my love for this pretty girl was, my need was greater. I think I thought that she somehow was a kind of angel standing at the door of eternity, holding me and telling me that I did not have to follow my father.

She said that she loved me. I'm not sure what she found to love in a twenty-year-old man more than half mad with grief. Need was not so much a part of her love. She came from a big, warm family out in West Newton, a suburb of Boston. When she invited me there shortly after my father's death, I fell in love not only with the girl, but her whole family, all the neighbors and the suburb of West Newton itself.

Her family lived in a big white Colonial house much like the one I had been born in. Her parents collected antiques, as my mother did. As soon as I walked through their front door, I felt at home.

Elise's father was an investment banker who belied all stereotyped notions of what a banker is. At first glance he resembled a Prussian general, for he kept his iron-gray hair cut short, and seemed to be standing at attention all the time. His deep voice had a ring of command to it, and I was a little scared of him until I learned how gentle he was with his two daughters and two sons. His elder son, Carl Pickhardt Junior, was a painter, a fact which gave his father great delight.

"I wish I could have been a painter," the father said, "and if I couldn't be a painter, I'd like to be a writer. Those are the guys who have all the fun."

Elise was the youngest member of her family and the only one who had not married. Every Sunday morning the whole clan gathered at the Pickhardt house. Carl Senior changed into the formal morning coat that he wore to the local Congregational church, and his wife, a tiny little woman with big brown eyes, wore a severely simple dress of white, gray or black with a hat to match. No pressure was put on the young people to go to church. Usually Elise stayed home with her brothers and Agatha, her elder sister, who was also a strikingly good-looking girl. Often Elise played the grand piano which stood in a corner of the living room while the rest of us lounged over coffee in the dining room and argued about politics, art and books. That was a wonderful family for arguing, no matter what the subject was. No one ever got angry, but often we all talked at once, and Carl Junior, a small man who took after his mother more than his father, fairly jumped up and down with indignation when someone scored a point against him in a debate. Carl Junior also jumped up and down with enthusiasm when the rest of us agreed with him. To me it seemed that Carl Junior was always jumping up and down, trying to rid himself of an excess of vitality.

When Carl Senior came home he went directly to his room to change his clothes. In summer he wore white linen suits and in winter dark gray or blue ones with pin stripes. His shoes were always shined and his pants perfectly pressed. I doubt if Carl Pickhardt Senior was ever really rumpled in his life.

An hour before dinner Carl Senior stirred a large pitcher of martinis in the library. Everyone drank, but I never saw anyone get really drunk, despite the fact that Carl Senior kept asking us whether we wanted "a little dividend" and assuring us that the pitcher in which he had mixed the martinis now contained "only a little ice water."

During this cocktail hour the family often became nostalgic and retold stories from earlier days. One of their favorites was about the time Carl Junior and his brother, Fowler, got hold of a sailor suit and contrived to make the bell-bottom trousers about seven feet long. After much practice, Carl was able to stand on his brother's shoulders and don the uniform, part of which covered Fowler's head. Beside a big highway on Cape Cod, they were able to give motorists the illusion that a sailor about nine feet tall was leaning nonchalantly against a tree, with a big cigar firmly clenched in his mouth.

Carl Junior was married to Meg, a beautiful dark-haired woman who was the daughter to Paul Sachs, who was, among other things, the head of the Fogg Art Museum at Harvard. Meg had been a national indoor tennis champion and through her father she had undoubtedly learned more about painting than the rest of us put together, but she had cultivated the art of silence. Because she listened with a smile of understanding, all the other people in the room often gathered around her. Meg was the audience while all the rest of us tried to be players.

After the cocktails, we all trooped into a big, paneled dining room, where a stout Nova Scotian woman who had been Elise's nursemaid served a New England boiled dinner or a roast. The excited conversation and laughter continued.

The Pickhardts' house seemed to me to be an island of cheer in an ocean of despair. I hated to leave, even for a night, and was finally almost adopted by the family. Student marriages were uncommon in those days, but my inner needs were given an excuse by the obvious approach of war. The allowance my mother had given me to finance my education and my participation in the elaborate social world of Boston would be enough to allow a young married couple to live simply. So why not get married and have a year or two together before the storm broke?

I was twenty years old at the time and Elise was eighteen. A great many sensible people were able to answer the question of why we shouldn't get married, but our ears were deaf during such debates. The discovery of our own sexuality shocked us, and we ached to become respectable again. Stern moral codes have the effect of forcing people into marriage when they are far too young to know what they are doing. I know that now, but I did not know it then. Perhaps that's just as well. The party the Pickhardts gave to announce the engagement of their youngest child to me was the greatest day of my life. Many of the people who came thought the festivities were part of the coming-out process and were surprised to learn that Elise was sort of going in before she had a chance to come out fully. Cynics guessed that she was pregnant or that I was getting married to avoid being drafted into the army. They were wrong on both counts. We got married because of the intensity of my need and our code of morality left no other choice. Or to put it another way, Carl Junior said, "Elise is marrying Sloan because it's the only way we know to get him out of the house."

We were married on February 4, 1941, and had fifteen months together before I went overseas. We spent those months in a two-room apartment at Holden Green, a housing complex for young instructors and graduate students which was owned by the university. I was so blindly happy that I did not realize that my young wife was experiencing many kinds of regret and fear. She told me once that she kept dreaming of being caught in a rushing river and being dragged far out to sea. A strange kind of passive melancholy sometimes overcame her normally high spirits. Often she felt nauseated and was always surprised when the doctor said she was not pregnant.

I assumed she was going through the "period of adjustment" which, I had read, many brides have to weather. When spring came we walked hand in hand along the green banks of the Charles River, and I was always proud to introduce her to friends as my wife. Her warmth gave me the strength to try to cope a little with the problems of my mother, who still was almost dumb with grief over the death of my father. All day mother sat staring out a window of her apartment in New York, her features frozen into a mask of despair. My sister, who lived with her, kept having mother examined by doctors, but none could find a prescription that could ease her pain for long.

Every Sunday Elise and I returned to the home of her parents for cocktails and the big dinner. To me that fortunate family seemed to live in the middle of a charmed circle into which illness, madness and death could never penetrate. The war itself failed to frighten them, for Carl Senior said there was a good chance that it all would be over before we had a chance to get into it. He himself was of German ancestry, and had taken his family to Berlin for the Olympic games. Although he had no admiration for Hitler, he had many German friends, and it was hard for him to believe that people of his own kind were running over Europe like a huge pack of mad dogs.

On December 7, 1941, Elise and I slept very late in our apartment. We started to get ready for the usual Sunday celebration at her family's house. Our clock said it was a little before two PM, and I thought it was a little fast. To get the right time, Elise turned on the radio. Instead of the time, she got the first news of Pearl Harbor.

"What does it mean?" she asked.

"War," I said, and I remember being very conscious of the brevity of that word. It's always those short words that get people into trouble— war, sex, hate and love.

"How soon will you be going?" she asked.

"Soon," I said, another short word that meant too much.

We drove silently to West Newton with the car radio giving us more bulletins. Carl Senior was sitting in his library with a martini glass in his hand. For the first and last time in the years that I knew him, he looked utterly defeated. At dinner that day there was no laughter. Carl Junior said he was going to try to get a commission in the navy.

"I suppose you'll be doing that too," he said to me.

"No," I replied, still for some reason conscious of the power of the shortest words.

"What will you be doing?" Carl Senior asked.

"I'm going to join the coast guard. They have small ships. I'll be at home there."

"Then maybe you won't even have to leave Boston," Elise said.

"In time of war the coast guard becomes part of the navy. I don't have any idea of where I'll be sent."

"Well, I know what you should do," Elise's mother said to her. "You should move right back with us when Sloan leaves. I'm not going to have you moping around some apartment alone."

"That would be nice," Elise said.

We finished the meal almost in silence. Afterward we sat around a radio in the library and listened to a recording of one of Hitler's speeches. I couldn't understand a word and the voice sounded more like the ululations of an hysteric than the pronouncements of a head of state.

"Can you understand what he's saying?" Elise's mother asked her father.

"Only a little," Carl Senior said. "The son of a bitch doesn't even speak pure German. Who knows what he's trying to say?"

Part 2
"Ignorance Is Death"

8

In those days, when there was such a need for young officers, it was possible to get a commission in the coast guard by taking a twelve-hour examination in navigation and seamanship at M.I.T. I had learned the navigation before I dropped out of the Naval Reserve unit at Harvard to look after my own vessel, and I had picked up a little seamanship during our summer cruises. I passed the examination with such high marks that I began laboring under the dangerous illusion that I was an experienced old salt.

With the notice that I had met the requirements for a commission, the coast guard sent me a list of clothes and equipment I should buy. My mother gave me the money for this, and I bought the full regalia, including an impressive sword.

"Why in the world do they make you buy a sword?" Elise asked. "Are you going to try to fight submarines with that?"

"I think they sometimes use swords in parades," I replied. "Anyway, it will make a nice souvenir for our children."

In those days we had fallen into the habit of talking about "our children" as though they already existed. The concept of them lying in wait to be born somehow comforted us.

In our apartment I tried on the handsome dress uniform, the blue uniforms with their single gold stripe and the gold shield, which was the coast guard emblem, on the cuffs. One thing I couldn't figure out was the way to attach the shoulder boards to the great coat and the khaki uniforms. It somehow seemed right to have the tapered ends out and the broad ends in. That's the way I fixed them and when my orders came a few weeks later, that's the way I wore them when I went aboard the United States Coast Guard Cutter *Tampa*, which was moored at a shipyard in Boston. Somewhere I had learned that one is supposed to salute the quarterdeck when one boards a cutter. I had very little practice at saluting, and instead of making it an informal gesture as most officers did, I stopped in the middle of the gangway, assumed as statuesque a position as possible and snapped my hand from the visor of my cap to my side. To the men who were watching me from the deck of the cutter, I seemed typical of all the reserve officers who were pouring into the service. I had my shoulder boards on backward and exaggerated the salute to the quarterdeck so much that I was burlesquing it.

Surprised by the laughter which greeted me, I asked the quartermaster who stood at the gangway where I could find the officer of the deck. This—*The Naval Officer's Guide* had taught me—was the correct procedure.

"He's in his stateroom," the quartermaster replied. "The exec will want to see you if you're coming aboard for duty. He's up on the flying bridge."

The quartermaster told a seaman to show me the way to the flying bridge. After climbing several steel ladders, I found myself standing on a broad deck where a stocky man about fifty years old was pacing in circles. On the cuffs of his uniform he wore two gold stripes which were so worn that they had turned almost to silver. His close-cropped hair was also silvery, and his wrinkled face resembled that of an English bulldog.

Without a word the messenger left me there and disappeared. For perhaps a minute—which seemed very long—the executive officer paced without seeming to notice me.

"Sir," I said finally.

"Now what the hell do you want?" he demanded.

"My name is Wilson, sir. Ensign Wilson is reporting aboard for duty."

"Oh no!" the exec said, and clapped his hand to his forehead.

"Sir?"

"I asked for an officer, god damn it, and they send me a boy with a gold stripe. Did you get that along with the gold stars the teacher used to give you in school?"

"No, sir."

"Have you ever had any experience with this big pond out here which we call the North Atlantic ocean?"

"I have had considerable experience, sir, with small vessels."

"What the hell kind of small vessels?"

"Yachts, sir."

"Oh, sweet Jesus Christ!" the exec thundered. "They've sent me a yachtsman! Dear sweet Jesus Christ, what have I done to deserve this?"

The man's rage was so great that he was making faces at me. His lips drew back in a snarl and his shaggy eyebrows almost covered his piercing blue eyes.

"A yachtsman," he repeated. "Yachtsmen are what the coast guard has to go out saving every day. If they have to commission yachtsmen, why in hell don't they give them to the other side? All of Hitler's admirals put together couldn't run a navy if they had yachtsmen for officers."

"Yes, sir," I heard myself saying.

"Now how did you get that gold stripe on your arm? It took me twenty years as a chief boatswain's mate to get a gold stripe. How did you get yours?"

"I took a twelve-hour examination at M.I.T., sir."

"Jesus, *sweet* Jesus, sweet Jesus Christ," the exec thundered, and he actually clawed his hair as though he were trying to pull it out.

"It took me twenty years to get a gold stripe, and it took you twelve hours. Now where did you get the book learning for that examination?"

"Harvard College, sir."

"Harvard! *Harvard!* I ask for a coast guard officer and they send me a Harvard boy. Are you a fag, boy? They say they got a lot of fags over there at Harvard. We'll have no fags aboard this ship. How could we sleep at night knowing there was only a Harvard fag standing watch on the bridge?"

"Sir! I'm not a fag. You have no reason to worry about that."

"Not a fag, eh? Well, I bet you're a rich little bastard. A snotty rich little prick. That's what they *specialize* in at Harvard, isn't it? That and fags. Of the two I think I'd prefer the fag."

He resumed his pacing and started circling around me like a wolf ready to close in for the kill. His face was still contorted with rage. At first I had thought that this was only some kind of hazing that met all newcomers, but I realized now that the executive officer's anger was real.

"I've only got two officers on this goddamn ship now that are good enough to stand a watch at sea," he continued. "How long do they think it will take me to make a coast guard officer out of a Harvard boy? This is only the second world war, boy! Even if I worked day and night, I doubt whether I could get you ready in time for the third one!"

I couldn't think of anything to say to this. I made a timid attempt to smile.

"What are you laughing for, boy? Jesus Christ, look at you. You've got your shoulder boards on backward. By god, you're an *original*, I'll say that for you. How dare you walk aboard a coast guard cutter all ass backwards like that?"

To my horror the blood rushed to my·face.

"I don't know anything about uniforms, sir, sir," I stammered. "The examination was only in navigation and seamanship."

"Book navigation and book seamanship, you mean. You think you know seamanship, eh? Can you launch and pick up a whaleboat in thirty-foot seas?"

"No, sir."

"Well, what the hell can you do? Please enlighten me. The government is giving you more pay than I got after my first twenty years in the service. Now, god damn it, you must know something. It stands to reason.

The people up there in Washington are crazy, but they can't be *this* crazy. What can you do to justify that gold stripe?"

"I think I can learn fairly fast, sir."

"*Learn!* You go to school to learn! On a coast guard cutter we save lives! We sink submarines! We stay out in hurricanes to send weather reports. This is no schoolhouse, boy! Maybe you got confused because we got a ship's bell. That's not a school bell, boy! We just ring that when we're anchored in a fog."

"Yes, sir."

"What can you do besides learn?"

"I can navigate fairly well, sir, but I need more experience in identifying stars."

"So you've come here to learn and to get experience. Can you piss in the head, boy, without missing it when the ship is rolling forty degrees?"

"I hope so, sir."

"Can you keep your vomit off my decks when we get out of this harbor? I'll have no Harvards vomiting on my decks. Makes them too slippery. We had a Yale aboard here once, and all he did was vomit on the decks. Had seamen sliding all over the place. I hear the Harvards are even worse than the Yales, more faggoty. Can you keep from vomiting on the decks, boy?"

"I'll try, sir."

"Oh Jesus, sweet Jesus Christ! Get out of my sight, boy! I have worries enough without you. I have this whole ship to put in shape, and they've given me only a week. I got women welders aboard. Have you ever heard of a woman welder? They sent two aboard to weld them twenty millimeters on the deck. I got women welders and I got Harvards and Yales, and who knows what's going to happen next? You know, it wouldn't surprise me one goddamn bit if they sent me a *monkey* in an ensign's uniform tomorrow. I got to get out of this port or we'll have the whole fucking zoo aboard here, all decked out in brand new uniforms!"

His ferocity was such that there was no temptation to laugh.

"Get out of here!" he finally said. "Go below! Hide! At least I don't have to *look* at you, do I?"

"No, sir," I said, and quickly skinned down the ladders to the deck. A thin, craggy-looking lieutenant junior grade came up to me.

"I see you're still alive," he said. "I'm sorry I didn't get a chance to warn you about the terrible tempered Pop Hart."

"Pop Hart?"

"That's what everybody calls him. He's great with the enlisted men, but he's hell on junior officers, especially us reserves."

"You mean he puts on that sort of display for every ensign who comes aboard here?"

"I don't know just what he did for you. He had one ensign locked up in the brig five minutes after he came aboard."

"What was the charge?"

"Impersonating an officer. He acted real surprised when the guy turned out to be legit."

I laughed.

"Come and I'll show you your stateroom," the lieutenant junior grade said. "My name is Carter. I'm glad to see you come aboard. Frankly, I hope you turn out to be completely incompetent. That might keep some of the heat off me."

9

I am writing these words thirty-three years after I walked aboard the United States Coast Guard Cutter *Tampa*. Although I was aboard the vessel only about six months, I have many more memories of her than I have of the four years I spent at Harvard College, and I think she taught me more.

The *Tampa* had been old even before the start of World War II. Two hundred and forty feet long, she had a plum stem and a stern like the tail of a seagull, a graceful configuration which showed its recent descent from sailing vessels. The ship had not yet acquired the arctic camouflage of pale blue and white. She was painted battleship gray, which was really the only warlike thing about her. Partly because of the heavy construction which made her an efficient rescue ship, the *Tampa* was painfully slow for an escort vessel. When the engines were running well, she could reach a speed of only thirteen knots—a limitation which meant that she could barely get out of the way of her own depth charges. To make matters worse, there was no modern method for aiming the two three-inch and two five-inch guns that had recently been welded to our decks. When we tried to sink a derelict barge, we couldn't hit it even when we sailed right alongside it. When we used a small iceberg for target practice, it survived intact. These displays did little to improve the morale of the crew.

The duty of the *Tampa*, during that spring of 1942, was to escort merchant vessels from Sydney, Nova Scotia, to our air bases in Greenland. As soon as the *Tampa* got to Greenland, she was ordered back to Sydney to meet a new convoy. Rarely did her crew get ashore.

Conditions at sea were so difficult that few men of the *Tampa* had time to worry about the German submarines which were reported in our area. During the summer months, those arctic seas were foggy most of the time, and in winter the endless night and almost endless gales reduced visibility as much as the fog did. In those early days of the war, the *Tampa* had no radar and only the most primitive sonar. Completely blind, the ship had to zigzag around a convoy which was itself zig-zagging. In retrospect, the fact that the ship did this without collisions appears to be a miracle.

It was a miracle which few of the *Tampa's* men expected. On the starboard side of a deckhouse some profound student of military morale had placed a bronze plaque in memory of the first *Tampa*, a coast guard cutter which had gone down with all hands during World War I. The men made grim jokes about the fact that one plaque could be used to commemorate both *Tampa's* if we sank.

When I first went aboard the *Tampa* and was lambasted by Pop Hart on the flying bridge, I assumed that this was some sort of hazing which was dished out to all newcomers, or that the grizzled executive officer was insane. I was wrong on both counts. Pop Hart's difficulty was simply that he understood the situation. He knew what it was like to convoy ships through arctic seas, and he also knew that the *Tampa* had no more than four competent deck officers in addition to an ever growing swarm of reserve officers who had been hastily commissioned before the coast guard even had a chance to start effective training programs.

"Do you know what this is like?" Pop Hart said to me the day after I had come aboard. "This is like going to some goddamn football stadium and dressing everybody in the audience up like players. You can put old ladies and fat men in helmets and jerseys, but, god damn it, that's not going to make them play ball!"

I never saw the commanding officer of the ship until a few minutes before we were to get underway and leave Boston Harbor for Nova Scotia and Greenland. Our skipper appeared to be the direct opposite of Pop Hart. Small, delicately made and dapper, he used as few words as possible. I watched the two of them in action, for I was stationed as a junior watch officer on the wing of the bridge.

The captain seated himself on a stool near the wheel. He gripped his knees, and the three gold stripes of a commander looked too big for his short arms.

"Mr. Hart," he said in a voice that was barely audible. "You may get underway when ready and proceed to the fuel barge."

"Aye, aye, sir!" Hart bellowed. At the top of his voice he began to give orders as he paced back and forth on the bridge.

"Quartermaster! Tell the engineroom to stand by. Messenger! Ask the chief if the decks are secure and ready for sea. Pipe mooring stations!

Mr. Wilson! Please get your ass off the bridge. The one thing I had hoped is that you at least would know enough to stay the hell out of the way!"

"I was told . . ."

"Never mind, god damn it. Get out of my sight. I got work to do."

I retreated to a ladder leading to the deck, where I could hide but still see a good deal of what was going on.

"Right full rudder," Hart bellowed to the helmsman as though he were standing a thousand yards away. Coming to the wing of the bridge over my head, he called, "All right, Boats, take in one, three and four."

"One, three and four, sir," the chief boatswain's mate repeated.

The heavy lines splashed. Mr. Hart started bawling orders to the quartermaster who stood by the engineroom telegraph. The ship trembled to the rhythm of her heavy engines as we backed away from the wharf and headed out of the slip.

That first short journey from the wharf to the fuel barge in Boston harbor taught me a lot. The channels were crowded with tugs, barges, tankers and every other kind of wartime shipping. Mr. Hart stood on the port wing of the bridge and barked brief orders to the helmsman and quartermaster as we threaded our way through the traffic. He stood straighter than I had ever seen him and his voice had lost its fury. He was, I realized as he threaded his way past a tug's string of barges and an aircraft carrier which occupied most of the channel, a superb ship handler. He smiled as we passed the carrier with only a few feet to spare at the very edge of the channel.

"Boy!" he said to me, despite the fact that I had thought myself safely hidden halfway down the ladder.

"Sir?"

"I doubt if it will ever happen, but if you ever learn enough to conn this vessel in crowded waters, you just remember that that uniform of yours is the uniform of the United States Coast Guard, and this is the United States Coast Guard Cutter *Tampa*. Other ships can walk or run, boy, but a United States Coast Guard cutter has to *dance!*"

And dance the old *Tampa* did as we zigzagged through the crowded harbor and finally arrived at the fuel barge, from which a destroyer was just pulling clear. A tanker was made fast to the other side of the barge, her ensign flat in a brisk breeze which was coming from the mouth of the harbor. As we passed a buoy I saw that it was leaning to a swift current. With such a wind and tide it would not be easy to take a single-screw vessel alongside a barge, and the task would be harder because the barge itself was anchored to long lines, on which it was slowly swinging in a broad arc.

"Ahead slow," Mr. Hart said, and almost immediately added, "Ahead half."

The cutter approached the barge briskly.

"Mr. Hart," the captain said in his oddly dead voice. "Don't try a smart mooring now. I just want a safe one. Reduce your speed."

"Aye, aye, sir," Mr. Hart said, and he made a face, a fierce grimace with bared fangs. Fortunately he had his back to the captain. "Ahead slow," he said to the quartermaster, and made his face again.

The curious thing about Mr. Hart was that when he made a face he managed to be truly terrifying, not just funny. There was nothing fake about Pop Hart. He hated all reserve officers because they didn't know enough, and he hated our captain because he was timid and did not act according to Hart's romantic ideal of a coast guard officer. Whether his romantic ideal of a coast guard officer went around making faces at people, I had no idea, but Pop Hart's all-consuming rage was so powerful that it had to erupt somewhere.

I have for some reason some intense need to make the war appear funny. There was, of course, nothing humorous about the half year I spent as a junior watch officer aboard the *Tampa*. In the first place, I was seasick almost all the time. Summer cruises on yachts had not fitted me for arctic gales. To obey Pop Hart's command that I keep his decks clean, I carried a bucket on my arm when I went on watch and quietly retched into it every few minutes. No food would stay down. Soon my uniform hung on me as loosely as though my shoulders were a wire hanger.

Worse than the seasickness was the fear of death. A large troopship, the *Chatham*, was sunk in Davis Strait just before we got there. Submarines appeared to me to be lying in wait for us everywhere. Thousands of icebergs seemed to me to constitute an even greater menace. It seemed clear to me that the odds were much in favor of my getting killed, and though I knew I should be brave, I was obsessed with thoughts of what it must be like to be on the deck of a ship when she was hit by a torpedo. Everyone said that a man couldn't live more than thirty seconds in the freezing seas of Davis Strait. What did he think about for those thirty seconds?

Lying in my bunk, retching in my bucket and trying to imagine death, I felt unabashedly sorry for myself. Damn it, I was much too *nice* to die, and actually, I was too nice to be seasick month after month. Somehow God had got his plans all mixed up. Here I was going to be eaten by sharks and crabs and even minnows, while evil old men prospered ashore. My wife would soon remarry someone smart or sick enough not to go to war. I would be erased without a memory. Even the sharks and crabs and minnows would soon be hungry for more.

Worse even than the seasickness and the fear was the realization of my own incompetence, my own worthlessness as an officer and as a man. Every day brought me new problems which I could not solve. Handicapped by my seasickness and by the murky skies, I hardly ever could make my star sights work. I couldn't read Morse code or signal flags. I knew nothing about the maintenance or use of the ship's guns. On and on the list of my inadequacies ran. When on watch I hid as much as possible behind a door on the bridge, and the rest of the time I retreated to my bunk.

When we were in Sydney, Nova Scotia, that autumn, the *Tampa* took aboard a load of six-hundred-pound depth charges—twice the normal weight. They were said to be effective against submarines, but almost every man in our crew suspected that because of her slow speed, the *Tampa* could not drop such large amounts of TNT without blowing off her own stern. Almost every man jack was just as scared as I was, I realized with some relief. In fear at least I was not alone.

At general quarters, I was stationed four decks down in the stern of the ship, where I was supposed to supervise five black steward's mates who were passing ammunition up to the five-inch gun overhead. Pop Hart told me to be sure to wear the forty-five automatic which every officer was supposed to wear during general quarters.

"It doesn't take much to make those niggers panic," Mr. Hart said darkly. He was, among other things, a cornucopia of racial prejudice. When he told me that he wanted me to shoot the steward's mates if they panicked, I was not a bit surprised.

Among the many things I didn't know was how to shoot a .45 pistol, and I had been unwilling to pull the gun from its holster for fear it might go off and hit me in the leg. Beyond this, I rather liked the steward's mates, who brought food to my stateroom when I felt well enough to eat, and who were the only people on the ship who did not keep sneering at my incompetence. Every time we went to general quarters, the steward's mates sat in the magazine waiting for the call for ammunition, and I sat a few steps up the companionway presumably waiting to shoot them. There was only one small blue bulb down there in the magazine and the eerie light it cast contributed to the lack of reality I felt. Once when all our machine guns opened up overhead, the steward's mates leapt to their feet and looked as though they might panic, but then I found myself backing up the companionway toward the deck—a reaction which was quite involuntary, and which was interrupted when one of the steward's mates said, "Suh, I think you better stay down here."

The machine guns, we soon learned, had been sinking a floating mine which probably had drifted over from Europe. None of us had expected to encounter a floating mine in the middle of Davis Strait, and the discovery of such a menace, in addition to all the others, did little to increase our sense of well-being.

Only a few days later, another coast guard cutter which was helping us to escort the convoy signaled a submarine alert and began dropping depth charges. We went to general quarters, and I again found myself sitting in that blue light with the five steward's mates, who appeared to be taking all the excitement so philosophically that they prepared to light cigarettes, until I reminded them that we were surrounded by ammunition. That was my most officer-like deed of the entire voyage, and I felt quite proud of it. Down there in the bowels of the ship, we felt the thump of the other cutter's depth charges in addition to hearing them. Then our own engines suddenly speeded up.

"Here we go," the tallest of the steward's mates said. "Now we going to find out if we can drop them six-hundred-pounders."

"Oh, we can drop *one*," a small, lighter-colored man said. Dark laughter.

There was a lot of clatter on deck, followed by silence broken only by an increase of the engines to what I guessed was flank speed. The motion of the ship changed as she shifted course. I vomited into my trusty bucket —my way of meeting all maritime emergencies. While I was still suffering from the dizziness of nausea, there was the loudest explosion I had ever heard and the stern of the vessel was thrown so high in the air that the decks became almost perpendicular. The blue light went out. In the complete darkness I was kicked several times as the steward's mates climbed over my body to bolt for the deck. I knew that this was when I was supposed to shoot them, but I was hanging precariously from a ladder, and it was too dark to shoot anybody, even if I had had any real stomach for that kind of military activity. The steward's mates did not seem very important, because the ship obviously had received an enormous blow, either from her own depth charges or a torpedo, and I was sure that I was about to die. The stern of the ship suddenly came down as violently as it had gone up, and all my strength was necessary to hang tightly to the ladder. I was surprised to find that my head was clearer than it had been in weeks, and I felt oddly calm. My calmness in the face of death delighted me. It would of course be a short-lived triumph, but at least I could die with the first glimmering of self-respect. As the ship steadied into a normal position, which is to say, a heavy roll, I listened to see if I could hear a rush of water through a hole left by the explosion, but there was none. All I could hear was the rolling of heavy objects on the deck below. It dawned on me that the steward's mates had dropped the explosive shells they were supposed to be passing to the gun overhead. Rolling about, they of course constituted a danger almost as bad as a torpedo. Feeling highly heroic, I captured the shells and stowed them. As I ran my fingers over the pigeon holes in which bags of powder and the shells were kept, it occurred to me that only a crazy man would

66

start shooting a pistol in a magazine. That is what I would tell Pop Hart if he asked me why I had not shot the steward's mates.

Only a few minutes later I heard the signal to secure from general quarters. In the wardroom, where the unrepentant steward's mates were serving sandwiches and coffee, I heard the cause of the enormous explosion: when the signal had been given to drop a six-hundred-pound charge, a frightened seaman had held the big "ashcan" back by putting his hand on it. Whereupon the signal had been given again, and in the end two of the lethal charges had been dropped together. Pop Hart was furious about the mix-up, but his anger was lightened by pride in the fact that the old *Tampa* had survived without serious injury.

"You tell me what ship except a coast guard cutter can survive twelve hundred pounds of TNT under her ass when she's only making thirteen knots!" he said.

I was apprehensive for days, but he never found out about the panicking steward's mates, or my dereliction from duty in allowing them to escape. In the lightheadedness induced by my continued seasickness, I sometimes imagined being ordered by Pop Hart to stalk through the ship, shooting steward's mates wherever they could be found. I even imagined a citation I might be given by President Roosevelt himself.

> "For shooting all six steward's mates aboard the United States Coast Guard Cutter *Tampa* while engaged in combat with German submarines off the coast of Greenland, the Distinguished Service Cross is hereby awarded to Ensign Sloan Wilson, USCGR, who bagged his men despite extreme seasickness."

Despite the lack of such a citation, I found that the memory of my performance in the after magazine of the *Tampa* gave me pleasure to help combat the depression of seasickness. There had, after all, been about three minutes there when I actually had been brave, the only three minutes in which I could feel pride during the months I had been aboard the *Tampa*. The nonsense about shooting the steward's mates was the first example I had of the fact that war is ridiculous far more than it is heroic. When one came right down to it, I saw, the steward's mates had been sensible enough to panic when the *Tampa* had come close to sinking herself with two giant depth charges while pursuing a whale, for that is what the man on the sonar machine finally decided that his target was. The only good thing about this whole burlesque was that despite the explosion of twelve-hundred pounds of TNT, both the steward's mates and the whale got away.

10

After about five months aboard the *Tampa,* I began to recover from sea-sickness. On a stormy day I stood on the flying bridge of the vessel, watched her struggle to the peak of mountainous arctic seas and dive into the valley which followed, burying half her length in green water and foam, all without making my stomach contract. With the nausea gone, I found that I could learn a little about the workings of the ship, but Pop Hart still did not trust me enough to do more than supervise the passing of ammunition and serve as a junior watch officer, which meant little more than acting as an extra lookout on the bridge.

Mr. Hart's worst excesses were saved for Mr. Carter, who offended Hart's sensibilities even more than I did. Mr. Carter's chief sin was that he had somehow contrived to enter the coast guard directly from civilian life as a lieutenant junior grade. In his late twenties, he was a tall thin man who kept getting thinner and more haggard as the months of stormy weather wore on. I was rather slow at overcoming seasickness, but Mr. Carter never did get to the point where he could go on watch without his bucket. When we donned steel helmets, life preservers and pistol belts for general quarters, Mr. Carter's gaunt bent figure looked like a caricature of an officer.

"Don't worry, men!" Pop Hart would explode as Carter entered the wardroom after we had secured from general quarters. "You don't have to worry about the Germans. They may have battleships and submarines, but we have Carter!"

Instead of going through variations of this routine, Hart sometimes would just watch Carter as he entered the wardroom, trying to make his way to his stateroom. The old coast guardsman would track Carter's fumbling progress the way a cat might track an injured mouse with his eyes. Just before Carter touched the doorknob of his stateroom, Hart smote his own forehead and shouted, "Jesus, Sweet Jesus, oh *Sweet* Jesus Christ! What did I do, God? Why did you let me live to see the day when coast guard officers look like that?"

Carter would jump into his room as though kicked.

Mr. Carter and I got to be good friends. On stormy days we sometimes stood in the lee of the deckhouse near the bronze plaque to the first

Tampa, which had been lost with all hands. Exercising a rather bizarre sense of humor, Mr. Carter liked to sing the old song about the [wreck of] the *Titanic*.

"It was sad," he'd chorus in his surprisingly strong tenor,

"It was sad, it was sad when that great ship went down,
TO THE BOTTOM,
Oh, husbands and wives, little children lost their lives, it was
    Sad when that great ship went down."

Carter knew dozens of verses and the only thing which could make him stop singing was a new spasm in his stomach, and the need to use his bucket.

Once when we had moored at an army base in a fjord near the southern tip of Greenland, a trawler which had been converted into a coast guard cutter moored alongside us. She was painted with sharp angles of blue and white to make her hard to see in the ice, and there was an air of jaunty independence about her tough little hull. Her skipper, a lieutenant junior grade who didn't look much older than I, asked if he could borrow some of our charts. While that request was going through channels, I offered him a cup of coffee in our wardroom.

"Where do you operate?" I asked.

"All up and down the west coast of Greenland and sometimes the Canadian arctic."

He was wearing a non-regulation sealskin cap and high jackboots. Obviously he was his own man, with no Pop Hart to worry him.

"Is it hard to get stationed on a trawler?" I asked.

"God no. It's just hard to get off one."

"Do you like it?"

He grinned.

"It's rough duty, but I like having my own ship."

That day I decided to request duty aboard one of the coast guard's armed trawlers. The idea of roaming the coast of Greenland aboard my own vessel obsessed my imagination so much that I never wondered whether I was sailor enough to command a ship in arctic waters.

It took about six months for my request to be acted upon. For some reason I was stationed for a few months on a buoy tender in Chesapeake Bay before I received orders to fly to Argentia, Newfoundland—there to report for duty aboard the United States Coast Guard Cutter *Nogak* (which in the Greenlander's tongue means "reindeer").

It was May of 1943, when I arrived aboard the *Nogak*. I had been in the coast guard just a year, but felt I had grown far beyond the awkward ensign who had reported aboard the *Tampa* with his shoulder boards on backward. I already boasted the stripes of a lieutenant junior grade, and was quite sure that I would never get seasick again.

No one in the huge naval base in Argentia appeared to know just where the *Nogak* was moored, but I finally found her at the end of a high pier. Only 114 feet long, the converted trawler looked much like an ocean-going tug. No one could call her beautiful, but there was a tough, no-nonsense quality about her that I found appealing. Swinging myself aboard with one hand on the rigging which supported a stubby mast, I asked an enlisted man who stood by the gangway for the officer of the deck.

"The officers are all ashore except the captain, and he's asleep," the seaman replied. He appeared to be only about eighteen years old, and had buttoned his peajacket tightly under his chin to ward off the Newfoundland breezes.

"I'm reporting aboard for duty," I said. "Do you want to log me in?"

"I just got here myself," he replied. "Maybe you better get one of the officers to take care of you."

I glanced at my watch. It was a little after three in the afternoon. In spring and summer, time was hard to estimate in the arctic; it never got dark.

"The officers' quarters are aft," the seaman said. "I guess you'll be bunking there."

I walked aft. The decks were of heavy pine planks caulked with pitch in the old-fashioned way. The stern was U-shaped in the classic manner of trawlers, and she carried a rack of three-hundred-pound depth charges. I wondered if she went fast enough to get out of their way. Because they are made to drag massive nets, most trawlers exchange speed for towing power. I descended a steep ladder and came to a cabin only about fifteen feet long and twelve feet wide. On each side there were two bunks. An ensign's uniform hung by one, while that of a warrant boatswain hung near the other. That made me feel good. I'd never met a warrant boatswain who didn't have years of experience. The bunks on the port side were filled with unopened canvas sacks of mail, some of which spilled over to the cabin sole. The place smelled of unaired bedsheets and old clothes. I climbed back on deck and walked forward. The little ship had a forty-caliber machine gun near her stern, two twenty-millimeter antiaircraft guns on a new steel deck which had been built forward of her pilothouse, and sort of a sawed-off, three-inch gun on her bow. Certainly this was not enough armament to fight off a submarine on the surface, but the *Nogak* could probably give a low-flying airplane a bad time. Sticking my head in an open hatch, I found myself at the head of a ladder leading to the forecastle, a fairly large V-shaped compartment with bunks stacked around both sides and a long table in the middle. Perhaps a third of the bunks were full of men sleeping or reading. At the table a man in a tall chef's hat—of a sort I had never seen in the service—was playing cards with a muscular, red-haired young boatswain's mate.

"Sir," the man with the chef's hat said in an accent which sounded German, "you want something?"

"I'm just looking around," I replied. "I've just reported aboard for duty."

The boatswain's mate, who had not paid much attention to me, began studying me carefully. Several men who had appeared to be asleep in their bunks propped their chin on an elbow to stare. Well, what is more important on a small ship, I thought, than the arrival of a new commanding officer? If he is unskilled, he can easily sink the ship with all hands. If he's a bastard, he can make everybody aboard miserable for months or years.

"You want a cup of coffee, lieutenant?" the man with the chef's hat asked. "I got some nice fresh apple cake. You want a piece?"

"That would go fine."

Taking my cap off, I sat down at the table. It suddenly occurred to me that I must look damnably young. My light-colored hair made me look even younger than my twenty-three years. I swallowed. In almost no time at all the man with the chef's hat brought me a mug of coffee and a plate with a large square of apple cake. The coffee, I found, was much better than the stuff one ordinarily gets aboard ships and the apple cake obviously had been made by a skilled pastry cook.

"This is great," I said to the man with the chef's hat. "What's your name?"

"Everybody just calls me Cookie," the man said. "I'm glad you like the apple cake. I do as well as I can with the G.I. stores we get. If we could only...."

He was interrupted by the seaman whom I had first seen at the gangway.

"Skipper's getting up!" he called from the top of the companionway. "He says he wants his usual. Don't bring it to his cabin. He'll eat it down here."

Cookie dashed to his galley. The boatswain's mate hurried on deck after putting the cards in his pocket, and the men in the bunks disappeared like groundhogs ducking into their holes.

After a few minutes of silence, there was the sound of jackboots approaching on the pine deck overhead. The jackboots were what I saw first of our commanding officer as he descended the ladder. They were black and polished. I next saw the carefully pressed uniform of a senior lieutenant who was tall and gracefully built. He was wearing the sealskin cap which so many of the officers on the Greenland Patrol sported. When at the foot of the ladder he turned toward me, I saw that he was about a third bald. He had piercing dark eyes and a thick black beard which was meticulously trimmed. The eyes bored into me.

"My name is Wilson," I said. "I'm reporting aboard for duty."

For what seemed a long time he said nothing. His eyes seemed to analyze me right down to the marrow of my bones. Suddenly I wanted to apologize for being only twenty-three years old and for looking younger.

"Do you have your orders?" he asked. His voice was oddly professorial, but I could not believe that he was the kind of reserve officer who had been commissioned after no experience at sea. It was impossible to guess his background.

I handed him the envelope with my orders. He studied the document carefully. I guessed that he was rereading the key sentence: "Lt. (j.g.) Sloan Wilson will report aboard U.S.C.G.C. *Nogak* as executive officer and prospective commanding officer." That could mean almost anything the skipper wanted it to. If he wanted to get off the ship, he could turn her over to me within a few days after certifying that I was competent for command. If he did not think me capable, or if he did not want to give up his ship, he could delay the matter for months or could quickly certify me as unfit for command. Usually, I had heard, the skippers of trawlers were so anxious to go to a bigger vessel which might be expected to serve in milder climates that prospective commanding officers were rarely made to wait long.

"I'll have you logged in," the skipper said, putting my orders in his pocket. His voice told me nothing. Cookie put a large platter of chicken livers and scrambled eggs with toast and a cup of coffee in front of him. The captain ate in silence, taking small precise forkfuls. He did not look at me. There were many questions I wanted to ask, but his face was forbidding. When he had finished the last bite of food and the last drop of coffee, he wiped his mouth with a linen napkin which Cookie provided and turned to me.

"Mr. Wilson," he said, "your first duty here will be to open the official mail and file it. We've been so busy that a good deal of the stuff has piled up over the past few months. As a matter of fact, I think you better devise a new filing system and start from scratch. I never have been able to find anything when I wanted it."

"Aye, aye, sir," I said, trying to keep my voice even. Wasn't I supposed to be executive officer, even if he disapproved of me as skipper? Since when were executive officers turned into filing clerks?

"I would do the job as fast as possible if I were you," the captain continued. "We'll be putting to sea any day now. You'll find that these little ships are pretty lively. It will be easier to do the filing in port."

"Aye, aye, sir," I repeated.

The captain got to his feet and went on deck. I followed, hoping to get a chance to ask him for permission to go ashore to look for my footlocker, which the baggage handlers had somehow mislaid.

"Is Mr. Mondino aboard yet?" the captain asked the man at the gangway.

"Yes, sir," the seaman said.

"Please tell him to come here."

His tone was studiously polite, but the seaman ran to the after cabin. In a few moments a short, bedraggled appearing ensign about my age appeared.

"Good afternoon, Mr. Mondino," the captain said, and I never heard so much disdain compressed into so few words.

"You want me?" Mondino asked, his round face doughy and sullen.

"I want you to relieve me. I'm going ashore."

"I relieve you, sir."

"If they should want you to move the ship, call me at the officers' club."

"Aye, aye, sir."

The captain put one hand on the rigging and with the grace of a gibbon swung himself ashore. At the moment his feet touched the wharf, a seaman on the bridge ran up the third repeater, a black and white pennant which means "the commanding officer is not aboard." Pleased by the precision of this bit of etiquette, the captain smiled and began striding on his long legs toward the officers' club.

"You're the new officer?" Mondino asked me.

"Yes."

"Who are you supposed to relieve?"

"I don't know."

"I was hoping it would be me, but they wouldn't send a j.g. to relieve an ensign."

"Probably not."

"You're probably supposed to relieve the old man. I sure hope so. I don't care what's the matter with you, you couldn't be half as bad as that crazy bastard."

"How is he crazy?"

"You'll see. He's crazier than a Kee bird."

"What's a Kee bird?"

"It's an arctic tern. It cries 'Kee, Kee, Christ but it's cold,' and flies in concentric circles until it finally disappears up its own asshole."

When we got to the after cabin Mr. Mondino opened two large lockers which held more sacks of official mail than the bunks did.

"There's more in the cargo hold," he said. "That's all he does with official mail—hide it someplace in case there's an admiral's inspection."

"Why doesn't he have you file it?"

"I tried for a while, but he doesn't like the way I do it. Thank god. My eyes aren't very good and I go blind before I can get through one sack of the stuff."

Since there was nothing else to do, I opened the first sack of official mail. Some of it consisted of codes, most of which were rated "top secret." Locating a filing cabinet with a lock, I started to do my best at what appeared to be an impossible job. Because none of the mail had been read, I had to scan it all and it took me more than an hour to empty the first bag.

After I had filed two more bags the pile of the canvas sacks on the bunks and in the lockers did not seem in the least diminished. Trying not to think of the additional sacks in the cargo hold, I made room for myself on a bunk and without getting fully undressed, lay down to catch a nap. My flight from Boston and my reception aboard the *Nogak* had left me so tired that I sank into a deep sleep. How many hours passed, I had no idea, but I was suddenly awakened by the hysterical clang of a high-pitched electric bell. Dressed only in long woolen underwear, Mr. Mondino rolled out of his bunk and dashed out of the companionway. He was followed by the warrant boatswain, a short, rotund man with ruddy cheeks and white hair. Pausing only to tighten my belt, I followed. Outside the sky was bright as ever. My watch said it was a little after four o'clock, and in the confusion of being awakened suddenly, it took me a few moments to realize that it was four in the morning. Men in all stages of dress and undress were crisscrossing the deck. On the bridge the captain stood leaning against a twenty-millimeter gun.

"Come on girls," he said. "If this weren't a drill, we'd be burnt to the waterline by now. How long is it going to take you to get pressure on those hoses?"

I was almost knocked down by the red-haired boatswain's mate and three seamen who were unrolling a coil of hose.

"You people *like* working in slow motion?" the captain asked.

"Sir," the boatswain's mate said, "this thing is frozen."

"What the hell do you think it will be in Greenland? Come on, give me water, boys! I want water! It's been three minutes since I sounded the alarm."

It was almost another minute before the first hose spurted. The spray nozzles had to be tried. A brisk wind blew the spray on deck, where it quickly froze, causing several seamen to fall painfully. Throughout all this confusion, the captain stood erect by the twenty-millimeter gun, stroking his beard and watching with sardonic detachment.

"All right, men," he said finally. "Secure from fire drill. I want pressure on those hoses inside a minute and a half. Until I get it, you can expect a fire drill every night."

Turning on his heel, he went into the pilot house.

"The son of a bitch!" Mr. Mondino was saying when I got back to our cabin. "A fire drill at four o'clock in the morning! The son of a bitch just gets tanked up at the officers' club and can't wait to come aboard and wake everybody up."

Charles Mahn, the warrant officer, scratched the round mound of his belly.

"Most of the boys are new to the ship," he said. "I don't blame the old man for breaking them in."

I took my trousers off, climbed into my bunk, shoved a mail bag away from my feet and went back to sleep.

In the morning I got permission to look for my footlocker. It took me several hours to find it and a jeep which would help to deliver it to the *Nogak*. In my absence a subchaser had moored alongside the converted trawler, and a big tanker had moored astern of her. A strong wind was blowing on the *Nogak*'s port beam, pinning her to the wharf. Before going aboard, I studied the situation, wondering how I would get the vessel out if I were in command of her. A single-screw vessel isn't easy to maneuver in a situation like that. Ahead of her was a rusty fuel barge. The little trawler was effectively boxed in on all four sides.

I had no sooner stowed the gear in my footlocker when there was the shrill call of a boatswain's pipe and the gruff voice of the boatswain's mate calling, "Mooring stations! Mooring stations!" I had been assigned no mooring station, but I went up to the bridge to see what was going on. The captain was engaged in a brisk conversation with the captain of the subchaser.

"God damn it, we're working on the engines, and we can't get underway for at least an hour," the captain of the subchaser said.

"I didn't ask you to get underway," our captain retorted. "I just said I was going to get underway."

"But you can't just leave me hanging out in the middle of the stream!"

"I'll put you right alongside the wharf, port side to. Just have your lines ready."

"I don't approve of this!" the captain of the subchaser said. "You can't move my vessel without my permission!"

"But you think you can tie my vessel up for at least an hour without my permission?"

"This is an emergency! My fuel pumps aren't working right!"

"So fix them," our captain said. "Hang on. You're going for a nice little ride."

Leaving that rail, the skipper looked down on the well deck, where the men were standing at mooring stations.

"Chief," he said to the red-haired boatswain's mate, "take in all lines except number two."

"Take in all lines except number two," the chief echoed. On the subchaser the entire crew was watching us, and several men were looking down at us from the bow of the tanker. Our skipper was standing out on a wing of the bridge with a look of complete satisfaction on his face. His orders to the helmsman and the man at the engineroom telegraph were just loud enough to be heard, and all the men on deck were quiet. As though controlled by more than her single propeller and the wind, the little trawler backed into the harbor, just missing the big tanker. With the subchaser still alongside, the *Nogak* turned, went back to her narrow berth, and nudged the subchaser gently into it.

"Now get your lines out, skipper," our captain said, and a few minutes later added, "You feel safe enough now for me to go about my business?"

The men on our deck laughed, drowning out whatever reply the other captain made.

"Cast off the subchaser," our skipper said. "Quartermaster, give me three blasts of the whistle. Back slow."

For so small a ship, the *Nogak* had a very loud air horn. By some quirk of physics, the smokestack was blowing smoke rings. With her newly painted pattern of blue and white triangles for camouflage in the ice, the little ship looked like a well-dressed bantam prizefighter as she turned and headed for the mouth of the harbor.

"Sir," I said to the captain, "I have been assigned to no watch."

"I know," he replied. "You'll stand no watch until you clean up that official mail. You better get below and get started on it."

Even in the protected waters of Argentia Bay, the *Nogak* rolled so hard that the drawers of the filing cabinets kept rushing back and forth on their tracks. Aboard the *Tampa* I thought I had recovered from seasickness for good, but the *Nogak* was less than half the *Tampa*'s length and had many nimble tricks of her own. During the months I had spent on a buoy tender on Chesapeake Bay, I apparently had lost much of my hard-earned immunity to motion sickness. Whatever the reason, I was queasy in Argentia Bay and went into real convulsions of seasickness the moment we turned the headland and sailed into Davis Strait. After asking a seaman to bring me a bucket, I went to the afterdeck to get a breath of air. Unfortunately the captain was there. Puffing a big cigar, he was looking at the foaming path of our wake on the glittery blue sea with satisfaction. Sardonically he looked at the galvanized bucket I had hooked over my right arm and my pale, sweating face. He said nothing about the state of my health, but his silence was almost worse than any verbal insult. Here I was, the "prospective commanding officer," barely able to stand up, even in weather that was normal for the North Atlantic.

"Mr. Wilson," he said finally, "do you have that filing job done?"

"No, sir."

"Well you better get to it. In a few days we might hit some weather. You better get it done while it's calm."

The next four days were the worst I had ever spent in my life. The drawers of the filing cabinets kept banging in and out. Sacks of mail which I was trying to empty slid back and forth. My bucket banged back and forth unless I wedged it into a corner of my bunk with pillows. My eyes almost burned out as I tried to scan all those sacks of mail. A filing drawer closed on my thumb, almost breaking it. And during all this time I realized that I was the laughingstock of the ship. Messengers could hardly keep a straight face as they brought me cups of bouillon. Mr. Mondino thoughtfully offered me raw bacon or "a cup of warm gin with a hair in it."

Charlie Mahn was the only officer to show kindness. He chatted with me about his family in Gloucester, where he had been a fisherman for thirty years. During the first world war he had been a senior lieutenant, a fact which he did not mention to the coast guard when they made him a warrant boatswain, because he wasn't sure he wanted to be a commissioned officer anyway.

"I can carry the rank of warrant officer," he said. "With a commission, I'd be faking half of the time."

While I, on the other hand, was faking all of the time, I reflected miserably. Whatever had led me to believe that I could command a ship of my own?

When the last mail sack had been emptied and sorted, I reported that fact to the captain. He immediately went to inspect the job. In my desperation I had let some of the pages stick up a little too high in the manila folders.

"Go through this again and fix it right," he said.

That took two more days, during which the weather was particularly rough. After another inspection, the captain said, "It still isn't a good job, but I guess it's adequate under the circumstances."

He told me to stand the eight-to-twelve watch, which he had been standing himself. We were not traveling in convoy, and as we made our way slowly toward Greenland, there was not much to do. The seas were still rough, but my seasickness began to subside. As soon as I was free of the nausea, my good spirits and ambitions returned. After all, why should I be ashamed of seasickness? Admiral Nelson was just one of many famous sailors who had had to keep a bucket handy.

A wide belt of ice surrounded the southern coast of Greenland when we got there. The *Tampa*, which usually was leading merchant ships, would have tried to go around it. The *Nogak* simply butted her way through it. The way the captain managed this without straining the hull fascinated me, for I had never seen an ice pilot at work. The belt of ice, which looked solid from a distance, was made up of thousands of icebergs of all different sizes which had been jammed together by the wind and current. Going very slowly, the captain placed the bow of the ship between two icebergs, rang for enough speed to push them apart, and then stopped before charging into the next iceberg. Twisting and turning, we cut through the ice field in only about five hours. Ahead of us the wind-smoothed rust-colored mountains of Greenland loomed, but instead of heading for them, the captain went back into the ice floe, where he purposely jammed the ship between two icebergs about as big as the ship.

"They'll keep us busy when we get back to the base," he said. "We might as well have a little homecoming celebration here."

Whiskey was broken out from some secret supply of the captain. Obviously forewarned, Cookie came forward with a tray of canapés which looked as though they had been prepared in the kitchen of a first-class hotel.

"Where did you learn to cook stuff like this?" I asked him.

He glared at me.

"I was head chef in the Palmer House Hotel in Chicago," he said. "Like a damn fool I joined the coast guard, and you know what they made me? Second class cook! Me! I was trained in the best hotels in Switzerland, but here I am a second class cook!"

He went off with his tray, his head still shaking in indignation. I went up to the bridge, where the captain was sitting on a stool, glass in hand.

"Hey you, Mr. Wilson," he said. "Have you got a drink?"

I didn't and he told me to get a glass from his cabin. That was the first time I had seen the captain's cabin, which contained little more than a berth and a chart table, but which seemed to be the gilded throne room of the mighty. In a rack on a bulkhead I found a heavy glass tumbler. The captain filled it a quarter full from a bottle he held in his right hand.

"Did you ever hear of the *Natsek*?" he asked.

"I'm afraid not."

"The censorship works better than it should. The *Natsek* was a sister ship of ours. So is the *Nanok*. The two of them sailed together from here to Boston last fall. The *Natsek* didn't make it."

"What happened?"

"Nobody knows for sure. Her skipper was a fine man. His name was LaFarge. Maybe you've heard of the LaFarges. They're an old Boston family."

"There's a writer and a poet . . ."

"That's the family. This fellow was a painter. I knew him pretty well, but I don't know his first name. When you're a captain you don't have a first name. Everybody just called him Captain LaFarge."

There was a pause while our captain took a drink.

"LaFarge had been a yachtsman, a good one. He ran his ship well. But he died with all his crew, and Maggie lived."

"Who's Maggie?"

"Magnusen, the skipper of the *Nanok*. Maggie used to be the skipper and owner of trawlers in Iceland. I have no idea how they got him into our coast guard, but he knows ice. And ice is what killed LaFarge, I figure."

"How?"

"I'm not talking about icebergs. I'm talking about icing up. There are certain conditions during which ice can form all over your ship. The ice finally makes her top-heavy, and she rolls over. These two ships, the *Natsek* and the *Nanok*, were sailing in company with orders to go through the Strait of Belle Isle. It was blowing like hell and the ice from the spray was building up fast. The fresh water from the St. Lawrence would make icing conditions worse as they approached the Strait of Belle Isle, and that's a bottleneck where you've got Labrador on one side of you and Newfoundland on the other, without any sea-room. You can often reduce icing by running before the wind, if you have the space for it. Of course Maggie knew all this. He suggested that they haul off shore and go around Cape Race. LaFarge signaled back, 'I shall follow my orders.' The *Natsek* disappeared in the haze and that was the last of her anyone ever saw, except for the body of one drowned seaman."

"Maybe a sub got her. They hang around the Strait of Belle Isle."

"In a raging gale? What sub is going to bother with a damn trawler anyway?"

"I guess you're right."

"You don't get my point yet," the captain said after taking another drink. "LaFarge was a fine man and we don't really know what happened, but the point is that in the arctic ignorance is death. It doesn't matter what good intentions you have. Ignorance is death, and if the captain of a ship in the arctic is ignorant, his whole crew doesn't have a

79

chance. The men know this. The arctic is one place where the men don't want an easy-going nice guy for commanding officer. When the wind pipes up to maybe 150 knots and it's either dark or foggy most of the year, the men want a captain who knows his business, even if he's the worst bastard in the world."

While I tried to digest this and figure out why the captain had told it all to me, I accepted another drink. A story like the captain's could be told to a man who was about to take command of a ship or to a man who would soon be told more formally that he was not fitted for command. I waited for the captain to tell me more, but he turned and walked down to the well deck, where a group of men had gathered to sing. Sitting on a hatch cover, he tilted his bearded face back and in a strong baritone which was slightly off-key launched into the chorus of, "You Are My Sunshine." The whiskey was starting to go to my head and I tottered aft to my bunk.

11

For about three months we sailed up and down the western coast of southern Greenland. Our duty was to supply weather stations and some mysterious installations (which we later learned were the highly secret Loran stations which gave both ships and aircraft a precise system of navigation). My seasickness decreased, and I enjoyed the long hours of working the ship through the ice. The ability to pick the best leads and to navigate while we were proceeding at no steady speed or course was nothing one could acquire in a book, and the discovery that I possessed this talent more than did Mr. Mondino or even Charlie Mahn built up my self-confidence. When I was off duty, I lay in my bunk reading books from the ship's meager library or sat in the forecastle drinking coffee and talking with a few of the enlisted men who became my friends. Aboard the *Tampa*, the officers had remained aloof from the enlisted men, but on the trawlers this rule was relaxed. This was fortunate for me because one of the most interesting men aboard the ship was a third class quartermaster named Charles Seymour Alden. A man barely more than twenty-one years old, Charlie Alden was about six feet tall and had a handsome, open face with a red birthmark. He spoke with almost an upper-class British accent. He drank coffee and ate his meals with a delicacy which some judged to be effeminate. Because some of the personnel men in

Boston considered Greenland a kind of Siberia, they often swept out the brigs to man vessels on the Greenland Patrol. We had a crew which was tougher than most, but none of our bully boys bothered Charlie Alden, despite his genteel mannerisms. The reason I soon discovered. Charlie Alden was that war-time rarity, an almost perfect seaman who was rated far below his ability. When we were creeping into poorly charted anchorages after our fathometer had been put out of commission by ice, Charlie could heave a deep-sea lead so fast and so accurately that we hardly had to slow down. When the gyro compass went on the blink, Charlie knew how to fix it. He deciphered flag signals without having to look them up in the book, and could talk by blinkerlight as fast as most can converse. He knew how to compensate a magnetic compass in the arctic, and could handle a sextant better than I could.

"Why didn't they make you an officer, Charlie?" I asked.

"I don't know," he said with a shrug. "I didn't push it much."

It was a long time before Charlie told me that he was a direct descendant of the Alden of "Speak for yourself, John" Alden fame. He was also a nephew of John Alden, the famous yacht designer, and the son of an Alden who was a four-striper in the navy. He had been brought up aboard all kinds of vessels. Now he wanted to make his way alone, and had picked the coast guard because he knew too many high-ranking officers in the navy.

During those first months I spent aboard the *Nogak*, Charlie Alden often made me feel envious. He seemed living proof that it was better to be under-ranked than over-ranked, as I obviously was. His character, which seemed innocent of ambition, was a reproach to me. If he was content to serve as a third-class quartermaster, why did my whole desire to live seem to depend on my ability to command a ship?

Deny it as I tried to, I began dreaming more and more of the day when the captain would turn the ship over to me. There would be a little ceremony on the well deck as we read our orders to the men. The next time I went ashore, the little black and white pennant, the third repeater, would fly at our masthead to tell anyone interested that the commanding officer was not aboard. At the officers' club, I would join the special group of skippers that seldom admitted anyone who did not have his own ship. My first name would be forgotten and I would be Captain Wilson, the Skipper or the Old Man. Aboard ship, Cookie would be quick to prepare any special dish I might want. I would never find it necessary to raise my voice when giving a command, for despite all the caricatures of captains, most of them can afford to exert their authority quietly. I would write my wife and tell her to address letters to "Lt. (j.g.) Sloan Wilson, commanding officer, United States Coast Guard Cutter *Nogak*." My mother, the daughter of a naval officer who, so far as I knew, never had commanded his own ship, would, I was sure, be especially appreciative of my accomplishment.

These dreams of glory were rudely interrupted one afternoon when I was drinking coffee in the forecastle. A messenger came in and told me that the captain wanted to see me "immediately" on the bridge. "Immediately" was a word the skipper rarely used. I ran to the bridge and saw him sitting on a high stool near the wheel. Apparently he had dismissed the enlisted men who usually stood watch on the bridge while we were at anchor. We were alone.

"You wanted me, sir?" I asked, hoping that he had finally decided to turn the ship over to me.

"Mr. Wilson," he said, "it is my sorry duty to inform you that I consider you unfit to take command of this ship, and even unfit to be executive officer. You are beyond question the worst officer I have ever seen, and one of the worst men."

I had the distinct sensation of sinking. I was in a whirlpool that was spiraling me down. I also had a terrible feeling that I was going to cry, a reaction which would be sure to confirm the captain's disgust. To counteract this horrifying return to childhood, I came to attention and stood as erect as though I expected to receive a medal.

"You are intensely disliked by every officer and man aboard this ship," the captain continued, and there was a small splinter of pleasure in my realization that this accusation was not a hundred percent true. Charlie Mahn and I were friends and Charlie Alden had shown no sign of disliking me. Out of forty-two men, I could be sure of two. There seemed no point in trying to interrupt the captain with this news.

"You don't even look like an officer," the captain continued. "You are dirty and disheveled most of the time."

Well, I had been while I was seasick. There was no way to get clothes washed or cleaned aboard the *Nogak* unless a man did the scrubbing himself. Still, the captain himself always managed to appear spotless.

"I shall not take the time to list here the many areas of your incompetence," he thundered, and I noticed something peculiar then: his hands were shaking. Somehow the fact that his hands were shaking while he read me off brought a little comfort. This was not the dispassionate judgment of a man forced to dismiss a subordinate. Something beyond reason and duty was at work here.

"You know nothing about ship handling," he went on. "You know nothing about the coast of Greenland. You know nothing about stowing cargo. You know nothing about ice, except for the light fields of storis we've been passing through."

He paused, took a deep breath and put his hands in his pockets.

"Ignorance itself is no crime," he continued, "but it becomes a crime when an officer does not recognize it in himself and pushes himself forward to take command of a ship. There are thirty-nine men and three officers aboard this vessel. If you allowed yourself to take command you would be guilty of forty-two murders and your own suicide. If I placed you in command I would have all that blood on my own hands."

I continued to stand like a wooden Indian. The desire to cry had gone and a curious kind of calm was coming over me, like that I felt when I thought the *Tampa* had been torpedoed.

"It is very probable," the captain continued, "that this vessel will soon get orders to Thule to build a weather station. Thule is just about as far north as a ship can get, way north of the Arctic Circle. If I allowed you to take that voyage as commanding officer of this ship, I would be hopelessly irresponsible. For this reason I shall transfer you with a bad fitness report the moment we return to base. Until that time you are relieved of all duties aboard this ship, and you are confined to your quarters. I have never before been forced to take such drastic action, but I have never before seen an officer who is so completely unfit to command a ship."

He took his hands from his pockets and realizing that they still were trembling, he put them back. I continued to stand mutely at attention.

"Well?" he demanded. "Any comment?"

"I can't be *that* bad," I said, my voice sounding curiously casual. "May I go now, sir?"

"Yes."

I went to my quarters, the small stateroom which I shared with Charlie Mahn and Mr. Mondino. Fortunately, Charlie was not in the cabin and Mondino was asleep. Feeling suddenly dazed and a little dizzy, I took off my uniform and climbed into my bunk. My thoughts were revolving faster and faster. When they stopped, several facts seemed clear. First of all, the captain must have something the matter with him, for there was no need for so much emotion and cruelty to surround the act of dismissing an officer. That was his problem. My problem was that something like ninety percent of what he said was true. I was an incompetent with ridiculous dreams of glory and could endanger any ship I tried to command. Undoubtedly that danger was gone, for the bad fitness report the captain had promised would forever remove me from being considered for command. It also might block all future promotions in rank. Probably I would end up a communications officer on some big cutter where there would be plenty of competent officers who would make sure I didn't do any harm.

That is what was going to be, I figured, and with that I would have to learn to live. In time I thought I could get used to the idea. If it was a return to truth, as I suspected it was, there would be no choice but to learn to live with it.

Feeling suddenly exhausted, I slept. I awoke when Charlie Mahn came down to get his parka.

"Nice evening out," he said, "but just a mite chilly. Never thought I'd be wearing a parka in summertime."

That meant he knew about my debacle and was trying to be nice about it. Charlie was never one to make small talk in ordinary circumstances.

A few minutes later Mr. Mondino came down. He had always been cool toward me, and I guessed that he himself had hoped for command of the ship. This was borne out by his greeting.

"How are you, captain?" he asked with a smirk.

"Watch out, Mondino," I said. "I'm certified incompetent. That means I can't even control my temper."

Suddenly I jumped out of my bunk and lunged for him with a fearful growl. He disappeared up the companionway as though jerked by strings. I sat on the edge of my bunk laughing. For the first time I was sure I was going to live.

A few hours later I heard the windlass take in the anchor and the steady thumping of our big diesel. It was five minutes to eight in the evening. It was time for me to go on watch, I thought, and was halfway up the companionway before I remembered that I was confined to quarters. In about two days, I figured, we would be back at the base, and I would be transferred. Maybe I would be sent back to Boston to await my next assignment. I might see my wife!

This thought filled me with all kinds of conflicting emotions. In letters I had boasted a lot about the phrase "prospective commanding officer" in my orders. Perhaps the intensity of my ambition had been related to the thought that my wife would be proud of me if I became a skipper. I had built up in her mind a picture of me as a great sailor, the man who passed the examination in navigation and seamanship at M.I.T. with flying colors and before that, the man who sailed an eighty-seven-foot schooner up the coast when he was still in his teens. Now this conception of me as the Viking prince would have to be preserved with lies or shattered with the news that I had been transferred from the *Nogak* as an incompetent. Lies could play no part in the idealistic conception I had of my marriage. My disgrace would have to be admitted.

As I write all this more than thirty years after the events I describe, I am astonished at the concept I had of marriage, of my wife and women in general. It seems obvious to me now that most wives would be little disturbed by the military failure of a husband in time of war, and would be quick to give sympathy. When I was twenty-three, I could not imagine that. Perhaps I was still prisoner of my childhood notion that women must be won like loving cups, and only a winner can be expected to keep a pretty woman for long.

As soon as we reached the base, I put on my uniform and waited for the arrival of my orders. None came. On deck I could hear a fearful clatter as some sort of cargo was brought aboard. This continued day and night for about forty-eight hours. At the end of that time the captain came to my cabin. His uniform looked soiled, I noticed with satisfaction, and he had not been trimming his beard lately.

"Mr. Wilson," he said, "I cannot get you transferred here. There is no coast guard personnel officer here at the moment and nobody seems to know what to do about you. I'm going to have to keep you aboard. Meanwhile, I have orders to proceed directly to Thule. If we don't get in and out of there soon, we'll be frozen in for the winter."

"I see."

"Of course your situation will remain unchanged," he continued. "You still will be confined to quarters."

"Aye, aye, sir!" I replied, hoping that there was irony in my heartiness.

Almost as soon as the captain went on deck, we got underway. It was, I knew, almost two thousand miles to Thule. Ordinarily the *Nogak* could cover such a distance in about twelve days, but if there was ice, any amount of time could be required. For about two days we rolled along with a stiff easterly on our beam. Then the sea grew calm and I heard the grinding of ice along our sides. Peering out the small porthole which gave me my only view, I saw a field of storis ice (small icebergs), stretching as far as I could see. With a sigh I returned to my bunk. If these conditions continued or worsened, my incarceration would begin to feel like a life sentence.

"Hey," Mondino said one night. "How long is the old man going to keep you down here?"

"I don't know."

"According to the regulations, an officer can be confined to quarters no longer than ten days. Why don't you pull that on him?"

"Maybe I will," I replied, but I knew that I would not. There was more dignity in acting the part of a martyr being illegally punished than in trying to be a sea lawyer.

The tenth day of my incarceration came and went without any word from the captain. I had read every book in the library at least twice, and learned to sleep at least twelve hours a day. The rest of the day I subsisted on a mixture of fantasy and memory. For my own protection, the memories of my wife had to be edited. When I had been stationed aboard the buoy tender in Chesapeake Bay before joining the *Nogak*, Elise and I had rented a small apartment in Baltimore. There had been joy and pride in seeing her, but she had suffered mysteriously from nausea and dizziness, especially in crowded places, like theaters, and had gone home to West Newton before my brief assignment on the bay was over. Before flying to Argentia, I had had a ten-day leave in Boston. Elise had wanted to have a baby, a prospect which had filled me with conflicting emotions, for I was worried about her health, and I had over-dramatized the possibility that I might be killed in the war. After I had come aboard the *Nogak*, the mails had been slow, and only about a month ago I had received an enthusiastic letter from her saying she was pregnant. Perhaps there was something wrong with me, but the prospect of having a baby annoyed me as much as it delighted me. After the war I wanted to charter a yawl and cruise the Bahamas before settling down in Paris for a few years to try writing a novel. A baby would change all that.

Sometimes my dreams went back to my boyhood. In Florida, when I was about twelve or thirteen years old, my father bought me a new Ratsey sail for my Moth, an eleven-foot catboat. The sail smelled the heady way that sails did when they were made of Egyptian cotton and tarred hemp—before the days of dacron. When I put it on the boat to try it out, it fitted perfectly, as one would expect from anything made by Ratsey, the finest sailmaker in the world. I could hardly wait to try it out in a race.

The next regatta was in the Indian River. The committee boat was an ancient motor yacht which boasted an old-fashioned brass signal cannon instead of the modern kind which merely shoots a blank shotgun shell. To shoot the old brass signal cannon, a charge of gunpowder was measured into the muzzle and was followed by a wad of paper or rags like those used in a gun on a pirate vessel. This old cannon boomed impressively as it sent classes of larger boats over the starting line. The Moths were last to go. We got a three-minute gun as a stand-by signal. I started my stopwatch. My new sail was drawing beautifully and I seemed to scoot away from my competitors as I approached the line. Choosing the windward end, I sailed close to the committee boat. I was close abeam it when the starting gun boomed, practically in my ear. A cloud of smoke gagged me. When it cleared, I saw that the wad from the cannon had torn a hole as big as a basketball in my beautiful new sail!

"Well, I guess that took the wind out of your sails," my father said when I told him about it. Suddenly I guessed that he might say something similar if he were alive now and I told him about being relieved of all duties because of incompetence. Somehow the episode of the cannon-torn sail seemed a fit prelude to my present dilemma.

I do not know how many days I was confined to quarters before the captain suddenly appeared at the companionway. He looked tired, and I guess that he had been on deck almost all the time in this apparently endless ice field.

"Mr. Wilson," he said, "I am going to put you back on duty. You're still drawing pay, so you may as well earn it."

"Aye, aye, sir."

"Now this isn't going to change anything. I'm still going to transfer you as soon as I get a chance, and I'm still going to give you a bad fitness report."

"Even if I do a good job now?" I wanted to ask, but I had made up my mind not to argue.

"Aye, aye, sir," I said again.

"Relieve me as soon as you can," the captain said, and disappeared.

I had had plenty of chance to do my laundry, and I made sure that I was well dressed when I climbed to the bridge. From my porthole I had not been able to appreciate the full extent of the ice field. For as far as the eye could see in all directions, the ice jam stretched. Most of the icebergs were no bigger than the ship, but a few continued for miles. The wind had streamlined them into thousands of shapes, and the ice came in all shades of green and blue, as well as the prevailing white. The sun sparkled on this great field of ice with such brilliance that it was literally blinding to anyone without dark glasses or the wood with narrow slits which the Eskimos used to reduce light.

"My god, it's beautiful!" I said.

"I'm glad you like it," the captain replied. "If we can't get through it pretty damn soon, we're liable to be here all winter."

He gave me the course he was trying to make good and said the speed should be "as much as possible."

"I relieve you, sir," I said and climbed to the flying bridge to conn the ship, which at the moment was lying dead in the water with small icebergs pressing against both sides and the bow. Through binoculars, I studied the sea ahead and to both sides of us. On our starboard bow there seemed to be a pretty good lead, a long finger of black water pointing through the ice.

"Ahead slow," I called down the voice tube. With a heartiness I had never heard from him before, the quartermaster replied, "The engine is ahead slow, sir!"

"Rudder amidships."

"The rudder is amidships, sir!" the helmsman sang out.

For some reason the cheerful ring of these voices almost made me cry. I wasn't sure what those men had thought of me when I first came aboard, but apparently I had become an underdog during my incarceration, and they were welcoming me back to their fold.

The *Nogak* dutifully pushed the small iceberg which was ahead of her out of her way. I stopped the engine and we glided toward two icebergs which were the size and almost the shape of small houses. There was a jagged crack where one iceberg was jammed against the other.

"Helmsman," I said in the voice tube. "Steer for the crack between those two bergs ahead."

"Steer for the crack, sir," he said.

The captain was leaning on the rail of the bridge below me. He looked as nervous as he was exhausted. The vessel was, I perceived, moving too fast.

"Back slow," I said into the voice tube.

"The engine is backing slow, sir."

I waited a moment, studying the ice we were passing.

"Stop the engine."

"The engine is stopped, sir."

The bow of the *Nogak* nestled against the crack between the two icebergs so gently that there wasn't a sound or a jar.

"Ahead slow," I said.

"The engine is ahead slow, sir."

The propeller churned, but the big bergs did not budge.

"Ahead half."

The vibration of the engine increased and white water spumed out astern as though we were making knots, but still the big icebergs did not move. I waited five minutes.

"Ahead full," I said finally.

The beat of the engine was now loud. Suddenly the big bergs gave way, opening like a great gate to let us through. The *Nogak* lunged ahead. Before she could crash into the next icebergs, I said in a voice which sounded much calmer than I felt. "Ahead slow."

"The engine is ahead slow, sir."

"Stop the engine."

"The engine is stopped, sir."

"Back slow."

"The engine is backing slow, sir."

"Back half."

"The engine is backing half, sir."

The bow of the *Nogak* came gently to rest against the next row of icebergs. I was sweating. Slowly the captain climbed the ladder to the flying bridge.

"Mr. Wilson," he said, "I'm going to get some sleep. I want you to keep the deck until I wake up. Mr. Mondino and Mr. Mahn are fine officers, but they have had very little experience in working a ship in ice."

"Aye, aye, sir."

He did not give me any direct compliment, but there is no compliment a captain can give to a watch officer that is more sincere than going to sleep in difficult conditions. If he preferred to have me work the ship through ice rather than Mondino and Mahn, why did he give me such hell while sparing them?

The answer of course was obvious. Mondino and Mahn did not aspire to be commanding officer, not openly, at least. It was only a prospective commanding officer who the captain would judge with the same stern standards he applied to himself.

For the next two weeks the captain worried that we would not get to Thule on time to unload our cargo and get out before the whole bay froze. I, however, was in a strange, exalted frame of mind which admitted no anxiety. The ice field continued to be beautiful in an infinite variety of ways. If one can imagine a handful of jewels blown up to the proportions of a great city, that is the way it sometimes looked. There was no dawn or dusk during that arctic summer, but sometimes clouds turned the sun red enough to make the whole ice field gleam in every tone of gold and copper. Often there was fog, which made the ocean look like a vast graveyard dotted by marble tombstones on a scale to mark the graves of giants.

I conned the ship twelve hours a day, six on and six off. In my relief at being enabled to escape some of my disgrace, I found myself beginning to love the *Nogak* as though she were some sort of ark which was saving my life. To other people she might appear to be nothing but an ugly little trawler, but her sturdy bow, made of oak which had been reinforced with more oak and heavy plates of steel, could push aside icebergs which would sink a proud destroyer. The *Nogak's* top speed was only eight knots, but her huge, slow turning propeller would let her maintain her eight knots through two feet of harbor ice or into the teeth of a howling gale. When I prayed, she would turn in her own length for me. She was the kind of vessel which could go to the ends of the earth and back if her captain and crew gave her any understanding at all.

The voyage to Thule was so enjoyable to me that I was sorry when we saw the strange conical mountain which is its chief landmark. Thule, or *Ultima Thule*, I had read, was the Greek term for the end of the world. It had been applied to various islands as exploration expanded maps. For a long while it had been used to designate Iceland, but now for a century at least it had been applied to this desolate harbor on the northwestern end of Greenland.

Shortly after World War II, an airbase which housed seven thousand men was built at Thule, but when I was there in 1943, there was nothing but a tiny house which had been built for the Danish administrator of the region and a dozen sod huts inhabited by Eskimos, or Greenlanders, as they preferred to be called. The temperature was already falling to twenty degrees, and the captain urged everyone to rush the job of unloading. There was no wharf. Lumber for the construction of the weather station was towed ashore by our motor launch and carried to the top of a knoll, where three army carpenters who had been our passengers worked frantically to build the small house which would house a generator and radio equipment. The heavy machinery was loaded into the launch and muscled out by Red, the boatswain's mate, and his entire deck gang.

My job was the unglamorous one of dropping a hundred fifty-two-gallon oil drums from our deck into the sea, hitching them to a long line and towing them to the beach. There they had to be rolled through the surf and over the tundra to the site of the construction. This task was made more difficult by the fact that the Greenlanders' sled dogs kept nipping at our feet and depositing their feces over the land we had to cross. No one who has not had to roll a fifty-two-gallon oil drum through a sea of dog droppings can appreciate the sheer messiness of this situation.

"The bastard has no right to make us do this," Mr. Mondino said bitterly as he tried to wash his hands in a bucket of sea water. "Nowhere in the regulations does it say that a commissioned officer has to roll oil drums through dog shit."

"Go tell him that," I said.

"I'll die for my country if I have to," Mondino continued, "but I'll be goddamned if I'll wade through shit for it."

"Do your best, and maybe you'll get a medal, the great dog shit medal with two oak leaf clusters."

The last thing we had to unload was about a ton of supplies which were supposed to last the Danish administrator and his wife for a year or longer if the winter turned out to be severe. The Dane was a tall man about fifty years old and his wife, a native Greenlander, was a young woman with a round, copper-colored face and glossy black hair. Both wore classic Eskimo clothing: thigh-high leather boots with brightly colored geometric designs around the tops, britches made of polar-bear fur and jackets made of delicate lighter furs such as fox and ermine. These magnificent get-ups were made comic by the insertion—for some unknown reason—of a dark piece of fur in the crotch of the white britches which from a distance made the whole outfit a burlesque of nudity. This made some of our men roar with laughter.

The Dane was so glad to get his year's supplies that he invited the ship's officers to his home for a celebration. Although our discharge of cargo was completed, we could not sail until the carpenters finished the weather station so the captain gave Mr. Mondino and me permission to go. Charlie Mahn, who did not drink, volunteered to stay aboard the ship, which was safely anchored.

The captain, Mondino and I spent a lot of time cleaning and pressing our uniforms before we presented ourselves at the Dane's red house. It was little bigger than a child's playhouse, for every stick of lumber had been imported from Denmark. Inside it was as neat and efficient as a ship's cabin. The Dane knew almost no English, and his wife knew only the Eskimo language. To dress up for the occasion she had put on a many-stranded necklace of beads carved from walrus tusks. We could not talk with our hosts, but when they put out whiskey bottles which had been part of their annual supplies, we began to do pretty well with sign language. To increase our thirst there were smoked salmons and salted sides of cod. Little water was served with the whiskey, and no ice. In Greenland, which is pressed by the sea ice, the great glaciers and ice cap, almost no one asked for ice in a drink.

The Dane remembered enough scraps of English to explain that he had had no whiskey for more than a month because he had drunk up the previous year's supply. He thanked us for bringing him a new supply and drank toasts to us, to the *Nogak* and to the United States, which would soon free his native country from the Nazi scourge. Quite soon he sank down on a sofa, apparently dazed by a wealth of whiskey to which he was not accustomed. Every once in a while he got up to wander around the room in search of the bottle, which his wife had hidden in a bookshelf, where we could see it, but he could not—his wife had removed his glasses while he was napping. Feeling sorry for him, the captain gave him a drink, which made the wife glare fiercely.

At about this point Mr. Mondino, who was not a drinking man, had the sense to return to the ship. The captain and I continued to drink and one of us, I'm not sure which, got the idea that it was not democratic for the officers of the *Nogak* to go to a party without asking the enlisted men. Using semaphore, at which he was expert, even when drunk, the captain stepped out the door and signaled the ship. Before long about twenty-five thirsty members of our crew arrived. By now our host was soundly sleeping on the couch and his wife had beat a retreat to the bedroom. The case of whiskey was found in the kitchen, and more cases were found in a storeroom which adjoined it.

The enlisted men drank and sang and soon one of them decided that it was not democratic to give a party in Thule without inviting the Eskimos. A messenger was sent to their colony of sod huts. Soon we were joined by about fifteen furry men and women. Most of them stood just to my shoulder, but they were hearty drinkers. Someone found a phonograph with Danish records that offered lively tunes, even if the words were unintelligible to us. Packed into those tiny rooms, we took turns dancing with the Eskimo women, who kept laughing uproariously.

It was a good party with an odd sense of timelessness, for it never got dark. When my watch read twelve o'clock I had no idea whether it meant noon or midnight. Between sessions of drinking and eating, most of us slept curled up on the floor with the feet of the dancers pounding around us. The captain and I had long conversations with the enlisted men, who told us one minute that they hated us and the next minute that we were the best goddamn officers in the whole coast guard. I experienced a wonderful sense of communion with the men. They were the goddamnedest best crew in the whole coast guard and the navy too. Together we could take the *Nogak* to hell and back again.

Every time we ran out of whiskey, someone rummaged through the storeroom and found more. When no more of the black bottles could be located, we drank gin, rum and all sorts of liqueurs before we had to content ourselves with some cases of beer.

Finally we could find nothing to drink and tottered back to the beach, where Charlie Alden came to get us in the motorboat.

"That must have been the longest party of all time," he said to me.

"Long?"

"You guys were in there *three days.* The carpenters have almost finished the weather station."

This didn't make much sense to me at the time. I fell into my bunk. About ten hours later, a messenger woke me with the news that we were getting underway. On the bridge I found the captain, looking as alarmingly fresh as he always did after a drinking bout.

"Good morning, Mr. Wilson," he said.

"Good morning," I replied weakly. My head was throbbing.

"I'm glad to be getting out of here," he continued. "I feel too guilty to stay."

"Guilty?" Somehow I could not imagine the captain feeling guilty.

"Do you know what we did?" he asked.

"We got damn well good and drunk."

"That doesn't bother me. What we did was to drink up that poor bastard's whole year's supply of booze. He won't have a drop until the next ship comes in here sometime next August."

"That's awful," I said.

"If anyone should wear sackcloth and ashes, we should," the captain continued. "I've never been so goddamned ashamed of anything in my life."

"Isn't there any way we could make it up to him?"

"I could have given the poor bastard some of my private supply, but I don't have much left. When you come right down to it, you can carry this guilt thing too far, can't you?"

12

When we got outside the bay at Thule, we found that most of the ice pack had drifted far off shore. The sea was calm and mirrored the intense blue of the sky. Everything was reflected in the water. A ghost image of the *Nogak* raced beside her and the icebergs stood above their doubles. If the weather held, we would be back at our base in twelve or fifteen days. The thought made my breath come short, for then I would learn what fate the captain would contrive for me. Before leaving for Thule, he had made a point of reminding me that I would still be transferred with a bad fitness report, but he had thought enough of me to leave me on watch while he was sleeping. I had no idea how he would reconcile his contradictory actions.

About two days after we left Thule, I was on watch. The sea was still calm, though long clouds of autumn were closing in the blue sky and turning the surface of the sea to slate gray. I was studying a distant headland with the binoculars when suddenly the engine stopped. The absence of sound and vibration was ominous and unbelievable, for such a thing had never happened before.

"The engineroom says they've got trouble," the quartermaster said. "It will take a while to figure out what it is."

Jumping from his cabin, the captain took a quick look around the horizon to make sure that we were in no immediate danger. Running to the engineroom, he came back a few minutes later.

"We've scored a cylinder liner," he said to me. "The engine will be out of commission until we get a new one. Lower the motorboat. If this calm lasts, I think the boat can tow us into Upernavik."

Within ten minutes, the boat was out ahead of us towing the trawler, which now looked huge. Using all her power, the boat could tow us at only about two knots. If a sudden wind sprang up we would be driven against the high cliffs which lined the shore, or would drift helplessly out to sea. The men stood on deck watching the sky and each cat's paw of wind which occasionally ruffled the polished surface of the sea. The red cliffs toward which we were heading seemed to get no closer. For five hours we continued our painfully slow progress before we saw an opening in the barrier of cliffs.

"Is that Upernavik?" I asked the captain.

"You've seen the chart, haven't you?" he snapped. "What the hell would you do if I weren't here to lead you by the hand?"

Upernavik was a small harbor, it turned out, with several of the red and white houses which the Danes built. We anchored under the lee of a headland.

"Get out the bower anchor," the captain said. "Mr. Wilson, why didn't you think of that? We've got no power and we may be here for months. Were you just going to let her swing to her regular anchor?"

"I thought you had the deck, sir," I said. "Do you want me to start trying to give you advice?"

"When you know something I don't know, give me advice."

He went into the radio shack. When he emerged an hour or so later, he said that a new cylinder liner was being flown to Base One, where another trawler would pick it up and try to deliver it to us.

For almost two months we were stuck in Upernavik. For a few days the Danes entertained us, but perhaps in fear that they would suffer the same fate as their colleague in Thule, they soon stopped. Although we were in no danger of starvation, we ran out of coffee, which is almost as indispensable to a ship as fuel oil, and we were short of all kinds of meat but Spam and Vienna sausage. To relieve the monotony of this diet the men hunted for seal and a seagull with black wing tips which was delicious to anyone accustomed to Spam and Vienna sausage.

The captain tried to keep the men busy painting the hull, but he found no therapy for himself. As the long days of idleness wore on, he became more and more short-tempered.

"Mr. Wilson," he said when I went to the galley to get a cup of tea, "I have finally found something you're good at."

"Sir?"

"Leisure! You seem to be born to it. I never saw anybody just lie around so well."

"There isn't much for me to do, is there?"

"Why don't you use this little holiday to fill the vast chasm of your ignorance? Just for starts, get Charlie Alden to teach you something about the blinker light. Ask guns to show you how to break down a twenty-millimeter."

It was a good idea, except the thought of trying to learn so much filled me with a kind of despair which led to indolence. Navigation, seamanship and ship handling were the skills the captain of a trawler needed most, while the other disciplines could be left to specialists. Trying to learn *everything* about a ship would drive me crazy and sanity was one of the first requirements for a skipper.

Nevertheless, I tried to follow the skipper's orders. Finding Charlie Alden and me hard at work with a blinker light, the captain was so approving that he asked us up to his cabin for a drink. He grew so mellow that I dared to ask him a question I had long pondered. "Captain," I asked, "what did you do before you joined the coast guard?"

"The Depression..." he said. "My father went broke. I had to leave Harvard. Best thing that ever happened to me."

"What did you do?"

"I got a job delivering yachts. Then I was captain of a research vessel out of Woods Hole, the *Atlantis*. You may have heard of her."

"Of course," I said reverently. The *Atlantis* was a huge sailing vessel, one of the most handsome I had ever seen. How had he gone from delivering yachts to a job that would be the envy of almost any seagoing man? The people at Woods Hole, I knew, were even more strict about the way their research vessels were run than the coast guard was about its cutters. Apparently they had recognized a man with a certain genius for seafaring when they saw him. I did not feel so bad about failing to measure up to our captain. The captain of the *Atlantis* would be apt to think any hastily commissioned coast guard officer a vile impostor.

Finally a trawler arrived with our cylinder liner. She put to sea as soon as she handed it to us, because her skipper was afraid of being caught in the ice. As soon as our black gang fixed the engine, we followed, but to our surprise the captain did not hurry. We had several bits of cargo to deliver to small settlements along the coast if weather permitted, and the skipper obviously took pride in playing the part of a mailman, whom neither fog, sleet nor gloom of night could deter from his duty.

There was plenty of gloom of night, for September was turning into October, and we were approaching the long polar darkness. Fall gales lashed the sea into spray that often kept our well deck awash.

One day, just as it was turning dark, the captain ducked between two boulders which weren't even shown on the chart and followed a narrow fjord to an Eskimo settlement.

"What have we got for this place?" I asked.

"Dog food. They've been short of dog food a long while."

"You mean you go into a place that isn't even on the chart to bring dog food?"

He grinned.

"These people need dog food the way other people need gas for a car. Beyond that there is a certain satisfaction in bringing my list of assignments up to the operations officer with the simple notation, *All done*. Most of the bastards on the other trawlers come back to base with a bunch of excuses."

As we approached the settlement, Eskimos appeared on the shore with beaming faces.

"Sound the horn," the captain said.

The horn blew, and the Eskimos cheered.

"Flash the searchlight," the captain said.

The searchlight swept the shore and the Eskimos cheered.

"Send a round of three-inch ammunition into that little iceberg over there."

Our three-inch gun spat fire, and the Eskimos again were so excited that they jumped up and down clapping.

At the captain's direction, we also fired our twenty-millimeters and our little forty-caliber gun. Never has a performer had a more enthusiastic reception. Looking at the captain's face, which was as delighted as those of the Eskimos, I realized one secret of his success: he loved his ship, he loved his men, he loved Greenland, which most people hated, and he loved the Eskimos. No wonder he resisted the thought of turning the ship over to me. It would be like giving up a beloved wife and children.

Only a few nights later the captain subjected me to a major crisis. We were headed toward another obscure harbor. Just looking at it on the chart led me to believe that no sane man would try to enter it in darkness. The channel led through groups of small, rocky islands, from many of which granite reefs extended. Greenland's high cliffs all but surrounded this little nightmare. If the opening were missed, any ship would be ground to pieces.

I expected the captain to stay off shore until daylight, but imperturbably he followed a course to the entrance. Although I was not on watch, I stayed on the bridge to see what kind of miracle he was about to perform. A brisk wind was blowing and the *Nogak* was rolling uncomfortably, throwing up icy spray. Slowly a half-moon rose over the ice-capped mountains of Greenland. The captain dashed to the wing of the bridge and in its dim light took several bearings on landmarks which must have been known only to him.

"Come left to 083," he said to the helmsman.

"I am coming left to 083," the helmsman replied and a moment later added, "Steady on 083, sir."

"Very well."

The captain sat on his stool staring out an open window of the bridge.

Standing near him I could suddenly hear breakers ahead. There is no sound more terrifying than that to any sailor. In the remaining light from the moon I could see breakers ahead, breakers to our left and breakers to our right.

"Captain, breakers ahead, breakers to the left and breakers to the right!" I said, my voice tense.

"Very well."

A long minute went by before he added, "Mr. Wilson, I understand that you want to take command of this ship. All right, you're in command now. What are you going to do?"

"Sir, I would never get a vessel into this position," I answered, showing real anger at him for the first time.

"All right, but you're in command now. Say I dropped dead of a heart attack. What are you going to do?"

The breakers sounded louder. Through my panicked mind came an old sailor's adage: "You can always go out the way you came in." The course was 083. The opposite to that would be 263.

"Right full rudder," I said to the helmsman. "I want the engine ahead half."

"The rudder is coming right full, sir," the helmsman replied imperturbably, and the quartermaster added, "The engine is ahead half."

"Steady on course 263."

"Coming to course 263, sir."

The captain said nothing. I went in to check the chart. Although the captain had made several small course changes on the way in, the new course would take us out without any danger.

"We are steady on course 263, sir," the helmsman said.

"Very well. Ahead full."

"Now what would you do?" the captain asked.

"I'd go off shore about five miles and steam back and forth at slow speed until morning."

"Well, that's what a good second-rate seaman would do. Let me show you what a first-rate seaman can do. I relieve you."

I never did figure out the way he did it, but he conned that ship right through all those islands and shoals in almost total darkness and anchored in the inner harbor with no trouble at all. One thing that explained his prowess was that he had been in that harbor several times before and had a photographic memory when it came to places and charts. His was still a remarkable performance.

Why had he done it? For all his skills, wasn't his method more risky than mine, more sure to lead to disaster if repeated often enough?

He had done it mostly for bravado, to flaunt his uncanny ability and to put me in my place, I thought. It was certain that his method was more risky than mine, but how did that square with the fact that he had never run any ship aground? Who would dare run the proud *Atlantis* or even the most humble coast guard cutter aground?

The whole experience depressed me because it dramatized the fact that I could never live up to the captain's expectations for a man to replace him. I felt as though I had been sent, after a short cram course in mathematics, to replace Einstein. The situation had worn my nerves thin, and I suddenly longed to get back to the base, accept my transfer, bad fitness report and all, and see what lay ahead for me. Whatever lowly position would be found for me, it might at least offer a kind of work I could do without constant recriminations.

When we finally returned to Base One, we moored alongside a Norwegian freighter, which towered above us. As he always did upon returning to base, the captain put on a blue uniform which was newly pressed and a crisp cardboard collar on a freshly laundered shirt. His beard was neatly trimmed, and he looked as though he had just returned from a weekend cruise aboard a yacht. He headed toward the office of the admiral and the operations officer. From messengers who had accompanied him, I had heard his routine. Drawing himself up, he would say, "I wish to report the return of the United States Coast Guard Cutter, *Nogak*. All assignments have been completed and we are ready to go to sea again on twelve hours notice."

Only this time he would have another message, and I could almost hear him give it: "I have an incompetent officer, whom I want transferred immediately and I request a replacement."

Well, fuck him, I thought as I wearily shaved and began to pack my gear. When would he give me the bad news? Probably he would stop at the officers' club first to celebrate the completion of his voyage and his success at ridding himself of an incompetent officer.

Hours went by and the captain did not return to the ship. I sat down for dinner in the forecastle but could not eat. Both Mr. Mondino and Charlie Mahn were lying in their bunks writing letters. I had not yet been able to bring myself to write my wife and mother about my debacle, but that would be necessary as soon as my address changed. Fatigued by despair, I took off my uniform and wearing only my long winter underwear, climbed into my bunk and slept.

I do not know how long it was before I was awakened by a peremptory shout from the companionway.

"*Mr.* Wilson!" the captain called. "Come up here!"

I thought he was going to bait me about my incompetence and feigned sleep. I heard him come down the steps to the cabin.

"*Mr.* Wilson, I tell you to get up!"

In the dim light from a porthole, I could see he had a glass in his hand

and his words were slurred. I turned over in my bunk to face the other way.

"Mr. Wilson, I order you out of that bunk this minute!"

"Captain, I don't have to obey you while you're drunk," I said.

"Now don't give me any more of that crap! Get out of that bunk!"

For so many months I had avoided being a sea lawyer or deliberately antagonizing him. Why start something up now on my last night? Feeling ridiculous in my long underwear, I crawled from the bunk.

"Put on your uniform."

"Why?"

"Because that's an order."

I put on my blue uniform and a shirt that wasn't very clean.

"Now follow me."

A light snow was falling, covering the decks of the *Nogak*. He slid a little, caught himself, drained his glass and threw it overboard. With agility he then began to climb the Jacob's ladder which led to the decks of the Norwegian freighter, thirty feet above. As I followed him, snow which he kicked from the rungs of the ladder got in my eyes. The decks of the freighter were covered with snow which reflected the pale light from the portholes of the deckhouse. Following the captain there, I found myself in a large compartment which was lit only by kerosene lanterns—apparently the vessel's generators had failed. In the shadows were overstuffed leather chairs occupied by perhaps twenty men, many of whom I recognized as the captains of other trawlers and larger ships which called frequently at that base. They were drinking and hardly glanced at me. These men made up the informal "club" of skippers which I had longed to join, and I had the sickening thought that perhaps my captain had gathered them here for a little drunken baiting of a man who had tried to become one of them but who had failed. Walking to a group of bottles which stood on a mahogany table, my captain filled a tumbler full of whiskey and handed it to me.

"Drink up," he said. "We're all ahead of you."

"I can't drink a whole damn glass!"

"Do your best."

I took about three sips and shuddered.

"Gentlemen!" the captain said.

The other officers all looked in our direction.

"I would like to introduce you to Captain Wilson, who as of tomorrow will be commanding officer of the United States Coast Guard Cutter *Nogak*, the best little cutter in the fleet if you will pardon my pride."

There was polite clapping, some "Cheers!" and a reaching for glasses.

"So here's to Captain Wilson and the *Nogak*," a thin lieutenant-commander said.

"Do you mean it?" I asked my captain.

"Who would make jokes? Here are your orders. We'll go through the change of command thing tomorrow morning if either of us can wake up."

He stuck a long white envelope in my breast pocket. Going to one of the kerosene lanterns, I withdrew a piece of the rather pulpy paper the coast guard used. My eyes skipped through the service jargon until it hit the key words, my name and the phrase, "Commanding officer, USCGC *Nogak*."

"Do you think I can do it?" I asked the captain.

"Do you?"

"Not the way you do. I'll have to go slowly and carefully, but the men will be safe."

"That's what I figured. Drink up!"

One might expect that a lot of meaningful conversation would have taken place on such an occasion, but we drank so much that I can't remember anything at all except the singing. For some reason the favorite tune was "Under the Bamboo Tree." The captains of all those ships gathered around the table and chorused endless verses.

> We'll build a bungalow big enough for two,
> Big enough, my darling, big enough for two,
> And when we are married, happy we'll be,
> Underneath the bamboo, underneath the bamboo tree.

The next morning, "Under the Bamboo Tree" was practically all I remembered of the great moment in my life. Even now I am transported back to that dimly lit compartment every time I hear that old song, and I feel again the sense of triumph that soared and soared the more I turned it over in my mind. The infinite satisfaction I felt came essentially from the knowledge that for a little while at least I had conquered my own weaknesses and had become what I had longed to become. To me the symbol of that frozen waste called Greenland will always be a bamboo tree.

13

In the morning, the ceremony of changing command was an anticlimax. The men lined up on the well deck in two rows. The captain, who had, as usual, recovered completely from his drinking bout, read his orders in a monotone. I stuttered a little as I read mine. Then the captain shook hands with me briskly and also shook hands with every member of the crew before disappearing up the ladder. I think we all knew that we would never see him again.

My head was aching. I busied myself first with carrying my gear up to the captain's cabin, which he had left spotlessly clean. One advantage of my new situation was the comfort of a stateroom to myself with a private shower and head. I sat at the chart table and tried to make lists of first steps. One thing I wanted to do was to get a direct commission for Charlie Alden. Another thing I thought of doing was trying to get Mr. Mondino transferred, for, if anything happened to me, he would not be qualified for command. The thought that I was trying to jump into the old captain's shoes in too many respects gave me pause, and I decided to wait before making major personnel changes.

At about five o'clock I started to the officers' club. As I climbed up the ladder to the deck of the Norwegian freighter, I looked over my shoulder and sure enough, the little black and white pennant, the third repeater, was just going up to the *Nogak*'s masthead to tell the world that the commanding officer was not aboard. Few things in my life had ever made me feel anywhere near as large. When I went up to the bar of the officers' club, I looked around for the other captains, but apparently they all remained aboard their ships. There was no group I could join. When I finally struck up a conversation with a sad looking lieutenant, I asked where he was stationed.

"I'm gunnery officer on a freighter," he said. "What are you?"

"Oh, I'm the skipper of the *Nogak*," I replied in a very off-handed manner.

"The *Nogak*? What's that?"

"It's a trawler which the coast guard converted to a cutter."

"A trawler! You mean one of those little fish boats? How can you stand it?"

Crushed, I headed back to my ship. It was true, I realized, that most of the world would consider her nothing but an ugly little fish boat, but there were lots of things which most of the world did not understand at all.

Only a day after I took command, we received orders to pick up a load of depth charges and carry them about three hundred miles up the coast to a destroyer, which had anchored there after dropping everything she had on a submarine. The destroyer could not come to the base where more depth charges were stored because it was currently ringed by ice.

This appeared to me to be as easy an assignment as one could wish for one's maiden voyage as skipper. Because we had not received an additional officer when the captain left, I took the eight-to-twelve watch. This meant that I acted as watch officer as well as captain when we pulled away from the wharf, after loading the depth charges, and headed down the eighty-mile fjord to the sea. It was late enough in the year for the still waters of the lake-like fjord to be lightly frozen. The *Nogak* broke her way effortlessly, leaving a long black path through the gray ice. Snow had changed the red rock of the high mountains which loomed on each side of the narrow fjord to a pewter color which changed to a dazzling silver when the sun came from behind a cloud. When Mr. Mondino relieved me at noon, he said, "It's a bitch of a day, isn't it?"

By that he apparently meant that this was the first cold spell of the fall, I guessed. Our breath was frosting and it was necessary to keep the hoods of our heavy parkas over our heads.

"It's a winter wonderland, Mr. Mondino," I said, "a regular winter wonderland."

He gave me a look of sheer loathing. We had never got along well, and now he was quite sure to hate me as he had quietly disliked the prior captain. I walked forward, where the red-haired boatswain's mate was putting the hatch cover over the hold. Remembering that the captain, as I still thought of my predecessor, had accused me of knowing nothing about cargo stowage, I said, "Hold it a minute, Boats. I want to take a look down there."

"Nobody ever checked up on me before," Boats replied.

"I'm not checking up on you, but when we're carrying explosives, I don't think everything should be left to one man."

The depth charges filled almost the entire hold, and Boats had done a good job of securing them.

"Everything in order, sir?" he asked as I stepped back on deck.

"Everything looks fine."

"I been a boatswain's mate for eight years, sir. I think I know my job."

"I know you do. We're lucky to have you aboard."

He looked sullen as he turned back to replacing the hatch cover. Well, a lot of the men, including some of the best ones, would not be easy to convince that I was an adequate commanding officer. Without thinking what I was doing, I walked toward the after cabin where I had lived so long. I was almost there before I remembered that I had been promoted to the captain's cabin. As I walked forward, I was struck by the beauty of the curve of the hull as it slid through the thin ice, sending up jagged fragments which looked like glass as they sparkled in the sun. The great diesel below her decks made the ship tremble like a stallion. From the vents of the engineroom came the smell of hot diesel oil and a flood of warmth. Most people find the smell of diesel oil repulsive, but anything which I associated with the *Nogak* in those days seemed pleasant. The bend of her caprail at the bow appeared to me to possess almost the grace of a racing yacht.

We emerged from the fjord just at dusk. The wind was blowing harder than I had realized in the fjord, and the ice pack had drifted only a mile from the coast. I relieved Mr. Mondino to take the vessel through the ice. A mackerel sky had been turned gold by the setting sun. As it sank beneath the horizon the sky between the long formations of cloud was green, an intense darkening green which seemed almost to pulsate as the wind-torn clouds wove patterns around it. It was a trouble sky, but at the moment I was more worried about the ice than the weather. The ice field was not as tightly packed as most I had seen. At the edge of it small bergs rolled in the seas and occasionally collided with other bergs, sending up a fearful crashing sound. If I got the *Nogak* between two such bergs, I thought, she could be smashed in a second. Fortunately I was able to pick my way around such bergs. As darkness closed in completely, Charlie Alden took the bow watch as I always asked him to do in difficult conditions. Even when there was no light except from that of a few stars, we could see ice remarkably well when our eyes got used to the night. I had always been amazed at how far the human eye can see at sea in what appears to be pitch darkness, and Charlie's vision was particularly keen. We played a game of dodge 'em with the icebergs for about an hour before emerging from the pack. There was a great sense of safety as I headed into the open sea, where there was nothing to hurt us. When we were well clear of the ice, I charted a course to the harbor—where the destroyer awaited us—and turned the ship over to Mr. Mondino. The wind was piping up but was nothing exceptional for Greenland in the fall.

Going to the galley, I had a cup of coffee and a piece of Cookie's freshly baked Danish pastry. The conversation of the men in the forecastle bunks stopped as I came in, something which had never happened before my elevation. Rather missing the easy give and take with the men, I returned to my cabin, which was just abaft the bridge. The anemometer there told me that the wind was blowing forty miles an hour, a good stiff breeze, but hardly much cause for worry to the sturdy *Nogak*. Still, I didn't take my clothes off as I lay down in the captain's bunk. The emotional events of the preceding days had tired me, and I soon slept.

I was awakened about two hours later by drops of cold water falling on my face. Dressed in a yellow southwester, Mr. Mondino was leaning over my bunk and shaking me.

"Captain," he said. "You better get up. It's blowing like hell, and Sparks has picked up a hurricane warning."

I jumped out of my bunk, threw on my parka and dashed to the bridge. The first thing I saw in the gleam of a cloud-obscured moon was heavy spray which was arcing from the weather side of the well deck clean across the ship. It took me a moment to realize that the wind had changed from east to west. The vessel was rolling heavily, despite the fact that we were now in the lee of the ice pack and the Greenland coast. The anemometer told me that the wind was blowing fifty-three miles an hour with gusts up to sixty-five. That still was not much for a heavy old trawler to brood about, but when I opened the pilot house door, I found I had to hold it with all my strength to keep it from flying out of my hand, even though it was on the lee side. On deck the wind felt danger-ous, no matter what the anemometer read. I saw Hoffman, the radioman, gripping the rail of the companionway as, head down, he struggled to get to the pilothouse. He handed me a piece of yellow paper on which he had typed, "To all units, Greenpat. Winds of hurricane velocity expected west coast of Greenland any time from present to next three days. Take ap-propriate action. Commander, Greenpat."

My first reaction was completely childish. This isn't fair, I thought. It's not fair to hit a man with a hurricane the first time he has ever com-manded a ship. I'm only twenty-three years old, God. Take your hurri-cane back and give it to somebody else.

My next reaction came with the realization that a captain must, to some degree, be a liar. He never can admit fear or ignorance. When Hoffman gave me a clip board with a pencil, I initialed the radio message and handed it back to him.

"It looks like we're going to get a hatful of wind," I said.

"Yes sir," he replied with a grin.

"Pass the word amongst the men, and remind them that the *Nogak* was built for just this kind of weather. These trawlers were not designed for weekends on Long Island Sound."

"Aye, aye, sir."

Sticking the clipboard under his coat, he went forward, losing his cap in the process.

The next problem was, what did I do to take "appropriate action"? It would be dangerous to try to beat my way back through the ice pack to the fjord we had recently left. If the wind shifted again, it could easily pin us against the ice or a lee shore. The safest thing would be to run for sea room. If we could get fifty or even a hundred miles off shore, a hurricane wind could push us in any direction without driving us on the rocks.

Straight before the wind we sped away from Greenland. The seas were high but long. The vessel was rolling the scuppers of her well deck under, but the motion was not much worse than plenty we had seen. The barometer, which I had begun to consult every fifteen minutes, was falling fast and was already past the lowest point I had ever seen it. The anemometer was gusting above eighty. Gradually the *Nogak* became harder to steer. As the great gray combers became steeper, the helmsman had to keep spinning the wheel frantically to keep on course and avoid broaching. The well deck was full of white water now. Boats was out there with two seamen rigging a safety line from the forecastle aft. The men were shouting at one another, but no voice could be heard above the roar of the wind.

When my dead reckoning showed that we were fifty miles off shore, I decided to turn the *Nogak* and let her jog slowly into the wind. Turning any vessel in a gale can be dangerous. Some refuse to round up and are caught broadside by the seas. I didn't think the wind was yet strong enough to do that to an old trawler, and I was right. With full left rudder and full speed ahead, the *Nogak* seemed almost bored as she waddled in a tight circle and looked the wind in the eye. Ringing up slow speed ahead, I figured that there was nothing to do now but wait.

Gradually the wind increased to 100 miles an hour, and then to 120— the top of the scale on our anemometer. The seas grew steadily larger, and for the first time the *Nogak's* hull appeared to be under a strain. Although she was steaming just enough to maintain steerage way, she was crashing into the big steep swells which hurled themselves upon her with a series of thuds which reminded me a little of the noise made by a fast speedboat in a chop. In every other swell or so she buried her high bow, and washed the canvas cover from our three-inch gun. Shortly afterward I was astonished by the sight of a long tongue of fire which the wind sucked from the Charlie Noble, the smokestack of the galley range. Over the telephone Cookie told us that he turned the range off as soon as he realized that the cast iron monster was glowing a ruby red. The fire from the Charlie Noble gradually receded, but it left the whole stack glowing for several minutes.

When the seas started to crash over the bow to the well deck, I decided that the ship might do better if she took care of herself. Picking a relatively calm spot, we turned her again, cut off the engine and let her drift. The ease which her motion acquired was unbelievable. Her great propeller acted as a sea anchor. Her big round stern rode the unrushing seas without taking any green water aboard. The helmsman lashed the wheel and was given permission to go below.

It gave me a curious sensation to reflect that the best thing I as captain could do was absolutely nothing until the gale subsided. For a long time I had been anthropomorphizing the ship. Now it was impossible for me to think of her in any terms but that of a great stout mother who took care of her children and in times of stress knew exactly what to do.

I have no idea how far above 120 knots the wind blew, but after about 24 hours, it began slowly to subside. At the end of three days it was blowing only about fifty miles an hour, but the seas were still mountainous. I could do no more than guess to what position we had drifted, but I charted a course to the port where the destroyer waited for us—and we started the engine. The wind continued to decline, and there was an hour of complete calm before it began to snow. Soon we realized that we were in the grip of a real blizzard.

"Well," Charlie Alden said, "I don't think that any of us really thought that Greenland was going to turn out to be like Palm Beach."

The heavy snow had the effect of calming the seas and the men appeared cheerful as they threw snowballs at each other. Apparently I was the only man aboard the ship who was miserable. The snow was so thick that I could hardly see the bow of the vessel. After days of drifting, I had had no chance to determine my position and had only the most approximate idea of where we were. In theory I could drift around until the weather cleared enough for celestial navigation, but in Greenland at that time of the year, that wait could be long. Both the captain of the destroyer and the commander of the Greenland Patrol would demand to know where I had been. My superiors at the base would be keeping an especially sharp eye on me on the occasion of my first voyage in command. Without admitting it to myself, I wanted to convince them that I was as good as the *Nogak*'s prior captain.

Perhaps I was too afraid of authority, but I determined that I would close with the coast. My chart did not show any radio direction signals near the fjord where I wanted to go, but a recent booklet which had come with the official mail did. Apparently a new radio beacon had been built to help naval vessels find the very harbor in which the destroyer was waiting for us.

The radio operator was able to pick up the signal the booklet gave, but he warned that to his knowledge our direction finder had never been used. He didn't even know whether it had been calibrated.

In a bookrack in the captain's cabin I had found a notebook with graphs showing the deviation of the ship's two magnetic compasses. Checking that, I also found in the prior captain's precise hand a graph showing the errors of the radio direction finder. Feeling as though the old man himself had come aboard to show me the way, I began to home on the radio beacon. We had drifted close to one hundred miles off shore, I guessed. In about twelve hours we would reach the harbor we wanted, if all went well.

Tired as I was after weathering the hurricane, I sat hunched on the stool on the bridge, staring into the thick curtain of snow ahead. When I thought we should be entering the ice pack, we saw nothing but the empty sea. Were my calculations wrong, or had the hurricane dispersed the ice pack? The men stood on deck in the snow clapping their hands together and talking. I wondered, what about? Was my nervousness visible? Did they know that I feared we would barge onto some outlying rocks as we blindly groped for the coast? Although I had read plenty about radio direction finders, I had never actually used one. Was I doing everything right?

Apparently the hurricane had pushed us farther off shore than we thought. The hour when we were supposed to reach the harbor came' and went. The snow, if anything, was thickening. Suddenly I seemed to see a shadow on the falling snow. I stared at it and gradually could see the outline of a mountain.

"Land ho!" Charlie Alden called from the bow. "Land to port and land to starboard. There's a little island with a white tower on it broad on the starboard bow."

That was the radio beacon that had guided us here. I had been both foolish and lucky to enter a harbor under such conditions, even if the mouth of it was a good mile wide. I vowed never to do such a thing again, but I was mightily thankful for this initial success.

The destroyer which awaited our cargo was only a few thousand yards farther into the harbor. Charlie signaled for permission to come alongside. When this was granted, we approached her low, flat stern and passed lines to her deck gang. While the depth charges were being unloaded, a messenger from the destroyer came to tell me that his captain would like me to have coffee with him in his cabin. I said yes before realizing that I had not shaved in three days and had been catching naps in my uniform. All my blue uniforms were dirty, but I had some clean khaki ones which were used for summer wear. After a shave so rapid that it left my chin bleeding, I put on the khakis, shined my shoes and presented myself aboard the destroyer.

The captain was a sleek, slender man about twice my age. His cabin looked to me like a suite in the Grand Hotel, and the coffee was poured from a silver pot by a Filipino mess boy in a spotless white coat.

"Well, captain, we're grateful for the depth charges," the destroyer's captain said.

"We're glad to be able to bring them to you."

"We've been having quite a hurricane here. We dragged three anchors. One of our sister ships caught it at sea and took such a beating that she had to go back to Boston for repairs."

"I'm sorry to hear that."

"Where were you when the storm hit?"

"At sea."

"Did you have any trouble?"

"Trouble?"

"Our anemometer clocked it at 150 miles an hour."

"That's about what it was. Nothing to worry about, sir. You can't spend much time on the Greenland Patrol without getting used to that sort of thing."

"I've never been to Greenland before," the captain of the destroyer said. "Do you get such extreme weather conditions often?"

The prior captain of the *Nogak* had enjoyed telling tall stories about Greenland to newcomers in bars, and I remembered some of his tales, all of which were true. I told the captain of the destroyer about the fahn winds which strike suddenly from the ice cap and are strong enough to lift a forty-foot liberty boat loaded with men right out of the water. I told him a story told by Magnusen, the Icelander who knew all about ice. Once Magnusen steered his *Nanok* too close to an iceberg that was about five miles long. He knew that ocean currents melt the bottoms of icebergs, causing them to turn over frequently, but he did not know that this particular iceberg had a shelf of ice which projected under the water for a quarter of a mile. The *Nanok* was right on top of that shelf when the iceberg decided to turn over. The shelf picked up the heavy trawler as though it were a toy, and the first thing Maggie knew about it, his ship was a hundred feet up in the air. Luckily it slid off, and being a trawler, wasn't hurt.

The captain of the destroyer looked at me in complete astonishment. "God damn it, is that true?" he demanded.

"We have things like that happen all the time around here."

"Well, I'll be glad to get the hell out of this place."

"It's no place for a destroyer, sir, as you know better than I do. The ice in the pack isn't just ordinary ice. Some of it is formed under thousands of tons of pressure at the bottom of the ice cap before it is forced down the glaciers into the sea. It's as hard as case-hardened steel."

"How do you handle that kind of ice?"

"Well, sir, we push those blue icebergs aside very gently. My little *Nogak* is so used to the ice pack that the icebergs actually try to mate with her every once in a while."

The captain of the destroyer laughed.

"I've got to be getting back to my ship," I said. "I'm sorry to wear my khakis aboard a destroyer this time of year. The truth is that we get such bad winters up here that we try to make summer last as long as possible. I don't even get my blues out of mothballs until sometime around November."

The captain of the destroyer gave me a courteous farewell, and we steamed back to our base without difficulty. By that time I had cleaned up my blue uniforms, and like my predecessor, I was spotless when I walked up to the office of the admiral and the operations officer, who turned out to be a fatherly looking bald commander.

"I just want to report that the *Nogak* has returned, and our mission has been accomplished," I said.

"We've been worried about you," the commander replied. "Did you have any trouble in the storm?"

"Not a bit, sir. We are ready to go to sea on twelve hours notice."

He looked amused.

"Very well, captain," he said. "I trust that all your assignments won't be as rough as your first one."

I thanked him and headed straight for the officers' club. This time the captains of several other trawlers were gathered at one end of the bar, and one of them beckoned me to join them. In a few minutes I saw the great Magnusen himself come in the door and join us. He was a man of middle size with warm brown eyes and prematurely white hair. In deference to this dean of the trawler captains, all conversation stopped. He ordered Scotch and sipped it slowly.

"I've just been up to the admiral's office," he said. "They want to send a bunch of trawlers back to Boston this fall for refits. They've decided that the *Natsek* was just a fluke."

"What did you say?" a tall, haggard-appearing man asked.

"I told them that November is the wrong time of year for a small vessel, even a trawler, to make the passage from Greenland to Boston, and I suggested rather strongly that they not route small ships through the Strait of Belle Isle this time of the year."

"Did the admiral seem to agree with you?" the tall man asked.

"I doubt if admirals ever agree with anybody. He just thanked me for giving my opinions, and dismissed me."

"I bet the bastard will send us right in the *Natsek*'s wake," the tall man said.

I drank with them for more than an hour. I couldn't forget that sentence: "I bet the bastard will send us right in the *Natsek*'s wake."

I had a vision then, one which had been plaguing me ever since the prior skipper of the *Nogak* had told me about the loss of the *Natsek*. I could see this ship, which was just like mine, icing up until she looked like a trawler carved out of ice. I could see her crew trying to free her from this burden with huge mallets and axes, but the ice formed faster than they could knock it off. Every time the ship rolled, she took longer to come back, until finally she took one sickening lurch, lay on her beam ends in the gray windswept sea and her captain, bracing himself in the pilothouse, realized that she would never come back.

The vision of such a death terrified me far more than the possibility of meeting German submarines or floating mines. When I returned to the *Nogak*, I added "icing stations" to our watch and quarter bill. When we went to icing stations, the chief machinist's mate stayed in the engine-room alone. The senior radioman stayed in the radio shack alone, and I alone remained on the bridge, taking the wheel myself. Every other man jack armed himself with an ice mallet or an axe and worked under the direction of the boatswain's mate at chipping ice.

As Magnusen had predicted, the *Nogak* soon got orders to return to Boston. It was mid-November. The men of course were delighted by the prospect of Christmas at home and so was I when I got my mind off worries about the voyage. As we waited at the base for the convoy we were to join, two things happened which complicated my state of mind. First of all, Charlie Alden's commission came through. I was proud of the speed with which my correspondence had achieved results until I saw in Charlie's file letters which the prior skipper of the *Nogak* had sent. Every commanding officer whom Charlie had ever had recommended him for a commission, and finally it came through. Charlie seemed both embarrassed and pleased. Other officers gave him spare uniforms and insignia which enabled him to be transformed into an ensign on the spot. Charlie had been so respected in the forecastle that not a man there showed any jealousy or derision. Since we had a vacancy for an officer, I planned to give Charlie the midnight watch and looked forward to many nights of sound sleep. This, as I should have known, was not to be. Within twenty-four hours of the time that Charlie was commissioned, he was transferred to another ship. Through long experience the coast guard had learned that a newly commissioned officer should not be asked to command his old messmates. The rule was probably a sound one, but when Charlie walked ashore I lost not only a friend, but the only man aboard the ship whose knowledge and judgment I could completely trust. Charlie Mahn was fine on deck and could pilot a vessel expertly in waters which were familiar to him, but he knew little about ice and did not really trust the ability of the instruments of navigation to take him to regions he had never seen. Mr. Mondino I had never understood well. Except for communications, which he handled well, he had never been an adequate officer. His hatred for the Greenland Patrol, the *Nogak* and me made him withdraw into himself more and more. When he was not on watch he spent most of his time in his bunk writing endless letters to his wife, a chubby, pleasant-faced young woman whose photographs lined the bulkhead by his bunk. Instead of learning more about the operation of the ship, he actually seemed to be forgetting rudimentary skills he had possessed when I first reported aboard. Once when I asked him to take bearings on some prominent headlands, he fussed with the small task for an hour before I got disgusted and did it myself, an action which made him sulk for days. He was hardly the kind of man on whom the captain of any ship could lean when the going got tough.

My worries about the voyage were interrupted a few days before we sailed by a messenger from the communications center of the base, who brought me a terse radiogram from my father-in-law. It said, "Elise fine but baby stillborn. When can you get home?"

To some people this might not sound like a first-class emergency, but I had some idea of how much my wife wanted that child. I wanted to ask for emergency leave, but Mr. Mondino would be in charge of the ship the minute I left. Of course the *Nogak* would soon be heading for Boston, but the censors could not allow me to radio that. There was nothing I could do but radio what love and compassion I could put into words. The censor even cut the phrase "Home soon."

In only a few days I was asked to the operations office, where the commanding officers of the other ships in the convoy were to meet. As I saw their rank, which ran from lieutenant commander to four-striper, I knew that the *Nogak* would be surrounded by much larger vessels. A glance at a small-scale chart which had been tacked to a sort of bulletin board showed me that our course would take us well to the east of Newfoundland, instead of through the Strait of Belle Isle. On one particular at least, the admiral had listened to Maggie.

The operations officer announced that the *Nogak* would act as an antisubmarine vessel and a rescue ship. He did not seem upset when I told him that we had depth charges but no sonar.

"You just follow the convoy," he said. "The subs have been coming in on the surface at night, following the wakes of the convoy. They will encounter you first. You may not have much armament, but you can tie a sub up for a few minutes and alert the rest of the convoy. If any of the other ships is sunk, however, your first priority is to pick up as many survivors as you can."

This painted a rather gaudy picture of the *Nogak*'s future activities, I thought, but it didn't worry me. Like many other officers on the Greenland Patrol, I could not take the possibility of German action seriously when the weather and the ice were clearly the real enemies.

"There is a probability that you will encounter icebergs during the first half of the voyage and a strong possibility that you will see floating mines," the operations officer said. "To maintain radio silence the commodore will sound whistle signals for emergency turns. I strongly recommend that you refresh your memory of these whistle signals and make sure that your watch officers know them. At night or in fog, you can imagine what a foul-up could do."

Before we left, the operations officer gave us mimeographed instructions which included the whistle signals for emergency turns, which I had never seen. After memorizing them, I gave them to Mr. Mondino and Charlie Mahn. To make sure they knew them, I tested them a couple of hours later. Both men appeared to have learned their lessons well.

There was great excitement when we began to make final preparations for getting underway the next day. One of the men invented a song which began, "I'm wishing for a brown Christmas, white is not the best at all. . . ." When I told a seaman named Cady to check the base post office to see if there was any mail, official or otherwise, for the ship, he returned to the *Nogak* with such eagerness to sail that he jumped aboard in too much of a hurry and broke his nose when he collided with some of our steel rigging. Holding a rag against his bleeding nose, Cady begged me not to send him to the base doctor, for he was scared of being hospitalized and being left behind when his ship headed for home. I was not dead sure that his nose was broken and guessed that Cady could survive without medical attention for the next ten days. I was cheered by the fact that the men did not seem at all worried about the dangers of the voyage to Boston.

14

As so often happens in wartime, there was an unexpected delay. When we were just about to cast off our lines, a messenger dashed to the wharf in a jeep and gave us a message from the operations officer. The convoy was held up because the destroyer escort which was supposed to meet us had experienced trouble with her engines, and was putting back to Argentia.

The delay stretched for almost a month. I had no more news from home and was worried about my wife. I also felt that the closer we got to the dead of winter, the more perilous our voyage would become. Already we had only a few hours of daylight and the fjord where we lay froze like a great lake. The wind that howled from the ice cap was driving the temperature down to thirty and forty degrees below zero. The men wore rubber boots over many pairs of woolen stockings, parkas and woolen face masks whenever they appeared on deck.

During this period of waiting, many of the men in the forecastle sat polishing narwhal or walrus tusks which they had obtained from the Eskimos in exchange for tinned food or cigarettes. They played cards, told stories about the Eskimo women they had bedded and made bets on the day we would finally reach Boston. I was constantly amazed and cheered by the fact that these men, many of whom were experienced seamen, never appeared to give a thought to the *Natsek*, which by now almost everyone knew about. They were as casual as men waiting for a passenger liner to take them home in time of peace.

In the after cabin Mr. Mondino lay in his bunk, writing so many letters to his wife that I wondered how she could ever get time to read them. Charlie Mahn, the oldest seaman of us all, walked up to the supply base, where he somehow found forty of the biggest ice mallets any of us had ever seen. Nicely varnished, they looked as though they were made as part of a croquet set for giants. We stowed them in the hold.

Finally the order came to sail. I had been waiting so long that I felt much as a prizefighter must feel when he awakes on the morning of a much delayed championship bout. The men cast off the ice-sheathed mooring lines with a will, and unable to coil them, secured their shiny lengths in the motorboat. The *Nogak* cut a straight path through the ice in the inner harbor. In the outer harbor, which was still free of ice, several large freighters and a big tanker, the *Laramie*, were steaming in single file toward the mouth of the fjord. Their signal flags made a colorful show, as though this were a Fourth of July regatta. With three hours to go before dark, the sky was like a blue canopy suspended from the tall, snow-covered mountains which rose steeply from each side of the fjord, dwarfing even the biggest ship.

The clear sky made me hope that even though we were going from Greenland to Boston in December, this might miraculously turn out to be a fairweather voyage. I had always believed in my own luck. Perhaps all we would have to do would be to follow these big ships right into Boston harbor.

Before we were out of the fjord, the pulsating northern lights and the gleam from a half-moon made the dark waters and the white mountains clearly visible. At the mouth of the fjord the destroyer escort met us and led the way to the open sea. The wind hit us as soon as we left the lee of the land and the sea was exactly as rough as one would expect on the coast of Greenland in December. The *Laramie*, which we were to follow, was running without cargo or ballast. She was having trouble steering, and also seemed unable to adjust her speed to that of the convoy, which was eight knots. For some reason she kept falling behind, causing us to reduce speed, then charging ahead, leaving us several miles behind the convoy. When the moon went down, it was hard to see this huge gray vessel, and my nightmare of being run down by this twenty thousand-ton monster began.

There was something almost mystical about the *Laramie* at the beginning of that voyage. During the long nights, one could see the outline of her vast bulk illuminated only by starlight. Suddenly she would vanish as though she had disintegrated, and soon would reappear in some entirely different place. She was to the right of us, to the left of us, ahead and behind us all the time, it seemed to me. Sometimes she came so close that we could see and hear the great white waves her bluff bow made as she rolled through the sea, and we had to look almost straight up to her bridge, where in those cold days no watch officer was ever visible. The fact that she seemed to be sailing without human help made her appear all the more sinister in my state of heightened imagination. As her scuppers spouted water and the red of her bottom glistened when she rolled, she sometimes appeared to me to be a great wounded beast hot in pursuit of our poor little trawler.

Tired of trying to keep station on a ship which was so erratic, I asked the commodore for permission to steam on the tanker's port beam instead of trying to follow her. This would reduce the chance of collision caused by the big ship's constant variations in speed. Since we sailed about two-thousand yards away from the tanker, only her most extreme variations in course could endanger us.

When we had been at sea about four days and nights, most of which I had spent on the bridge out of sheer nervousness, I retired to my bunk, which was directly abaft the pilothouse. Mr. Mondino had the watch, but the realization that he was actually headed home to his wife had awakened him from his long stupor, and he seemed to me to care as much as I did about keeping the *Nogak* alive. When I went to my cabin, it was snowing heavily and the night was black, but these conditions were normal for that place and that time, and I told myself that I could not stay awake forever. As soon as I crawled into my narrow bunk, I fell into a deep sleep. I had no idea how long I slept before I awoke as suddenly as though I had been slapped. Faint in the distance ahead I had heard a whistle signal. At first my sleep-drugged brain couldn't make much sense out of it. Then I heard Mr. Mondino say calmly to the helmsman, "Come right half rudder," and at the same time I realized that the whistle signal which still seemed half-dreamed had called for a forty-five-degree emergency turn to the *left*. My mind was suddenly full of that great tanker on our right which was now turning left and heading directly for us. While I was thinking these thoughts I was jumping out of my bunk and pulling open the cabin door.

"Reverse the helm!" I shouted at the helmsman. "Left full rudder!"

"I am coming to left full rudder," the helmsman said as he rapidly spun the wheel.

"Ahead flank," I said to the quartermaster.

"I am calling for ahead flank, sir," the quartermaster said.

Ignoring Mr. Mondino, I dashed to the wing of the bridge through the darkness to find the tanker. The snow was falling thicker now. There was a flash of white which I took to be a sea breaking close alongside, but suddenly I realized that this was the *Laramie*'s bow wave, not more than five-hundred yards away. Even in the snow, the vast bulk of the twenty thousand-ton ship could be seen looming above us like the outline of a mountain. The *Nogak* had already spun on her stern and was drawing away. Hurrying to my chart table, I figured out a new course and gave it to the helmsman. All of a sudden Mr. Mondino, who had been standing in a corner of the pilothouse, let loose.

"It's illegal!" he said with great emotion.

"What's illegal?"

"The commanding officer may not give orders on the bridge without relieving the deck officer first!"

I was angry. Taking his arm, I pushed him out on the wing of the bridge. The *Nogak* was increasing her distance from the *Laramie*, but the big tanker was still visible like a great mountain in the snow and the massive bow could still be seen cutting through the sea with irresistible force.

"If I hadn't heard that signal in my sleep," I said to Mr. Mondino, "we'd all be dead by now. I doubt if the men on the bridge of that tanker would even know that they'd hit us. In the morning we'd just be missing."

I don't know what I expected Mr. Mondino's reaction to be. Perhaps I thought he would apologize to me, like me better and try harder to be an effective officer. Instead he broke into tears. The snow-filled wind was bitter, and I helped him into the warm pilothouse. There his paroxysm continued.

"No!" he suddenly shouted, clenching his fists against his belly. "No, no, no!"

"You better get below," I said.

"You bastard! You're a worse bastard than the old bastard you relieved, and I thought he was the worst bastard I could ever see!"

"Go get some sleep," I said. "I relieve you."

"You've never liked me any more than the old bastard did. You think I don't know why?"

"We'll talk about it tomorrow."

"I want to have it out with you now, you Harvard bastard, rich kid. The old man went to Harvard and you went to Harvard. Both nice Protestant bastards. You don't like Italians, do you? I heard the old man making fun of the Italian navy once. You don't have any niggers here, so you've made me the nigger. Well, I won't stand for it!"

In the distance I heard the thump of depth charges. I had been so excited by the near collision that I had not had a chance to wonder why the emergency turn had been ordered. Apparently the DE had contact with a submarine up ahead.

"Sound general quarters," I said to the quartermaster.

Almost immediately there was the urgent cry of the horn we used to call the men to battle stations. The door from the forecastle flew open and men came running, buttoning their parkas as they slipped and slid in the snow on the well deck.

"I'm going to hang you," Mr. Mondino continued. "You've broken every regulation in the book!"

"Go to your cabin immediately," I said. "That is a direct order."

"I don't have to obey your goddamn orders. Who the fuck are you to give orders to me?"

The helmsman was a giant of a man named Kelly.

"Kelly, take Mr. Mondino to his bunk," I said. "I'll take the wheel."

"Aye, aye, sir."

I took the polished spokes of the wheel.

"Don't you touch me!" Mr. Mondino said as Kelly approached him. "I order you not to touch me."

He drew back as the big man neared, but in that tiny pilothouse there was no place to retreat. Kelly grabbed him. There was a brief, futile struggle before Kelly hoisted him on his shoulder and walked toward the after cabin. In the distance there was the sound of more depth charges. Well, there was little we could do except keep a good lookout for submarines on the surface. Suddenly I was glad that there were no decisions I had to make. For the moment I was nothing but a helmsman, with the wheel kicking in my hands. There was an art to keeping the lubberline of the compass on the course we were following. I had achieved command of the *Nogak* without ever steering her. Her blunt stern was being slapped around by the quartering seas, and she was acting like a dog trying to lick a wounded tail. It took me a few minutes to straighten her out. In the next war, I'm just going to be a helmsman, I thought. The pay is not so hot, but at least the problems of a helmsman can usually be solved.

Kelly returned and silently relieved me at the wheel.

"Did you have much trouble?" I asked.

"No sir. I put him in his bunk. He acted like he was unconscious or asleep. I didn't have to rough him up at all."

It was only a short time before the commodore of the convoy ordered us to return to our original course. We never learned whether the DE had been pursuing submarines or whales. The whole maneuver which had almost resulted in a collision with the big tanker and which had accomplished the undoing of Mr. Mondino, was just one of those routine exercises which anyone who sails in convoy soon learns to expect.

The day after Mr. Mondino had been carried from the bridge, I went to the after cabin to talk to him. The sight of him lying in his bunk and staring at the overhead reminded me of the weeks during which I had been in a similar position and I felt sorry for him.

"Mr. Mondino," I began, "there's no reason why you can't recover from a thing like last night. Everybody makes mistakes..."

"Get out of here, you bastard! I don't want to talk to you!"

His eyes blazed. I had never been openly hated before, at least not to my knowledge. My ego was such that I couldn't understand *why* Mr. Mondino hated a fine, kind, upstanding young character like me. The only reason I thought he might have a right to hate me was that I did not really have the skills and experience necessary for commanding a ship and might inadvertently kill him with all the other men, but he did not seem to realize or worry about this. His hatred was intensely personal. I turned all this over in my mind for a long while before I realized that he hated me in large part because I couldn't help but be contemptuous of him. He thought I was contemptuous of him because he was of Italian descent. My reason was because he was a bad officer who predictably had almost killed everyone aboard the ship. The intensity of my feeling for an officer who appeared to me to be a potential murderer caused me to hate everything about Mr. Mondino, from the fact that he rarely washed the back of his neck, which had become gray from diesel smoke, to his habit of writing so many long letters every day to his plump, innocent-looking wife. My hatred for Mr. Mondino had become as irrational as his for me.

Suddenly I remembered that the hands of the prior captain of the *Nogak* had shaken when he was relieving me of my duties because of my many inadequacies. I had fallen into the habit of assuming that that whole exercise had simply been a method to fit me for command. But that wasn't true. The prior skipper had hated me for all the reasons that I loathed Mr. Mondino.

When I find I dislike a man intensely, there is a temptation to compensate for negative feelings with positive actions to soften my own guilt. I found myself thinking of returning Mr. Mondino to duty and giving him a good fitness report. The result of that, of course, might be the elevation of the man to command of the *Nogak* the minute I got transferred. That, I felt, could be a tragedy for every man aboard. I would have to force my mind to do exactly what my emotions wanted to do: transfer Mr. Mondino with a bad fitness report, the same fate which had been planned for me.

I did not feel that the middle of the North Atlantic Ocean in December was the best place and time to discuss Mr. Mondino's future with him, and soon the weather gave me other things to worry about. Veering around to the southwest, the wind blew up to sixty knots. There was no great difficulty about that except that the big ships were able to maintain their speed against a headwind better than the *Nogak* could. Gradually they forged ahead. When he was almost beyond signaling distance, the commodore signaled, "Are you maintaining your best speed?"

We replied: "Affirmative."

The big ships signaled to each other, and soon I realized that they were slowing down for us. I felt absurdly grateful, like a child whose parents wait to give him a chance to catch up.

The wind increased and the seas built up to the point where even the big tanker disappeared from our sight entirely when she sank into a valley between two combers. When the destroyer escort circled the convoy at dusk, sniffing for submarines, I saw that she was plunging the first third of her hull into the sea when she hit the bottom of the roller coaster ride offered by the big graybearded swells. The blunt bow of the little *Nogak* was doing better than that. We bobbed along in about the same fashion we had been doing for months. There was only one trouble: our speed against that wind and those seas continued to decrease. At dusk we were a mile behind our station. When dawn came not a ship was in sight, and the gray North Atlantic looked like the loneliest place in the world.

"Where is everybody?" Charlie Mahn asked.

Before I had a chance to answer, a lookout reported the destroyer escort just coming over the horizon dead ahead. Hurrying back to try to round up her flock, the narrow gray vessel soon came within signaling distance.

"Are you all right?" she blinked.

"Yes," we replied, and somewhat roguishly added, "Can we be of any assistance?"

Destroyers do not have a highly developed sense of humor. "Are you proceeding at your best speed?" she inquired.

"Affirmative."

There was a wait of several minutes.

"Proceed to destination independently," the destroyer finally signaled.

"Will comply," we said.

"Good luck," she added.

"Same to you."

Perhaps offended by our brashness, the DE sped over the horizon to the larger ships.

"At least we don't have to worry about collision," Charlie Mahn said. Ever since the voyage had started, he had kept almost as long hours on the bridge as I had. He had to wear glasses, but he had the eyes of an experienced seaman which seemed to penetrate darkness uncannily.

Hardly had the destroyer disappeared when the wind began rapidly to abate. The sun shone between fragments of fast scudding gray clouds and turned the jumble of confused seas into glittering masses of jade, like hills of broken glass.

"Maybe we'll get a spell of good weather now," I said to Charlie Mahn.

"No. Now she'll come from the north."

Unlike Greenland, this was his part of the ocean, latitudes in which he had worked aboard fishing vessels since the days of sail. He understood the weather. Only about an hour after he spoke, heavy gray clouds built up on the northern horizon. The sun soon was gone. A wind from the north hit with such force that it ripped loose some parkas which the men had lashed loosely in the rigging to dry, and sent them soaring high in the sky with their arms flapping frantically like those of frightened, flying men. The temperature plummeted suddenly from fifteen degrees above zero to twenty-below. First hitting us with quick gusts which subsided after a few minutes, the storm grew into a steady roar. The anemometer told me that it was blowing seventy knots. That was only about half the wind we had experienced during the hurricane, but in the middle of the North Atlantic the seas were bigger than anything I had seen. Perhaps to avoid submarines, our orders required us to head in toward the coast of Maine before turning south to Boston. The course kept the ship with the wind on her beam, causing her to roll the bulwarks of the well deck under. We had recently rigged a new aerial which the radioman thought would increase the range of our radio transmitter. Perhaps this mass of wires caused the wind to howl louder than it had during the hurricane. As though the storm were playing a devil's harp, it kept rising almost unbearably in pitch, only to fall into a dirge which seemed suitable to mourn everyone who ever died at sea.

There was little on the bridge which I could do. Leaving Charlie

Mahn on watch, I turned in. For some reason I slept better than I had since leaving Greenland. When I awoke I could see daylight through my porthole. The wind seemed even louder than it had been when I turned in. Filled with a vague sense of apprehension, I hurried to the bridge. The red-haired chief boatswain's mate whom I had chosen to take Mr. Mondino's watch was wiping the inside of the pilothouse windows with a rag to clear them of condensation. When I looked out, the first thing I saw was the wire topping lift which ran from the truck of our mast to the end of our cargo boom. Usually it was a half inch in diameter. Now it was covered by six inches of gleaming white ice. The rigging of the mast was similarly decorated. The three-inch gun and the twenty millimeters all looked as though they had been carved from ice.

"She's been icing up for the past couple of hours," Red said. "I was going to call you, but I figured it's not thick enough to start chipping yet."

My anxiety took the form of fury for not being called. Why in the hell had I tried to turn a chief boatswain's mate into a watch officer? Even Mr. Mondino would have called me if we started icing up. Yet Red was right: the ice was not thick enough in most places to start chipping. The energy of the men should be preserved.

Putting on a heavy parka, I went out on the wing of the bridge. It felt as though it was raining, but this rain was salty, and came not from the sky, but from the sea. The brutal wind was blowing the tops off the waves and was creating a swirl of spray that reached at least as high as our masthead, which was swollen to twice its size. The spray glazed every vertical surface the ship offered, and it turned our three-hundred-pound depth charges on the stern to great white cylinders the size of the *Tampa's* six-hundred pounders. The spray also froze the moment it hit the deck, and I could walk only by hanging onto every handhold I could find and moving my feet like those of a beginning skater.

"When do you think we should begin chipping?" I asked Red when I returned to the bridge.

"We could start with the rigging and the guns pretty soon."

It occurred to me that in all probability Red had never experienced the phenomenon of icing up. Why had I asked him for his advice? Did I want to avoid the responsibility of command as much as I for some reason craved its honors?

"I'll take over, chief," I said. "We don't have to go to icing-up stations yet, but take a crew of about six men and clean her up as best you can."

The men started forward with the big mallets and worked their way aft. It was hard work in the cold wind, and unable to support themselves while they wielded the mallets, the men took many falls on the icy decks as the ship rolled. One man, his identity hidden by the hood of his parka, almost fell overboard, and I yelled at Red to use safety lines. These took a long while to rig and hampered the men so much that they chipped little ice. It took the crew three hours to work from the bow to the stern. When they were through the bow had again iced up almost as badly as when they started.

"How long do these conditions usually last?" I asked Charlie Mahn.

"It can be a long time. Hurricanes hit and run. A North Atlantic gale can go on for a week or two, sometimes more."

If these icing conditions lasted a week, I could easily see that every man aboard would be exhausted by chopping, and would have to lie with the apathy of weariness while the ship became more and more top-heavy. On this return from Greenland we had nothing but a few mailbags in our cargo hold, where the *Nogak* would have carried many tons of fish or ice during her days as a working trawler. Without ballast below, the *Nogak* had to carry the weight of her guns and depth charges far above her well deck. No wonder the *Natsek* had rolled over: all these converted trawlers were top-heavy even before they began to ice up.

I was sweating, despite the chill of the drafty pilothouse. For several weeks I had tried not to think of the *Natsek*. How accurately I had imagined her as a ship carved from ice! Already my own vessel was duplicating my nightmares.

It is necessary to remember, I thought, that the *Nanok* survived, and she too has the same design as the *Nogak*. Old Maggie knew what to do. He ran. He turned his stern to the wind and let her run clean around Cape Race where there was plenty of searoom.

Well, I was not far from Cape Race, that cutting edge of Newfoundland, and searoom was one thing I had. Charting a course due south instead of west to the coast of Maine, we ran with the wind at our stern.

Old Maggie knew a thing or two about trawlers in frozen seas. With only her stern presented to the storm, the *Nogak* suffered much less icing. When the long gray combers grew too difficult to ride, we drifted as we had in the hurricane. With the wind on our quarter, there was a little more icing, but nothing we couldn't handle.

For five days I sat on the bridge every moment I could stay awake. About every half hour I tapped the barometer with my finger and checked the anemometer. Never had I seen such a static storm. The wind remained between sixty and seventy miles an hour, and the barometer stayed shockingly low.

The driving spray which caused the icing somehow penetrated corners of the ship that rain had never touched. The after cabin took the brunt while we were drifting. In every locker and drawer the clothes of Mr. Mondino and Charlie Mahn were soaked. My cabin, which had a port facing aft, did not fare much better, and even the forecastle, which was most protected from the stinging spray, was damp as a dungeon. Our chief machinist mate rigged clothes lines in the engineroom. From these our uniforms arrived warm, dry and stained with oil and grease.

Finally the wind and spray let up, but the heavy cloud cover remained, giving me no chance for celestial navigation. While the men asked me what their chances were for getting home in time for Christmas, I puzzled over my charts, trying to come up with some sort of estimated position. We had steamed two-thirds of the way from Greenland to Newfoundland, and had cut to southwest before the convoy left us. Then I had run south and drifted until we were probably well on our way to Iceland, but it is difficult for any man to guess the speed of a drifting vessel. I had done it with a fair degree of success after the hurricane, and I gave it a try now. Charting a course from my estimated position, I gave it to the helmsman. My hope was that we could get close enough to Boston to pick up that city's signals on our radio direction finder.

While we were still much too far at sea to get accurate radio bearings, I turned on our direction finder to see if it was working properly. I got a surprise. The dampness had got to it so much that I couldn't even get a light behind the dial. The radio operator said it would take time to dry it out. He sounded quite casual about it.

I hoped that the sky would clear, but instead it started to snow. We steamed toward what I hoped was Boston through calm seas with a swirl of snow decorating every porthole. Some of the men had radios which picked up stations from New York to Ohio, including Boston. After December twentieth, they played almost nothing but Christmas carols. The men began ironing uniforms and shining shoes for the great homecoming.

"What's our position, captain?" many men asked me. "When are we going to make our landfall?"

I could not tell them that I did not really know. Again I noticed that one of the civilian virtues that the captains of ships can rarely afford is the habit of complete honesty. A commanding officer of a ship cannot come forward and say, "Look, men, the truth really is that I don't know what I'm doing. To put it bluntly, I think we're lost. I don't have a clue about our position, but I hope to blunder through one way or another."

Instead of saying that, I told them my best estimated position and said that we would sight land on the morning of December twenty-fourth, weather and other conditions permitting. The Christmas Eve date delighted them. They started cutting each other's hair. The machinist's mates began to soak their hands, cleaning fingernails which had long been used to working with oil and grease.

The snow reduced visibility as much as a thick fog would. When I tried to sleep, I had visions of the *Nogak* crashing up on the beach of Cape Cod, or perhaps Sandy Hook.

"Is this Boston?" I would ask as I waded briskly ashore.

When I awoke with the shakes, I would curse the day we had lost our electronic sounding machine, an accident which happened to almost every vessel which worked in the ice pack. I also rued the day when Charlie Alden left, for he was the only man I knew who could handle a deep sea lead without causing the vessel to creep along as though she had a broken screw. I mentioned this to Charlie Mahn and he said, "I can take your soundings for you. It's been quite a while, but I used to be thought pretty good with a leadline."

The old warrant officer soon proved that he had not lost his skills. He stood up on the bow and sent the heavy lead whistling ahead. When we started, we got bottom at fifty fathoms, which showed me that we probably were somewhat ahead of my estimated position. As I pored over my chart, I needed every scrap of information I could get. I became so intent at piecing together the various clues the bottom provided that I entirely forgot the hard physical effort necessary for heaving a deep sea lead. Suddenly I glanced at my watch and realized that Charlie Mahn had been up there on the bow for more than three hours. I called him to my cabin and thanked him. His right hand had been deeply cut by the leadline and his nose was blue with cold.

"I can't thank you enough," I began weakly.

"Did you figure your position?"

"A lot better than I had."

"We never used to have more than a leadline and a compass when we came in here. I know we ain't far off. You'll pick up lights as soon as it gets dark. Then we'll know where we are."

His confidence cheered me. Soon darkness fell, as snowy and as cheerless as countless nights in Greenland. As soon as the clouds lost their last glimmer of light, Charlie Mahn climbed to the flying bridge with a pair of binoculars. Maintaining a steady eight knots toward the coast, whatever part of North America it turned out to be, I sat hunched on my stool on the bridge, feeling more and more nervous. Weren't there plenty of sections of coast which would offer the same soundings which we had taken? Perhaps just behind the curtain of snow ahead there was a group of rocky islands with granite reefs. Our first knowledge of them would be a sickening crash which would knock us all off our feet.

"Captain," Charlie Mahn said casually into the voice tube. "I see Cape Ann light. She's bearing 293 on the standard compass. That light's got a range of more than twenty-five miles, and it's right on the horizon. I'd say we were twenty miles out at least."

"Charlie, are you sure? Are you sure it's Cape Ann?"

"The day I don't know Cape Ann light, I've forgotten my father's name. Why if I had a dollar for every night I helped my father sail his schooner into Gloucester with the help of that light, I'd be a rich man."

Rushing to the chart, I plotted our position according to Charlie Mahn's bearing and range. It put us about twenty miles north of my estimate, but twenty miles north of Boston was not a bad place to be.

"Captain," Charlie Mahn said in his curiously matter-of-fact way a short time afterward, "I got Minot's Rock and the Boston lightship. You want to stand by for bearings?"

"Shoot."

"These are standard compass bearings. You'll have to monkey with the deviation and variation yourself. Now let me start with Minot light..."

In Greenland I had not been impressed with Charlie Mahn as an officer, much as I liked him, but on his home grounds he appeared to be an entirely different man. All the characteristics of lights near Boston he had long ago memorized, and he seemed almost able to smell his way along the New England coast.

On the way in I was amused that Charlie Mahn gave me bearings he had taken with the standard magnetic compass, despite the fact that a repeater of our gyroscopic compass was on the flying bridge. Charlie had never really trusted gyro compasses, even in the arctic where a magnetic compass spins in confusion over the magnetic pole. Now Charlie was back to civilization, where the magnetic compass made sense, and perhaps he felt that he shared many qualities with it.

Charlie and I made a good team, I thought, as we approached Boston harbor. He remained on the flying bridge calling bearings to me while I plotted them on the chart and gave courses to the helmsman. Never in Greenland had I enjoyed a partnership with an officer I trusted, and I found this new procedure a relief.

The only trouble was that the snow fell heavier as we reached the lightship and visibility was far from good. Only a few miles away from us, the lights of the city of Boston blazed, an inferno of every dazzling color. It had been a long time since I had seen the lights of a large city. They looked beautiful but infinitely confusing as they obliterated the navigational lights, which were already faint in the snow.

"I think we better stay out at sea and go in in the morning," I said to Charlie.

"A lot of the boys are going to be awfully disappointed," he replied. "It's Christmas Eve..."

Already careless about the need for a blackout until we passed through the submarine net, the men had left the forecastle door open. In its yellow rectangle, I could see a man sewing new insignia on his uniform to show that he had been promoted. My name would be mud with these men if I made them stay at sea another twelve hours with the lights of Boston clearly in sight. I also thought of my wife, whose home was only a few miles away. Because of naval censorship I had been unable to tell her when I would return. I had tried not to worry about her, but I knew that the experience of having a stillborn child was likely to add seriously to the tensions under which she had long lived. Suddenly I wanted to be with her so intensely that it was hard to think of anything else.

"Look, captain," Charlie Mahn said, "if you're worried, let me take her in. I've been coming in and out of Boston Harbor all my life."

"All right, Charlie," I replied. "Take her in."

The channel through Boston's outer harbor is crooked and full of so many lights that it is confusing to a stranger, especially one who had grown used to entering the unlit fjords of Greenland. Charlie made his turns with precision and without hesitation. Ahead of us the net tender lay at the opening in the scramble of steel cables which barred submarines from the inner harbor. With a signal light she asked for our identification. Upon receiving it, she said, "Proceed to Growski shipyard."

I had never heard of that shipyard and neither had Charlie Mahn. He said he knew where all the shipyards in Boston Harbor were, however, and guessed that one of them had had its name changed. We proceeded to the inner harbor. The water there was smooth as black marble and reflected the millions of lights which ringed it. After taking a look at the chart, which showed no shipyards, I went to the flying bridge. Ahead of us was a dry dock with a ship on which workers were using welding torches that made an intense blue light.

"There's some kind of yard up ahead," I called to Charlie, who was on the starboard wing of the bridge.

We steamed closer, staring through binoculars. Finally we saw a big sign on a shed. It was not the yard we wanted. Seeing a wharf, I moored and sent a man up to ask for directions to the Growski shipyard. None of the late-working welders knew.

I don't know how long we circled the harbor. I suppose we should have opened up on our radio, but I had been so used to maintaining radio silence that I never even thought of it, and none of the others suggested it. We just kept crisscrossing the harbor, figuring that by trial and error we must find the Growski place some time. On the flying bridge I was filled with a variety of intense emotions. After the rigors of the voyage from Greenland, I was grateful to be circling in this pond-smooth harbor. This was what the *Natsek* was trying to reach when she went down. My fear that the *Nogak* would follow exactly in her wake was not to be justified, not this year at least. The relief of realizing this brought a kind of peace and also a curious let down. With no immediate dangers to confront, the exhaustion resulting from the many nights I had spent on the bridge since leaving Greenland took over. It was hard even to stand erect up there on the flying bridge, and I found myself leaning against a binnacle for support. My eyes burned. It was painful to keep them open, and suddenly I was furious at the authorities who had assumed that the officers of a ship just in from Greenland would know the location of some obscure shipyard.

"Damn them!" I found myself repeating, and I took to jamming my right fist into the palm of my left hand.

Charlie Mahn was conning the ship and he started on a long tour of the waterfront. I went into my cabin to study my chart once more and to see if Growski's shipyard was mentioned anywhere in our orders or the convoy instructions. I was so tired that I studied the chart to try to find a good anchorage, regardless of the emotions the men would suffer if I made them swing to the hook on Christmas Eve within almost an easy swim of their goal. The last thing which was worrying me at that point was the possibility of running aground.

The *Nogak* was going at slow speed when she hit the mud bank. The thing was clearly marked on the chart, and if we had been sailing by the book, taking bearings every fifteen minutes, we wouldn't have hit it. I, however, was thinking of other things, confident that Charlie Mahn knew what he was doing, and Charlie Mahn, for all his many strengths, was at least as exhausted as I was, and trapped by his dependence on local knowledge. He had known Boston Harbor just as well as he said he had, but the war had brought changes in lights and in channels which confused him. He had taken off his glasses to polish them when the ship hit the mud bank.

There was no shock, and most of the men aboard had no idea that we had hit anything. They were changing into their best uniforms now and brushing each other off. Up on the flying bridge, I was the first to know we were in trouble. The lights from our ports shone onto the surface of the water and told me that we were not moving.

Charlie stopped the engine. In the sudden silence we could hear Christmas carols and the honking of automobile horns ashore.

"Captain," Charlie said into the voice tube, "I'm afraid we've run aground. There's a mud bottom here. We shouldn't be in too much trouble."

"Let's get some bearings and find out where we are," I said. "I'll do that. You get the tide table and figure out whether we're lucky or unlucky."

We were unlucky. We had eased into the mudbank only a little after flood tide. Already I had waited too long to get her free. The water was an inch below our normal waterline. Going up to the flying bridge, I called for back slow, back half and back full, but not even the eight-foot propeller of the *Nogak* could break the grip of the suction that held her bottom in the mud. Suddenly the chief machinist's mate called to say that the main intakes for water to cool the engine were plugged with mud. We would have to stop the engine or ruin it.

Dizzy with exhaustion, I could not understand all that had happened to me. The ship was safe, even though she was beginning to heel over on her side like a sailing vessel. A tug could take her off the mud bank in no time, but that would mean official reports which could do me no good. I preferred to clean out the engine's intakes and back the *Nogak* off myself at the next high tide.

I had only one worry during that strange befuddled night. I was afraid that the ship might go so far over on her beam ends that her whole interior would be a jumble of everything from batteries to beer cans, and that the mud might hold her in that position until the tide came back, rushing like a great river at every hatch, port and door. More than one ship had been sunk that way. We should get some timbers to shore up the vessel. . . .

In the after cabin I sat watching the inclinometer, which showed how far over the vessel was heeling. Mr. Mondino watched me from his bunk. There was a slight sardonic smile on his face, but he said nothing.

When the inclinometer had convinced me that the *Nogak* was probably not going to fall completely over, with the top of her mast in the mud, I at last fell into my bunk. I was too tired to take even my shoes off.

In the morning, I was told later, a coast guard commander came into his office in a building which overlooked Boston harbor, saw a small vessel stranded on a mudbank and studied her through his binoculars. It was a coast guard vessel, the ice camouflage told him, probably one fresh in from the Greenland Patrol, but what was a coast guard cutter doing lying on her side in the mud?

The commander made many telephone calls and many pairs of binoculars were trained on the poor *Nogak* in her moment of humiliation.

I was not aware of all this. At dawn I forced myself to get up to check the damage to the vessel, which seemed unhurt, and to make sure that the black gang was working on the intake pumps which cooled the big diesel. After all this was done I went to the galley where Cookie had contrived to cook a bountiful Christmas breakfast despite the fact that his stove was at a forty-five-degree angle. To my relief, the men did not blame me for ruining their Christmas return from Greenland. Instead they kept giving me condolences, as though a member of my family had died.

Shortly after I had finished my late breakfast, I sat on the flying bridge, watching the tide come in. There was some comfort in watching the *Nogak* begin to straighten up. She had not had time to come far, however, when a coast guard picket boat came and stopped near us. Her cockpit was packed with officers, some of whom had scrambled eggs on their caps to show their exalted rank. They studied the *Nogak* through binoculars as though she were a strange prehistoric beast which had been dropped from the moon. An enlisted man took photographs, perhaps because they would come in handy when the board of inquiry met to decide what had caused the United States Coast Guard Cutter *Nogak* to run aground in the middle of Boston harbor on Christmas Eve in 1943.

I had been so tired and so worried about the ship I had not fully understood that the grounding of the *Nogak* was bound to bring me some official reprimand or punishment. Perhaps I would never be promoted to full lieutenant. Perhaps I would be transferred from the *Nogak* and would never again command a ship. Why, after all, should the coast guard give a man command of a ship if all he does is run her aground in Boston harbor?

The picket boat carrying the officers disappeared. It was not long before a small tug came along and expertly passed us a heavy line. With surprisingly little trouble he towed us off, despite the fact that the tide was not yet full. He took us to the Growski shipyard, a small establishment which had recently been started. We were immediately hauled out of the water. To my relief I found that the only damage done by the great grounding incident was to my ego and reputation. The stout hull of the *Nogak* remained unscratched.

In the forecastle Charlie Mahn was trying to adjust the claims of all those who wanted a ten-day leave without giving us a deserted ship. He seemed to be doing pretty well and offered to take the deck himself for the next twenty-four hours to satisfy the requirement that an officer always be aboard. Accepting this offer, I went to the after cabin to make up a schedule for the remaining days with Mr. Mondino. He had gone, and so had all his uniforms. For a commissioned officer to be absent without leave was a serious offense, punishable by a long prison term. Probably he hoped to avoid that kind of trouble by running directly to coast guard headquarters in Boston, and telling the officers there as lurid a story about the indignities he had suffered aboard the *Nogak* as he could contrive.

Well, I've really done things up brown, I thought. I have handled an officer in such a way that he wants to destroy me, and after having survived all those voyages in Greenland, a hurricane and icing up at sea, I have returned to Boston to run aground in the most public place possible—short of a football stadium. Soon I shall be known as the greatest fuck-up in the entire Greenland Patrol.

That's just the way things sometimes work out, I told myself. In any case, I now had at least twenty-four hours before having to get back to the ship to relieve Charlie Mahn. Finally I could call my wife. Climbing down a rather rickety twenty-foot ladder which led from the deck of the ship to the ways, I felt in my pocket for a coin. Failing to find one, I went back up the ladder, took one from a drawer in my cabin, and again descended. There was no pay telephone in the yard, but a workman pointed the way to the main gate. In a small bar just outside it, I had a quick shot of Scotch before dialing the familiar number.

"Hello?" she answered.

"It's me," I said. "Believe it or not, I'm home."

Part **3**
"The War Isn't Over for You and Me"

15

Soon after the *Nogak* was made ready to go back to Greenland, a tall regular coast guard lieutenant appeared aboard with orders to serve as "executive officer and prospective commanding officer." Unlike me, he did not have to go through tortuous months of examination. He was competent, I realized, while voyaging with him only to Portland, Maine. After giving him command of the ship, which had seemed like father and mother to me for so long, I went back to Boston, where I was given orders to attend two navy schools in Florida.

This, as I guess it was intended, was a real vacation. I was allowed to take my wife with me and to rent a small house in St. Augustine. Although she had lost a lot of weight after her ordeal with the stillbirth, Elise was still a touchingly pretty girl. There was a quality of vulnerability in her large brown eyes and delicate bone structure that made me want to protect her, yet she had the narrow waist and sensual body of a knowing woman, not a child. She appeared frightened of many things: driving to Florida, living in a strange neighborhood ... perhaps of me, most of all. Both of us were still very young. I think I expected her to devote herself wholeheartedly to me—my thoughts, my emotions, my memories and my exuberant needs. Perhaps she expected me to devote myself wholeheartedly to her, the emotional ordeal of stillbirth, the strain of living with her parents. We had not really lived with each other enough to compensate for the differences in our personalities. I was by nature a slob, she was New England neat. I talked incessantly; she liked to sit quietly listening to music. My tastes were earthy, hers delicate. Sometimes we found conversation very difficult. Odd to recall, during that brief pause between two tours of overseas duty, the reunited war couple found itself going with surprising frequency to the movies, sometimes seeing two double-features in a row.

Never, however, did I feel any special or profound dissatisfaction with my wife. On the contrary, I was exuberantly proud of her beauty as I introduced her to my friends, and at home I was grateful just to have her there. Even when she was not feeling well, there was no loneliness in the cottage we rented near a school for the deaf. Outside a fence by the playground of the school, she often stood watching the little boys and girls swing and play tag.

"I wonder why those deaf children are so incredibly beautiful," she said to me once. "They really are beautiful. Maybe the rest of us *communicate* too much. Or try to . . ."

Her words hit me hard because I had constantly been trying to explain myself to her, and to get her to explain herself to me. It came as a shock to realize that all the talk in the world didn't really make up for what might be missing between two people. Well, we'd work it out, I told myself. I had no idea, of course, how many other young married couples who'd gotten married but not really *acquainted* before the war separated them, were going through the same experience, telling themselves, for better or worse, pretty much the same thing. . . .

After a few weeks in St. Augustine, I was assigned to the Anti-Submarine Warfare School in Miami. While I was there, I received the formal letter of admonition from Coast Guard Headquarters which was my punishment for running the *Nogak* aground. It angered me because a friend of mine had just received a citation for work he had done in Washington, while my reward for all those months in Greenland was a letter saying, "You are hereby admonished . . ."

Still, my routine promotion to full lieutenant also came through, and a little later I was assigned as commanding officer of a 180-foot supply ship that was to sail from Long Beach, California, to New Guinea. While I was celebrating this event I was surprised to see Mr. Mondino at the other end of the bar. Dressed in neatly pressed khakis, he didn't look anything like the officer who had been carried from the bridge of the *Nogak*. He too was going to the South Pacific, I later learned. Perhaps because of the marks I had put on his record, he was never given command, despite the fact that he was the only officer who had been with me aboard the *Nogak* who did not get a letter of admonition for running aground. Mr. Mondino, after all, had been off duty.

In Long Beach, California, a few weeks later, I took command of the *FS-158*, a supply ship that was owned by the army and manned by the coast guard. A year later I got pneumonia, and when I was released from the hospital in Hollandia, New Guinea, I was flown to the Philippine Islands to command the *Y-14*, a small gasoline tanker. Sailing these ships back and forth across the southwest Pacific was a fascinating and, frankly, often terrifying experience for a very young man. Still, despite the fact that I did see a little enemy action in the southwest Pacific, my whole experience there somehow felt like an anticlimax after Greenland and the *Nogak*. I am also somewhat embarrassed that, although I have spent only four of my fifty-five years in uniform, my memory seems to store more war stories than tales of love and peace. It still confuses me that a man who has always taken strongly felt stands against militarism finds so many of his cherished memories concern storms at sea and battles, although I am aware that I share this conundrum with a few million other men who really never got over the last of the "good" wars.

Nonetheless, I hasten to the end of World War II.

When the Japanese surrendered, the *Y-14*, my little gas tanker, was lying at anchor in Manila harbor. She was a battered old vessel, her jungle-green camouflage streaked with red rust, a ship that obviously had been wounded. During the first part of the invasion of the Philippines, a Japanese suicide plane had hit her bridge, killing her captain and many of her men. A destroyer had managed to put the fire out before it reached her tanks, and the vessel had been beached. Later she had been hastily repaired, and I had replaced the skipper who had been killed. Since then, I had been carrying gas around the Philippines and trying my best to enforce safety regulations aboard a ship whose gasoline often leaked into the pump room and bilge, and where neither I nor many of the men had any experience with tankers. The few experienced hands we had were worse than we novices. They had been aboard when the suicide plane struck and were still suffering from shock to one degree or another.

When Manila got the news that Japan had quit, all the ships in the harbor began shooting guns, Very pistols and emergency rockets. The wind blew a parachute flare right past our masthead vents, where escaping gasoline vapors could be seen by the shadows they left on our decks. Perhaps it was combat fatigue, but the idea of blowing up on the very day of the victory celebration possessed all of us. Wetting down our decks as protection from more flares, we took in our anchor and looked for a quiet spot. There was none in Manila harbor that day, but it did not matter much, for we soon got orders to deliver gasoline to San Fernando, a small port on the island of Luzon.

A thoughtful army colonel explained to me when we got to San Fernando that the occupation of Japan would require many planes and, therefore, much gasoline.

"The war isn't over for you and me," he said. "Not by a long shot. I bet they won't be able to give up any tankers for at least a year."

For several months we were busier than ever. More and more machinery began to break down, but apparently the supply of spare parts had dried up with the end of the war. Our radio hardly worked at all. The generators limped. The main engine exuded thick black smoke, and even the hull began to act in a most peculiar way. When we hit a heavy swell at the entrance to Manila harbor, the deck plates began to bend, as though the whole ship were flexible.

"The trouble is," our engineer said, "she hasn't been hauled since God knows when. With the gas eating on the inside of her plates and the salt water eating on the outside, she hasn't got much metal left."

The men dubbed the ship, "The flexible flyer" and speculated about how long she'd last if she ever got into a typhoon. That was not a question I liked to consider. Fortunately our gas runs kept us close to a coast that had many harbors.

When we returned to San Fernando the pump which discharged our cargo broke down. It had happened many times before, but this time was final. My friend the army colonel was so hungry for gasoline that he used his own pumps to discharge our cargo. Since his pumps backfired frequently and had leaky connections, this was a highly hazardous piece of business. I told my men they could camp on the beach at a safe distance from the ship, but most of them were so hardened to the danger of explosion that they preferred to stay aboard, where they at least had comfortable bunks and a shower bath. Because the galley range made sparks, I ordered the cook to secure it until we were unloaded. We ate K-rations, stared at the gas running in our scuppers from the army pumps and cursed.

When I awoke in the morning the cook gave me a cup of hot coffee. Doing a kind of double-take, I asked who had told him to light our range. He said the engineer had given the order. The stink of gas still pervaded the ship and the monotonous sound of the army pumps continued. I went to the stateroom of the engineer, who was a friend of mine, and asked him if he had told the cook to light the range.

"You're goddamn right," he said from his bunk. "I'm sick of cold chow. If she's going to blow, she's going to blow. Meanwhile I intend to eat good."

I confined him to his cabin with an armed guard at his door and told the cook to close down the range. When the discharge of cargo had been finished, we went to the middle of the small harbor and anchored. There was no work we could do until the cargo pump was repaired and spare parts had to come from the States.

For more than a month we lay at anchor, a useless crew aboard a useless ship. I soon let the engineer out of his cabin, but he still lay listlessly in his bunk, his skin turned yellow by Atabrin, his hair gone gray. Much of the time I had nothing to do but watch the ship rust. To preserve my sanity I wrote a poem of sorts called, "The Soldiers Who Sit." On impulse I mailed it to *The New Yorker*, and was astonished when a few weeks later it was accepted. The check which the editor enclosed was for only fifty-six dollars, but I felt as though I had been given the keys to a kingdom which I had wanted to enter ever since I could remember. I was so elated that I typed day and night aboard that derelict tanker. Although most of my stuff was rejected, I managed to sell enough to make my ambitions appear realistic.

The men aboard the ship assumed that I was a little mad, as most skippers were supposed to be. They talked constantly about the possibility of being ordered to sail home and argued about the chances we had of getting our floating wreck across the Pacific. Sitting near the open door of my cabin, they debated the question of whether the Atabrin, which we were required to take to ward off malaria, would, in addition to turning our skin yellow, make us impotent, as some of the propaganda had said.

We also spent a great deal of time adding up the points which, according to a complex system, gave each man a priority for being discharged from the service. Having had almost continuous sea duty since May of 1942, I had the most points, but an ensign who had been in the coast guard only a few months felt a special ruling should be made for him because he had not yet had a chance to get married.

It was hot in that airless harbor aboard that badly ventilated iron ship. Many of the men developed heat rashes and "jungle rot," the worst heat rash of all, which occurred wherever one part of the body touched another, or where clothes were tight. There was little but canned Spam, dehydrated potatoes and beans to eat, and nothing but warm chlorinated water to drink. The news on the radio was full of stories of returning troops being welcomed by admiring crowds at home.

"By the time we get home, if we ever get there, all the celebrations will be over," a morose seaman said.

Many of the men blamed me for our endless wait at anchor. Finally I got tired of sending messages to inquire about the spare parts we needed. There were no officers' clubs in San Fernando at that time, but there were plenty of bars. Almost every evening I roamed these. Since the distilleries had opened in Manila, an event which occurred almost immediately after the city had been taken by American forces, I had been drinking fairly heavily. At last, in a way, this quest for oblivion paid off in an unusual way. An army officer whom I met in a bar said that several small tankers were going to be given to the Philippine government.

"You ought to get your ship on that list," he said.

The next day I went to Manila, a distance of perhaps three-hundred miles. I had no leave, no permission to quit the ship. It seemed wise to keep my mission a secret to avoid disappointing the men if I failed. They immediately assumed that I was going to Manila to seek my personal transfer, leaving them without a competent deck officer. They were cold and disapproving as they took me ashore in our small boat.

A crowded narrow-gauge railroad train took me to Manila. All day I wandered from office to office in both army and coast guard headquarters to find out whether a list of tankers to be given to the Philippine government was being made up, and if so, whether it was complete. Finally I discovered the name of the army officer in charge of the list, but he was not in his office. Hoping that I could see him the next day, I spent the night in bars and in a cheap hotel. I looked terrible when I showed up the next morning to ask for an appointment. Perhaps that helped—if anyone looked like a grizzled veteran, I did. At any rate, the officer saw me, listened to my description of the Y-14's troubles, and immediately added her name to the list of ships to be given away.

"I'll have a Filipino crew ready to take over in forty-eight hours," the officer said. "They can hardly wait to get their hands on these tankers."

On my way back to San Fernando, the narrow little train was so crowded that I slept in the aisle, awaking occasionally to see heavy boots or naked brown feet trying to step over me. By the time I reached my destination, I was red-eyed, as dirty and rumpled as any bum. Taking a small bottle of whiskey which had been aged overnight from my pocket, I walked down to the beach and caught a ride out to the ship aboard a launch from a vessel commanded by a friend of mine. There was no greeting from the man at the gangway as I stepped aboard. Giving me a stony gaze, he turned away and spat on the hot steel deck. I made my way up to the bridge and told the executive officer, who looked as though he wanted to kill me, to muster all hands on deck.

"You going to read your orders, are you, captain?" he asked bitterly.

"Yes," I said.

He passed the word and the men lined up on the tank deck. Unshaven, wearing only a few filthy rags, they were as piratical as one could imagine. As I stood before them in my rumpled uniform they looked at me as though they wished I were standing in front of a firing squad.

"The other day I learned," I began, "that several small tankers are to be given to the Philippine government. I went to Manila to check on this. It's true and I got this ship put on the list. We are to be relieved by a Filipino crew within forty-eight hours, and we will sail home on a transport."

Pandemonium interrupted me. I, who had been so unpopular, was picked up and paraded on the shoulders of the deck gang all over the vessel. Although alcohol had been forbidden aboard the ship, a great deal was suddenly taken from hiding places, and we had the greatest celebration I had ever seen in my life.

Two days later an army Duck brought out the Filipino officers and crew. We had made the decision to show the new men the weaknesses of the ship, but they seemed delighted with her anyhow. After signing a few papers, my crew and I got into the waiting Duck and headed for shore. While we churned toward the beach, I stared at the high-sided rusty hull of the *Y-14*. Ever since I had reported aboard her to replace her dead captain, I had had a premonition that I would never leave her alive, but there she was, growing smaller as she receded into the past. *I had survived the war!* As though I had been reborn, I could look forward to a whole new life.

16

A large troop ship took us from Manila to Seattle. The vessel was fairly fast, but the two weeks she took to complete the voyage seemed an eternity. The returning officers in my compartment had, like me, been away from home two years or more, and they were as nervous as though they were riding this ship into another battle. There was the same nervous laughter I had heard while men waited at battle stations. At night the men played poker for the same absurdly high stakes that were usual in war zones. To change their luck they played zany variations of poker, such as "baseball," with many wild cards that changed all the odds. At the end of the evening the losers borrowed money from the winners, and the next night the game started all over again.

I noticed that the men did not show photographs of their wives and children to new acquaintances, as they often did in the officers' clubs at Leyte or Manila. The thought that the pictures were about to come to life was almost unbearably exciting, but also frightening in many ways. We had all heard stories of men who had returned home only to find that their wives had fallen in love with somebody else. I think that every man was sure that such a thing could not happen to him, but no one could deny that occasionally such events occurred. And then, though it sounds crazy now, I think that many of us felt that the war had aged us prematurely, and that our wives would think us too old for love. There were many discussions of the possible effects of the Atabrin we took to ward off malaria, and of the amount of time required for the yellowing effect to wear off. A friend of mine repeatedly asked me to assure him that he was not growing bald at the back of his head, and though I had inherited my parents' full head of hair, I found myself peering in the mirror to see if it was growing any thinner. I, and perhaps others, worried about the unsightly patches of jungle rot which lingered like red burns on all the most sensitive areas of the body. The pharmacist's mate in the troop carrier's sick bay ran out of the calamine lotion which the doctors uselessly prescribed for these rashes.

Much of the time I lay in my bunk studying the photographs of my wife which I carried in my wallet. She had sent me new ones from time to time, but I still preferred the creased and dog-eared old ones which I had carried on the Greenland Patrol. These I knew so well that I hardly had to glance at them to see the sweet, still childlike face, the enormous eyes and the slender but womanly figure. The photographs were dearly familiar, and it was a shock to realize that I knew much less about the subject than I did about her pictures. After we had been married, we had had a chance to live together only a little more than a year before I went into the coast guard. There had been all sorts of mysterious tensions which I had put down to the inevitable "period of adjustment," but there never had been time to work out solutions. The few ten-day leaves I had had before sailing for the southwest Pacific had been like short honeymoons, periods in which a man and a woman try their best to live up to a fantasy that is impossible and are afraid to admit their failure. On the last day of our last leave we had gone to see a double-feature. In the theater we had sat eating popcorn and holding hands like teenagers, grateful to the actors on the screen for making conversation unnecessary.

Since then we had written hundreds of letters to each other. Because of censorship I could tell nothing of the work of my ships or of the places we visited, and I myself censored talk of the fear I felt, fear of being killed and fear of disgracing myself by proving that I could not do a captain's job. After these subjects were deleted, there was little I could say but the fact that I thought about her a lot.

Her letters, I suspected, had been just as subject to censorship because the women at home were urged not to write anything that would cause their men to worry. She wrote about teas that her mother gave, the doings of her sister and brothers. It is a terrible thing to ask a woman to write every day. I knew everything about the gossip in West Newton, the books Elise read, the difficulty in getting butter and gasoline. It was not her fault, but from her letters I could not guess what kind of a woman my wife had become.

Finally the troopship approached Seattle. When I went on deck to see the hills lying low on the horizon, I experienced that intensification of senses, especially the sense of smell, which is given to people who have been far from land a long time. Although it was winter, the fragrance of pine forests was strong. There was the warm, humid smell of the earth itself, mixed with all sorts of exotic aromas I could not even guess, but which combined to make the smell of the city, not a smoky stink, but in imagination at least, the essence of all the fine food being cooked, the rich coffee, the liquor, the perfume being worn by richly gowned women, all the things which the men on the troopship had not seen for years. I don't know how it affected the others, but I got a most embarrassing reaction. Inhaling the fragrance of the city, I got a mighty erection which was impossible to put down. Apparently I wanted to make love not only to my wife, but to the whole city of Seattle, the state of Washington, and the whole North American continent. After two years in the southwest Pacific, I felt just about ready.

As a final torture before releasing us, the coast guard insisted that we spend ten days in Seattle for the processing of our separation papers. After filling in countless forms, I wandered the streets, amazed at the beauty of the women and the luxury of the shops. The last city I had seen was Manila, which had yet to begin to recover from the ravages of war. The sunny opulence of Seattle was a wonder, but there was also a bitter feeling of loneliness as I walked through the city alone. Seattle was a city in which I knew no one and no one knew me. For months there had been hordes of returning servicemen, and the pretty girls in the streets tended to look at us as though we did not exist. Enough servicemen had cashed bad checks to make it impossible to get any money even with full identification and even if it were a government check. Toward the last of my days in Seattle, I stayed at the officers' club and joined the conversations of other men just back from the southwest Pacific. We talked about battles we had fought and storms we had survived. Oddly enough, not one of us mentioned his thoughts about returning home.

I had hoped for a plane to Boston, but instead I was put on a troop train much like the one which had taken me from Boston to California, where I had started my voyage to the southwest Pacific. The men going home sat awkwardly in their seats, and looked as preoccupied as the soldiers on their way out had appeared. Some of them sang the few songs that had become part of World War II, "Bless 'Em All" and "You Are My Sunshine." Their voices sounded mournful, I thought as I lay in a lower bunk and stared out the window as the painted desert and the ocean-like plains rolled by. To me, an easterner, the desert and the plains looked more foreign than the icy mountains of Greenland. I don't know my own country, I thought. I don't know my own wife, really, and I don't know my own country at all.

Those words came to my mind and seemed to echo there very much against my will. Still, Elise had sounded strange when I had called her from Seattle to tell her when I would arrive home. Her voice, naturally enough, had a strong upper-class Boston accent. I had ceased to hear it shortly after I had met her, but after so long an absence, and after so long a time in places where no one I knew had such an accent, my ear found my wife's diction peculiar, somehow incongruous with the pretty girl in my wallet.

Our conversation had been as awkward as was almost inevitable for such a momentous telephone call.

"Hello?" she said when the telephone rang.

"It's me," I replied. "I'm in Seattle."

"Seattle? What are you doing in Seattle?"

"That's where the troopship took me. I'll be home in a few days."

"Oh, *darling!* That's wonderful, isn't it?"

"It sure is. I can hardly wait to see you."

"I can hardly wait to see you, too."

"I've been thinking of you all the time."

"So have I. I mean I've been thinking of *you* all the time."

"Are you all right?"

"Sure. Are you?" . . .

So the conversation had continued. The next time the leaders of the world's nations consider a declaration of war, they should contemplate well the fact that war forces such inane conversations upon millions of innocent people. World leaders have shown themselves conspicuously careless about human lives, but they might respond to the horror of the words which wars wring from lovers.

Aboard the troop train I tried to forget the telephone conversation with my wife. In this I was helped by a red-faced railroad conductor who told a sergeant that he could not smoke in our car. The sergeant, who had just been discharged from the army, was in no mood to accept a new discipline. He growled something picturesque to the conductor, who said he would get some trainmen and have the sergeant arrested. The conductor, who had ridden many troop trains, had a few choice comments to make about returning soldiers "who think they're God almighty." Everyone in the car heard this. When the conductor started to go toward the engine, the soldiers and sailors simply held hands across the aisle. Infuriated, the conductor tried to charge this barrier, but he could not get past the arms of a navy boatswain's mate and a marine master sergeant. Howling with rage, he was stuck, and the men would not let him go until he apologized for badmouthing servicemen. When he finally choked, "sorry," there were cheers all around, and he was released.

When we got to Boston it was colder than I had remembered it, and the light raincoat which I had brought back from Manila did little to protect me. When I called my wife from the railroad station, the Pickhardts' maid answered the telephone. She was a kind old woman who had been Elise's nursemaid, and she inquired about my health for what seemed an endless time before she asked Elise to come to the telephone.

"South station," I said, so tense that my throat was closing.

"I'll be there in a minute. I've reserved a room in a hotel. The whole family is here, and I thought we should be alone for a few hours."

"Thank you. Hurry."

I figured that it would take her half an hour to drive from her family's house. I wanted a drink desperately but didn't want booze on my breath when I kissed her. My mind kept going crazy. What would happen if I had an erection the moment she came through the door? That is not the way a man should greet his wife after an absence of two years, especially when the wife speaks with the accent of a proper Bostonian. I had the drink—vodka, which I had never really liked.

It seemed to take her an interminable amount of time to drive from West Newton. Then I saw her trotting through the polished brass door of the station—a lovely young woman with a pale face that looked as tense as I felt. I hugged her. Even a hug felt strange, for I had not hugged anybody in two years and was suddenly unsure about how tightly I should squeeze. Too tight a squeeze might injure a delicate young woman, after all, and too light a one might seem to lack enthusiasm. I kissed her. After a moment she turned away and said, "Let's go up to the hotel."

The Ritz had been full, she said, and so she had reserved a room in a closer, smaller hotel. We reached the car, the same old green Ford which we had had before the war. It looked so familiar, so completely unchanged that I was tempted to kiss it, but when I got behind the wheel I found that my years aboard ships had caused me almost to forget how to drive a car. We pulled away from the curb jerkily and with a grinding of gears.

The hotel she had chosen was a luxurious one, full of ornate furniture, red cushions trimmed with ivory and gold. It was the kind of place in which virtually no one, except, perhaps, a well-heeled traveling salesman, could possibly feel at home. An old man whose seamed face appeared to reflect a lifetime of trouble took her small suitcase and my big one. Mine contained, among other things, a few of my favorite books, a file of short stories I had written and my portable typewriter. It was heavy, and the old bellman put it down after taking only a few steps and rubbed his shoulder. I tried to carry it for him, but he shook his head firmly, and with agonizing slowness struggled toward the elevator. On the way up to our floor he breathed so heavily that I feared for his life. His lips looked blue. Suddenly I was filled with the vision of his dropping dead the moment he opened the door of our room. Instead of embracing my wife, there would be efforts to resuscitate this old man; instead of love, there would be sudden death, just as there had been when my father died long ago when Elise paid her first visit to Rogers Rock, our place in the Adirondacks.

This premonition was so strong that I almost grabbed the suitcases from the man as he set them down to rest for a few moments in a long hall. Perhaps because he was no longer in view of the people at the front desk, he did not object. Directing us to a room at the end of the hall, he fumbled with a key for what seemed like a long time. Finally the door opened. In my wallet I had nothing smaller than a five-dollar bill. I handed one of these to the bellman, who gave me a jerky little military salute.

"I was in the first one," he said.

"What?"

"The first world war. You didn't have gas, did you? Chlorine. And trenches. You didn't have trenches, did you?"

"No," I said, pushed our suitcases into the room and locked the door. My wife was taking her hat off.

"Would you like some champagne?" I asked.

"That would be nice."

In response to my call to room service, the same tired old man brought an ice bucket of champagne. I had never liked champagne much and Elise never drank except on ceremonial occasions, but we both sipped it thirstily, as though it were some magic medicine. Finally we made love and were shocked, as were millions of others in our situation, by the discovery that even years of longing cannot be followed by more than a pitifully short reunion of the flesh.

"I'm hungry," I said. "How about some dinner?"

"I'll have just a bite," she replied.

The old bellman, who seemed to have adopted us, brought up a many-paged menu. Elise ordered tea and a chicken sandwich, but I was suddenly consumed by hunger for all the fancy foods I had done without aboard ship. This, the night of my homecoming, was a time when I felt free to indulge myself. I ordered a dozen oysters on the half shell, a large broiled lobster, cherry pie *à la mode* and a pot of black coffee. I also asked the old bellman to bring me a double martini while we were waiting for the meal and a bottle of chablis to go with it. While I was at it, I ordered a double brandy to cap off the dinner.

The bellman had been so inspired by the five-dollar tip I had given him that the martini arrived almost immediately. While I sipped it, Elise said, "We have so many plans to make!"

"I have a surprise for you," I said.

Shortly before leaving the Philippines, I had received a letter from a small, unknown publisher who had read two brief pieces I had sold to *The New Yorker* and wanted to know if I would like to try a novel. I showed it to Elise.

"That's wonderful!" she said. "Do you think you can write a novel?"

"I'd like to try."

"Don't you think you should finish up at Harvard first? It seems a shame to give up a diploma when you have only one semester to go."

I had not even thought of going back to Harvard, which I had quit after the midyear examinations of my senior year to join the coast guard.

"I have picked out a great house we could get," Elise said, "and Sinny wants to talk to you about a job. Of course, he thinks you should graduate from college first."

"Sinny" was Sinclair Weeks, of Hornblower and Weeks, the investment firm, and a bastion of the Republican party who would in due time become a marvelously undistinguished secretary of the interior. He was a cousin of Elise's mother and served as a sort of tribal chief, dispensing jobs to the husbands of third cousins, and lending large sums of money to closer relatives when absolutely necessary. He was a stocky bald man who had served in the first world war and had often led American Legion parades even on the hottest days. He was pleasant enough, but I could not see myself approaching him for help in forwarding my long-smoldering ambition to be the new Fitzgerald or Hemingway.

Before I could explain this the waiter arrived with the sumptuous dinner I had ordered. As I squeezed a wedge of lemon on the oysters, I reflected that it had been years since I had seen a fresh lemon. This reminded me of a small disaster which had affected a friend of mine, who had commanded an ocean-going tugboat in the Philippines. In Leyte, where water was scarce for several months after our invasion, he took on thirty thousand gallons in preparation for a long voyage. The shore authorities warned him that the water was impure and should be heavily chlorinated. Having no chlorine, he sent his supply officer, a young ensign, ashore to look for some. A sergeant who presided over a quonset hut where many supplies were kept showed the ensign a cardboard barrel which apparently had suffered rain damage, or had been briefly submerged in salt water during its trip from the States. The contents were perfectly dry, the sergeant said, and triumphantly the ensign loaded the barrel into the back of his jeep. It was dark when he got back to the ship and the blackout required him to feed the powder from the barrel into the tanks without a light. Since his skipper had told him to treat the water heavily, he spooned almost the entire barrel into the funnels which led to the big tanks at the bottom of the tug.

A seaman in the forecastle was the first to raise an alarm. Shortly after the ensign had poured the powder into the tanks, this man, who had been helping the cook wash dishes, ran a glass of water from the tap over the galley sink, tasted it, and tasted it again in surprise.

"How come we get lemonade out of the faucet?" he asked.

Other people tasted the water, and word of the strange discovery spread throughout the ship. Dragging his barrel inside, the ensign examined it in a bright light for the first time. The remaining powder was a light yellow, and if one studied the damp, wrinkled labels on the outside, one could see that the barrel contained powder for making lemonade.

At first the men aboard the tug considered the matter a joke, but then the tug got emergency orders to try to rescue a ship whose engine had failed far out at sea. Her skipper got underway, and for almost a month the crew of that tug drank lemonade, made coffee with lemonade, and even took showers in lemonade. After more than thirty days of this, the lemonade was no longer considered a joke. In fact, it was dangerous even to say the word "lemonade" to a member of the crew of that vessel.

Elise did not laugh as much as I had expected. Like a failing comedian, I plunged on with more laugh-a-minute accounts of World War II....

When I was aboard the small supply vessel which I sailed from Long Beach, California, to New Guinea, I had an executive officer who seemed unusually stupid. By this time I had understood the fact that small vessels rarely had competent executive officers because the nation was building ships so fast that officers were given command almost as soon as they could distinguish between the bow and the stern. It was up to me to train my executive officer. Since navigation was the most important skill for an officer to have, I told him that he was navigator of the ship, and that I wanted to see his calculations every day.

To my surprise the man learned to take star sights fairly well, but he kept forgetting to take the noon latitude sight that I valued highly because it did not depend on the accuracy of our rather erratic chronometer. Every day I would caution the fellow against missing the noon latitude sight, and almost every day he would fail to take it. Sometimes he would complain that after checking and rechecking his morning star sights, he would fall wearily to sleep and fail to wake up in time for the noon sight. At other times he would say that some small emergency in the forecastle had demanded his presence at the crucial moment when the sun was highest in the sky. Finally he complained that his eyes were so sensitive that the task of shooting the sun was painful. I explained the colored disks of glass on the sextant that make it unnecessary to stare into glare and said that I was completely fed up with his excuses. If he didn't give me a noon latitude sight the next day, I would relieve him of his job as navigator simply because he apparently was unable to perform it.

Early the next morning the commodore of the convoy in which we were steaming raised a flag signal which said, "Enemy planes are in the vicinity." At about ten in the morning a Jap bomber which came in at a very high altitude dropped a bomb which literally missed the convoy by a mile. Laughing about that, the men sat at their guns eating sandwiches and drinking coffee. In the hot sun we had such a long wait that some of the men wished that the Japs would hurry up and get the attack over with. Suddenly a torpedo plane came over the horizon toward us with its belly almost slapping the water. At the lead edge of his wings there was the flicker of machine-gun fire. Standing on the flying bridge, I gave the order to fire and through cowardice or intelligence threw myself flat on the deck. When I got up, I saw that the railing and binnacle had been shot away a few inches over my prone body. The men shouted and I saw that the plane had dropped its torpedo shortly before passing over our deck. The torpedo dived, went right under our shallow-drafted hull, and exploded on the stern of a Liberty ship. At about the same time the plane crashed into the sea. Without propeller or rudder, the Liberty dropped astern, where another Jap torpedo plane torpedoed the bow. Smoke boiled from her foredeck.

The Liberty ship was full of troops; they could clearly be seen donning life preservers on her decks. Sandhurst, the captain of a sister ship of ours, dropped out of the convoy and prepared to go alongside on a rescue mission. This was a hazardous undertaking at best. Sandy's ship, like mine, was loaded with ammunition. A big enough sea was rolling to jam the two ships together like two tin pans being banged. To take a ship loaded with ammunition alongside a burning vessel in a running sea was a genuine act of either foolishness or heroism. I knew, because I considered the idea thoroughly for about a fifth of a second before rejecting it.

But Sandy was born to be a hero. He even looked like a hero—a tall, elegant officer with the accent of an educated Virginian. He brought his vessel alongside the burning Liberty ship, hung there while the ships crashed into each other, and when the last man had jumped onto his deck, which he had thoughtfully covered with mattresses, he sheered off. As though waiting for him, the Japanese then finished off the Liberty ship with another torpedo. Sandy steamed back to his place in the convoy. The other ships were too busy by that time even to signal, "well done." The first suicide plane I had ever seen flew directly into the gun tub on the bow of a big freighter, disappearing for a moment like a pool ball shot at high speed into a pocket. A great balloon of pale yellow fire burst into sight and hung in the air, looking oddly like the balloons from the mouths of comicbook figures, as though the dying ship were being given a chance to talk.

More suicide planes approached. The guns on every ship in the convoy boomed and chattered. A ship near us exploded and at this moment my executive officer appeared on the flying bridge, a sextant in one hand and his navigation notebook in the other.

"What the hell are you doing?" I asked.

"You told me not to miss my noon latitude sight," he replied with simple dignity.

Thud. I had meant the story to be funny, but somehow it didn't turn out that way. There was a painful moment of silence. I wondered suddenly why almost all the war stories that soldiers and sailors tell at home or even to each other are presented as jokes. Or juicy romances. I had read so many stories about soldiers or sailors having these great love affairs in foreign ports, but all I had seen were Eskimo women who washed their hair in urine, and the women of New Guinea, who dyed their hair orange with peroxide. In Manila, I had seen only war-weary peasant women and dockside whores who offered a few minutes of dalliance under a truck or railroad car. Precious little humor and no romance would be in the war novel the publisher in New York had asked me to write. For the first time I began wondering how such a book could possibly sell.

"What are you thinking about?" Elise asked.

"Nothing, except the war wasn't really funny at all."

"But now you can forget it," she said.

I didn't reply but I was struck for the first time by the knowledge that I would never forget the war. It had been more than two years since I had left the *Nogak*, but I still remembered the name of every man in her crew. The story of my being first refused and then given command of that old trawler continued to plague me as though it were full of questions only half understood. The day the Japanese attacked our convoy in the Pacific still obsessed me, not as a joke about the executive officer with his sextant, but as a question: why hadn't I, instead of Sandy, gone alongside that burning ship to rescue men?

"Eat your dinner," she said. "It must be getting cold."

The lobster was good, and though it was the largest one I had ever seen, I ate it all with gusto. The crisp fresh lettuce in the salad seemed a newly invented delight and the cherry pie with slightly melted vanilla ice cream seemed the best ever made. The double brandy, served in a proper snifter, instead of the shot glass used at officers' clubs, seemed the essence of luxury.

"Do you mind if we make more plans?" Elise asked. "Maybe it's too early, but I'm dying to get started, and we have to be practical."

"Of course."

"Do you mind if we talk about money?"

"Of course not."

Nervously she lit a cigarette and told me that she had hoped to save money from the allotments I had sent her, but there had been doctor's bills. She hadn't written me about it because she had not wanted to worry me.

At this moment I realized that this meeting was perhaps more tense for her than it was for me. I told her that I had not expected her to save money, that there was no reason to worry about it.

No, she said, she wanted me to know the details. After the birth of her stillborn baby and after I had gone to the South Pacific, she had realized that something was the matter with her. She was afraid to leave her parents' home, afraid she would be sick to her stomach in public places. She had wanted to make herself a fit wife, she kept saying, and so she went to a psychiatrist.

I did not have much sense in those days, and I only half realized the amount of courage it must have taken for a woman only about twenty-one years old to seek a psychiatrist in a place and era where all the people she knew, including her own family, thought that only crazy people should seek psychiatric care. Unwillingly the thought of a psychiatrist brought memories of my mother's dark depressions during my childhood. The doctors who attended her called themselves "neurologists" to escape the dread of a more accurate term.

"I think you did just the right thing," I said, wondering why my sentences were beginning to sound false to my own ears.

Now, she continued, she was feeling much better. She was anxious to have a baby—maybe that would reduce the depression which had lingered after the stillbirth.

"Do you mind if I tell you about that?" she asked.

"Of course not."

"The doctor knew when I was only about seven months along that the baby was dead. He could hear no heartbeat, but he didn't tell me. He thought it best not to tell me, since he thought I should carry the baby full term. My stomach was strangely hard. I should have known that something was wrong. When the nine months were up, they took me to the hospital and put me on the obstetrical floor. I don't remember anything about the birth. When I woke up they told me that the cord had wound around the baby's neck and choked it. I didn't really believe that, and finally the doctor told me that the baby had been malformed and had been dead for a long time. No one, he said, knows the reason why that happens every once in a while. I had to stay in the hospital almost a week, and the hardest part was seeing the babies brought to all the other mothers. They shouldn't keep cases like mine on the obstetrical floor."

I tried to comfort her as best I could.

"So you can see that I want to have a baby," she continued. "We'll need a house, and I know of an awfully good buy in West Newton. I think we can get it for about eight thousand dollars. We could buy it with the twelve-thousand-dollar trust fund your mother gave you. With the four thousand left over, we can live at least a year. If you go back to college, the G.I. Bill will give you ninety dollars a month. At the end of a year we'll see how your writing is going, and if you can't make a living with it, you can go see Sinny."

"We'll have to think about all this a lot," I replied, and ordered another double brandy.

"Oh!" Elise said suddenly. "You have to call your mother. I promised her that I'd have you call as soon as you got in."

She had the number of my mother's apartment on 11th Street.

"Hello!" my mother said, sounding her usual, forceful self. "Welcome home! Home is the sailor, home from the sea, and the hunter home from the hill."

"I'm home, all right."

"I'm so proud of your commanding all those ships and of your wonderful work in *The New Yorker*. All my friends have seen those poems and the article. They all think they're wonderful."

"I'm glad."

"When do you have more stuff coming out in *The New Yorker*?"

"I don't know, mother."

"Well, keep at it. They don't have anybody who can write like you. I'm just *tired* of that James Thurber and S. J. Perelman. I don't know why they waste so much space on them."

"They're funny that way," I said, and, after promising to come to New York soon, bid my mother farewell.

My brandy was gone and I ordered another. There was more love making and more drinking and more attempts to make plans for our future. I was tired from the long train trip across the continent. The brandy was strong and suddenly my head began to spin. This was followed by acute nausea, which sent me running for the bathroom.

It was a terrible thing to do to a long-awaited homecoming, but my whole system went into some kind of a revolt. For more than an hour I knelt before the toilet as though I were worshiping it. I felt oddly as though I were back aboard the *Nogak*, on my first voyage from Newfoundland to Greenland. The bathroom seemed to be rolling in a heavy sea, and I grabbed a towel rack to steady myself when I stood up.

As the illness continued hour after hour, it seemed apparent that something more than the brandy was at work. Alarmed, Elise called the house doctor. A tall, bald-headed man who somehow looked more like a waiter than a physician, he examined me thoroughly.

"Could it be food poisoning?" Elise asked.

"Most unlikely at this hotel," he replied loftily, and gave me a sedative.

Before the sedative worked, Elise and I joked about our romantic reunion. I do not remember what we said, but our shared humor had the effect of bringing us together more than serious talk could. By the time I finally slept, her presence in the bed beside me did not feel so strange.

When I went to pay the bill the next morning, the hotel clerk smiled and said there would be no charge. Somewhere I had heard that where there is a chance of food poisoning, some hotels do not like to present a bill, for it is harder for a customer to sue successfully if he has not paid. I had no idea of the truth of that, but it was pleasant to find that we had had a night on the house. For a couple of hours I had felt pretty low, but the sedative had given me a sound sleep. Outside the towers of Boston were gleaming in the chilled sunshine of a January morning. Church bells were ringing. In a florist's shop, I bought my wife a red rose. As I pinned it to the lapel of her coat—the way I had often done during the days I had courted her—I felt that I had finally come home again.

17

During the war, I had often dreamed of taking a long vacation when I got home, but there were so many things to do when I got back to Boston that the thought of leisure was impossible. Within a few days I enrolled at Harvard and rented a one-room apartment near Harvard Square. Elise had longed to buy a house, but after long discussions, she regretfully agreed that we should not tie ourselves down so soon. In the basement of the apartment building, there was an empty coal bin which had not been used since the furnace had been converted to oil. I saw this when I took our suitcases to the basement for storage. After a somewhat surprised superintendent had given me his permission, I swept out this coal bin, scrubbed it and whitewashed it. With the addition of a sturdy table and chair, it made an excellent study. A long extension cord brought light. The furnace gave warmth, and there was never any sound but its hum. People often thought it was funny when I said I worked in a coal bin, but in some ways my first study turned out to be the best I would ever have.

Aboard my little tanker I had thought myself so close to total exhaustion, combat fatigue, or whatever one might call it, that I had occasionally thought of asking for a medical discharge. Now I found that hidden wells of energy kept me working day and night. It is still hard for me to believe the amount of work I did during the first five months of my return to civilian life. Although I had never been more than a middling scholar, I finished the four courses required for my degree with top marks. I wrote four short pieces for *The New Yorker* and a full-length novel, *Voyage to Somewhere*, which the publisher in New York accepted. I also tried out as a reader for Houghton Mifflin, the Boston publisher.

This strange venture began when Carl Pickhardt Jr., my wife's older brother, said he knew Paul Brooks, the editor of Houghton Mifflin, well. After all the work I had done, I felt written out, and was beginning to face the realities of trying to make a living as a full-time writer. If I couldn't think of more material for magazines or books, I soon would have to find some kind of job. The urgency of this was intensified when my wife happily announced that she was pregnant. The idea of going to "Sinny" for a job, presumably in some field entirely unrelated to writing, did not appeal to me. Working for a publishing house, however, might increase my knowledge of books, as well as provide a steady living.

A lean, tall young man who looked much like half the instructors at Harvard, Paul Brooks received me affably and gave me one of those brick-colored cardboard carrying cases the size of a briefcase—the ones that publishers so often used. In my coal-bin study at home I opened it and found a dog-eared, sloppily typed manuscript entitled, *The Captain's Palms*. It was, I found, the story of some men aboard a supply ship in the southwest Pacific. The captain of this vessel was an utter fool on whom the men played practical jokes. The other officers occupied themselves by leering at nurses and doing almost everything else but the job of running a ship. Since almost everyone in the book was a fool of one sort or another, it was difficult to understand who navigated this ship on her long voyages and who had the skill to bring her alongside a wharf when there was a stiff current backed by a strong wind. The boredom of the men aboard a supply vessel was well-expressed, but there was hardly a hint of the fear that so often is the prevailing emotion aboard a ship, even when she is rarely or never under fire. There is always the possibility, after all, of encountering a Japanese submarine or a far-ranging destroyer which could gun a supply ship down as easily as an outlaw can kill a fat lady. Every supply ship has a good chance of being ordered to join convoys which bring supplies to bases where fighting is still in progress and where Japanese planes do their best to sink any vessel bringing help to their enemies. The cargo on such voyages is often ammunition, and I defy any man to ride ammunition into battle without learning a little about the meaning of fear.

The men in *The Captain's Palms*, however, were mostly concerned with their practical jokes, their loathing of their captain and their rather delicate feelings for each other. Innocent of worry about the Japanese or their own questionable ability to run a ship well enough to avoid sinking her by accident, they just seemed to go from one gag to another, making the war one gigantic comedy.

The book offended me. I wrote a scathing reader's report and confidently sent it off to Paul Brooks. The next time I went to the offices of Houghton Mifflin to get more manuscripts, Paul looked at me oddly.

"I'm sorry that you didn't like *The Captain's Palms,*" he said.

"Fundamentally I think that it's a dishonest book," I replied. "The war was not like that."

"Maybe not, but there's a lot of advance interest in the manuscript. *The Atlantic* is going to serialize some of it. By the way, we're going to change the title to *Mr. Roberts.* What do you think of that?"

"Well, it's innocuous," I said. "Frankly, I shall be very surprised if the book goes anywhere."

The other manuscripts which I read for Houghton Mifflin proved to be almost as big a disaster for me. Almost invariably I hated the books which the editors of the big publishing house planned to publish and loved the manuscripts which they were in the process of rejecting. Still, it would be quite possible for me to write reader's reports which would agree with Paul Brooks, I realized. All I would have to do would be to praise all the manuscripts I loathed and knock hell out of those I loved. This did not seem a good way to start a career in publishing. When I told Paul that I had concluded that publishing was not the best career for me, he looked immensely relieved.

Often in the years that followed I joked about the fact that I had advised a publisher to turn down *Mr. Roberts,* but it was not overpoweringly funny at the time. Not only did it discourage me from entering a business which might be congenial, but it proved that my judgment at the time was obviously wrong. There was a temptation to tell myself that my artistic sensibilities were more acute than those of the editors of Houghton Mifflin, but they were professionals when it came to judging manuscripts, while I was only an amateur. If I had to buck the professionals all my life, the so-called literary world was likely to prove a hard place to make a living.

While I was pondering this, I remembered that my father, who had helped to start the School of Journalism at N.Y.U., had said that anyone who wants to write should work two years for a good newspaper. Not less than two years, he had cautioned, for one cannot pick up the skills of a reporter quickly, but not more than two years, for those who tarry in newspaper offices too long rarely get beyond simple journalism.

"I want to work for a newspaper," I said to my wife one night at dinner.

"I'm sure that Sinny will know somebody on the *Transcript* or *Globe.*"

"No. I want to try the *New York Times* or the *Trib*. I might as well start at the top." I smiled uneasily.

She frowned, and I remembered how much she hated the thought of moving to New York, a city which had frightened her when, as a young girl, she had visited it. In addition she had the traditional Bostonian's loathing of Manhattan and disliked the thought of giving up our frequent visits to her family in West Newton. She was now almost five months pregnant, and it did not seem a good time to force her into a move which she did not want to make.

"Providence," I said. "How would you feel about moving to Providence? It's only about an hour's drive."

"Why Providence?" she asked.

It was strange how many of the things my father had told me long ago came to mind when I needed them.

"The Providence *Journal* is one of the best newspapers in the country," I said. "And papers outside of New York are sometimes better than the *Times* or the *Trib* for beginners. In New York I might have to start out as a copy boy or a legman who just telephones facts to a reporter. In Providence I might start right out at a typewriter."

"Providence doesn't sound so bad," she said thoughtfully. "We could still come home weekends. Do you think it will be hard to get a job with the paper there?"

"I don't know. I have a cousin in Providence. Her husband is a real Rhode Islander. I bet he'd know somebody on the *Journal* I could see."

In principle I disapproved of the practice of using family connections to get jobs, but in practice I employed it as much as possible. That very evening I called my cousin, Carol Simonds, at her home in Providence, and after a few minutes of trading family news, asked to speak to her husband, Godfrey.

Although I had not seen him since the war, Godfrey Simonds had long been one of my favorite relatives. Tall, slim and elegant, he had had a bad heart since his twenties, much as my father had had, and like my father he had seemed unusually aware of the need to appreciate every minute. While still in his thirties he had made a great deal of money in the investment banking business and had used it to create a way of living for his family which had zest and style. He loved the theater, and when he went to New York or Boston to see plays with his family, they stayed at the best hotels, ate at gourmet restaurants which were soon to be fashionable and sat in the best seats. What impressed me most when, as a child, I had been included on these expeditions, was that Godfrey often knew someone in the cast, and after the last curtain, we were invited backstage to meet the wondrous people whom we had seen in the play.

Now, so many years later, I was not surprised when Godfrey told me that he knew Sevelyn Brown, the editor-publisher of the Providence *Journal*, Jeff Brown, the editor, and Watkins (whose first name I forget), who had the title of publisher.

"Why do you want to work for the *Journal*?" Godfrey asked. "The pay will be terrible."

"I figure that it will be a good training ground, and maybe I can work my way up."

"I wouldn't count on it," Godfrey replied. "The *Journal* is a good paper, but it seems to stay that way by breaking all the rules. I've never seen nepotism raised to such a fine art. Old Man Brown still runs the show. One of his sons is editor and another is in charge of the book page. His son-in-law is publisher, whatever that title means, while Sevelyn is still around."

"At the bottom of the ladder I don't think all that will affect me. I just want their training."

A few days later Godfrey set up a luncheon at the Turk's Head Club in Providence for the brass of the *Journal*, and me. Never did anyone start at the lowly job of cub reporter with more fanfare than I had. Proudly I showed the editor of the *Journal* my scrapbook of pieces I had had published in *The New Yorker* and *Harper's* magazine. I was just about to graduate from Harvard, I reported, and gave a brief summary of my service in the coast guard. The editor and publisher of the *Journal* seemed impressed, and told me to see the state editor of the paper the next day. What this meant, I had no idea. When I presented myself in the impressive Journal Building the next morning, I was directed to a bald man who sat in a plainly furnished cubicle. There were two telephones on his desk which he kept answering, barking short sentences into the receiver before slamming it down.

"You Wilson?" he asked. "You want to work here?"

"I think so."

"Forty dollars a week. Forty-eight if you have a car."

"I had hoped for a little more than that."

His telephone rang. "No," he shouted into the receiver. "Absolutely not."

Turning to me, he added, "Take it or leave it. With all the men getting out of the service, we have more help than we need anyway."

With a new baby coming, I didn't see how we were going to live on forty dollars a week, or even forty-eight with a car, but the training would be good and perhaps I could sell enough magazine pieces to tide me over. I accepted the offer.

"Okay," he said, took a handful of forms from his top drawer and handed them to me. "Fill these out. When do you want to start?"

❖ ❖ ❖

The next day Elise and I toured the area looking for a place to live. One of the men who had lunched with Godfrey Simonds and me at the Turk's Head Club had recommended Barrington. That suburb of Providence was beautiful because of a river which divided it from the more industrial town of Warren. Fleets of small yachts were moored in the river, down the channel of which heavily laden oyster boats came to unload at piers built on tall piles which looked as though they were falling down. There was one street in Barrington where the front lawns of the houses ran to the edge of the river. I set my heart on one of these comfortable old homes, but they of course proved too expensive for a man making the princely sum of forty-eight dollars a week, with car. All rents were too expensive, we found, but with a veteran's mortgage, it might be possible to buy. The real estate agent shrugged when I told her that I wanted something costing in the neighborhood of seven thousand dollars on which I could get a G.I. loan. Consulting her notebook, she suddenly brightened.

"I have something you might like," she said. "It's on the water too."

She took us across a bridge near the head of the river and turned onto a macadam road which got narrower and narrower until it turned to dirt. After jolting along for five minutes, we came to a row of dilapidated summer cottages, some of which were covered with weathered shingles, and others were painted in brighter colors than the rainbow ever offered. It was still too early in the spring for these to be occupied. A screen door on one cottage hung open like the mouth of an idiot and there was a splash of glass on one front lawn where someone had been smashing bottles.

"We need a year-round place," Elise said.

"I have one here that's winterized," the agent replied. She led the way to a freshly painted cottage which wasn't bad as inexpensive summer places go. There was a view of the river which, now at low tide, offered little more than mud banks and marsh grass. There was new linoleum on the floors, two bedrooms and a big sleeping porch which, the agent said, could easily be enclosed. The general effect was country tacky, but we wouldn't have to live in it long, I told my wife. Within a couple of years I would either succeed at the *Journal* or move on.

During the following days, we combed the countryside for better buys, but eventually settled on the cottage by the river. Elise's face was grim as a moving truck crew unloaded our furniture and some she had borrowed from her family.

"This place looks bad when it's empty and twice as bad when it's furnished," she said. "There isn't room for *anything!*"

156

The day after we moved into our newly acquired cottage, I finished up at Harvard and without waiting for the graduation ceremonies, went to work for the Providence *Journal*. Immediately I got two shocks. The first was that instead of being assigned to an office near Barrington, where I had been advised to live, I was told to report to an office in Westerly, a town at the other side of the state. Rhode Island is small but crowded. It would be difficult and expensive to commute from one side of it to the other.

The second shock was that I was expected to work a split shift. At nine in the morning I was to report for work on the Providence *Evening Bulletin*, which the company also published. At about one in the afternoon I could go home, but I had to report for work again at seven in the evening, to work until midnight on the next morning's *Journal*.

"That's crazy," my wife said.

"You know, I got this horrible job by using pull," I replied. "I wonder what the hell kind of a job I would get if I *didn't* use pull?"

The state editor was not sympathetic when I told him that my schedule and my place of work would make it almost impossible for me to go home.

"Get a hotel room," he barked and hung up.

Calling him back, I asked, "Who's going to pay for it?"

"You," he said, and hung up again.

For a while I thought of quitting, but decided to try to work things out for a few weeks at least. It was June and the *Journal's* Westerly man, whom I was to assist, gave me a list of weddings to write up. Feeling that I was being logical, I appeared at several ceremonies and wrote what I thought were colorful descriptions.

"Jesus Christ!" the Westerly man exploded, slapping his forehead. "You don't *go* to weddings you're supposed to report! You get the information over the telephone and write them up right."

"What's 'right'?" I asked innocently.

"The way we always write up weddings. Don't you know *anything*? I never can tell what the head office will send me when I yell for help, but god damn it, they never sent me anybody before that went to weddings as though he were some kind of guest!"

For a moment there I was swept back to the day when Pop Hart welcomed me aboard the *Tampa* in Boston Harbor. Apparently it was my lot in life to appear constantly as the novice who enrages his superiors with his ignorance.

It did not take long for me to learn the style in which the *Journal* wrote up weddings, a form which was almost as rigid as that of the sonnet. I was rather sorry, however, that I could no longer appear at the ceremonies. Two of them I have never forgotten. At one of them a man who wore clean overalls with the name of a gasoline station on them married a sweet-faced young woman who was both pregnant and deaf and dumb. No guests were present. The bride and groom were much at ease with each other and held hands with obvious affection.

The other wedding was a high society affair in one of the grand houses that help to make Westerly a fashionable summer resort. The bride was a genuine beauty and her bridegroom was an athletic appearing young man who wore his cutaway as nonchalantly as though he got married every day. In the living room of the big house, wedding gifts were on display. The crystal, china, linen and silver spilled over to several bedrooms. During the reception that followed the ceremony, the bride's mother, a thin-lipped woman who looked like a cruel caricature of her daughter, took many of the guests, including me, on a tour of what looked to me like Tiffany's basement. After describing each gift and telling the name of the donor if he was prominent, this lady gave me the price of it. I have no idea how she determined the worth of all those presents, but to her own satisfaction, at least, she had mentally assembled a sort of catalogue.

"Don't you think it would be lovely if we had a description of all these gifts in the newspapers?" the lady asked.

"Complete with price?"

"I think that prices interest people. I'm not snobbish about that."

Perhaps the *Journal* had the right idea when they wrote up this wedding and the one of the deaf and dumb girl in such a way that the reader would gather that the two ceremonies had been similar.

Soon after writing up the weddings, I made another mistake. I went to a forest fire. The sight of the firemen with tanks strapped to their backs trudging up a steep hillside to stop the river of fire which was flooding over the newly green trees and the withered winter foliage was stirring, as was the rescue of one man who almost became asphyxiated by smoke and had to be carried back to the firetruck. No matter. Reporters cover small forest fires by telephone. Since no one was seriously injured, my morning's work resulted in just one short paragraph, and the derision of my superior when I complained of an aching back.

Shortly after the June weddings let up, the state editor called me up and said, "You're going to work in Warren. Report to Charlie Hughes."

"Charlie Hughes, eh?" the Westerly man said when I told him of this development. "Old Charlie will eat you alive. If you start going to weddings and forest fires for him, he'll *skin* you."

At least I'll be near home, I thought, and hurried back to my wife, whom I had been seeing only once or twice a week. Now that it was July, the cottages around us were all occupied. Radios blared and children ran in packs through the bushes.

"Oh, I'm so glad you'll be coming home every night now!" Elise said. "You couldn't believe what's been happening."

"What?"

"Well, there's this woman, Margaret Drake ..."

With some agitation Elise went on to tell me that Margaret Drake was an alcoholic who lived two houses away. Shortly after noon almost every day, Margaret Drake came calling. At first she drank our booze, but when Elise stopped supplying that, she got into the habit of bringing her own bottle in a paper bag. Sitting on our couch, she cited her immediate troubles and worked her way back to the torments of her youth and those of her parents. Her immediate troubles concerned one of two situations: either she mourned the fact that her husband was home or she became furious when he was away. When he was at home he often beat her, a fact which she demonstrated by pulling parts of her clothing up or down to display bruises. When he was not at home she ran out of money, had to borrow groceries and a few dollars for liquor. Although she claimed that she hated her husband, she was obsessed with the fear that he had another woman. She once had had a son, but he had been killed by a car while playing with his sled on the street. Her mother, whom she loved, was dying of cancer. Her father had been fired from his job two years before the age of retirement and was drinking himself to death. This was more or less the beginning of Margaret Drake's recitation of woe.

"You can't listen to that sort of thing all day long," I said. "Tell her you're busy."

"She'd come right in anyway."

"Be firm. Keep the doors locked and don't answer when she knocks."

"I can't treat her like that!"

That summer Margaret Drake almost became a member of our family. Elise seemed half fascinated, half repelled by this great hemorrhaging of troubles. I suffered little from it, for I was kept busier than I ever had been at the Westerly office of the *Journal*.

Charlie Hughes, who ran the Warren office, was a tall, handsome Irishman about fifty years old. He had iron-gray hair and a club foot which made it difficult for him to climb stairs rapidly. Shortly after I went to work for him, I realized that he was a man something like the skipper I had relieved aboard the *Nogak*. That is to say, he was as good at his job as anyone could possibly be, took great pride in it and hated anyone who did it badly. That meant me, but only at first, for Charlie soon perceived that I was willing to learn and set about trying to teach me. He was as good a teacher as he was a newspaperman. His method was to send me on all kinds of assignments, blue-pencil my copy, tell me to go back for whatever information I had missed and to write the story again. Sometimes I worked two days on one short piece, but Charlie never tired until I got it exactly right.

There is a curious trick which my memory has played on me about Charlie Hughes. When years later I went back to Warren to see him, not long before he died, men who had worked in the office with the two of us said they were surprised to see me. Charlie and I had yelled at each other at the top of our lungs the whole time we worked together, they said, and everyone had supposed that we hated each other.

I don't doubt the truth of the neutral observers, but I cannot remember any shouting whatsoever. Of course there was the natural exuberance of getting a story right and the disgust of getting one wrong, and Charlie and I were not the sort to work in utter silence, but there was no *mean* mouthing, even, if as our colleagues said, we occasionally scared the life out of people who were walking down the hall outside our office.

It was not so hard to learn to write the clean English sentences which Charlie liked, but it was impossible to learn in a short time how to cover Bristol County the way he did. There was no one of any consequence in Charlie's territory whom he did not know. Not only the police chiefs but most of the patrolmen were familiar to Charlie by name, as were clergymen of all denominations, politicians—past, present and future—union leaders, plant managers, anyone who might provide a story or a lead. A man had to live in Bristol County a lifetime, as Charlie had, to acquire so many news sources.

Charlie often called himself "nothing but a hick reporter, a small-town scribe," but he knew better than that. What he actually was was a man doing a small job so well that he made bigger jobs look sloppy. Charlie could never cover New York or even Providence as perfectly as he could cover Bristol County, and that is why he never really tried to move up to the so-called big-time.

One of the biggest stories I did for Charlie was covering the burning of the Herreshoff yacht yard in Bristol. Many cup defenders had been built at that yard, as well as whole fleets of other fine yachts. For me and many other people the Herreshoff yard stood for quality and tradition, everything that was graceful and good about the past. When the yard burned, only people who knew boats were aware that nothing like it would ever be seen again. Hardly anyone could afford a Herreshoff yacht, and the skilled artisans who had built them had somehow disappeared.

Since Charlie had taught me to use the big speed Graflex, I took pictures of the fire before interviewing the fire chief, what owners I could find, and all the other people one has to interview when there is a big fire. I worked hurriedly because my deadline for the paper was close. Charlie had some history books from the library waiting for me, and had opened them to the pages which gave the background of the Herreshoff family and yard. When I sat down to my typewriter he said, "You don't have time. You'll have to dictate it."

This was the first time I had done that with a story of any size. Taking my rather crumpled notes from my pocket, I reached for the telephone. Speaking fairly rapidly, I dictated an article which turned out to take up about half of a newspaper page. When I had finished, I was exhausted.

"That was good," Charlie said. "You made it an obituary, which I guess it really is, though I don't hold much with all this yachting stuff. If my ancestors ever got close to a yacht, they probably tried to steal it."

I laughed.

"How about a beer?" he asked.

He did not often ask anyone who worked for him to have a beer. We went to the Warren Inn, where they served oysters fresh from the boat that docked across the street.

"Sloanie, drink up," he said as soon as the beer arrived.

No one before or since has ever called me Sloanie, but Charlie made it sound almost natural. Still, he seemed tense. My work had been going well for the past several weeks, and I wondered whether he was preparing to give me a raise.

"Sloanie, I'm going to do you a favor which I wish someone had done for me when I was your age," he said. "I'm going to fire you."

"What?" I asked incredulously.

"If someone had fired me at your age, I might have got somewhere in the world."

"I thought you loved this kind of work."

"Sure, I love it, and I love living here by the river, but Sloanie, I'll tell you something. I've worked for the *Journal* for close to thirty years, and my pay still isn't much more than twice yours. People *start* at more than that in lots of businesses. And hardly a week goes by that I don't work fifty or sixty hours."

"Maybe we need the guild in here."

"No, I don't hold with the guild. Reporters can't be treated like factory workers. What you should do is go to New York. That's where the future is."

"It's too soon," I replied. "I have only been here about five months. I intended to stay about two years."

"There's one good thing about that. You suck in all the training you can and then quit. That's really helping the cause."

"How's that?" I asked reddening.

"If all the young guys stuck the *Journal* like that, they'd have to pay beginners more and the raise would have to go right up the line. If I fired you, that wouldn't prove anything. If you intend to quit at the end of a year or so, that's okay, but if I see you hanging on here any longer, I'll belt your ass right into the street."

Only a few days after this conversation, I received more confirmation, if I needed it, that it was difficult for me to run my life in any logical way. Right after committing myself to leaving the *Journal* in a year or so, I bought a larger house in Barrington. Maddened by the continuing tale of woe from our neighbor, Margaret Drake, whom she could neither stand nor turn away, Elise had toured the area with a real estate broker and had finally found a house which she wholeheartedly loved. A comfortable Victorian structure, it had a front lawn which ran down to the river and a back yard with a good barn and several gnarled old apple trees. The price was twelve thousand—cheap for waterfront property in a fashionable suburb even in that day. Buying it involved the sale of the house we were in and cleaning out our savings account, including the remainder of the small trust fund which had been supplementing my small salary. When I pointed out that it was ridiculous to buy a bigger house while planning to move, Elise said that the house was such a bargain that we could consider it an investment. Her parents offered to pay for a new oil burner which was needed, and I sold a couple of pieces to *The New Yorker*. Somehow the whole transaction was put together, and much to my wife's joy, we moved into the charming old house. When I was not working, we could sit on the front porch and watch the oyster boats come in and slip sideways in the current as they turned to moor at the wharf across the river. In the summertime there was almost always a rainbow of sails near the Barrington Yacht Club and tall yawls often glided in to anchor for the night. Unable to withstand the temptation to join all this nautical activity. I bought a nine-foot sailing dinghy from Bill Dyer, whose famous little boatyard was right across the stream. Charlie Hughes' son, who was then about twelve and who longed to go to the Naval Academy (which in due time he successfully did), volunteered to be my crew on windy days. Even in January, we raced with a frostbite fleet which tacked across the gray river on snowy days with the enthusiasm of true fanatics.

That fall my first novel, *Voyage to Somewhere*, was published in New York. Most of the reviews of this little story about a supply vessel in the South Pacific were lukewarm and the sales were so disappointing that the publisher eventually asked me to refund most of the $500 advance he had given me, but E. B. White mentioned the book respectfully in a column called "Turtle Bay Diary" which he was writing in *The New Yorker*. For years I had been such an admirer of E. B. White that his brief mention of me seemed a message straight from Mount

Olympus. How could a book which E. B. White had noticed possibly be called a failure?

In many of the papers which printed faint praise of *Voyage to Somewhere*, there were glowing accounts of the fantastic success of *Mr. Roberts*, which I had advised Paul Brooks not to publish. This further proof of my bad judgment hurt, but after all, E. B. White had not praised *Mr. Roberts*, had he? If Mr. White had written a rave review of *Mr. Roberts*, I might well have drowned myself.

Elise was due to give birth at some time toward the end of November. The elaborate layette which she had prepared for the first child was carefully washed and ironed. Somewhere Elise had acquired a fancy four-poster crib with a crocheted canopy. We painted a room upstairs which was to serve as the nursery and read so many books on child care that I reckoned myself to be a master of theory, if not of practice.

The day before Thanksgiving, we drove to her family's house in West Newton, as we usually did on holidays. We were not there long before Elise felt contractions, and I rushed her to the West Newton Hospital. A nurse put her into a wheelchair, which made her look as though— with shocking speed—she had been turned into an invalid, and disappeared with her down a long corridor. I was left pacing in a crowded waiting room, the living cliché of an expectant father. Why, I wondered, are expectant fathers always treated as jokes? The worries I had were not amusing. Elise had suffered so much during her first effort to deliver a child that she might not get over the shock if something went wrong this time.

Pushing this worry out of my mind, I began wondering how I was going to pay the obstetrician's bill, which was all of three hundred dollars, and also the wages of a baby nurse, which Elise's mother said we should hire for a few weeks to give Elise a chance to get on her feet. I had hoped to sell enough magazine pieces to meet these expenses, but ideas never seemed to come when I needed them most.

After I had paced for three or four hours, a nurse told me that I could go home. Nothing much was happening, but someone would call me the moment labor started in earnest.

For some reason this seemed a bad sign. When I asked if I could see my wife, I was told that she was asleep. She must be drugged, I thought. Why would they drug her right at the beginning if everything is all right? Afraid I might be needed, I sank down on a couch. An old woman at my left was telling another old woman that her daughter had cancer of the uterus. The second old woman replied that her sister had had the same thing, and had lived about a year. The first old woman said that the doctor had not given her that much hope. It suddenly seemed strange to me that birth and death had to take place in the same building, and that sometimes they even involved the same organs. I wished the old ladies would stop talking, but instead they began to discuss many of the details of cancer of the uterus. I tried to focus my mind on the question of whether I wanted a boy or a girl. It was hard to visualize any child younger than about six years old. There was an old joke about a father who bought a baseball glove and bat for his infant boy. Well, I had always hated baseball and almost every other sport, so there was no danger of my doing that. If I had a boy I could teach him to sail, but plenty of girls learn how to do that. Although I was hardly a ladies' man, I had during most of my life preferred the company of women. Four years of male company during the war had been enough. In my imagination at least, little girls were pretty and little boys were scruffy. What would I do if I had a little girl who turned out to be very plain? Ugly women have a much worse time in life than ugly men, I had observed. Maybe it would be safer to have a boy, a tough little boy, who soon could learn to take on the problems of the world.

After a good deal of fevered thinking of this sort, I fell into a deep sleep. People kept getting up from the other end of the couch and others sat down. One old man stumbled over my outstretched feet and I began to dream of the narrow-gauged railroad car on which I had slept in the Philippines. It was strange to think that I was going to meet my child. I had a clear picture of one of those tattered Filipino children with big eyes in a thin starving face.

"A child can look like any of its parents or grandparents," I had read, and had a vision of a child looking exactly as my father had during the months before he had died—a gray-haired child with a pipe in his mouth, pince-nez glasses on a black ribbon and Malacca cane in his hand.

Hours went by before a nurse woke me.

"Your wife is fine and you have a beautiful baby girl," she said, and beckoned me toward a small private room which was empty. Rubbing my eyes, I couldn't come fully awake. It seemed terrible to ruin such a climactic moment by staying half asleep. In a few moments Dr. Clark, the obstetrician, appeared. He had on a white hospital coat heavily stained with blood. The fact that he looked much as though he had just come from a battlefield shocked me profoundly, seeming to knit the union of life and death closer than ever.

"They'll let you see the baby in a few minutes," the doctor said. "They still are cleaning her up. I just thought you'd like to know that the delivery was perfectly normal, no complications at all. Your wife went through some fairly hard labor, though, and I think she should sleep for as long as she can."

I thanked him. In a few minutes a nurse came in with an infant that was loosely swaddled in a white baby blanket. She handed the bundle to me. My first impression was of its incredible lightness. I felt as though I were holding something like a squirrel done up in a diaper, not a human being of any age. The books had warned me that newborn infants are rarely if ever objects of great beauty. Rather fearfully I peered between folds of the blanket. There was a face smaller than my fist, blue eyes already equipped with just a touch of dark eyelashes and blond eyebrows. There was a button nose and scarlet lips which opened from time to time to give a fretful whimper.

"She's a beautiful baby," the nurse said. "I'd swear she was a Caesarean if I didn't know better. There isn't a mark on her."

The baby stopped whimpering and I turned toward the window. Dawn was breaking. The first rays of sun were gilding a bank of gray clouds. Glancing at the baby, I saw that she appeared to be looking at the sky, too.

"I better take her to the baby ward now," the nurse said.

Handing my daughter to her, I walked to my car in a daze. Thanksgiving day was dawning in a blaze of sunlight, and I had a daughter. Lisa would be her name. My wife and I had decided on that, thinking that it was a little unusual, as indeed it was shortly after World War II.

As I drove toward the home of Elise's parents, I for some reason thought of the night my father had died and the leaden dawn which had followed. The most intense despair had engulfed the whole family that day. If death can bring such suffering, why shouldn't birth bring exaltation of equal intensity? Why can't there be some ceremony which can act as the reverse of a funeral, a formal event which will bring all the relatives running? A feast should be prepared and prayers offered at the beginning of life, just as they are at the end of it.

The Pickhardts were already up when I reached their home, for at their request the hospital had notified them as soon as the baby was born. They had already begun to prepare a feast, which of course was for Thanksgiving day. They congratulated me and gave me an early glass of their Thanksgiving day punch, a potent combination of rum, tea and lime juice. As I drank it I had a premonition, not of doom, but its opposite, whatever word that is. Lisa would be a good daughter and a beautiful woman who would lead an interesting life, I thought with conviction, and to take the curse of cockiness off that prediction, I prayed that it would be true.

So far it has come true.

It's hard to believe that twenty-eight years have passed since that Thanksgiving day. Like everyone else, I have of course had plenty of disappointments in life, but none have come from my children. Lisa, the first, is about to give me my first grandchild. When she first hands it to me, I plan to drink a glass of Thanksgiving day punch, no matter what time of the year it is. In so doing I shall feel as though I am drawing a large part of my life full circle.

18

There followed what in many ways were the happiest days of my life up to that time. Although Charlie and I continued to yell at each other in the office so horribly that our colleagues thought we were going to kill each other, we continued to be close friends. The routine of the newspaper was tiring, but I soon came to enjoy it. As soon as I unlocked the office at nine in the morning, I checked our primary news sources by telephone. Following a list, I called the police department, the fire department, the undertakers who might know of funeral plans and the clergymen who might know of weddings. If this produced no results, I consulted a notebook in which I had scribbled ideas for feature stories. On a side street I had seen a sign advertising canaries for sale, and had discovered that an old woman there raised birds in her attic. A cemetery with the graves of soldiers who had fought in the Revolution was choked with weeds and refuse. There was always something with which to fill the paper before crossing the bridge to my home for lunch.

The fact that I had afternoons off instead of evenings gave me unusual opportunities to watch Lisa grow. Long before she could talk, she appeared to enjoy picture books and liked to have the captions read aloud to her. Before she was a year old, she began to say a few words, many of them mispronounced but understandable to her parents. Soon I made up a set of flash cards and began teaching her the alphabet. The letters were of course meaningless to her, but in time she began to say "A" when she saw that letter.

In the evenings I spent a lot of time reporting the meetings of the many organizations to which almost everyone in the county seemed to belong. In addition to the churches, which had clubs to accommodate people of every age and condition, there were the Owls and the Odd Fellows, the Masons and the Knights of Columbus, the Lions, the Optimists and the Rotarians, the American Legion and the Veterans of Foreign Wars, the Kiwanians and God knew what else. Most of these organizations provided rostrums for solemn speakers. There were a great many oaths taken, and much pledging of allegiance to. Ornamental swords and scimitars decorated with simulated jewels were sported by the officials of some of the organizations, while the leaders of one group donned fake beards. It was impossible to tour the halls in which all these people met without wondering how they could stand so many earnest speeches and solemn ceremonies. When I finally asked Charlie Hughes this question, he laughed.

"They do it for the honor of the thing," he said. "Everybody in this town is honored by some outfit at least once a year."

The life of a small-town reporter was pleasant, but there were two serious drawbacks: I was not being paid enough to support my family, never mind save for the future, and the life apparently was not conducive to writing magazine stories or books on the side. On many days I wrote more than half a page of newspaper copy, which was enough to make the thought of a typewriter repugnant in my spare time. The afternoons at home were more full of distractions than the evenings had been. Although I had received one ten-dollar raise after being with the *Journal* about a year, Charlie kept reminding me that he himself was receiving little more than twice my salary, despite his decades of service. Obviously it was time to move on, but to where?

This question was so perplexing that I avoided it until, only three months after the birth of Lisa, Elise announced that she was pregnant again. If I were going to have two children, I would certainly need a salary of more than $50 a week.

"I guess it's time to see Sinny," Elise said.

The idea still appalled me, but deciding that I would be churlish to refuse to see the man, I made an appointment at his office.

Sinclair Weeks was bland-appearing—bald, plump and soft-looking—but like many rich men he had some very strong convictions. He believed in God, the Republican Party, the American Legion and the wisdom of most successful businessmen. Over his affable smile his eyes were penetrating as he greeted me. I was wearing a tweed jacket with leather elbow patches and gray flannel slacks, an outfit which had seemed suitable in Barrington, but which somehow became tacky in Mr. Weeks' opulent office. He was wearing a banker's suit, gray with pinstripes.

"You've got a good military record," he said, picking up a folder which I did not know he had. "You did well enough at Harvard. Why did you go in for newspaper work?"

"I thought it was good training for a writer," I said.

"Very risky career, writing," he replied, sensibly enough. "Maybe I can offer you something better."

His suggestion, it turned out, was that I go to work at a factory that plated table silver and which he owned. It was located in a small town in western Massachusetts. Naturally I would have to start at the bottom, but if I did well, there was every chance that I would rise rapidly. When I said that I would have to think this suggestion over, he appeared miffed and slapped my folder shut.

"I want to thank you for thinking of me, anyway," I said awkwardly.

He gave a smile of genuine charm.

"Nice to help a fellow veteran," he said. "Different war, but still a veteran. When you make up your mind, come in and see me again."

I went home feeling dejected. Elise laughed at the possibility of my entering the silver-plating business, but we both had the sobering thought that it might be the only opportunity available which would enable us to support two children. Maybe I could write in my spare time. . . .

It was not a decision I could make swiftly. This turned out to be fortunate, because I soon got an extraordinary telephone call from a man I had met at Harvard who now worked for *Time* magazine. *Time*, he said, was hiring. Would I be interested?

Part 4
"Let Me Off of This Thing
and Never Ask Me to
Go Back on It Again"

19

I was interested if not, according to friend and family, exactly well-dressed for my audiences at Time, Inc., with Mr. Darling and Mr. Fixx. Nonetheless, in the cheerless cubicle they put me in to write my autobiographical sketch, nobody was looking and, after spending ten of the sixty minutes they'd allotted for the task in worrying about the propriety of the thing, I managed to sweat through a fifty-minutes' speedy typing, hand it in to the young lady who rather magically appeared at the hour's end, and head back as fast as I could to Rhode Island to await whatever decision might be made about me.

At work again in Warren on the Providence *Journal*, I tried to tell myself that nothing had happened and nothing probably would, but the trip to New York had affected me. *Time* scared me, but now the *Journal* seemed more barren of opportunity than it ever had before. When, only a few days later, I got a letter from Calvin Fixx telling me that I could try out as a writer for *Time* if I wanted, I was damn near as scared and proud as when I first took command of a coast guard ship.

One of the first things that happened when I began working at *Time* was that a young man who worked with the personnel department took me to lunch.

"I hope you don't take this personally," he said, "but most of the people here are pretty careful about the kind of clothes they wear. Why don't you go down to Brooks Brothers and buy yourself a gray flannel suit?"

You too? I thought. "When they pay me enough to buy my clothes from Brooks Brothers, I'll do it," I said.

"That's not the way it works. First you fit in here well, and then you get your raise. This isn't official—it's just a friendly hint."

"But Brooks Brothers charge something like two hundred dollars for a suit!"

"I'll give you a tip," he said. "Go to the boys' department. The same materials cost about half as much there."

"Boys' department! I weigh more than two hundred pounds!"

"They have clothes for boys of all sizes," he said.

The clerk in the boys' department at Brooks Brothers did not seem surprised and fitted me quite well with a gray flannel that cost only eighty dollars. When my friend in the personnel department saw me the next day, he grinned.

"You look better," he said. "When you get another one, make it a charcoal gray. You may not believe it, but little things like that are important around here."

The first thing which Calvin Fixx asked me to do when I reported for duty at *Time* was to study the latest edition of the magazine and give him a sort of critique of it with some suggestion of what departments might interest me most. The magazine he gave me featured an article on the great victories of Chiang Kai-shek in China with the clear implication that the Chinese Communists were doomed. There was also a lot of praise for Thomas Dewey, who obviously was to be our next president, and some unkind words about Harry Truman, who was not a big enough man for his job. At the age of twenty-seven, I was, as I am now, an almost completely unpolitical animal, but during my years of running a small supply ship in the south Pacific, I had met a good many officers who had worked with Chiang Kai-shek's Nationalists in China, and I had received the impression that reports of their victories were mostly propaganda. I also, on instinct detested Thomas Dewey and admired Harry Truman. Clearly it would be folly to begin my career at *Time* by attacking their major heroes, but there was something about Calvin Fixx's mournful face and knowing eyes which made me think it would be foolish as well as immoral to try to lie to him. With a jittery attempt at self-confidence, I told him that I disagreed with *Time*'s views on China and Tom Dewey, and that I might be more effective if I were allowed to review books or report on some of the lighter news events. With obvious sincerity he said that he admired my honesty, and I found myself dreaming of turning the whole editorial policy of Time Inc. right around. This fantasy crashed when Calvin gently added that the best place for me to start at *Time* would be as a writer for *FYI*, the company house organ which was distributed only to employees. He said this would give me an opportunity to meet a lot of the editors and get sort of a feeling for the place.

Rarely has my pride suffered such a blow. The few pieces I had had published in *The New Yorker* and the one story which *Harper's* Magazine had accepted had given me the impression that I had at least a slender talent. Writing for *Time* had seemed a definite downward step which was necessary for financial reasons, but being assigned to *Time*'s house organ seemed to place me about as low as a writer could go.

Calvin's explanation that almost all beginners at *Time* were asked to serve an apprenticeship on *FYI* did little to cheer me, and reading some samples of *FYI*, which discussed all company happenings with wondrous enthusiasm, increased my depression. Aside from the fact that I did not want to write for *FYI*, I seriously doubted whether I could do it convincingly. My father had told me a good many truthful things about writing, and one of them was that a man's style is his personality and cannot be changed without risking parody. The bright-eyed eagerness of *FYI* about all the workings of *Time* would not be easy for me to contrive, no matter how anxious I was, as the saying went, "to sell out" for money. Glumly I returned to the small office which had been assigned to me and stared twenty-six floors down to Rockefeller Plaza. Our house in Rhode Island had already been sold and my wife was eagerly looking at houses in New Canaan. Perhaps a New York newspaper might have a job for me. The prospect of high pay would be less, but at least there might be work I could do well.

While I was wondering how I would explain why I had quit *Time* two days after going to work there, the telephone on my desk rang, and the firm voice of an executive secretary gave me a most astonishing message: Roy Larsen, the president of Time, Inc., wanted to see me. I could not imagine why such an august personage would want to see a young man who had just been assigned to his company house organ, but there was something about the brisk voice of the executive secretary which made it impossible to ask questions. She told me to appear at Roy Larsen's office that afternoon, and I of course said I would.

Too nervous to go to lunch, I sat in my office and thought. Although he was president of Time, Inc., and had once been publisher of *Life*, the name of Roy Larsen was not well known outside of the company, where most people seemed to think that Henry Luce got out all his magazines almost single-handedly. Still, I had heard Larsen's name recently in Cambridge. Suddenly I remembered that Professor Paul Sachs, from whom I had requested a letter of recommendation for the *Time* job, had said that he knew Roy Larsen well. Larsen was a Harvard graduate who made a secret virtue of giving a great deal of money and time to the university.

I had always despised the idea of "It's who you know, not what you know, that counts," and I had equally hated the thought that a Harvard diploma possessed magic qualities when it came to getting a job. If, however, Professor Sachs' letter meant that I was going to get a chance to meet the president of Time, Inc., before quitting in despair, I was grateful for the chance.

At the appointed hour I presented myself at Roy Larsen's outer office on the thirty-second floor. Miss Sugarman, his executive secretary, was a small, dark-haired woman who somehow gave the impression of being able to run vast corporations entirely by herself. She ushered me into a large rectangular room. Roy Larsen was sitting behind a desk the size and shape of a billiard table. A trim man who appeared to be in his late forties, he had iron-gray hair, a ruddy face with penetrating blue eyes and a smile of great warmth. He was in his shirtsleeves. When he saw me he got up, almost trotted around the end of his desk, gave my hand a hearty shake and spoke in fast short sentences which in my tense state seemed to merge.

"So you're the young fellow Paul Sachs thinks so well of. Sit down. Want to take off your coat? How long have you been here? Where have they got you working? How do you like it?"

With as much dignity as I could muster, I explained that I had been assigned to *FYI*, and that I didn't like it at all. Roy Larsen looked so sympathetic that I admitted I was beginning to doubt I belonged at Time, Inc., at all.

"I wouldn't get too downhearted about that," he replied, looking and sounding as though he had never been downhearted about anything in his life. "Our editorial departments require certain disciplines that are more congenial to some writers than others. How would you like to look for a spot in some other part of the company?"

"Like what?" I asked in surprise.

"It's a big company with many kinds of positions. As a matter of fact you might consider working with me on a project that has nothing to do with the company."

He talked so fast that I did not have to ask many questions. James Bryant Conant, the president of Harvard, was worried about the state of the nation's public schools, Mr. Larsen said. Conant was trying to get together a "group of national leaders" to form a committee that would study the problems of the public schools and recommend solutions to them. Larsen had agreed to head up "a sort of exploratory committee" which would try to bring people into a larger organization and form policies. He needed a young man to help him. How would I like the job?

"I'm afraid," I replied, stammering a little, "that I've never even been to a public school and I know very little about education."

"Fine!" Larsen said. "What we need is a reporter with an unbiased view. You can go around the country talking to educators and all kinds of leaders and report to me what they think we should do."

"It sounds interesting."

"Fine! Now why don't you go and talk to Barnie Barnes about the details? He's in charge of special projects around here."

Bernard Barnes was a handsome man who appeared to be in his late thirties and who comported himself with the briskness of a marine drill sergeant. If I took the job I would be his assistant and would start at five thousand dollars a year. The whole project had not "been firmed up yet" and I might be fired at any time. For the first six months I would, at any rate, be on probation. I could, of course, assume that Roy and "Jim" Conant could persuade almost anyone they wanted to join a committee for the improvement of public education. Not only people in the communications business should be included. Labor should be represented and industry. Money for the activities of the committee could easily be got from the big foundations. My first assignment would be to talk to as many educators as necessary, read as many books as necessary and come up with some suggestions about what such a committee could do. *How* would a committee of VIP's set about improving the public schools? He hoped that I could give him at least some sort of preliminary report inside of two weeks.

My mouth was so dry that I could hardly swallow. This was a job for which I felt I had absolutely *no* qualifications. In the past the whole subject of education had filled me with nothing but boredom. Even so, the idea of going around the country talking to all these great important men sounded interesting and the pay still sounded good.

"I'll be glad to give it a try," I said. "It certainly sounds like *important* work."

"You can start right away," Barnes replied. "Work in your office, in the library, any place you like. All I want is a report within two weeks. If it's good enough, it might get us a couple of million dollars from the foundations for a start."

That night when I returned to the inn where we were staying in Connecticut, I found that my wife had found a house she liked in New Canaan.

"I think I ought to tell you that I'm not even working for *Time* anymore," I said.

"What do you mean?"

I tried to explain my strange situation.

"You mean you're going to be some kind of an *educator*?" she asked.

"Sort of a reporter on education, I guess."

"Will you like that?"

"I don't know. It's still five thousand dollars a year."

"Let's go look at the house," she said.

The house she had discovered was on White Oak Shade Road across from a beautiful field. It had been built somewhere around 1835, had a big fireplace and great charm. It was tiny and the ceilings were so low that they brushed the top of my hat, though I am only five feet ten inches tall. There was no basement, and the logs on which the floor had been built had rotted so much that a gap was beginning to show at the bottom of the wall facing the porch. During World War II, someone had tried to raise chickens in the attic and had never cleaned up after the attempt. Still, the early Colonial charm was undeniable and the price was eighteen thousand dollars, which seemed high to me, but people said it was low for New Canaan, especially in view of the fact that a nice piece of land and a good barn came with the house. Having just sold the house in Rhode Island at a small profit, we figured we could swing the deal.

Only a few days later we moved into the house, and I began spending my days at the New York Public Library reading books on public education, which certainly are among the dullest in the world. When I could no longer keep my eyes open, I went back to my office at *Time* and tried to write stories for *The New Yorker*. The *Time* office was a good place for writing *New Yorker* pieces because my telephone never rang there, and a few of my minor attempts were successful. Sometimes it occurred to me that it was rather dishonest to be sitting at *Time* writing for *The New Yorker*, but I was beginning to realize that my morality, like the suits I wore, came in different shades of gray, and who could really worry about cheating an outfit as big and ferocious as Time Inc., anyway?

In the late Forties a reporter did not need much skill to describe the problems of the public schools. Almost any public school superintendent was quick to say that he didn't have enough buildings or teachers for the baby boom that followed World War II, and that there was a desperate shortage of money. Almost anyone who considered himself an intellectual agreed with the need for money for public schools, but went on to say that licensing procedures for public school teachers had been designed more to protect a guild than to provide good instruction for the children. In the unlikely event that Picasso, for instance, decided to be an art teacher in an American public school, he would be barred because he had taken no courses in education and in many states he would also be barred because he had not taken special courses in the state history. Public school teachers usually came from state teacher colleges or the education department of universities. Scholars who concentrated on their subject, and distrusted courses in the techniques of teaching, could not get jobs in public schools despite the much heralded teacher shortage.

One of the first things I learned is that teachers of all kinds, despite their reputation for mildness, shout a lot when talking to a reporter. Some yelled about the great need for federal aid to education, while others retorted that such help would turn the schools into propaganda mills. Then as now there was a lot of shouting about how, when or whether racial segregation should be stopped.

The seemingly dull subject of education also caused businessmen, parents and almost anybody one met at a cocktail party to start waving their arms a lot. It was commonly charged that the public schools were not teaching people to read, spell, or do much of anything. A special hysteria attended discussions of whether sex and religion could be taught or even discussed in public school classrooms.

For about a year I wrote a series of reports on this situation for Roy Larsen. He and James B. Conant got together an imposing committee to study the problems and recommend solutions. Walter Lippmann and George Gallup were among our stars. Mrs. Eugene Meyer, the imposing wife of the publisher of the *Washington Post*, and Mrs. Barry Bingham, the astringently intelligent wife of the publisher of the Louisville *Courier and Journal*, were among our most vocal members. Beardsley Ruml, who somehow had gone from being a professor at the University of Chicago to tax adviser for the government and treasurer of Macy's department store, was our most Johnsonian figure, huge and gross in appearance, but with mordant wit. *The Reader's Digest* sent us a senior editor, Robert Littell. Leo Perlis, an unassuming man with great knowledge, represented the C.I.O., and Lester Granger, a senatorial appearing black man, spoke for the Urban League. These people and many other luminaries met for many luncheons at the Waldorf-Astoria hotel, and discussed passionately the problems of the schools. They consulted college presidents and school superintendents across the land. For about two years they deliberated, and it was my privilege to sit at the end of the table and take notes for Roy Larsen, who was chairman. A great many brilliant things were said, but in the end this mountain of a committee agreed only on a mouse of an idea: billboards would be put up all around the nation saying, BETTER SCHOOLS MAKE BETTER COMMUNITIES, and the same message would be repeated in newspaper and magazine advertisements.

It took months for all these brilliant people to decide on a name for their group, but they finally settled on the National Citizens Commission for the Public Schools, which later was shortened to Better Schools, Inc. A staff of some thirty people was hired and an office rented on 45th Street near Fifth Avenue in New York. I was given the proud title of Assistant Director. My salary was doubled and I kept on scurrying around the country writing reports of school problems for the members.

The commission was under a great deal of pressure from the foundations which supported it as well as from almost every educator they asked to lunch at the Waldorf to come up with an actual plan for helping people who wanted to act on the slogan, "Better Schools Make

Better Communities." It was impossible to find a strategy which would not infuriate someone. Finally it was decided to encourage people to form local committees which could study their own schools and decide what to do. Since almost every American town had an official school board and a PTA, this suggestion that additional, unofficial and perhaps uncongenial committees be formed was thought by some to be less than original, but it was the best the commission could do. The advertising media which carried the slogan about schools making better communities added the suggestion that interested people should write our commission for advice on how to do it, and we prepared a lot of form letters and pamphlets about how to form a committee and study school problems. Answers to the problems we carefully refrained from trying to give.

To my knowledge no one seriously criticized the National Citizens Commission for the Public Schools for spending several millions of dollars of Ford, Carnegie and Rockefeller money for such meager results. It is possible that their advertising campaign for the schools and the many brief-lived committees which were formed across the country helped to get a lot of bond issues passed for new schools. Despite this, I could not help but feel that there was something fundamentally funny, as well as frustrating, about the vast amount of intelligence, time, money and dignity being wasted on nothing but an advertising campaign and the advice to form committees.

To fit in well with the foundation executives with whom I had to deal, I now found myself wearing not only a gray flannel suit but a Chesterfield coat and homburg hat. Because part of my job was ghost-writing speeches and magazine articles on education for some of our busier members, I found myself having midnight discussions with the presidents of large corporations in elaborate restaurants and flying in company planes to distant states where important executives wanted to help improve their schools without saying anything controversial. Within a period of only two or three years, so much of the prestige of my employers rubbed off on me that quite a few people started regarding me as an expert on public education. When more important members of our commission and staff were busy, I was sent out to make speeches to large gatherings of PTA members or businessmen. Since I had no experience in public speaking and suffered badly from stage fright, I was terrified— until I discovered that no one expected me to do anything but look earnest and decry the many problems facing the public schools. Both my pen and tongue soon became glib at this. I kept reminding myself that I had somehow landed in a good job which enabled me to meet many interesting people and travel all over the United States. Still I could not get over the feeling that I was an impostor and that the whole

178

enterprise, so driven by good will and so desperately afraid of controversy, was a colossal and expensive joke.

There were a few cynics on the staff of *Time* and some newspapers who thought that a lot of the members joined our commission more because of a desire for good personal or corporate publicity than because of any real concern for the schools. I often heard this charge leveled at Neil McElroy, who was president of Procter and Gamble and famous chiefly for his salary of $300,000 a year, which had been much publicized. Neil had climbed to the top of Procter and Gamble by distinguishing himself as a soap salesman, and a lot of the professional educators with whom I dealt couldn't understand why he had suddenly become so interested in the schools. Neil liked to make public speeches about education and as a ghost writer I found him one of my best clients, because he never argued about anything I suggested. He was not a dramatic speaker, but he was a most impressive looking man, trim, well over six feet tall, and with a Byronic profile. No matter what he said sounded like the truth. When as the years went by, Neil McElroy became chairman of Eisenhower's White House Conference on Education and then Secretary of Defense, he was placed on lists of potential presidents, and some of the foundation employees asked me whether I thought he had used our school commission as a way to get into politics.

I, of course, have no idea what went on in the intricate mind of the president of Procter and Gamble, but he seemed to me to be the least devious of men. When asked by a reporter what he thought about federal aid to education, which was then a hot issue, he said, "I don't like it," instead of providing our standard answer that more study was necessary. When a woman asked him how he could promote education on the one hand while on the other hand having his company sponsor soap operas on television, he said, "Lady, when I sell education, I sell education, and when I sell soap, I sell soap."

He was so blunt that he soon became surrounded by droves of public relations men, some of whom were on the Procter and Gamble staff. One of these I shall call Charlie because I would not like to cause him more trouble than he already has. Charlie lived in Cincinnati, where Procter and Gamble has its headquarters, and when I went out there to help Neil McElroy with a speech or magazine article, I was asked to stay at Charlie's house, which was an imposing mansion on a block crowded with huge Victorian houses. Charlie's big worry was that McElroy, far from improving the image of Procter and Gamble with his efforts on behalf of education, might be hurting it. Charlie had worked so long for Procter and Gamble and had done so well there that he spoke the name of the firm with a sort of hushed reverence, like a priest referring to his deity. Over cocktails in his living room one evening he begged me not to put anything controversial into the speeches I was writing for Neil.

"We always must remember," Charlie said, "that Mr. McElroy is not just a man. He is the personification of Procter and Gamble."

Charlie's wife, a pleasant if plain appearing woman, had not seemed to be listening to our conversation, and she gave signs of having started the cocktail hour at some time much earlier in the day. Pouring herself another martini, she spilled a little and said mildly, "Charlie, can't you stop talking bullshit for just one hour?"

"Please, darling," he said.

"I propose a toast," she said. "For just one night, let's fuck Procter and Gamble."

"Darling—"

"Fuck Procter and Gamble!" the undaunted lady shouted, and opening the front door, again shouted the words at the top of her lungs.

Charlie grabbed her, but while he was trying to shut the door, she got away, ran to an open window and again repeated her message at the top of her lungs. She was a strong woman, and while Charlie was trying to hold her and shut the window, she grabbed a telephone and began repeating her message into the receiver. Finally Charlie got her upstairs by promising to bring her a bottle there. When he returned his face was ashen, and I of course felt sorry for him, but his immediate fears apparently did not concern his wife.

"Do you suppose anyone heard?" he asked. "Did you notice if anyone was walking by out there?"

Except for this overzealous public relations man, I never saw anyone worry about the corporate images of the members of the school commission. Their employees were usually pleasant, but the only one I ever really liked and thought about afterward was Charlie's wife. I have often thought of her living out there at the headquarters of Procter and Gamble, married to a man who almost worshiped the company, and boiling with fury at the sanctimoniousness of so much that goes on in big business and big charity. Charlie's wife was one of many influences which caused me to work night and day on my own writing. Much of my stuff did not turn out well, but there was always the hope that someday I could make a living writing for myself, and could give up my oddly blossoming career as an educator.

20

The thing I can't quite believe about my memories of New Canaan, Connecticut, in the five years that followed World War II, is the ferocity with which everyone worked. The houses which the men bought after getting out of the army or navy soon became too small, for that was an era when few of us had even heard of the population explosion, and there was something about the war which made most of us want to raise a large family. My wife, Elise, and I had three children in less than four years, and though we were considered kind of speedy, we were not regarded as unusual. A real estate agent in New Canaan told me that the average small house in the village was sold every four years, because its owners outgrew it physically or financially and wanted something better.

The young men that I knew in New Canaan dressed as I did, either in gray flannel or in other drab hues. It often occurred to me that we looked like soldiers as we lined up to climb aboard the trains, and there was much else about those commuting trains which reminded me of troop carriers. There was, for one thing, the pervasive almost physical smell of fear, which was combatted by many jokes and nervous laughter. Some of my friends at *Time* openly admitted their dread of getting fired or of falling hopelessly behind in the race for promotions. The many advertising men I knew had more bravado, but they tended actually to lose their jobs more often. One public relations man I knew rode the rails for over a month looking for a job. He had a forty-thousand-dollar house with two mortgages on it, two cars which had not been paid for and several children. I was never able to make his case believable in fiction, but this mild-mannered little man eventually held up a bank in a nearby town and got away with it so easily that he tried the same crime again at the same bank a few months later. That time he was caught and sent to jail.

I don't think that many of us were afraid of reaching a point where we could find no work at all, but most of the young commuters had high ambitions in one field or another, and knew perfectly well that the odds against achieving them were large. I tried to write magazine pieces and started books on nights and weekends, but the young advertising men and bankers often worked as hard or harder than I. When there was no office work to be done, there was always a lawn that had to be cut, a porch to be painted, or a basement to be turned into a recreation room.

In those days there was not so much talk about careers for women, but most of our wives worked as hard as we did. Few had any help in taking care of the children and many took up paint brushes or buckets of wallpaper paste to make old houses more comfortable or attractive enough to sell. The women joined committees to start a nursery school, the PTA to help the public schools, and classes to teach them how to make their own clothes or to make slipcovers for furniture. On weekends many of the families gave cocktail parties with food which required elaborate preparation. If one did not give parties, one did not get asked to them, and a good many people regarded the thought of a mailbox without invitations as a calamity almost as bad as getting fired.

Most of us worried about money, and ignoring the conventional manners of our parents, talked about it incessantly. The bills were always piling up, yet as soon as we got a raise, which most of us during these years did fairly often, we either bought a bigger house, a boat, a new car or all three, if our credit could be stretched far enough. The financial tension which we brought upon ourselves sometimes became unbearable. A friend of mine who sold space for a magazine literally drank himself to death on a business trip to Chicago. He swallowed more than a quart of vodka at one sitting, and because he was not generally known to be an alcoholic, he was suspected of suicide. His wife knew little of his financial affairs, but upon investigation she found that their fifty-thousand-dollar house had the usual two mortgages, and that the twenty-thousand-dollar boat they had just bought was also mortgaged. This man belonged to a country club, a yacht club and several other expensive clubs in New York, and he had a guaranteed income of only fifteen thousand dollars a year. Most of the things he had bought he had acquired with nothing but loans from banks, relatives, and faith that high living would eventually help a space salesman to afford high living.

Although the suburbs were later written up as hotbeds of wife-swapping and all kinds of sexual excitement, when we men in gray flannel suits were in our twenties most of us were still in love with our wives and, in any case, were too tired for much extracurricular activity. After a hard day's work, the drill tended to be a couple of drinks and a few hours of blessed sleep before the children woke up and the 7:38, or whatever, left for New York, or wherever. Later on, when men got established in their businesses, and when their wives acquired maids or children old enough to take care of themselves, boredom often set in, and there was new-found time, energy and resources for the kind of experimentation that became the subject for so many sensational novels and movies.

Although I had been born sort of half in New Canaan I was also something of a misfit. For one thing, my house, beautiful as it was, seemed more burden than pleasure, and far from getting a bigger one, I kept hoping I could find one which would require less money and less work. For another thing, I soon came to detest a way of life which required me to travel almost a hundred miles a day. Enthusiasts said that some trains could get you from New Canaan to New York in little more than an hour, but it actually took at least two hours to get from the door of my house to the door of my office. Even before I started doing any writing of my own, I was often away from home from 7 A.M. to 7 P.M. A system like that was hell on marriage and relationships with children. My wife found it impossible to understand what I did in New York all day long. I wasn't really a reporter any more and I wasn't really an educator. I was just a man who woke up with nightmares sometimes, screaming, "Better schools make better communities, better schools make better communities!" She could not understand why I hated a job which continued to pay fairly well and to subject me to few of the strains about which the advertising men amongst our friends complained. Elise was sympathetic to my idea of saving enough money to take a year off to write a novel, but she was far too intelligent to imagine that such a gamble was smart for a man with three children. One legitimate complaint she had against me was that I hated either giving or going to cocktail parties. A supremely social being who could have a good time without drinking anything, Elise genuinely loved parties as a mechanism for building up a large group of close friends much like the one she had grown up with in West Newton and Boston. A misanthrope, I begrudged the time I had to take from my typewriter, and so many tensions were building within me that I found it almost impossible to go to drinking parties without getting drunk. Somehow the dreams of marriage which had kept Elise and me writing letters to each other almost every day during the four years I spent at sea during World War II, were fading into a kind of reality neither of us had imagined. I developed asthma, and when my wife went to a doctor, he told her she was suffering from simple exhaustion. One reason might have been that she did not agree with me that keeping up the lawn and house was not important. Along with trying to care for three babes in arms, she was often out there cutting the grass or plastering the living room walls, which tended to crumble under places where the roof leaked.

After we had lived about two years in the little house on White Oak Shade Road, I did two things which would have infuriated almost any wife, but which seemed sensible to me at the time. I talked Elise into selling our charming, if rotting Colonial cottage and buying a cheaper but more substantial house in a less fashionable part of town. What we were doing was trading charm for practicality, but charm in any form always meant a great deal to Elise, and it was a little embarrassing to move down in the real estate world while most of our friends were moving up. I also decided, more or less on the spur of the moment, to buy a boat. My idea was that all work and no play were making me a dull boy indeed. The little cabin of the boat I had in mind would make a quiet place for me to work, and when I wasn't working, the boat would provide a sport which the whole family could enjoy. These were the things I said, but the real reason I bought the boat was that I had loved boats all my life, and had fallen in love with an ancient Friendship sloop near my grandmother's house in Mystic, Connecticut. Boats were one thing I had known since early childhood and had learned more about during my four years in the coast guard. The children were getting old enough to enjoy a sail, and after being a subordinate in my office and the subordinate which almost every commuting husband is in his home, I guess I ached for twenty-eight feet of space where I was undisputed master.

Perhaps because she had been born into a family of naval officers, my mother always understood my passion for the sea. My need for a boat was the kind of emergency she could understand, and although it was against her principles and hard on her budget to give money to relatives, she offered to lend me part of the twenty-five hundred dollars that the ancient sloop cost. When I showed the boat to Elise, even she, who had never liked boats, became enthusiastic, for the *Yankee Trader*, which the old vessel was called, had undeniable charm for even a landsman. Those Friendship sloops were built in the town of Friendship, Maine, in the early 1900s as lobster boats, and they had—in miniature—the lines of a clipper ship. This one was painted a very dark green with a red boot top along the waterline. There was plenty of room in the cockpit for three sleeping bags, and a cozy cabin offered two bunks and a galley.

My wife's father, Carl Pickhardt, an investment banker whose hobbies were gardening and woodworking, had never had much use for boats, but he saw the beauty in this one. He often drove from West Newton to Mystic to help me get the old sloop ready, and he carved a beautiful gold eagle to put on her stern. The big cockpit made a good playpen for the children, and while the boat was moored in a quiet harbor, my wife seemed to enjoy fitting out the galley. I fancied that the old sloop actually might offer many hours which would bring the family together.

Late in May I had a three-day weekend, and Elise, her father and I left the children with a sitter and prepared to sail the *Yankee Trader* from Mystic to Norwalk, where I intended to keep her. As he often did, my father-in-law arrived with several boxes full of good food and liquor. After these had been stowed, I started the little auxiliary engine, took the big tiller in my hand, and asked the manager of the boatyard to cast us off. It was a cold day with a brisk fair wind, but I did not expect any rough weather in Long Island Sound. Before leaving the harbor we hoisted the big gaff-rigged mainsail, and Elise seemed to enjoy holding the tiller while her father and I hauled away at the halyards. When I turned the motor off, there was that good feeling of slipping silently through the water.

"This is wonderful," Elise said, and her father jovially opened some bottles of beer.

Ten minutes later we sailed past the headlands of the harbor and paid off on our course almost dead before the wind. The swell wasn't bad, but it was big enough to make the sloop roll sufficiently to dip the end of her big main boom occasionally, which made the blocks of the main sheet rattle and bang. The planks and frames of the old hull creaked. Elise said she felt cold and went below. Soon afterward we sailed into a bank of heavy fog from which we emerged only to enter another one which apparently filled the whole Sound. When Elise stuck her head up the hatch, she said, "I can't see *anything!*"

"No danger," I said. "I have a good compass, and we're picking up buoys every mile or so."

"It doesn't look as though there's any land at all," she said.

Although the wind did not blow away the fog, it increased, and soon we were bowling along at a good six knots, but rolling our scuppers under. Undaunted, Elise's father sat with a blanket tucked up to his chin in the cockpit and sipped his beer. His daughter came on deck, crawled to the rail and was seasick.

"Can't you *stop* this thing?" she asked. "Can't you put in somewhere?"

"In a few hours we can make New Haven," I said. "I like to pick a well-marked port like that to enter in heavy fog."

"A few *hours!*" she said in desperation, and again went below. As she disappeared into the companionway, I saw that her face was not only pale but had almost appeared to lose shape because of fear.

"There's no danger!" I called. "No danger at all. We used to spend months in fog like this on the Greenland Patrol."

Her only answer was a groan. If I had had any sense, I would have anchored in the shelter of a nearby island or felt my way into the closest harbor, but I had my heart set on New Haven, where we could easily tie the boat up and get a train home to wait for better weather. My navigation did prove accurate, and well before dark we tied up at a snug wharf in the inner part of New Haven harbor. I expected compliments on my seamanship, but as we neared shore, Elise said, "Let me off of this thing and never ask me to go back on it again!"

The children, it soon turned out, were too young to enjoy a boat and hated wearing life preservers and being yelled at about the danger of getting their fingers caught in blocks. That summer the family took a few sails with me on calm days, but for the most part, the boat turned out to be a place where I went to think and write alone. Elise busied herself making curtains and giving as much charm as possible to the plain old house we had bought. She became active on a committee which formed a nursery school and started to do a lot of painting and drawing under the guidance of her older brother, the artist, who visited us occasionally. Looking back, I think that both my wife and I were very lonely, but we didn't admit it or talk about it. Marriage, it seemed, often turned out like this, with two people traveling parallel lines that were close but never met. I told myself that things were bound to get better, when I really got started on my writing and did not have to hold a nine-to-five job.

The winter after I bought the boat I drove to a convention of school superintendents at Atlantic City, where the National Citizens Commission for the Public Schools was going to explain its activities or lack of them. What school superintendents talk about most of the time is budgets and bond issues, and I had to listen to a great many boring speeches, some of which I had written myself for our members. On the way home my car got a flat tire. Fortunately I was near a filling station, and I left it there to be fixed. Next to the filling station was a small resort hotel with a bar. It was a cold rainy day and the bar was deserted, except for a pretty young Italian woman who sat on a stool near the cash register. I ordered a beer. The woman had very large brown eyes, long black hair and a friendly if rueful sort of smile. I guessed that she was about twenty-five years old.

"Not much of a day, is it?" she asked as she put my glass in front of me.

"Not much."

"Are you staying around here or just driving through?"

"Just driving. They're fixing my car at the garage."

She sighed.

"This is a hell of a place in the winter," she said. "My mother owns this place. She took off to Florida and left me with it. My husband was killed in the war."

"I'm sorry," I said awkwardly.

"Were you in the war?"

"Yes."

"Well, you got back, anyway. My husband, Jack, was a paratrooper. He got it in Holland. One of his buddies said he was shot before he even hit the ground, never had a chance at all, but didn't suffer."

"That's better than the way it was with some," I said.

"Are you married?" she asked.

"Yes."

"Kids?"

"Three."

"That's the way I imagined it would be with us. I should get married again, but since the war, they're not many guys around here. This place used to be packed day and night with soldiers and sailors."

"Times have sure changed," I said, thinking how strange it was that I was half wishing to be back in the war again. God knows, there were a lot of terrible things about the war, but aboard the small ships where I served, there was a lot of companionship and there was always a sense of purpose, even if it was just keeping the ship afloat and getting home alive to the blissful existence which we were all so sure awaited us.

The girl went over and put a quarter in a jukebox. She played a record I had not heard in years, "It's Been a Long, Long Time," a Tin Pan Alley song turned to gold by nostalgia.

"I always liked that record," she said. "I won't let them take it out."

"It's a good song."

"Are you hungry? I got some good meatballs and fresh Italian bread."

I found I was hungry. She produced a bottle of chianti. After a few glasses of it, she showed me a tinted photograph of her husband, a thin young corporal in paratrooper boots.

"The truth is, I can't even remember what he was like any more," she said. "Do you have a picture of your wife?"

I was embarrassed to reply that I did not. During the war I had carried a whole wallet full of them, but somehow money and credit cards had taken their place.

"You don't look like a happy guy," she said a few minutes later. "I guess maybe marriage isn't always what it's cracked up to be."

"Not always."

There was a moment of silence while we drank the wine.

"I'm glad you don't complain about your wife," she said. "I hate guys who do that."

"I have nothing to complain about."

"Your job then. Don't you like that?"

"What do you mean?"

"I mean you look about as miserable as I feel."

I couldn't think of a damn thing to say that wouldn't be a lie or sound fatuous. "How can you tell?" I asked finally.

"Hell, anybody can see that. I can always tell whether a guy is happy or not right away. I don't even have to look at his face. I can tell by the way he walks. I don't see many happy guys come in here. There must be something awfully wrong somewhere."

We finished the bottle of wine. Getting up, she went to a window.

"The rain is turning to sleet," she said. "The driving will be rotten. If you want to spend the night, I have a room upstairs."

"I have to be getting home."

"It wouldn't cost you anything," she said, and to my surprise blushed.

"I know," I said, and added, "If I did stay, maybe I'd never want to leave, and think what a mess I'd be in."

She laughed and accepted money for the beer and food, but not the wine.

"It gets so lonely here I sometimes go a little crazy," she said. "Go home. And drive careful. You're the first nice guy I've met in weeks."

"That's the nicest thing said to me in weeks."

As I climbed into my car and drove away, I had the distinct impression that I would always regret leaving that girl, despite my whole Puritan up-bringing and the long established love I had for my wife, which always had made infidelity almost unthinkable. That girl had been offering some-thing which my wife and I had lost track of for a long time. At its lowest level it might be no more than mutual admiration, sympathy and the absence of the hostility that grows with conflicting goals in a marriage. Twice I almost turned back to that bar, but I sensed some fragility in myself. A lot of my Puritanism was really self-protection, a defense against emotions which got too intense at all the wrong times. In a sense I had been telling that pretty girl the truth when I said I was afraid to stay because I might never want to leave, and then where would I be? The solution to my problems obviously lay not in nights with lonely girls met in taverns, but in straightening out my situation at home. As I drove carefully over icy highways back to New Canaan, I began seriously plan-ning to get an advance from some publisher and to spend a year trying to write a novel. If the book didn't turn out to be any good, I would at least know that I had not failed from lack of courage. If it succeeded enough to allow me to make a living on my own typewriter on my own time, maybe my wife and I could heal some of the invisible wounds we had in-flicted on each other—wounds that at least were invisible to most, but not to a bar girl with penetrating eyes. Maybe if I wrote a book that sold a lot of copies I could buy Elise the kind of house she wanted which, I suspected, was a replica of the big Colonial house in which she had been raised in West Newton. Maybe she could get someone to help her with the children and devote more time to her drawing and painting. It hit me with a shock to recall that her own self-portraits always looked as sad as my face had appeared to that pretty girl in the bar. Looking back, it seems naïve for me to have thought that the writing of a book could cure all our ills, but it was partly that belief which soon caused me to give up a good job and risk everything on my ability to write a successful novel despite the fact that I knew perfectly well that most novels are never even published, and first-hand that those which do get into print rarely make the writer enough money to live for more than a few months.

21

My decision to leave the school commission was delayed by a man whom
I shall here call Bobbie Anderson, who walked into my office like a ghost
of my future self if I wasn't careful. Like me, Bobbie had been through
World War II and had started out as a newspaper reporter. Like me he
had written magazine fiction on stolen office time, during evenings and
weekends. He had been ahead of me, however, in that he had already
saved enough money to spend a year in Paris trying to write a novel.
He was a short thin man with an engaging spaniel quality of wanting to
be liked.

"In Paris I had everything necessary to write a great novel," he said.
"I had an apartment on the left bank. I had a great girl. All I lacked was
talent and a subject. So when I ran out of money, I came back here. Do
you have any idea where I can find a job?"

I arranged to have our school commission hire him as a publicity man.
The commission was beginning to give dinners and hold meetings in
large cities all over the nation to remind people that better schools make
better communities and to urge the citizens to form committees to answer their own educational problems. Maximum publicity was wanted,
and I thought that Bobbie Anderson would have more than the necessary
skills.

The trouble with Bobbie was that he was such a natural humorist that
I kept forgetting that he was fundamentally in trouble.

"I got married once," he said. "She was a teacher. We had a big
wedding ceremony, but I never could get used to the idea that she was
my wife. I like to spend a lot of my evenings in bars, and when I got
home late one night, she gave me a terrible lecture.

" 'Just who the hell do you think you are?' I asked her. 'The way you
talk, you'd think we were married. What makes you think you're my
wife?'

" 'We *are* married,' she said. 'And nothing else makes me think I'm your
wife.' I suddenly felt very sorry for her, for both of us I guess. Marriage
had been sort of like a vaccination that didn't take. We split up and I
hear she married a man who loves her. Same old story . . . I didn't have
the talent or the subject."

Bobbie's ambition, like that of many middle-aged, divorced men looking for a way out of their *weltschmerz*, was to meet as many beautiful young women in New York as possible. He didn't believe me when I said I had no idea how one would set out to meet beautiful girls in the city—I hardly qualified as a young man about town. Undaunted, he spent much of his salary on renting and fixing up an elaborate bachelor's apartment.

"I'm having no luck at all," he confided to me a few weeks later. "I even tried joining a church, for God's sake"—he smiled—"but the girls I met there were all very religious. I've toured about half the bars in New York, and most of the girls I find there are drunk. Do you think I would be arrested if I became a sandwich man and walked around with a sign saying, 'I WANT TO MEET A GIRL'?"

I thought his problem was solved a few days later when he went to a large city on the West Coast to arrange some publicity for us and fell in love with a young woman in a newspaper office. As soon as I arrived to help him make arrangements for the meetings, he told me about her.

"She's marvelous!" he said. "Intelligent! Beautiful! But she has sort of a strange history."

The lady, he said, had been born in Germany, and had married a German officer who had been killed on the Russian front. Later she had become engaged to an American Army Air Force pilot, who had returned to his home on the West Coast of the United States to find a job and make arrangements for their wedding. Before she could join him, the pilot shot himself—either by accident or on purpose, no one knew. The man's heartbroken parents asked the German girl to come over anyway and live with them as a daughter. The father of the pilot was an editor of the paper where the girl now worked.

Touched by this story and much moved by the lady's charms, Bobbie acted like a foolish young boy in love for the first time. Before he had known the girl much more than a week, he proposed to her and borrowed money to buy her an enormous engagement ring. When it came time for him to return to New York, he kept finding excuses to return to the West Coast. Plans were made for a wedding within three months, which they had decided to be a sensible waiting period.

On a cold April day which I shall never forget, Bobbie asked me to have luncheon with him at a small French restaurant near our office in New York. He seemed agitated, and I thought he was worried about his job of representing us at a national meeting of publishers, which was being held at the Waldorf-Astoria that afternoon. No, that task did not worry him at all, he said when we had ordered martinis. He was scared to death by the thought of his approaching wedding. Most prospective bridegrooms get the jitters at one time or another, I replied. No, he said, this was different. What did I really think of his German girl?

190

I reminded him that I had met her only once, but that she had seemed charming.

"I am becoming very suspicious of her," he said, tossed down his martini and ordered another.

"Why?" I asked.

"That newspaper editor, the father of the guy she was supposed to marry, acts very strange whenever I come to take her out. I think she's been his mistress ever since she came to this country."

"Do you have any real evidence for believing that?"

"It's just a feeling, the way she acts and he acts."

"If it's true, it's obviously an arrangement that she's trying to get out of," I said. "She must have been lonely when she first came over here. Such things can happen. Neither of you are kids. Even if she did have some sort of relationship with the old man, would that have to change everything?"

"I could never marry another man's mistress," he said with dignity, and ordered another martini.

"I didn't know that Chicago newspapermen were such Puritans," I said, and I have often wished that I had thought of some more compassionate reply.

Bobbie was quite drunk when he left the luncheon table, but I thought he could handle himself well enough to talk to the newspaper publishers at the Waldorf. One of the things I shall always regret is that I did not realize how disturbed he was and make him go home. I never saw him alive again, but I heard what happened.

At the Waldorf he kept on drinking, regardless of the fact that he was on duty and had never appeared to be an alcoholic. He was seen staggering down corridors, fending himself off the walls. Sometime late in the afternoon he took the elevator down to the main lobby and staggering very fast, headed for the stairs at the Park Avenue entrance. There he fell and hit his head on the marble floor at the bottom. Thinking he was simply drunk, many people passed his body without doing anything. Something like an hour went by before an ambulance was called to take him to a hospital. There it was discovered that he had fractured the base of his skull and was quickly dying.

"You ought to put Bobbie in a novel," one of the commission employees said to me after the funeral, which was attended by the German lady— a dignified woman of great beauty who while still relatively young had lost a husband and two American fiancés who came to bizarre ends.

"Novels are supposed to make sense," I replied bitterly. "That's why they almost never can honestly be based on what people call 'real life.'"

22

The gloom with which Bobbie's death left me was lightened a little when Roy Larsen called me into his office at Time, Inc., and without preamble said he wanted me to help Eddie Albert, the actor, to write a speech about sex education. I had admired Eddie Albert in the movies, but I had never met him, and I had no idea why he wanted to give a speech about sex education, a subject which always had confused me, since I had received very little of it in my youth and in my adult life knew it only as a subject for terrible fights in the PTA's of small towns and suburbs. Doing as I was told, however, I went to the luxurious hotel in New York where Eddie Albert was staying and presented myself to offer my services. Eddie looked exactly as he did in films and so did his pretty wife, the actress, Margo.

"Roy says you write good speeches," Eddie began.

"It's become sort of a specialty of my house," I replied.

"Well, I need a good speech to give before a big meeting of school superintendents," Eddie continued. "I'm in trouble and I have to get out of it."

"What kind of trouble are you in?" I asked.

"Margo here and I have both been very serious about the subject of sex education for a long while," Eddie said, pacing up and down the room while his wife curled up on a couch. "Margo was educated in convents and went directly from them to nightclubs when she started to work as a dancer. We both are very much aware of the danger of ignorance."

He went on to explain that in his opinion most parents get all upset when they try to talk about sex with their children. Public school teachers, many of whom are unmarried, also have a difficult time when asked to give courses about sex. The solution, Eddie thought, was an educational movie which could be shown at schools everywhere. He believed in this so much that he had spent a great deal of his own money in producing one. The trouble was in getting school administrators to accept it. A lot of school people refused to take an actor like Eddie Albert seriously when he entered the field of education. There were also a lot of strident complaints from a few of the teachers to whom he had shown the film. One lady had fainted when confronted by a diagram of a penis which stretched across a screen forty feet wide, and he was thinking of taking that part out, but the rest of the film was undoubtedly in good taste and he wanted it shown.

There was no doubt about the sincerity of Eddie Albert and Margo, and when they screened the film for me, I found myself wishing that I had seen it when I was about twelve years old. Everything was explained so simply and warmly that I found myself wondering why millions of books are sold every year to people who keep wanting to learn more about how to go to bed with each other. This, of course, was a few years before the time when books and magazines began making people feel inferior if they didn't turn sexual intercourse into a mixture of a Roman banquet and a professional wrestling match. Eddie Albert's film just showed people how to make love and how children are born. Still, I knew that he was headed for trouble. The only thing that can make a school superintendent angrier than a failed bond issue is the suggestion that he get parents fighting about the mildest exposition of human reproduction, never mind a fairly explicit film. I told Eddie that I thought he would find the school superintendents less than enthusiastic, but I would write the best speech I could.

For two weeks I worked on that speech almost day and night. It came out as an impassioned plea for enlightenment, a damnation of ignorance and a sales pitch for film as an impersonal way to present a subject which most people found difficult. Albert made some improvements and gave the speech before a huge crowd of school people with all the skill of a fine actor talking from the heart. A few schools decided to show the film, but it quickly slipped into oblivion. Today the law allows magazines and movies which rightfully or wrongfully extol almost everything I was brought up to believe to be either sick or sinful, but in countless schools parents still go hysterical at the thought of teachers telling children how life begins.

Those well-meaning people who oppose sex education in the schools could be more helpful if they started worrying about just plain sex in the schools—which goes on whether or not there is formal instruction on sex in the classroom. It is not unusual for about a third of the senior girls in many high schools to be pregnant at graduation, and pregnancy is not unusual all the way down to the freshman class. Statistically, teenagers who get married have a high divorce rate and many studies illustrate the obvious fact that children make pathetic parents. Sex education does not cause pregnancy—as many irate parents appear to believe— despite the fact that schools with no sex education have a high rate of pregnancy. Ignorance causes most juvenile pregnancy, as most pregnant children can testify. Ordering children simply to avoid sex commonly does not work. . . . Almost all children are told that.

I can remember the exact moment when I finally made up my mind that I could not work for the school commission any longer. A new billboard had been erected down near Canal Street in Manhattan with the slogan, "Better Schools Make Better Communities." For publicity purposes a picture was to be taken of Roy Larsen, the chairman of the school commission, and another imposing-looking man who was chairman of the Outdoor Advertising Council—with the billboard in the background. As he often did on such occasions, Roy asked me to go along with him, and we drove down to Canal Street in a large limousine. Soon another large limousine arrived with the Outdoor Advertising executive, who also had a young man in a gray flannel suit with him. It was a cold windy day. The billboard with the slogan about better schools making better communities looked a little ironic, because it had been erected on a slum lot and a group of derelicts was leaning against the bottom of it passing a bottle of wine back and forth. The Outdoor Advertising executive's young man helped the camera crew to chase these unwanted ghosts away. He took his boss's briefcase and I took Roy's briefcase as the two leaders stood up before the sign. While the cameraman fiddled with his lenses, the Outdoor Advertising executive's young man realized that the leaders would look better if photographed without hats. Leaping forward, he took his employer's hat and also Roy's. When he returned to my side, I felt outdone.

"Do you mind if I hold my man's hat?" I asked.

"Of course not," he said gravely, and passed me the fedora.

Something happened to me then without clear reason and I began to laugh. At first I was able to control my mirth, but finally it burst out in most unmannerly fashion and all the other people there looked at me strangely. When the photographer had finished, the executives got back in their limousines and the derelicts returned to the billboard, which sheltered them from the wind.

"What was so funny?" Roy asked.

"I don't know," I said, handing him back his hat. "I guess maybe this seems a strange place for that billboard."

"A lot of people drive by here," Roy said with dignity, and put on his hat.

I'll start writing to book publishers tomorrow and see if I can get an advance for a novel, I thought. It wasn't so much that I really felt I had a good novel to write. I just didn't see any other way to avoid standing by such billboards on tragic streets humbly asking if I could hold my man's hat.

In the early 1950s—or perhaps anytime—it was not easy for a young man who had only one slender novel and a dozen or so magazine pieces to his credit to get much of an advance. Finding that a great many editors did not care whether I had written a novel or not, I concentrated on my stories for *The New Yorker*, and finally sold ten in one year. Most of the stories were slight pieces about the war and life at home immediately after it. I told publishers that I wanted to weave that basic material into a substantial novel, but no one offered me more than thirty-five hundred dollars for a contract, and I didn't see how I was going to support a family long enough on that to write much of a book. Of course I could sell the *Yankee Trader* and maybe get a bigger mortgage on the house, but, though I don't think I suspected it at the time, an advance meant more than money to me. A large advance would mean that some publisher had confidence in me, might devote some time to helping me edit my book, and might make some special effort to sell it. At the age of thirty-one, which I was then, I fancied I knew a great deal about the publishing business. Of course I had no idea at all of the rapidity with which it changes nor of the enormous effect one powerful editor or publisher can have on a huge company.

One young editor of a large company said he could get me a good advance, but it would have to be paid out a little at a time as each chapter of the novel was finished and examined. This, I thought, would lead to a year of perpetual crisis, at best. Another editor offered a smaller advance, but said he would publish a collection of my magazine pieces. At least on the surface my ego was mammoth, but at heart I knew that the magazine stories were not substantial enough to be made into a book, and I suspected that collections of short stories rarely do well in the marketplace and could not be expected to help me make enough money to live. I had almost given up hope of finding a way to spend even a few months writing full-time when I got a letter from Richard L. Simon, the president of Simon and Schuster, a company I had always admired. Written by hand in green ink, it said simply, "I hear you want to write a book. Why don't you come up and see me?"

Before this I had dealt only with junior editors, and I had not even approached Simon and Schuster because someone had told me that they liked to deal mostly with established authors. Joyfully I assumed that Mr. Simon had read some of my *New Yorker* stuff or my forgotten little novel and had become spellbound. I telephoned him immediately, and he told me, casually, that if I had the time, why not come right on up and see him?

The offices of Simon and Schuster were only four blocks from the office of our school commission, and I almost ran the whole way, up Fifth Avenue. A secretary ushered me into Mr. Simon's office, which looked much like Roy Larsen's headquarters at Time, Inc., a large room with windows overlooking the city and expensive-looking, if simple, furniture. Simon himself was one of the most impressive-appearing men I had ever met. He was thin, six feet five inches tall, dressed like a preoccupied college professor, and full of so much nervous energy that he kept snapping his fingers. He looked down at me from the majesty of his great height, smiled and said, "I hear you're a pretty good writer. They're hard to find."

"What pieces of mine have you read?" I asked, defensively. I should have said, Thank you, and shut up.

To my astonishment he lay down on a couch in the corner of the room and stared at the ceiling for a moment before answering.

"Actually I haven't read anything you've written," he said, "but Roy Larsen says you're a person who might do something someday, and Roy has good judgment. Generally I tend to deal more in men than in manuscripts."

Larsen had never said anything to me about my possibilities for the future, and I had never told him that I wanted to write a book. My sense of astonishment was mixed with gratitude.

"Why don't you just go ahead and write your book?" Simon asked.

"I need time and that means I need money. I've been hoping to get an advance."

"I hear that you've sort of been shopping around the other publishers," Simon said. "That's no way to do it."

"What should I do?"

"How long will it take you to write this book?"

"About a year, I think."

"How much will it cost you to live for a year?"

"I have three children. We might get by on ten thousand."

"How much have you got in the bank?"

"Very little. I'd have to check."

"Figure out how much you need. I'll advance it to you. Then try to forget about money and concentrate on your book."

"Thank you," I said, hardly believing my good fortune.

"I'll have some of my people draw up a contract. Do you have an agent?"

An old man who had helped my father had been acting as my agent. I gave Simon his name.

"I'll get in touch with him," Simon said. "I hope you can get to work as soon as possible. If you get into any kind of trouble, either with the manuscript or with finances, come to me. My job is to help writers finish books."

"I will," I said.

"Meanwhile drop in and see me at my place out in Stamford whenever you feel like it. I like to know the men I'm working with. We have a pool and tennis courts. Quite a few writers come there whom you might want to meet."

"Thank you," I said again.

He got up from the couch, took my hand in his enormous one, smiled again and said, "I bet we get a darn good book. I have a nose for talent. I've based my business on it. I have a feeling that everything is going to turn out great!"

Except for a few kind words that had come with small checks from *The New Yorker*, I had never had any real encouragement before. To my chagrin I found myself near the point of tears. Thanking him again, I sort of floated out of his office to the elevators. I had reached Fifth Avenue before I realized that he had never asked me what kind of book I planned to write. Apparently Roy Larsen's recommendation had been enough. As Dick Simon had said, he really didn't deal in manuscripts. He relied on his judgment of men, and the opinions of men he respected. I had had a good many snide thoughts about Roy Larsen, Time, Inc., and the school commission. Whoever would have thought . . . ?

When I got home that night I was so happy it didn't occur to me that few wives with three children would be overjoyed by the news that their husband was quitting a good steady job with the promise of only enough money to live for a year which would be spent on the great gamble of writing a novel. Elise took the announcement with good grace, though she looked worried and asked if I could get a leave of absence from the school commission. I had already explored that possibility, and had been told that I would have to be replaced when I left, and there was no way of keeping my old job on ice.

"What will we do if the book doesn't work out?" my wife asked.

"It's bound to," I said. "Guys like Dick Simon don't lay out thousands of dollars for no reason. He knows what he's doing and so do I."

After winding up my affairs at the school commission, where most of my friends thought I was crazy, I rented a room in an attic near our house in New Canaan to assure perfect peace and quiet. I put my typewriter on an old table there, bought two reams of paper and a large supply of carbons. Instead of getting on the early train to New York the next morning, I walked up to my silent office and set out to enjoy my favorite dream, a whole year in which I had nothing to do but write one book.

It took only about two weeks for the dream to turn into a nightmare. The first chapters I wrote were so bad that they went straight from the typewriter to the wastepaper basket. Writing badly was torture enough, but soon the day came when I couldn't think of anything at all worth putting into words. The hope that I could somehow expand and fit together the magazine pieces I had written obviously was false. They had no characters and no situations in common. When I tried to outline one long narrative about my experiences in the war and my work in New York, I seemed to have lived a very dull life that could not be translated into any kind of drama at all. My mind went blank every time I put my fingers on the keys of the typewriter and a deep depression settled over me which made nothing I could remember or imagine seem in the least interesting, never mind exciting. The panic caused by the apparent loss of my ability to write was increased by the thought that every month our bank account grew slimmer.

I had read enough about the lives of writers to know that something called a "block" could happen, and I tried to pretend that before long my mind would be teeming with ideas, but at heart I had a terrible conviction that I could never write a book of any kind, much less a good one, and that my ambitions had been inherited from my parents rather than grown from the consciousness of any real ability. Much against my will, I kept remembering my friend Bobbie, who said he had gone to Paris to write a novel, only to find that he had everything but talent and a subject.

Every morning I walked up to my attic room, paced, thought, stared at the typewriter for ten hours, and then walked back to my house. I tried to maintain a facade of confidence, but my wife knew me too well to be fooled. My depression was catching and soon the two of us were struggling with the same sense of disaster.

My mother occasionally came out to visit us, but she had the misfortune of not being well that year either. Perhaps because she lived alone so much of the time, my mother's vice and virtue was almost non-stop talking about the family's past, which should have interested me as a novelist, but which was sad enough to increase my depression. Apparently we had been nutty people as far back as anybody could remember, eccentrics who occasionally did brilliant things, but who usually ended up in disaster.

After about a month of failing to write anything, I took Dick Simon up on his offer to visit him at his summer home in Stamford. I had thought of myself as being raised in rather opulent surroundings, but I had never seen anything like the luxury of Dick's estate, which had so many buildings that it seemed to me to be more like a village than one home. Dick greeted the glum news that I had accomplished nothing in my first four weeks with imperturbable cheer and introduced me to a group of people by the pool who seemed to me to have entered the Utopia of successful writers, from which I probably would be forever barred. Most of the names of those minor celebrities of that day have been half-forgotten now. Among them was John Crosby, who wrote a brilliant column on television for the New York *Herald Tribune*, and Jerome Weidner, whose books on the garment center endure as minor classics. Not all the guests were literary. Jackie Robinson, the baseball player, was there with his beautiful wife and children, and there were several television performers who were celebrities at the time. The star attractions, however, were the members of Dick's family. His wife, Andrea, who seemed to be a great earth mother, embraced my wife like a long-lost child. Dick's two elder teenage daughters were conspicuously beautiful. Only Carlie, who is nowadays such a famous folk singer, seemed at the age of eleven or twelve to be plain.

I learned later that Dick Simon had more troubles than most people do, both in his office and in other aspects of his life, but during those first visits I paid him at Stamford, he seemed the very embodiment of all kinds of success. The warmth of his and Andrea's hospitality scared me a little because I did not feel I had earned it, and I feared it would disappear as soon as Dick found I never was going to be able to write a book. Like a sinner in heaven, I felt out of place among all the glittering people who gathered around Dick's pool, and I didn't take him up on his invitation to come over every weekend.

23

The only good part about these months I spent vainly trying to pull a novel out of myself was that I got to know my children better. Lisa, who was six, and Becky, who was only a year and two weeks younger, looked alike as two daffodils, and David, at four and a half, was such a solemn, silent little boy that I didn't know whether he was unnaturally wise or too scared to talk. After hours of failing to fill blank paper in a typewriter, it was fun to take walks with the children, or just roll on a big double bed with them, hugging and laughing. I never found much to say to young children, but our bodies seemed able to communicate joy when that was a scarce commodity in our house. In those dark days my children seemed my only accomplishment, but they also made the idea of trying to live without a steady job all the more terrifying. At six, Lisa was already beginning to notice that our house was nowhere near as grand as those of her friends at school, and I heard the daughter of an acquaintance of mine ask her why we drove such a funny old car. I saw the hurt look in Lisa's eyes and heard her retort that she loved our car. If the materialism of the suburbs didn't get to men and women directly, it got at them through their children. Most of my neighbors had moved to the suburbs "for the sake of the children," and many of them thought or imagined that they were working for bigger homes, membership in the country club, and all the rest only in order to give their children advantages that they, the parents, had never had. Now, twenty years later, it gives me a peculiar feeling to reflect that many of those children grew up to be rebels against their suburban parents and their apparently rampant materialism—itself the basis of the well-being against which they had the luxury of rebelling.

In those bleak months during which I tried vainly to write without holding a steady job, I suppose I was, despite early gray flannel, in some ways a kind of hippie who had come along a generation too soon. Perhaps because my parents had brought me up in fairly handsome houses, I did not have the illusion that fancy real estate offered mysterious opportunities for happiness. I had no ambition to join the country club, which—as New Canaan grew—necessarily became more selective in choosing new members. My parents had belonged to that country club in the days when almost anyone who lived nearby could join it, and they had quit it because at one wild party many of the guests had used their table knives to flip butter balls at the ceiling, where they stuck and dripped on the guests for the remainder of the evening. My mother said that one of her main memories of New Canaan was a room crowded with people in evening clothes on which butter was raining. That seemed to her to sum up the town; though I knew that was unfair, I came to agree with her opinion more as our money ran out and I felt that my family was more and more shunned. New Canaan is not a friendly town in which to go broke.

Although I tried not to mind the fact that invitations to parties which my wife had enjoyed receiving trickled to a halt as we stopped entertaining, I worried about my inability to save for the education of the children, the fact that I had almost no life insurance, and that unexpected bills from doctors and dentists kept piling up. There was always the comforting feeling that in an emergency, either my mother or my wife's parents could help, but though they all enjoyed the idea of having a writer in the family, I could not blame them for dreading the thought of being asked to support my entire brood for an indefinite period. We were all basically New Englanders, and our eleventh commandment was Support Thyself. The very rich or the very poor somehow had the freedom to break that commandment, especially if they aspired to be artists of some sort, but the people in my family and my wife's ranged from lower- to upper-middle class, and though they were kind enough not to say it, they clearly thought that a man who could not afford to support his own family was a bum. Some of them began asking me nervous questions about what I planned to do if my book did not "work out."

I tried to sell the *Yankee Trader*, but despite my long experience with boats, she turned out to be one of my many mistakes. Having fallen in love with her looks, I had not looked hard enough for dry rot. More careful purchasers found that her whole stern was growing soft under the beautiful gold eagle my father-in-law had made. To rid myself of the expense of the boat, I lent her to a cousin who had been to the Naval Academy, and offered to spend some time fixing her up.

To make our money last longer we mixed dry milk for the children and tried buying cut-rate groceries in bulk. I thought of asking Dick Simon for another advance, but did not see how any publisher, despite his kindness, could give more money to a man who produced nothing, not even a sample chapter or outline. In strict confidence I asked some old friends at the school commission if they knew of any job which might open up for me. None did. A rumor, which proved to be true, was spreading that the members of the school commission had decided they had done about all the good they could, and were planning to fold up the organization.

I made some timid inquiries amongst school and newspaper people I knew, but the fact seemed to be that I was sort of half a reporter, a quarter of an educator, and a quarter of a novelist with unrealistic aspirations. No personnel man seemed eager to hire such a person. My money was almost gone and I was at my wit's end when a letter arrived from a man I had met at a meeting of educators more than a year before. This man did not know that I had quit the school commission to try to write a book. He had recently become an administrator at the University of Buffalo and was looking for a public relations man for that institution. Would I like to be interviewed for the job?

Feeling that I was being saved by the hand of God, I immediately telephoned the University of Buffalo and arranged to go there the next day.

"I guess I ought to warn you," my friend said, "that the salary we have in mind is only eight thousand dollars a year, but you'll find that the living is cheaper here than near New York."

In the days when I had been working for the school commission and writing for magazines on the side, I had ended by making close to twenty thousand a year, but with nothing in my bank account, no job in sight and no ideas for stories or books in my head, I was in no mood to quibble. My only worry was that I might not be hired after the interview.

At the time I had been married to Elise for eleven years, and it is impossible to understand how little I knew her. Like me, she had been miserable during the months I had failed to write a novel, and I assumed that she would be as delighted as I by the chance for a new start in a new place. I forgot that some women have a very strong feeling for home and place which can become more powerful than ever when a marriage is strained. I had few friends in New Canaan who meant anything to me, but she had many. Furthermore, New Canaan was close enough to West Newton to permit frequent visits with her family. She had never been to Buffalo, but I think the name did not sound very civilized to her, and I believe the city seemed to her to be at the edge of a distant, hostile world.

"*Buffalo!*" she said to me in horror. "You mean we'd have to sell the house, take the children out of school and move out there *forever?*"

"I think we might like university life," I said. "If we stuck it out, it would solve one problem: the children could go to college free."

"My father used to go to Buffalo on business," she said. "He thought it was one of the ugliest cities he had ever seen—"

"Oh come on, every city has some nice parts," I countered, but my wife looked almost as she had aboard the *Yankee Trader* during the fog, as though all hope were gone. Nevertheless, she agreed with me that we had small choice, and that I better investigate the new opportunity.

The University of Buffalo was a private institution in those days and consisted mostly of some gray stone buildings on a bleak field on the edge of the city. Nevertheless, the "chancellor," as they called the man who headed it, and the various deans greeted me cordially. My job would be to distribute news of the university, help to raise funds, devise plans for better public relations, edit the catalogues of the university's fourteen colleges, help to supervise a student newspaper and a student magazine, and teach a course in writing. This seemed a lot, they knew, but they were trying to find the money to hire two women to help me. Because a lot of people were suspicious of public relations men in academic life, my title would be "director of information services."

Without asking many questions I accepted and agreed to report for work as soon as I could sell my house in New Canaan and find a place to live near the university.

"You mean you *committed* yourself?" my wife said when I got home.

"Don't make it sound as though I were entering a mental institution."

"Maybe you ought to. You haven't tried to find a job in Boston. I'm sure that dad and Sinny would help."

There was no way I could explain either to her or to myself why I did not want to live in Boston, despite some happy memories of my days at Harvard. Boston and Harvard always somehow made me feel unusually small.

My wife accepted the idea that I didn't like Boston with dutiful grace, but there was no getting away from the fact that I was saying I disapproved of everything she loved most. She had a bad cold and asked if she could go home to her parents for a rest while I saw to putting our house on the market and packing. A sitter was found to help me take care of the children, and I drove my wife to the train.

In those days houses sold fast in New Canaan, and within a few days I made a sale which gave us a small profit. Calling my wife, I asked her if she would like to fly to Buffalo to help me choose a house there.

"No," she said, her voice sounding oddly dead. "My cold is worse. I'll trust your judgment. Buy or rent whatever seems best."

A neighbor agreed to help the sitter with the children and I hurried to Buffalo. The friend who had offered me the job in the first place showed me a house in a nearby suburb which a real estate agent had recommended. With the bottom half built of granite blocks and the top half of brown clapboards, it stood on a spacious lot on a quiet street of substantial homes. Most of the interior was nicely paneled. It was by far the finest house which my wife and I had ever owned, and when I learned the price and mortgage arrangements, I realized that we would have enough cash left after buying it to give Dick Simon back his advance. A publisher's advance is legally nothing but a loan, and one thing which had been bothering me was the thought of going the rest of my life owing money to a man who had misplaced his trust in me. At that time the idea of my ever writing a novel seemed not only impossible, but crazy. I was vowing never to try fiction again.

Sure that my wife would like the house, I dashed back to New Canaan and gave her an enthusiastic description over the telephone.

"Fine," she said with that curious apathy in her voice. "I still don't feel very well and the doctor thinks I should rest for a few more days. Do you suppose you could get some professionals in to arrange for the packing and moving? Dad says he'll pay for it."

I did not like the idea of having professionals do all the packing and attempted to do much of it myself. The sitter who was taking care of the children slipped on the stairs, hurt her back, and quit. The neighbor who had been helping said that one of her own children was sick and she couldn't get over to our place very much. My own children all seemed to have colds. They kept crying a lot and asking for their mother.

With the house full of boxes and barrels, I soon got to the point where I couldn't find the clothing they needed nor the toys they wanted. My friend in Buffalo called to say that the deal for the house there was going through without trouble, and he hoped I could get on the job as soon as possible because the person I was replacing wanted to quit. At this point the children were all crying and arguing so much that I could barely hear him, but I promised to start my job as soon as I could. My daughter Lisa shouted from upstairs to say that David had just vomited. After cleaning up that mess, I couldn't find any new clothes for him and discovered that I had forgotten to turn on the clothes washer, which I had filled with garments from the day before. Wrapping David in an old flannel shirt of my own, I found that my nerves were beginning to give out, and hurriedly put in a call for my wife.

"I'm afraid you've just got to come home," I said.

"I'm not sure I can," she replied, and suddenly we both burst into tears. This did not reassure the children, and they joined the chorus. Hearing that, Elise took a deep breath and said, "I'll come right away. Dad will drive me."

"Thanks," I said, finding the one word hard to get out through my throat.

When Elise arrived five hours later, she looked sicker than I had ever seen her, and her father said he was worried because he had never seen her so depressed. With real courage but few words she comforted the children and started to finish up the packing, a job with which her father helped. I went up to the attic room which I had rented for the purpose of writing a novel, and sent Dick Simon a check with a brief note thanking him for his confidence in me, and regrets that it had been misplaced. For several months I had not been able to muster the courage to visit him, and I figured that I would never see him again.

The final packing took another twenty-four hours. Neighbors dropped in to say good-by, and the gathering was about as cheerful as a funeral with Elise as mournful as any widow. I seemed to myself to be the corpse.

"*Why* are you leaving?" a neighbor asked.

Tired of evasions, I said, "Because I tried to write a novel and found I couldn't."

Only a few minutes later there was a knock on the door. A special delivery messenger gave me a letter from Simon and Schuster. It contained my check to Dick torn in half and a note which said, "Don't worry because it takes time. I know a good writer when I see one, and I predict that you'll be world known inside of a few years. I don't want your money. I just want an option on your book whenever you finish it.

I know we're going to have a fine book much quicker than you think. That's the way it goes."

Those few lines hit me like an injection of the most powerful drug of all, a miracle drug which replaced despair with hope, defeat with self-confidence. Showing it to my wife, I said, "Don't worry. Once I get established in Buffalo, I'll write every night. Someday we'll get a book and then you can live anywhere you want!"

Elise's father was cheered by the letter.

"The man certainly must have confidence in you, or he wouldn't return your money," he said.

I went out and bought a bottle of Scotch. We finished our years in New Canaan with a real celebration. The next day as we drove to Buffalo I kept the torn check and Dick's letter in my pocket, and patted it every time I got a case of the doubts.

Years later people often asked me why I thought Dick Simon was a good publisher, and did I really think he could teach people to write novels? I never was able to explain convincingly that Dick's gifts of hope, self-confidence and enthusiasm backed by money which guaranteed their sincerity were worth more than any kind of editorial help. He worked with men, not manuscripts, and he helped men, not manuscripts. Once a writer with any talent at all really got on his feet, he told me once, the manuscript would take care of itself.

24

One of my jobs at the University of Buffalo was to advise the chancellor on the effect some of his decisions might have on the public. Why he thought I understood the public any better than he did, I never knew, but when he had a tough problem he often asked me down to his big, stately office and discussed his alternatives. He was a tall, thin man with an ascetic face who had a distinguished record as a scholar, but who had little experience at heading a university. He was one of the most moral men I had ever met, but as an administrator, he had a fatal weakness: he yearned to be liked by everyone associated with the university. Never could he really bring himself to face the fact that decisions which would please the conservative men who made up his board of trustees and who gave large sums of money to the university, were almost bound to infuriate the many members of his faculty who prided themselves on being liberals. It was also true that decisions which pleased the students rarely pleased anyone else. The alumni, many of whom wanted the college to have winning athletic teams even though we had almost no money to support them, contributed to the chancellor's troubles. Never had I met such a harried, unhappy man.

Those were the days when Senator Joseph McCarthy was terrorizing academic folk. Shortly after I arrived in Buffalo, one of our associate professors was asked to testify before a committee in Washington because his name had appeared on committees which had been declared un-American. The professor was a mild little man who did not appear to be much of a danger to the Republic, but many of the businessmen of Buffalo insisted that he be fired and said they never would give money to the university if he were kept. The faculty, almost to a man, rose to defend academic freedom. The associate professor was on tenure, the professors pointed out, and if he were fired, they would do everything possible to bring discredit on the university.

I had no knowledge of such matters, but the laws and customs concerning tenure seemed clear, and the people in Washington never proved that our man had done anything more than lend his name to some fairly innocuous committees, most of which had not been active since the Spanish Civil War. It seemed clear that we should refuse to fire the man, but we were in the middle of one of our incessant fund campaigns, and the chancellor wanted to do something to ease the anger of the rich conservatives who were calling for blood. As a result, he contrived a solution which infuriated everybody: he did not fire the man, but removed him from tenure so that he could be fired with relative ease if he ever slipped from grace again. Because I had just arrived, a lot of the professors blamed this decision on me, despite the fact that it was far more ingenious than anything I could have contrived, and the chancellor rarely took any advice I gave him anyway.

Before the echoes of this controversy had died away, the university's literary magazine published a short story about a priest being seduced by a prostitute. Buffalo is a predominantly Catholic city and soon all the telephones started to ring with indignant complaints and outraged promises to cancel schedules of contributions. This time the faculty arose to defend not only academic freedom but the freedom of the press. The story would cost the university hundreds of thousands of dollars, the chancellor figured, and it was all the harder to defend because it was badly written and in the worst possible taste. For fear of outraging the faculty, he did not criticize the story publicly or abolish the magazine, but somehow most of the copies of the edition with the story about the priest disappeared from the bookstore and newsstands. I am still not sure who accomplished this piece of business or how. Such decisive action was unlike the chancellor, and I certainly did not run around snitching magazines. Any one of a number of infuriated groups could have committed the deed, but the chancellor was blamed for book burning, and I was widely suspected of being his accomplice.

Not long after this debacle the student newspaper published an edition with an anti-Negro cartoon. That got a lot of people mad, and the whole issue of freedom of the press was raised again, this time mostly by the students. The Buffalo *Evening News*, the most powerful paper in the region, was not enthusiastic about either the troubles of the university nor the chancellor's attempts to solve them. Since both the editor and publisher of the *News* were trustees of the university, the chancellor rarely ignored them, and one of my jobs was to go to the stern old man who edited the big paper and explain our actions, or lack of them. Our chancellor had been hurt so much by the book-burning issue that he did nothing about the student newspaper except to give its editors a lecture, which infuriated them. While trying to please everyone, the chancellor succeeded in earning the contempt of a great many people. Sadly he told me that on the average, the presidents of universities last only about four years, and the time for him to resign was probably growing close. This scared me because I had been hired as one of his assistants, and if he went, there might well be a clean sweep of the administrative offices.

The fear of finding myself in a strange city with no job increased my energy to almost manic proportions. My mind seemed to work faster than it ever had before, and perhaps the fact that I had left New York and New Canaan gave me a better perspective of the life I had led there. Every morning I got up at about five-thirty and went to a typewriter we had put in a spare bedroom. Although my hands had seemed almost paralyzed while I had been trying to write full-time, they now flew over the keys with a life of their own, and the first pages of a novel which seemed to make at least a little sense began to appear. At nine I went to my office at the University, wrestled with the chancellor's problems, wrote newspaper releases about the university's activities, edited the catalogues and tried to teach a class of about twenty students how to write. When I got home at about five-thirty, I gulped my dinner and went back to my typewriter, where I worked happily until about one in the morning. In this way and in only about two weeks, I completed the first hundred pages of a novel about a harried suburban couple. My working title was *The Sky Watchers*, because even after the Second World War was over, some nervous people in Connecticut organized groups to stand on rooftops and keep an eye out for enemy planes. Hurriedly retyping and editing these pages, I mailed them to Dick

Simon. I did not have much confidence in them, and I expected that after a wait of two or three weeks, I would get a letter from Dick which might give me some advice on how to improve them. In my heart was the fear that he might say that I was so far off the track that there was not much point in continuing, and I was also frightened by the knowledge that I really had no clear idea of how to go on to the second hundred pages, never mind the third or fourth. Of course I had written many outlines, but I had made the sad discovery that I was the kind of writer who could not make an outline come alive, and just had to plunge ahead as best I could, keeping chapters which seemed to work and throwing away the rest.

I was so nervous when I mailed the manuscript that the idea of waiting two or three weeks for a response seemed torturous. To get my mind off it, I drank a good deal that night and struggled through the next day at the university with a terrible hangover. It was best to brace myself, I thought, for the worst news. If Dick didn't like the pages I had sent him, maybe I could try something entirely different, like science fiction.

I had quite a few drinks at lunch that day. When I got home that evening, my head ached and I poured myself a glass of the cheap port which had been my main sustenance. It was a little before six in the afternoon when the telephone rang. My wife answered.

"It's Dick Simon," she said. "He says the book is great and he wants to speak to you."

I grabbed the receiver.

"You've done exactly what I hoped you would do," Dick said. "Great stuff! Keep it up and I'm sure we'll have a best seller on our hands, and probably a movie too!"

After my experience with my first novel, which had sold only sixteen hundred copies, I had not allowed my dreams about my second attempt to grow very large, but Dick's words suddenly transported me from Buffalo to Key West or Cuba, where I would go fishing with Papa Hemingway for a few weeks before going to Hollywood, where I would write and maybe direct my own film to get it just right. I don't know what else Dick said, but when he had finished, I almost flew back to my typewriter. I pounded the keys so hard that night that the letter "e" flew off the part of the machine that hits the paper. Not wanting to waste the night, I went next door to a neighbor who, I knew, had an elaborate workshop in his cellar. He attempted to solder my "e" back, but when I started to work again, it flew off like a bumblebee. For the rest of the night I inserted each "e" by hand, and in the morning I took the last dollars from our savings account to buy a new typewriter. Nothing could be allowed to delay the arrival of my greatest triumph.

I worked so long at night that I wandered around the university in a daze during working hours. The two women who had been hired to help me had learned their jobs well and carried out almost all my duties except the task of going down to the chancellor's office and agonizing about the conflicting opinions of the university's supporters.

In another two weeks I had the second hundred pages done. They were terrible because there was no real action. My suburban couple just kept sitting around agonizing about their problems, but nothing ever seemed to happen to them. That seemed realistic for little had happened to the couples I had known in New Canaan, but somehow it did not make good drama. Reassuring myself with the thought that I was at least writing a highly realistic novel, I sent this second section off to Dick Simon. This time he took about forty-eight hours to call, which seemed to me to be a long time.

"Fine!" he said. "Everything's going fine!" But his voice sounded more subdued, and he added, "Why don't you come down and see me next weekend? This might be a good time to talk the book over."

Elise stayed in Buffalo with the children while I drove to Dick's winter home in Bronxville. His hospitality and that of his wife, Andrea, was as warm as ever. He still seemed exuberantly enthusiastic about my book, but he thought it might be possible to speed up the action a little bit. I listened with sinking heart to this advice, for I had no idea how to carry it out. Then Dick went back to saying how sure he was that we had a best seller on our hands and maybe a really great book, and my courage started to come back. That, I was beginning to realize, was Dick's method of dealing perhaps not with all writers, but with me. My enemy was always despair, depression and the apathy that came with it. By curing that with vast infusions of enthusiasm and hope, he persuaded me to rewrite again and again and again, as a more experienced and talented writer would have done without his help.

"I'm *sure* we're going to have something big here," he kept saying. "The only thing is not to go to the printer before you're really ready. I'll make you one promise: when you say print, I'll print. Don't worry about working for years and having nothing published. For both our sakes, I just want to make sure that you work on this long enough to give it your best."

That reassurance and cautioning was the sum of his help, and for me it did wonders. Without regret I threw away the second hundred pages and by the time I got back to Buffalo I had a brand new idea which was really fiction, not thinly disguised autobiography, which the first hundred pages had been. I would bring the war into the book, not the war at sea as I had known it, but the more violent war a friend of mine had told me about, the combat of the paratroopers. This could be done in a flashback. To give it relevance to the rest of the book I could use the plot of a short story named "Bygones," which long ago I had sold to *The New Yorker*. I had written that story after reading an article in *Life* about the hundreds of thousands of illegitimate children American troops had left behind them in every country where they had been stationed. In the short story, the German mother of one of those children had written the American father several years after the war to ask for financial help. The American father had been unable to provide regular donations without the knowledge of his wife. Moved by pity for the child he had left behind in Germany, he had told his American wife about the affair he had had while he was in the army and the son who had resulted from it. In the short story, the wife had furiously refused to send money, and had said the German woman was probably just a whore. The point of the bitter little tale was that the American ended by thinking his wife was really the whore, and secretly sent what money he could to his ragged son in Germany.

While driving back to Buffalo the idea came to me that not all American women would react so cynically in such a situation. In my novel I could get action by making a crisis of telling the wife about an illegitimate child, and could make her a more sympathetic woman by having her agree to help support the boy. For the first time I had a plot of sorts. When I got back to Buffalo, I continued to work day and night, and in only about six months finished a first draft of the novel. With his mixture of extravagant praise and caution, Dick Simon talked me into rewriting it a total of twelve times without ever getting discouraged. The whole process took almost two years. When I sent in the final draft, I felt that my hands would drop off if Dick asked me to do any more work, and I had gone over the story so much that it had stopped making any sense, like a word endlessly repeated.

"Great!" he said to me on the telephone a few hours after he had received the manuscript. "Your work is done and now mine begins. Hold tight. I think you have a fine book here. Just give me a few months to see what I can do with it."

Without the routine of working at fever pitch on the book, I felt strangely empty. The chancellor at the university was leaving, and to my surprise the man who replaced him decided to keep me on, at least for the time being. He allowed me to put into action some plans of mine which his predecessor had shelved. One of these was to invite the publisher of the Buffalo *Evening News* to ask one of his editors to take a part-time job as an adviser to our student paper, which the *News* had been criticizing. This would give our student editors the help of a professional newspaper man and would also have the advantage of making it difficult for the *News* to criticize our journalistic efforts.

"Marvelous!" the new chancellor said with a laugh. "Probably there will be a few outraged cries about bringing in a censor, but it's good to stir up the animals once in a while."

The new chancellor, whose name was Clifford C. Furnas, made decisions quickly, never worried about being liked, and was immediately admired by almost everyone. Just as I had had to share some of the unpopularity of the other chancellor, I basked in the approval given this one. The university could give me a pleasant and useful life-long career, I told myself. It was absurd to spend all my time dreaming of having a great best seller. As weeks went by without word from Dick, I tried to brace myself for the publication of a book which, like my first one, would be forgotten after a few lukewarm reviews.

It was at about this time that a contingent of foreign graduate students arrived to study at the University of Buffalo. One of my jobs was to find rooms for them in the homes of faculty members who, it was hoped, might help them to understand life in Buffalo. The American government paid a modest rent for the foreign students, and I easily found lodging for all but one tall, ebony-black Nigerian. Our faculty members prided themselves on their liberal views, but somehow I couldn't find anyone who wanted this black giant as a house guest. Tired of trying, I decided to take him into my own home. My wife seemed a little surprised, but she did not object. We put him in the spare room which I had used as a study.

Our Nigerian guest had come to America with the impression that Buffalo had a tropical climate, and owned few clothes but his native robes. I lent him some of my old uniforms and a gray flannel suit. He was so tall that the sleeves came little below his elbows and the cuffs of the trousers reached only halfway between his ankles and his knees, but he had such immense dignity and assurance that this comic costume did not seem to bother him at all. The Nigerian government had provided him with little spending money, and since my old clothes kept him warm, he wore them to even the most formal occasions.

"I do not care what people think of me," he said with an accent he had picked up during years of study at the University of London. "I have come here to study America, to see, not to be seen."

Shortly after our Nigerian guest arrived, Dick Simon called to ask for some minor changes in the manuscript. We had not yet chosen a title from a long list of suggestions I had provided. *The Man in the Gray Flannel Suit* was on the list, but Dick thought it was too long and sounded too much like Mary McCarthy's story *The Man in the Brooks Brothers Shirt* and the movie, *The Man in the White Suit*. For some reason I wanted to call the book, *A Candle at Midnight*. We decided to reserve decision on the title until I finished the new revisions. Moving my typewriter to the cellar, I again started my routine of working at the university all day and typing at home until one or two o'clock each morning. Our Nigerian guest watched this process with interest, and also heard it, because my typewriter was almost directly under his room.

"Mr. Wilson," he said to me with astonishment one day, "I have often heard that Americans work hard, but I never imagined anything like this. Apparently you never sleep. Is this a common practice here?"

I assured him that not everyone was trying to finish a novel and keep about three jobs going at the university at the same time. I also assured him that I myself rarely went to such extraordinary efforts. He seemed greatly relieved.

"I would hate to think that Nigerians would have to give up sleep to achieve progress," he said.

The weeks of readying the book for the printer seemed endless. Dick called both my wife and me to his home in Bronxville for a final conference on the title. My wife held out strongly for *The Man in the Gray Flannel Suit*, and she was so convincing that I agreed with her. Dick was still dubious, and we went home with the matter still undecided. The following Monday he telephoned me at my office.

"On the train going to work today I counted more than eighty men wearing gray flannel suits," he said. "*Eighty*, and I walked through only a few cars. It's a uniform for a certain kind of man, and I think it will make a great title for the book. We'll go to press just as soon as we can."

"How long before publication?" I asked.

"I'm shooting for sometime in April," he said. "From now on, we're going to do everything fast."

April was still three months away and that sounded like a long time. A friend of mine who recently had had a novel published told me not to get my hopes up. His publisher had been wildly enthusiastic, but they had ended with bad reviews and almost no sales.

"Publishers just try to egg you on," he said morosely. "It's their business."

I had been so busy with my work that my wife and I had lived in the house together almost as strangers. Her housework was made more difficult by our Nigerian guest, whose religion forbade him to eat pork or food from dishes which pork had touched. The three children were still young enough to demand a great deal of her time, and the new chancellor's wife expected her to help a lot at the faculty club and at dinners she gave for trustees and other dignitaries. Although she liked parties, my wife rebelled at the idea of being a sort of professional hostess for people she had never met. She missed her friends in New Canaan, her family in West Newton, and her husband, who sort of ran away with a typewriter, she said once, and never came back. She hated the weather in Buffalo, where the skies were almost always gray, where fall came early and spring came late. Because I had no time for such activities, she shoveled snow, raked leaves and made plans for a garden. My small salary left little room for clothes, and she made many for both the children and herself.

"At home," our Nigerian guest said to her at dinner one night, "I have three wives, and I'm going to tell them that all three together don't do as much work as one American woman."

Elise laughed.

"You do work awfully hard," I said guiltily. "I at least ought to take care of the yard."

"You stick to your typewriter," she said. "I will put up with *anything* if it helps us get out of Buffalo."

Although it probably was not fair, I now shared some of her dislike for the city, especially the people who considered themselves the local aristocracy. As a fund raiser I was introduced to a lot of the leading people in Buffalo, and I found them far more arrogant and stiff-necked than the men and women who had made up the old school commission in New York. It was next to impossible to raise money for the University of Buffalo, partly because it was "only a place where the cook's children went," one of the local social leaders explained to me. People who were anybody in Buffalo sent their children to Ivy League colleges, and had small interest in their local university.

Unlike Rochester, which had an enormously rich university, Buffalo was a city of branch offices, and few businesses had their headquarters there. Large corporations, it was explained to me, give money to universities near their headquarters.

Few of the rich men I met in Buffalo had much interest in their university. One of them thought that the fact that he was a trustee of the university meant that I should work, at least part-time, as his personal public relations man. He had a problem and he asked me to solve it. The problem was that the government wanted to put a Nike site for the defense of the city on his polo field. The government officials I approached assured me that the gentleman's polo field was, for all kinds of technical reasons, the best place for launching missiles, and they called upon him to be patriotic enough to give it up. This made him indignant, and he wanted me to advise him how best to fight the case. It took me hours to convince him that there was no way he was going to look good if he went to court to save his polo field from the defense department.

"The trouble is," he said finally, "that no one thinks polo is important any more. The army used to think it was a fine way to condition men."

A good many of the leaders of Buffalo declined to give money to the University because they considered it a hotbed of socialism. Not only did we have that one associate professor who was called to appear before a committee in Washington to discuss his un-American activities, we had all kinds of men on the campus who were beginning to speak out for ecology, for racial integration, and God knew what else. If there was one thing that made these leaders angry, it was the thought of being asked to give money to a university which was full of socialists. The result was that few people gave large amounts of money, and it soon became evident that the university could not afford to expand its facilities enough to accommodate the increasing number of young people who wanted to study there. Somewhere along the line, someone had the great idea of how to solve the problem. Because no one liked socialism, the final solution for the University of Buffalo, a private institution, was to give it to the state.

Rumors that the university was to become part of the State University of New York were flying while I was waiting to find what was going to happen to my novel. If that happened, the whole administration would be changed, and again, I realized, my job would be in great danger.

"I'm *sure* you could find something in Boston," Elise said, and I had visions of that silver-plating factory again.

Weeks went by during which I tried to keep myself busy rewriting college catalogues, which is certainly one of the dullest jobs in the world. Because I worked with the chancellor on many problems, some of the faculty members assumed that I knew all kinds of secrets about the future of the university, and they gave me little peace when I visited the faculty club. As a result I usually ate lunch at a workingman's bar named Bitterman's which was just across the street from the campus. One cold March afternoon I was drinking beer there when the bartender said there was a telephone call for me. It was my secretary. A man named Richard Simon had called, she said, and he wanted me to call him right back. There was only a pay phone at Bitterman's and I didn't have enough money with me to call New York. I ran all the way back to my office, and when I had recovered my breath, I called Dick.

"Good news!" he said. "The Literary Guild has taken your book. That will only mean about thirty thousand right away, but it's a good start. I've got magazines and movie people asking me for copies of the galleys. I was always sure we had something big, and now I know it. Relax and celebrate and give your wife a kiss for me."

"You're really pretty sure about all this?" I asked.

"Nobody ever accused me of not knowing a best seller when I saw one. Relax. By the way, I've been handling all this without your agent. It's easier at this stage. Do you want me to bring him in on every deal?"

"No need," I said. "He's not my agent any more."

At the time I had returned the advance money to Dick in New

Canaan, I had naïvely asked my agent to return his ten percent. He had refused. Angered at having to repay one hundred and ten percent of what I had received, I had exercised my option of severing our contract.

"So you've got no agent," Dick said with satisfaction. "If you'll give me a free hand, I'll guarantee I'll never make a deal you'll regret."

"You've got a free hand," I said.

Friends who thought they knew a lot about the literary marketplace told me I was a fool to deal with a publisher without an agent, but Dick was as good as his word. He made many deals for me, but never one I had any reason to regret.

Leaving the financial aspects of publication in Dick's hands did not even seem odd to me that afternoon when he told me about the Literary Guild. Running to my car, I drove home as fast as I could. My wife was washing dishes in the kitchen.

"Dick Simon called to say that the Literary Guild has taken the book," I said. "He's dead sure we're going to have a great success."

"Thank God!" she said. "When can we leave Buffalo?"

"Well, I guess we better stick around until a few more eggs are actually hatched."

"You told me that if the book went well, we could live wherever I wanted," she reminded me.

"That's right," I said a little regretfully, because I was not at all sure where I wanted to live.

"Boston!" she said. "Not necessarily West Newton, but somewhere near Boston. It's back to civilization again!"

25

As it turned out, I went from an income of eight thousand dollars a year to several hundreds of thousands of dollars for the next few years. Still, even Dick Simon's printer was quick to point out that *The Man in the Gray Flannel Suit* was something less than a literary masterpiece, and along about the time I read the page proofs, the euphoria of completing a novel wore off and my critical abilities, which have always been sharper than my creative ones, told me that no one was about to make marble busts of me to set up in libraries. Still I had made what most of my friends and relatives thought was a great success. I changed almost overnight from a minor functionary at a struggling university to a man 35 years old who was praised a lot, criticized a lot, and asked to discuss the phenomenon of success on television shows. In an era, the mid-Fifties, when Americans were much criticized for being materialists, I suddenly had the means to buy almost anything material I wanted.

A great many people asked me how this sudden change in my fortunes felt. At the time I was too confused to give coherent answers, but now, twenty years later, the phenomenon seems to fall into a drama of three well-defined acts.

My first reaction when Dick Simon told me that he was sure the book was going to be a success, was wild elation. All my immediate problems disappeared. Suddenly it didn't matter whether my job at the university lasted. I had long worried about finding enough money to replace our ancient Jeep station wagon and the blower on the furnace of our house, which made odd noises. The knowledge that problems of this kind would not bother me for a long time was a joy. There was also release from a hidden worry I had had that the unusual energy which had allowed me to write the book while keeping a full schedule at the university was only a manic phase which followed the depression I had felt in New Canaan. I had seen my mother go through such swings of emotion with disastrous consequences, and had feared a dark inheritance. Months of manic energy could not really be called crazy, I figured, if they resulted in what almost everyone considered to be a success.

A mixed blessing which I immediately felt was the freedom that money brings. Suddenly we could live anywhere we wanted, and the intensity of my wife's desire to return to Boston seemed to increase every day. I felt guilty, because more and more I regretted my promise to live wherever she wanted. The success of the book pulled me toward New York, where I could talk with Dick Simon about future books, appear on television programs and become a sort of minor celebrity for a few months at least, a prospect which both intrigued and terrified me.

The success of the book also opened up another possibility. Unlike some universities, the University of Buffalo appeared to like the idea of having a director of information services and teacher of writing who was also a novelist. Suddenly my academic title was changed from instructor of English to assistant professor. I heard talk that if the university were to be reorganized, it might have vice-presidents and I might be one of them. Perhaps by coincidence, I even got an offer at about this time to become president of a small college in the south. There was a temptation to continue my academic career with writing as a part-time business. This would reduce the pressure, which was already building, to start another novel. As I always had after finishing even a short story, I felt that I had written myself completely out in *The Man in the Gray Flannel Suit,* and would never have anything to say again.

Dick Simon also called to warn me that one great worm in the apple of success was the tax collector. He had dealt with several writers who had made hundreds of thousands of dollars, only to find themselves broke or in debt within a few years. Through the dean of the university's law school, I met a tax expert who scared me badly. We could try a plan for spreading the income of the book over a number of years, he said, but for various reasons, he was not sure that the government would approve it. At any time within a period of something like six years, the government could disapprove the plan and demand something like eighty percent of everything the book made. Despite the fact that so much money was rolling in, I did not seem to have any long-range financial security at all, and I was the sort who worried about things like that.

There was also, I knew, some mystical, black side of literary success which I did not understand, but which had caused three writers whom I admired to commit suicide soon after publishing a popular book, and which had caused many other writers I knew about to follow publication with divorce. The phenomenon of a writer killing himself at a time in life when he was most admired became a little less mysterious as the days went by. There is an intensity to writing which makes it a little like making love. A book in progress is exciting, and there is always the hope or illusion that one is creating something really great. When the last chapter is finished, a kind of *tristesse* sets in. There is nothing that stimulating to do any more, and time hangs heavy on one's hands. Even before the critics flash their knives, most writers, I believe, realize that their work is much worse than they had hoped it would be. Money is fun, but it doesn't make up for the shock of discovering that a book one wrote with the secret hope of greatness is at best popular. Furthermore, a novel exposes a writer's weaknesses, which may be one of the causes of his popularity. If he is at heart sentimental and if his thoughts are shallow, his novel will not allow him to hide those facts any more. Deep in their secret beings, I believe that most writers are their own worst critics. I have rarely met a writer who could stand reading anything he had written, because all the weaknesses show too much.

Popular success, it seems to me, is often accompanied by a sense of private failure—in the case of a novelist—literary failure, which deepens the feeling that it may be impossible or useless ever to try to write again. The exhaustion which follows the final efforts to finish a book makes a person all the more vulnerable to such depression.

It also may just be true that many writers are to some degree manic-depressive. I do not know whether I get depressed when I can't write, or whether I can't write simply because I occasionally go into a depression. There is something manic about splattering words out with fine abandon, sometimes at the rate of twenty or thirty pages a day, as many writers do when working on a first draft, and it's not surprising that such high periods are followed by low ones.

Another strange aspect of success turned out to be the effect it had on relatives and friends. I should not be surprised by this because I know that I am jealous enough myself to be as secretly hurt by the triumph of anyone close to me as I am delighted. When I had my success, however, I was surprised that many old friends shunned me, and a few relatives were even more critical of my book than the most caustic reviewers or myself. When one suddenly is making hundreds of thousands of dollars a year, the friends one had when one was making eight thousand a year no longer feel at home with you, and hate the idea of seeming to curry favor on the basis of old acquaintanceship. When one loses old friends in this manner, one does not acquire new friends who are also striking it rich right away, but one does find an awful lot of people turning up to sell insurance or automobiles. It is easy for a newly successful man in any field to find himself suddenly friendless and a mark. It is even easier for him to forget how much he longed for this perilous condition.

One reason why divorce often follows success became obvious almost immediately. Partly because of the loneliness which had come from my father's death and my mother's illnesses, I had been married at the age of twenty to Elise, who was then eighteen and, even by the most objective standards, a spectacularly beautiful young woman. I had been brought up to be a Puritan, and even during the four years I was away from home during the war, I was never unfaithful—an act of virtue which was made easier by the fact that my ships operated mainly out of Greenland and New Guinea, where the natives offered few enticements to a rather prudish young officer. In the fifteen years I had been married to my wife, I had, after my fashion, been in love with her, and had been too caught up in the drama of trying to write and make a living and support children to pay any attention to other women. I was an average-looking, if somewhat distraught, young man, and the sad truth is that beautiful young women almost never paid any attention to me, and I had little temptation to resist. The girl who flirted with me in the bar while my car was being fixed in Atlantic City remained in my mind because that sort of thing happened to me so seldom.

As soon as I became known as the writer of a popular book, however, all that changed. Apparently I had grown six inches taller, lost thirty pounds, and straightened out my profile. Pretty graduate students and secretaries at the university flocked around me. Perhaps one reason was that the book gave me more self-confidence than I had ever had, and I suspect that this is a quality which most women admire. There may also have been a certain curiosity about what kind of man writes a book and gets his name in the newspapers a lot. Whatever the reason, I seemed to change overnight from a man who found little opportunity for attractive sin to something called an author who was often surrounded by temptresses. For quite a while I did nothing about this, but my mind was suddenly full of all kinds of fantasies which, I knew, could easily be turned into reality.

This, I was well aware, was not at all fair to my wife, who had stuck with me through all the hard times, and had worked unusually hard herself to give me the opportunity to do two jobs. At the many cocktail parties to which we were suddenly asked, she watched me stand surrounded by women. At the age of thirty-three, she was still an unusually beautiful woman, but like many women that age, she felt she had passed her peak while I mysteriously was just reaching mine. After a while she said she did not like going to parties with me.

The new attention I received from women subtly changed my relationship to my wife even at home. Both my mother and my wife's mother had strong personalities, and we were both used to seeing a home dominated by a woman. It had not seemed strange to me to be rather meek around the house, and I don't think I ever expected to be admired, flattered or catered to by any woman. Suddenly I got the idea that I had been too passive all my life, and that that might be one reason why my marriage had lacked the excitement I had sometimes dreamed about. My wife knew too much about my bad qualities. She had endured my depressions, felt my fears, suffered from my uncertainties. I do not think my success seemed either real, reasonable or permanent to her from the start, and she certainly could not bring herself to look at me with the adoring eyes of strangers who knew only that I had written a popular book. Whether it was fair or not, I enjoyed basking in the adoration of people who didn't know anything bad about me. Almost any gathering of people began to offer more excitement than my home. My students and strangers listened to me with such attention that I was rather annoyed when my wife challenged my opinions. Despite my growing awareness of the weaknesses of the book, I had a new, if sometimes false consciousness of my strength as a man. I, after all, had gone to Harvard, commanded ships and written books. Who was any woman who had accomplished no such miracles to ask me to take out the garbage or criticize me because I drank too much? The book gave me a sense of male liberation I had never had before. A little of it may have been justified, for I had grown up with exaggerated fear of displeasing women and of the emotional storms which could follow, but success changed my personality in a way which must have been less than a comfort to my wife.

We began to fight about where we were going to live because I thought that the business demands of the present and future outweighed any promises I had made in the past. This battle was tragically resolved when we paid a visit to her home in West Newton and found that her father—whom I loved almost as much as she did—had cancer of the pancreas, and was given only about six months to live. She was determined to spend that six months with him, regardless of what I did, and I of course accompanied her when she moved with the children to a house she had rented near her father's home.

Suddenly the triumph of the book was dwarfed by the gloom of terminal illness. Carl Pickhardt had been such a benign power to his whole family, that his approaching death seemed to many of them like the end of everything. I worried about the impact of so much sadness on my children, and the effect of making them change schools once again in the middle of a year. I knew few people in West Newton and after talking with my father-in-law the few minutes the doctor allowed each day, I had nothing to do but try to draw another book out of my empty head. Understandably enough, the sight of her father wasting away before her eyes plunged my wife into almost as deep depressions as those my mother's troubles had taught me to dread. Success does strange things, I thought. Without it, we could not have afforded to give up my job in Buffalo and move to West Newton. Our new freedom had somehow compelled my wife to endure a six-month death watch. The last thing her father wanted was to make anyone else suffer, and though he was often under heavy sedation, he determinedly remained cheerful when his children were present. I often thought it would have been easier for both him and my wife if we had remained in Buffalo, but with circumstances as they were, my wife had to spend half a year making heartbreaking attempts to comfort a man she adored while he was in ever deepening pain.

I was able to catch my book just before it went to press and dedicate it to Carl Pickhardt. That and all the news of the movies bidding for the book pleased him. He himself had known a good deal of success and enjoyed the triumphs of any member of the family even more than his own.

When I told Dick Simon that my father-in-law was dying and was pleased by the dedication of the book, Dick asked if the sick man would enjoy a visit from him. As an investment banker Carl Pickhardt had dealt with important men many times in his life, and he had deep respect for anyone who had accomplished anything. I had told him how much Dick had helped me and, as an inveterate reader, he was familiar with the firm of Simon and Schuster. The news that Dick Simon wanted to visit him delighted him.

A few days later there followed one of the most terrible yet admirable scenes I have ever witnessed. My father-in-law had been bedridden for several days, but he made up his mind that he had to get up, get dressed, and go down to the living room to greet this important guest who had done so much for his family. After putting on a suit which now was pitifully too big for him, he rested on his bed while I met Dick at the door. When Dick was seated, my father-in-law got up and started down the stairs, holding firmly to the banister. He had told me he wanted no help. About halfway down the stairs he fell, and tumbled head over heels, landing at Dick's feet. Appalled, Dick and I helped him up. Straightening his back, Carl Pickhardt said, "Well, Mr. Simon, you can't say that I don't make dramatic entrances. It is a pleasure to welcome you to our home."

For a few minutes Dick told him how great he thought my book was, and what a fine future he was sure was in store for me. Then Dick left, and my wife and I helped her father back to his bed. He never left it alive again, but during his last days he often said what a pleasure it had been to meet Dick Simon and to know that all was well with me and my career.

26

The fact that I had nothing to do in West Newton kept increasing my depression, and I was delighted when I got an unexpected call from my old acquaintance Neil McElroy, the president of Procter and Gamble. President Eisenhower had just asked him to head up a White House conference on education, and would I like to sign on as its writer with the title of assistant director? When I explained my circumstances and said I could not leave West Newton for long, he said I could work anywhere I liked as long as I was free to travel to occasional conferences. My wife agreed that this was a good idea, and her father loved the idea that however indirectly, I was going to do something for President Eisenhower, whom he admired. Even Sinclair Weeks thought that this placed the final stamp of authority on my success, though he was shocked to read in the papers that I had been appointed despite the fact that I was a Democrat. This rather surprised me too, for I had never been politically active, but the Democrats had asked me to serve a brief stint on the school board in New Canaan. I had accepted, and so I was branded. Sinclair Weeks, who prided himself on his lifelong devotion to the

Republican party, told my mother-in-law that it was lucky my writing had worked out well, because no Democrat should ever come looking for favors from him. There went the silver-plating job.

President Eisenhower's White House conference on education, which I started to help prepare in 1955 and which took place a year later, has long been forgotten, as have virtually all White House conferences. When I started to work on it, it was highly controversial. Its enemies thought it was simply a mechanism to allow the President to delay making a decision on federal aid to education, which most knowledgeable people knew had to come sooner or later, since states like South Carolina produced so little money and so many children. The supporters of the conference, which included Roy Larsen and most of the members of the old school commission, hoped it would give the President as much knowledge as possible about the problems of the public schools before he had to start signing bills.

I must confess that from the beginning, the great conference, like so many government operations, seemed absurd to me. The basic idea was that each "community" (a word that I had somehow come to hate), would have a "workshop conference" to discuss school problems, and so would each state. Some two thousand delegates would be appointed to go to Washington for two or three days and have a giant "workshop conference" which would provide a report with recommendations for the President. I had no idea what a "workshop conference" really was, but it turned out to be a mechanism which allowed large numbers of people to report their opinions without ever taking a vote to see what ideas prevailed. Votes might be dangerous because they could appear to force the President's hand, and, anyway, they would be meaningless since the delegates were chosen not by popular vote but by appointment, usually by local school boards.

It seemed quite clear to me and to many members of the committee for the conference which Neil McElroy headed that if two thousand delegates came to Washington for two or three days to talk about schools, they were not going to end up with a coherent report. Since there was going to be no voting, they would conclude with a statement of every possible opinion on every issue. Specific recommendations for the President would not come from two thousand people talking for two or three days. They would have to come from a special report from McElroy's committee itself. My job was to gather expert information and write a report which McElroy's committee would sign.

I never had any idea that I knew enough about education to tell Neil McElroy what he should recommend to the President, but, through my work with the school commission, I had met one man who, I knew, could make more sense than any committee or "workshop conference."

His name was James R. Killian, Jr., then head of M.I.T. in Cambridge, Massachusetts. In many meetings where I had served as a reporter, Dr. Killian had shown himself not only an expert on anything to do with education, but that rare kind of man with no ambition to advance, no ego to satisfy, nothing but a rather weary hope that he could help his country during the few years of active life he had left. The first thing I did when I got my new job was to ask Dr. Killian what those two thousand delegates would tell the President if they were all as smart as he was. Taking a few hours from his busy schedule, he almost dictated a report to me. I translated it from the language of college presidents to the language of newspapers, and gave it to Neil McElroy. My job was done almost before I started, but the political process of local meetings and appointing all those delegates and sending them to Washington still had to continue for about a year. Probably McElroy was right when he said that these meetings stirred up a lot of interest and support for the schools, even if they did not result in coherent recommendations. He suggested that I visit a lot of the state meetings, so that a final report could be written with a knowledge of local feelings in addition to Dr. Killian's recommendations. I was urged to travel anywhere I wanted within the United States.

"Workshop conferences" on education were, I quickly discovered, much alike wherever one went. They were held in big hotels. People sat around tables in ballrooms, argued all the problems, and solemnly reported all possible solutions to them without deciding which one was best. There were a lot of cocktail parties and dinners to ease the tension of the debates. At the state conferences representatives of the outlying "communities" lived in the big hotels on government expense accounts, and the party atmosphere of a big business convention prevailed. In the end, it seemed to me, the White House conferences on education pretty much came out on every side of every issue.

I did not seem to be doing much good for anyone. In West Newton my wife was being drawn more and more not only into the tragedy of her father, but also that of her mother, who was so overcome with grief that, to the surprise of no one in the family, she died soon after her husband had. My wife's two brothers and her sister were all nearby. Elise did not try to discourage me from traveling. At first she used to meet me at the airport when I came home from a week of conferences, but she soon became too depressed to leave the house. Once when I came home, after telephoning my time of arrival, she seemed startled to see me.

"To tell the truth, I sort of forgot about you," she said.

I tried to provide her some support, but as the months went by and the excitement about the book—which was being serialized in advance of publication by a magazine and which was constantly being bid up by the movie and soft-cover book people—built, I became increasingly restless. No one ever did a better job of advance publicity on a novel than Dick Simon did with my book. Newspaper advertisements appeared weeks before publication. *The Man in the Gray Flannel Suit* was famous and perhaps most appreciated before anyone had read it.

At the conference on education my old colleagues on the school commission talked a lot about my great good fortune. At the cocktail parties which followed the debates I continued to get the special kind of attention which had astonished me in Buffalo when news of the book had first come out. Despite all the sympathy I could muster for the concern of my wife for her parents, I began feeling neglected and lonely as the months went by. This was not fair, I realized all too keenly, but I was beginning to realize that my emotions did not always have much to do with what was fair, reasonable or moral. For some reason I could think of almost nothing but having an affair with a responsive woman like the one I had avoided in the bar in Atlantic City, and like the one I had imagined in order to give a plot to my book. I was thirty-five years old and suddenly had both the time and the money to run a little wild without hurting anyone, I liked to think. For fifteen years I had been a faithful husband, and it occurred to me that in addition to being virtuous, I was quite probably simply square. There was also the beguiling excuse that a writer really has to live intensely if he is to gather grist for his novels. Awash in such rationalization, sin could become almost a professional obligation.

It was, I suppose, almost inevitable that in a city I shall have the sense not to name, I met an extremely beautiful young woman who came up to me at a cocktail party to discuss books and schools, and who ended by spending the night with me, talking most of the next day, and teaching me more than I thought I would ever learn at a state conference on education.

(Parenthetically I might say here that it seemed to me until recently that I never in my life made love to a woman who was not extraordinarily beautiful. A few months ago I came across a box of old photographs which convinced me of something better: any woman who loved me even for one night seemed to me at the time and in memory to possess breathtaking beauty.)

I shall here call this lady who first introduced me to what she wryly called "the great new world of adultery," Patience, because she was really very patient with me and my confused emotions. She was in her early thirties, had long black hair, and was wearing an unadorned dress of black silk when I met her. She was a member of a school board in a prosperous suburb and began by telling me that she had three children and was happily married to a man who was very successful in some sort of business—just what kind I forget. She had read some of my book in the magazine installments and a few of my pieces in *The New Yorker* and frankly said she was curious to see what writers are like. Instead of asking the usual questions about how writers get ideas and what they eat, she asked me whether I went through strange depressions when I couldn't work and crazy elations when anything seemed possible. She also wanted to know whether I really believed that marriage was as happy an affair as I generally presented it in print. When I reminded her that she herself had just said that she was happily married, she replied that she and her husband did not fight, that they were like good business partners. Did I believe that there was more in or out of marriage that people should seek, or was all the talk about romance and passion nothing more than a dream of youth? I said that I was not at all sure of that. Like the woman in the bar in Atlantic City, she said that I looked like a very unhappy man, and how could this be true, since everything was apparently going so well for me? I told her about the illness in my wife's family and she told me that one of her children had a serious, probably incurable disease. Part of her charm, I realized, was a look of melancholy in her dark eyes which she kept trying to counteract with a wry smile which really seemed to make a joke of almost everything. We started to tell each other our life stories, and before long we found that the room, which had been crowded with drinkers, was empty except for a bartender who kept glaring at us. She said she was staying at a hotel a block away, and accepted my offer to walk there with her. When we got to the lobby there was an awkward pause. I asked her if she would like a drink in the bar, and she said she preferred simply to talk. Would I like to come up to her room with her? I was both eager and with the stirrings of all my Puritan ancestors, profoundly scared. As soon as we got into her room, I kissed her, and looking genuinely surprised, she said, "That's really not why I asked you up here at all."

I apparently looked as disappointed and embarrassed as I felt. For an instant she studied me critically.

"You need someone," she said. "I'm not sure it's me."

"Right now I'm sure," I said.

"Are you capable," she asked, "of an affair with absolutely no consequences, no telephone calls, no letters, no attempts to meet again?"

"I guess that's the only kind I could be capable of right now."

"Good," she said, and put out the light.

I suppose that a great many people have had similar adventures without finding that they had any lasting effect. One thing that the lady taught me is that anything that happens betwen a man and a woman in bed is predetermined by what they think of each other before they go there. Suddenly I found myself receiving all the passion which this woman apparently felt for almost all writers, all creative people, few of whom she had ever met in a suburb inhabited entirely by businessmen. Somehow I had received the idea early in youth that the duty and pride of a man is to give pleasure to a woman in bed. In my ignorance and innocence, I had never met a woman who thought it her duty and pride to give the maximum pleasure to a man. I think that in some ways we both felt sorry for each other, and maybe we felt sorry for ourselves for promising to make this a one-night stand. At any rate, we both acted as though we were releasing emotions which had been stored up for decades.

"There's only one thing I feel guilty for," she said in the morning.

"What?"

"Somehow I know you as though we had been brought up together. You are going to feel guilty. You are going to worry that you've made me pregnant like the girl in your book. And damn it, you've had such a good time that you will do this again, not with me because I can't afford to have affairs where I live, but with the next reasonably good-looking woman who comes along. Fidelity is a habit which is hard to recapture once it's broken."

"I suppose so," I said.

"I have maybe an affair a year," she said. "Frankly, the hope and memories of these affairs are all that keep me really alive. I think you'll be the same way—highly selective, careful not to get involved or to hurt anyone, but always looking. I just hope you'll learn to get over the guilt. That isn't hard for me because I know my husband is out doing the same thing."

"Sometimes that must be tough," I said.

"Sure it is! This is no dream life, but it's the best way of living we've been able to work out."

We did a lot more talking and made love once more before she chased me out of her room. The only time I ever heard from her again was when I got a formal letter from her asking for my photograph and autograph. I was often tempted to call her, but finally decided that she was right when she said we should never see each other again. A man with three children ought to have enough sense to stay away from another man's wife with three children of her own.

Part 5
"How is Your Wife Taking the Big Apple?"

27

In the spring of 1956, Elise and I took our children to Florida for a vacation. Elise had been drained by the torturous death of her father. I had been affected by that almost as much as she, and I was tired by my efforts to finish up my work for the White House conference on education. A final report for Mr. McElroy to give to President Eisenhower was now in the hands of the typists and I figured that my services would no longer be needed.

Events had hit us with such force since the publication of *The Man in the Gray Flannel Suit* that we had had little chance to enjoy this strange phenomenon of success. Now I bought a black Buick "estate wagon" which caused Elise to speculate on the question of where we would eventually get an estate to go with it. After putting a crib mattress in the back for the children, we headed south.

Any trip to Florida was a journey home for me. The big white house in which my father had spent the last winters of his life still stood on the banks of the Halifax River in Ormond Beach, as unchanged as the ancient live oak trees which surrounded it. Farther south, the east coast of Florida was already so built up that I couldn't find many of the places which my father and I had visited when we had gone cruising up and down the Intracoastal Waterway. Restlessly I crossed the state and began exploring the west coast, which I had rarely visited. Before long we came to Sanibel and Captiva Islands. In those days they were connected to the mainland only by a ferry and a mail boat. No telephones were on the islands, and there were no tall apartment buildings or hotels. We fell in love with Sanibel and Captiva the moment we drove off the ferry boat and were disappointed when a real estate agent told us that she had nothing for rent. At the urging of my wife and children, I stopped at the offices of other agents, and finally was told that a beautiful new house had just come on the market, and could be rented until it was sold.

The grounds of the house stretched across the narrow island of Captiva from the ocean to the bay. It had a large terrace of red tiles, and was surrounded by pines, palms, orange and bamboo trees. A better place for a vacation could hardly be imagined.

Our holiday started well when David, immediately upon seeing the beach in front of the house, begged to go fishing. Although I was tired after driving most of the day and unloading our baggage, I was determined to draw closer to the children after so many months of hard work. With only a few grumbles, I drove to a small general store, where I bought a package of frozen shrimp, hooks, some heavy sinkers and several long hand lines. When I returned to the beach I noticed that the surf was surprisingly gentle and saw that there was a barrier reef a few hundred feet off-shore. This was a place where a small boat could be of help to a fisherman. Having none, I rigged up a line for heaving into deep water. David watched with interest as I twirled the end of the line, which had been weighted with heavy sinkers, around my head and let it fly. It landed about a hundred feet out in the ocean, which was darkening to purple in the setting sun. I handed him the other end of the line.

"If you get a bite, just hang onto this and run inland," I said.

Almost immediately he began to run.

"Wait till you have a bite!" I called.

"I have one!"

He kept on running and, to my astonishment, a sea bass about three feet long suddenly flopped out of the surf. David continued to run until the big fish was high and dry. Then he dashed to it, lifted it to a position in which it seemed to be his dancing partner, and dragging the line, rushed to show his catch to his mother and sisters.

The catching of that sea bass was one of those small events which can have unexpected consequences. It made David a dedicated fisherman, though while still in his teens his interest shifted from catching fish to studying them.

Lying on the beach slapping at sand flies that spring, I had plenty to think about. First of all, there was the history or mythology of the island, which I read in books from the local library. Captiva Island got its name because a pirate named Gasparilla kept his female captives there. Most pirates sought gold, but Gasparilla sailed mostly in search of women. On this little island he was said to have assembled a fine harem. The amorous pirate seemed a rather sympathetic character to me and I was sorry to read that, when he realized that he was going to be captured, he wrapped himself in a heavy anchor chain and jumped overboard. My father could have contrived no better end for a passionate pirate.

When I tired of thinking of the island's past, there was the short history of the house in which we were living to consider. After I had signed a lease, the real estate agent told me that the wife of a busy corporation executive had had the place built as a surprise for her husband, who had had a heart attack. What better place for rest could be found than Captiva Island? On his first visit the executive had admired the estate.

"Where's the telephone?" he had asked a few minutes later. "I better check in with the office."

"There's no telephone," his wife had replied happily.

"Where's the mail?" the executive had asked. "Do I have any mail?"

"The mail comes only about once a week."

For a moment the executive had considered the fact that his wife had given him a house on an island with no telephones and only irregular delivery of mail. His face grew red, his breath came short and he had a fatal heart attack.

My fear was that I was growing more and more like the executive whose death had been responsible for the availability of this beautiful house. I missed the telephone calls from Dick Simon and my lawyer—who had kept me informed of the surprising speed with which the people in Hollywood were making the film of my book. I kept expecting them to ask me out there for help on the script or technical advice on the sets, but except for asking me to pose for publicity shots with Gregory Peck, they remained silent. I had no idea what kind of film was being made.

The irregular mail service was a headache. Recently the mail had begun to act almost as a powerful drug on me. There were newspaper and magazine reviews of *The Man* sent by my clipping agency. Sometimes whole handfuls arrived, and I found myself reading them as feverishly as though they were going to tell me my future. As usual, I tossed unkind reviews aside and treasured the flattering ones. A lot of wits were carving up my book, but Orville Prescott of the New York *Times* said I had a "style like cream poured from a Georgian pitcher." This, with E. B. White's notice of my first book, made me as nearly impervious to the slings and arrows as I could get, but bad reviews still left me feeling miserable for hours, even when I crumpled them up and threw them away half-read.

One thing about the reviews made me cynical about the men who wrote them: most of them said either that the book was marvelous or terrible. Instinctively I knew that the novel really didn't deserve superlatives of any kind. Reviewers, after all, are journalists of a sort, I concluded, and are out to make their columns as newsworthy as possible. The publication of a great book or a terrible book can be considered news, but who would hurry to read a column about a so-so book?

When I wasn't worried about the reviews, I was concerned about my wife, who sat in the sun, half-dazed by the death of her father. Long ago when my own father had died, she had been quick to comfort me and had, indeed, seemed to me to be the only comfort in life strong enough to balance the memory of my father's last heart attack and my mother's long depression. I wanted to give her some of the strength she had given me, but somehow we had withdrawn from each other and sat as though under separate glass bells. The mysterious hostility between us was stronger than it had ever been. She knew that probably I would not honor my promise to settle down near Boston, despite the fact that I was financially able to do that now. I thought she resented my preoccupation with the mail. One bulging manila envelope which I received contained the papers of a whole college class which had been asked to review *The Man in the Gray Flannel Suit*. Not one of some twenty students had found anything good to say about the book. The teacher who had sent me the papers wanted to know if I had any reply to make. For some reason the denunciations of a whole English class bothered me even more than the criticisms of professional reviewers. I imagined that they looked much like my students at the University of Buffalo. If they all made fun of my work, what would I say? If I told them they they left me crying all the way to the bank, I would be cheap, and lying as well. If I told them that a class which voted entirely against almost any book must lack individualists, I would be taking refuge in a dim kind of wit. If I did not answer at all, I might appear to them to be a coward, and although it might seem ridiculous, I found myself caring a good deal about the opinion this unknown class of English students had of me. Finally I decided to answer with a question: If the book is as bad as these students think, why is it proving so immensely popular all over the world?

That answer did not satisfy me even after I had sent it off. In conversation with Elise I wrestled with alternative answers, until finally she said, "Don't you ever get *sick* of it all?"

It came as something of a shock to realize how self-obsessed the book was making me, but that did not mean that I became cured of my malady. Letters from Dick Simon told me that my book was being translated into Japanese, Icelandic and Hebrew, as well as dozens of other languages. I somehow liked the idea of a Japanese an Icelandic and a Jewish scholar all perusing the words I had laboriously written that night when the "e" flew off my typewriter like a small bumblebee. It was fun to think of great printing presses all over the world roaring along to produce something I had tapped out in our spare bedroom and in our cellar.

"Yes, it's an interesting thought," Elise said with a sigh.

The woman with whom I had spent the night at the state conference on education had been fascinated by my thoughts about the book. Of course, she had known me only about twelve hours, but my mind kept going back to her. Our affair, she had said to me, would have to be without consequences. Perhaps a more experienced person than I could enjoy a chance night like that without being changed by it, but I was consumed by guilt every time my eyes met those of my wife, exactly as my friend had predicted. No matter what its quality, my existence had always been fairly consistent. Monogamy had always seemed to me to be the only way of life for any sensible, affectionate head of a family. That still seemed to be true, but it was also true that one night with a woman I had just met had contained more excitement and joy than some of the years which had preceded it. Guilty I might feel, but I also had a new kind of sexual self-confidence which I never had missed until I acquired it. A gay dog was I, irresistible to attractive women at state conferences for education. Although I had never worn a hat, I bought one made of coconut fiber and wore it at a rakish angle. Pretty girls behind store counters seemed to me to return my bold stares with interest.

The pose of the successful author turned gay dog was rather enjoyable, but I was not quite sure where it was going to lead me. The idea of having a lot of affairs with young women I happened to meet at lunch counters seemed highly risky. Perhaps I should seek an unattached woman somewhat nearer my own age and condition in life who would like a continuing friendship. The word "mistress" sounded exploitative to me, reminiscent mostly of French novels about noblemen who kept women in elaborate houses, and who drove around Paris with them in carriages with curtained windows. That was a bit fancy for my taste, but there might be this continuing friendship with a woman who for one reason or another did not want to get married.

Never in these fantasies did I think of divorce. Even to consider that word was unthinkable as I played with my children or tried to find a subject other than my book to discuss with my exhausted wife. Even the thoughts of having a mistress, who would appear cloaked in some other more congenial name, I tried to banish, as I did dreams of using the money I was making to buy a schooner and sail around the world, as I had planned to do when I was very young. If my wife had to choose between my acquiring a mistress or a schooner, she would probably prefer the mistress, I concluded. Why was it that all my dreams would seem as hateful to her as her dream of a quiet life near Boston was hateful to me?

While I was pondering all these questions, the mail boat delivered to me a telegram in which Neil McElroy invited me to attend the ceremony during which he would present the report of the White House conference on education to President Eisenhower. Since members of the staff of such committees were rarely honored by invitations to White House ceremonies, I was much flattered.

"But you don't even *like* President Eisenhower," Elise replied when I said I wanted to interrupt my holiday and fly to Washington.

It was true that I had voted for Stevenson, but there was something about an invitation to the White House to see the President, no matter who he was, that I for one could not refuse. The telegram had taken so long to reach me on the island that I had to start right away. Leaving my wife and children on Captiva, I took a railroad train when I found that no plane reservations were available. So many young people were returning from their Easter vacations in Florida, that not even an upper berth was available. Figuring that my dignity had grown so bloated that I could not sleep in the aisle, as I had done on the narrow gauge railway in the Philippines, I sat up all night in the club car, sipping whiskey and thinking, for some reason, of the little tanker I had commanded during the last part of the war. Always she had seemed to me about to explode. In some strange way the mood of that strange little ship had returned to me. Safe ashore, I still felt that somehow my whole life was about to explode. The only comfort was that the premonition of doom I had suffered aboard that ship had turned out to be false.

By the time we pulled into Washington, I was red-eyed, rumpled and irritable, but the train had been so late that I did not have a chance to get a hotel room and change before hurrying to the White House. I felt downright eminent, however, as I climbed into a taxi and told the driver my destination. He stared at me with suspicion before starting off.

When we were only a few blocks from the White House, we passed a large movie theater which, to my astonishment, was advertising the newly completed film of "The Man in the Gray Flannel Suit." No one had informed me that the movie was already showing, and my sense of being kept an outsider during the whole process of making a movie based on my book was increased to the point of outrage. Nevertheless, the movie was there, where I could undoubtedly see it after the ceremony at the White House. Certainly a man who could in one day meet the President of the United States and see a major movie based on a novel he had written was doing pretty well, wasn't he? An objective answer had to be yes, but why did I feel only nervousness about meeting the President in my rumpled clothes, and anger at a system which kept a writer from even a preliminary viewing of a movie based on his own work? It was curious to remember, but I had never enjoyed a sense of success as strong as that I had felt when I first took command of the old *Nogak* in Greenland. Honors there might be for writers, but no one hoisted a little flag whenever they left home.

The guard at the White House gate looked at me even more suspiciously than had the taxi driver. After I had shown him my credentials he made several telephone calls before telling me to go in. Inside the front door of the great mansion there was a crowd of people, many of them distinguished educators and famous businessmen, like Neil McElroy, who had made up the committee for the conference. Steve Haggerty,

Eisenhower's press secretary, was ordering these personages about as though he were a master-of-arms aboard a coast guard cutter.

His purpose was to get people in line before the closed door of the Oval Room and to control the pack of photographers who were trying to cut a few celebrities out of the herd. We all milled around for what seemed a long time. Then a tall door opened and President Eisenhower appeared. Such a profound hush happened that the whole building appeared to be holding its breath. The President stood just inside the open door, ready to shake hands with those who filed in. My first rather stunned impression was that this man, whose politics I had rarely admired, was the most attractive human being I had ever seen. He was much taller than I had expected, and though he was old enough to be my father, he still had the body of a young athlete, broad-shouldered and narrow-hipped. The banker's suit he wore was unable to disguise his military bearing. Somehow he looked both at ease and at attention at the same time. A photographer held up a camera, and he gave that smile of his, the charm of which was that it transmitted a kind of warmth and kindness which no one ever expected to receive from a professional soldier. The smile was even more vivid in person than it was in all those millions of photographs.

While I was thinking these thoughts, I shuffled along in the line that led to the President. The question of what I should say when I shook hands with him bothered me. How about, "Boy, sir, you sure are a great looking President!"?

The line ahead speeded up, and suddenly I was holding my hand out to the President.

"Hello, sir," I said.

"Hello," he replied.

The man behind me gave me a slight push, and I moved on. The great moment of meeting the President was over.

Inside the Oval Room, Steve Haggerty still trotted about like a shepherd dog lining up sheep. Finally the President sat behind his desk. Photographers were allowed to kneel as though they were worshiping him. Then Neil McElroy stepped forward, as handsome and impeccably groomed as a matinée idol. He was carrying the report which with a few changes was essentially the one which Dr. Killian of M.I.T. had more or less dictated to me. I still thought of the report as a small mound of much edited typewriter pages, but now it was bound in leather with a glint of gold lettering.

Neil McElroy said, "It is a great honor, Mr. President, to present to you the report of the White House conference on education, which you asked me to convene."

The president did his smile as he reached for the oddly bulky book, and the photographers flashed their bulbs.

"Well, Neil," the President said easily as he leaned back in his chair with the book on his lap, "I guess this means that you've finished your tour of duty and want to be a civilian again."

"Yes, sir," Neil replied with a trace of uneasiness.

"Well," the President said, "That reminds me of a story. Back in World War II, I had a trusted old master sergeant. When a division was doing very badly, I'd assign this old sergeant to its headquarters, and after a few weeks he'd call me up and tell me what was wrong.

"One time," the President continued, "this old sergeant called me and said, 'The trouble with this regiment, General, is that the officers are no damn good.'

" 'Now sergeant,' I said, 'officers are almost always good for something. Give me your recommendations for reassignments.'

" 'No, sir,' the sergeant said. 'These officers are good for *nothing*. They ain't even worth being civilians!' "

There was a confused silence as the President finished this anecdote.

"Well, Neil, you can be a civilian again if you want," the President concluded, smiled again, and put the report on his desk. Steve Haggerty herded us all through the door.

I never did figure out the meaning of the President's story. When before long Neil McElroy was made Secretary of Defense, its meaning became perhaps a little clearer, but I never did figure out whether the President, like his sergeant, really thought civilians ranked lower than any creature on earth. Smile and all, maybe he did.

After leaving the White House, I took a taxi to the movie of "The Man in the Gray Flannel Suit." Many people have asked me how it feels to see a movie based on a book one has written, but I have never been able to give a very coherent answer. It is not, as I found that day, an experience to which I can react rationally. First of all, there was the title in huge letters which seemed somehow to throb. By their sheer size they seemed to have an awe-inspiring importance. Slouched in my seat while I stared at it, I thought of all the titles we had debated in Dick Simon's living room. I recalled the exact moment when I had scrawled *The Man in the Gray Flannel Suit* with a pencil on a list of possible titles. I also remembered the fact that my wife had backed this particular title when Dick Simon was arguing for another and I wondered whether she was coming to think of the blossoming of those seven little words as a flower of evil.

The title disappeared, to be replaced by my name. Who is it with ego so small or sense of security so great that he can be unmoved by the sight of his name in huge, throbbing letters which run the whole length of a movie screen? I found that the pleasure of this was sensational, but it was marred by the thought that this man who had his name up there on the screen had never been consulted about the movie which was to follow it.

Finally the movie began. The first scenes were a shock, for the color had gone wrong, and there was Gregory Peck in a light blue suit. *All* the men in his office sported light blue suits. What in the world would happen if all the executives of Time, Inc., came to work in light blue suits? The whole building at 9 Rockefeller Plaza would fall down.

The movie disconcerted me because Nunally Johnson, who had written the script, had done an admirable job of following my plot and inserting much of my dialogue, but the personality of Gregory Peck was so different from that of the hero I had imagined that the whole story was thrown off. Tom Rath, my leading character, had been desperately afraid of losing his job and of being unable to make even $9,000 a year with which to support his family. Gregory Peck talked much as my character did, but who could ever imagine that Gregory Peck was afraid he couldn't make $9,000 a year?

Sometimes the backgrounds made my dialogue seem ridiculous. My heroine, Betsy, had stood in a shabby house which had been worth only $14,000 when it was new, and had said that she couldn't raise children in such a place. The movie kept the dialogue but put Betsy in a mansion which obviously was worth about $100,000. Poor Betsy on the screen sounded like a terrible bitch.

The only scenes in the movie which came startlingly close to the ideas in my head which I had tried to transfer to paper were the war scenes and the sequence about the love affair in Italy. This was curious, for those parts of the story were the least autobiographical and the most based on fantasy. Apparently, I concluded, a writer's dream can be made into a fantasy on the screen far easier than can a writer's attempt to portray a world he really knows.

Suddenly the film ended and I found myself one of a few hundred people who were trying to struggle into raincoats. Hurrying to the railroad station, I got a compartment on a train going to Fort Myers—the stop nearest to Captiva Island. Although I had had no sleep in more than twenty-four hours, I was so keyed up that I lay for a long while in my bunk, sipping Scotch and watching the dreary buildings which line southern railroad tracks fly by. Our engine had only a diesel's air horn, but it was easy to imagine the steam whistles on the locomotives which had towed my great-grandmother's private car, and many other trains in which my parents had taken me south. Despite his bad heart, my father had always appeared masterful on these journeys as he kept track of the luggage and carried tickets for the whole family in his briefcase. What, I wondered, would he think if he knew that I had won the popular success which forever eluded him? Perhaps he would be contemptuous of my book, as he had been for the success of his pupil, Dale Carnegie. Certainly he would be indignant, if not furious, if he knew about the night I had spent with the lady at the state education conference. Seeing myself mirrored in the window of the train, I observed that as I grew older, I looked more and more like the last memories I had of my father. How strange to think that the image of such a puritanical man was now an adulterer who, no matter what he pretended to himself, was busily trying to figure out how he could repeat his crime as often and as soon as possible.

Fantasies, just fantasies, I told myself, the same kind of spun sugar which can so easily be blown up for the screen. Finishing my pint of Scotch, I slid under the covers and dreamed of President Eisenhower in a light blue suit taking care of the luggage and holding my whole family's tickets on the train. Those who said that President Eisenhower was a father image were apparently right.

28

Our last days on Captiva Island caused us to feel oddly homeless because we were not sure where we were going when our holiday ended. Until we made up our mind where to settle down, we decided to return to West Newton, where the children could finish their school year. To some extent I looked forward to moving back to the Pickhardts' big Colonial house at 281 Otis Street. More than any other building it was home to me, a repository of some of my happiest memories. I remembered the warmth behind that big black front door when I first entered it, shortly after my father had died. In the apple-green library I had sat for hours arguing about books with Elise's father, one of the few men who could strongly disagree with a much younger man without a hint of rancor. Down the front stairs Elise had walked on our wedding day to stand with me near the grand piano in the living room to exchange vows. In the paneled dining room there had been parties at Christmas and Thanksgiving days, with much singing and laughter.

Now when we returned to the house it was cold, as though the whole building had died with its owner. Turning up the furnace did not dispel drafts which we had never noticed. The liquor cabinet was still full of bottles, but the cocktail hour for me amounted to nothing more than solitary drinking. At night the whistling winds made sounds too much like the groans of a man in his death throes.

"We've got to get out of here," I said.

Elise wanted to look at houses in a small town near Boston where her brother lived. Although I was still anxious to move to New York, I accompanied her on tours with a real estate agent. Soon she fell in love with a miniature Colonial mansion, an ancient structure which was no bigger than a cottage, but which had the proportions and the elegant woodwork of a much larger place. When I complained that there were not enough rooms for us, Elise suggested that we also buy a small house across the street which had great charm. Her idea was that we could sleep in one house, while we used the dining room and living room in the other. The novelty of this concept appealed to the children. In questioning the practicality of the plan, I found myself to be the family ogre. Faced with tearful entreaties, I delayed.

"Well, we can live anywhere we want, can't we?" Elise kept asking. "Why not here?"

"Because at the very instant of my so-called success, I don't want to bury myself in the country."

It was not an answer calculated to bring cheers. "Success" is often considered a dirty word, I was learning, an open affront and threat to many people who are close to it.

"Damn your *success!*" It was a sentence I was to hear more than once.

The weeks rolled by while we waited for the children to finish school in West Newton and debated our eventual destination. The man who lived next door to us complained to a mutual friend that I never said hello to him or waved when I came out in the early morning to pick up my newspaper. Success had changed me, he said, though to my knowledge I had never exchanged greetings with anybody before breakfast.

The dean of the School of Education at Harvard University, whom I had come to know well during the preparations for the White House conference on education, called me up and asked me if I would like to work for Harvard. Since I had usually been happy to see "C's" and "D's" on my report card when I was an undergraduate at Harvard, this flattered me, and my self-esteem continued to grow as the dean told me how much he admired the work I had done on the report to the President.

"What would my title at the university be?" I asked.

"I guess you'd be sort of a special assistant to me."

"What kind of salary would go with the job?"

"Two thousand dollars."

"Two thousand dollars a *year*?"

"That's about all I can squeeze out of my budget, but I didn't think that money would be one of your primary considerations these days."

My training at the knees of my parents had been such that I never had to think much about grammar, but now I suddenly found myself indulging in a spree of triple negatives.

"I ain't going to work for no two thousand dollars for no Harvard University," I said.

Elise did not agree with me on this decision and became especially indignant when I said that salary was an emblem of prestige at a university, just as it was anywhere else. Prestige, she said, was a word which had begun to concern me much too much.

This was true, but prestige, I was finding, was a tricky word for a man who had just written a best seller. When I went out on a speaking engagement I never knew whether I was to be treated like a king or a criminal. Soon I learned that librarians and the people who arranged speakers for women's clubs were almost always admiring. High school and college students were usually friendly, but many of their teachers apparently thought that I was a low, conniving type who ranked somewhere below the copywriters who composed advertisements for substances to reduce body odor. With animal-like cunning I had devised a few thousand words which would so titillate the base instincts of the masses that thousands of poor ignorant wretches would come running to buy my book while all sorts of pure-minded poets and novelists starved. One thing that numerous college professors seemed to want to prove was that they *knew The Man in the Gray Flannel Suit* was neither *Hamlet* nor *War and Peace*. Nobody was going to fool *them*.

This churlishly put me in mind of a line from a book by a playwright which Dick Simon had given me. Though I could not remember either the title of the book nor the author's name, these words came clearly to my mind: "English professors often want to prove that the books an author has written are nowhere near as good as the books the professors plan to write."

No words did much to restore my spirits after an evening with English professors. Sometimes when I got home I telephoned Dick Simon just to hear an encouraging word.

"When are you going to come here and see us?" he often asked.

Thinking of the famous writers and other successful people who lounged around Dick's pool, I wondered if I would feel natural in joining them, now that I had in a way earned the right. I don't think it was social ambition which made me want to join the celebrities as much as curiosity about the way these gods and demi-gods lived. Just as I had as a boy been fascinated by H. G. Wells, I was anxious to learn as much as I could about these later-day denizens of Mt. Olympus.

The trouble with my conversations with Dick was that he almost alway asked me how plans for my next book were coming. My mind went absolutely blank when I tried to think of writing another novel, but I didn't think that I should admit that my cupboard was bare. After all, a writer who has no ideas for a book is something like a banker who has no money. There are certain kinds of emptiness which it does not pay to advertise. Usually I chatted with Dick about a new book as though it were already flowing smoothly from my typewriter, or discussed ideas for novels as though my only problem was to make a choice from many riches. I am sure he knew what I was doing, but as usual, his voice was richly enthusiastic and congratulatory. Only after I had hung up did the deception of trying to sell an empty box bother me.

I was not (and have never been) bitter about the special problems brought by success, for they of course are easier to bear than the problems brought by failure and poverty. Still, I was unprepared for one of the fundamental problems which success can bring to a writer: idleness. Usually I had gone to work before nine in the morning. Now I had no office but a room with a typewriter which seemed to have frozen keys. The give-and-take with business friends which often had proved distracting now was missed. Suddenly there were no people in my life but my immediate family and the men and women whom I met at neighborhood cocktail parties. Even at festivities in the houses of old friends, I appeared to be becoming more of a personage and less of an individual. If I wore a gray flannel suit, which I soon refused to do, I was kidded about advertising my own product. If I did not wear a gray flannel suit, a few people asked me whether I was afraid to appear in my old uniform, and whether I was next going to write a book with a hero in blue serge.

Never in my life had I been clothes-conscious, but the good-natured kidding I took about gray flannel soon made me recoil from *any* suit remotely resembling it. I was dumbfounded when the representatives of the manufacturers of gray flannel suits began calling me to offer me free samples of their wares. When one persistent tailor kept dropping in, I agreed to accept a brown flannel suit. He seemed astonished, but measured me for what turned out to be a fine garment.

The peak of the hysteria about gray flannel came when my entire class at Harvard agreed to wear gray flannel suits to our next reunion. A special invitation was sent to me, but though I knew this was an honor of sorts, the thought of some twelve-hundred members of the Harvard Class of '42 marching across the Yard in serried ranks of gray flannel absolutely flabbergasted me. I had no idea of what my response could be.

The very thought of standing up on some platform to say, "Thanks, fellows..." made me flush with embarrassment. Feeling churlish, I did not go to that reunion. Several friends were disgusted with me. For some reason they would not believe me when I said that I simply could not force myself to attend.

Elise too received certain unwanted playbacks from the book. For some reason a great many people assumed that the chapters I had written about the heroine of the novel forgiving the hero for siring an illegitimate child in Italy during the war were entirely autobiographical. Some people congratulated Elise for her tolerance while others sympathized with her for having to put up with an unfaithful husband. Tired of trying to explain that the book was fiction, Elise ended by thanking her public for their admiration or sympathy.

The business about the illegitimate child in the book brought me confessions from the fathers of illegitimate children who were sure that I would understand their problems and their sense of guilt. One of these secretly penitent sires of illegitimate children was a famous magazine editor whose sophistication about the difference between fact and fiction evidently stopped when he read scenes which approximated his own situation. For a man who never had an illegitimate child and who, for better or for worse, went through the whole war without even a brief affair, I dispensed an unusual amount of advice and sympathy concerning bastardy.

Pacing up and down the room in which I had put my silent typewriter and brooding about all the odd ramifications of my book was about to drive me nuts. I was saved by a telephone call from an editor of the New York *Herald Tribune*. Would I like to be education editor for them? They assumed that I would be doing writing of my own, and they would not expect me to give them all of my time. Eagerly I accepted. The job would answer the question of what I was supposed to do with my time when I had no fiction to write. It sounded interesting and it gave me a reason for seeking a home near New York, not Boston.

Elise and the children agreed to the decision with less opposition than I had expected.

"Why don't we go back to New Canaan?" Elise asked. "Wouldn't it be good to go back there, now when we can afford a really nice house?"

Only about five years had passed since we had held a kind of wake in our plain old house in New Canaan to mourn the fact that for several months I had failed to write a novel. The gray asbestos-shingled building looked as dreary as ever. An old friend in the real estate business drove us around the curving roads of New Canaan, a Connecticut village which somehow had lost all trace of New England, like a preacher's son who had gone to New York and got rich in the advertising business. On impulse I asked to see the house on the Norwalk line in which I had been born. It still stood there, a sturdy farmhouse which had been built somewhere around 1680 and which had been rebuilt many times to make it into this sleek suburban mansion. The owner, it turned out, was Austin Goodyear, a man I knew slightly and who sometimes identified himself as "the non-blimp Goodyear." Graciously he took us on a tour of the new-old structure. The enormous fireplace I remembered, perhaps because my father had duplicated it in his summer cottage on Lake George. Nothing else was in the least familiar. Thinking that I might recognize the kitchen, where I had spent most of my time with the servants when I was a small boy, I walked through a pantry door. The kitchen, of course, was now modern, and there was nothing for me to remember there at all. Somehow discomfitted by the fact that there was no nostalgia to be wrung even from the house where I had been born, I got back in the car to continue the tour of New Canaan. The post boxes before houses in which friends had once lived now usually bore other names, and I was reminded of the agent who had once told me that houses in many such suburbs tend to change hands every four years.

To one who had been away five years, the houses of New Canaan were almost as monotonous as the row houses on Long Island, where all the homes had been built to one design. New Canaan houses of course differed in size and shape, but there was a sense of sameness, nonetheless. Apparently no one in the whole area had original taste. Everything was Colonial or fake Colonial or something called "ranch," which appeared to have very little to do with any time or place except here and now. Almost every house was painted white. Lawns were invariably manicured and hedges were closely clipped. Certain stigmata of the region were everywhere: fake coach lanterns on poles, white wagon wheels, sleek station wagons in almost every driveway. There was nothing wrong with it, of course, but suddenly it seemed a part of my past which I wanted to escape. To my surprise Elise agreed with me.

"I hope that the place we get this time will be a permanent home," she said. "We better look everywhere until we find a place we really like."

As it turned out we did not have to look long. In Pound Ridge, a village which was only a few miles from New Canaan, we discovered an old New England farmhouse which was little different from many in New Canaan but which had the advantage of being perched on the edge of some unusually beautiful grounds. The two acres or so which came with the house lay naturally in the shape of a tiny valley. At the bottom of the valley was a small pond which was surrounded by lawns. Across the pond from the house was a red barn which had been converted into a year-around guest house. A small operating barn stood a few hundred feet away. The children greeted all this with delight and Elise said that it was the kind of place she had been waiting for all her life. Immediately upon entering the kitchen she began making enthusiastic plans for renovating it. The price for the whole place was only about $45,000, which seemed low to me even in 1956, but when I called my lawyer about making the payment, he again reminded me that when I had paid my taxes, I would not have money for more than about five years of living at my current rate of expenditure. As it was his job to do, he set me to pinching pennies as best I could during the peak years of my earning power. The only trouble was that I failed at actually saving the pinched pennies, and succeeded only in making myself miserable whenever any member of the family bought anything expensive. If I had had any confidence in my ability to write another book, all this worry about money in the midst of riches would have been unnecessary. As things were, I kept envisioning myself taking my family directly from our new home to the poorhouse. When Elise said that I was becoming more and more neurotic about money, I told her that she simply did not understand the situation.

As often happened in my life, events began to speed up like a great Ferris wheel out of control. Every morning I went in to New York and read mountains of news releases which almost every college and school system in the nation sent to the *Herald Tribune*. After making a few of these into articles, I wrote a Sunday column and walked across town to the offices of *Parents' Magazine*, the publisher of which also wanted me to be a part-time education editor. Most of the articles designed for *Parents'* seemed to me to be entitled, "Breast or Bottle?" or "Does Spanking Hurt?" A few hours of contemplating this sort of thing weighed heavy. In the evening I often was scheduled to appear for radio or television performances which were the last gasps of the publicity campaign for my book, or which had been arranged by the magazine or newspaper which employed me. Since I suffered from intense stage fright when confronted by a microphone or camera, these appearances were painful, but I had a sort of theory that mike fright is like seasickness and will go away sooner or later if one does not give in to it. My preoccupation with controlling my own feelings made it difficult to defend myself when, as happened from time to time, I found myself confronting a hostile interviewer. Tex Mc-Crary, who with his wife Jinx used to broadcast a radio show from Peacock Alley in the Waldorf-Astoria, was usually friendly, but without warning he once asked, "How does it feel to be a 90-day wonder?"

The question stunned me, for it took me back to the first day I walked aboard the *Tampa*, and got verbally battered for being, in effect, a 90-day wonder. Why did I keep finding myself in the same position over and over again? This time it was not fair, I thought, for I had worked all my life to be a writer, despite the fact that I was new to the world of publicity.

"How does it feel to be a ninety-day wonder?" McCrary asked again, fearing, perhaps, that I was going to sleep, for I was sitting in front of the microphone with my eyes closed to help me to think.

"I don't know, Tex," I replied. "How does it feel? Why don't you tell me?"

Jinx laughed and stepped in to cover the situation with lighthearted chatter. That was a moment I always remembered because it was the only time I actually made a riposte of that sort during a show instead of thinking of one later.

When I had no television or radio programs, I drove home to Pound Ridge, where Elise was often giving a party. All her life she had loved to give parties, but usually she had been frustrated by our small houses and modest budgets. The fairly large kitchen, dining room, living room and library of the old house in Pound Ridge were almost as good for parties as her father's house in West Newton had been. Like her mother, she prepared for festivities by filling each room with flowers. Elaborate trays of canapés were covered with damp towels in the kitchen, and our bar would have been a credit to the officers' club at Pearl Harbor.

Dozens and dozens of guests always appeared when Elise gave a party. Where they came from was always a mystery to me, for we had not lived in Pound Ridge long enough to meet many people. The guests seemed to spring up as spontaneously as dandelions on the lawn. No one ever dressed formally in Pound Ridge, but they apparently threw their informal clothes away after wearing them once. Never did I see anyone wear anything stained or rumpled. The men often appeared in sports coats of raspberry or light blue material, with white flannel slacks and white shoes which never looked dirty, even when they had to hop over mud puddles in our driveway on rainy days. The women commonly wore cocktail dresses which really were evening gowns with short skirts. Most were in their thirties, like us, and though many were beautiful, they almost all had a harried, worn look, as though they were expecting bombs to rain down from the sky at any time.

The people in Pound Ridge were different from any I had ever known, I reflected as I got to know some of them well. Although still in their thirties, most of the men were making a great deal of money, some of them considerably more than $100,000 a year. Almost all these men had started life in humble circumstances, and several of the most successful had never gone to college. Many were the vice-presidents of advertising agencies. There were two writers whose work had earned far more money than praise and who, like me, brooded about that. There were network officials, an actor who had become a television star, a publisher, a physician and several tax lawyers.

If these people received so much money, I found myself thinking as I watched them dance and drink in my low-ceilinged living room, they must be putting out a great deal of energy and running a great many risks to earn it. Although they were far from old, there was nothing youthful about their faces. Perhaps, I thought, they were disillusioned by the fact that it was not enough to climb to the top of the heap in America. Even more struggle was required to stay on a high perch. If they fell off, there was not even a guarantee of financial security. Taxes and high living made mincemeat of even the biggest salaries. Divorce beggared some of the most successful. It was easy to tell which men had been married two or three times: their wives were younger and their cars were older. In an unguarded moment I suspected that this might not be such a bad arrangement for a man who refused to be a materialist, but I rebuked myself. In those days I still could not stand even the thought of divorce.

The parties at our house were much like such festivities anywhere with certain exceptions. Although few people actually fell down, there was a good deal of heavy drinking, which I could not criticize, because I was in the forefront. The advertising men walked around telling jokes. Advertising agencies must employ comedians to train their vice-presidents, I concluded. The jokes often sounded extremely funny, but even when I could remember them the next morning, the humor seemed to have evaporated like the dew on the lawn. Sometimes I envied the ability of the advertising men to make such bad lines sound side-splitting. Often they spent hours roaring at each other's jokes.

The writers talked mostly about agents and contracts they had made. Clearly they were haunted and self-obsessed, the way people accused me of being. Their jokes did not sound anywhere near as funny as those of the advertising men, and I talked to them as little as possible.

There was one aspect of those parties in Pound Ridge which I detested from the start. In the dining room about a dozen couples danced. There was nothing wrong with that, of course, but some who regarded themselves as young bloods conducted themselves much like sailors in taxi dance halls. The embraces were considerably more passionate than those I had learned at Miss Darlington's Dancing School. There was much steamy staring and whispering in ears. All of this might have been acceptable, of course, if the wives of the male dancers and the husbands of the female dancers had not been sitting on the sidelines. Usually they tried to behave as though nothing was happening, but occasionally there was a murderous glance which cut right through the smoke that swirled around the hand-hewn beams of the low ceiling.

Elise was dancing. She was a good dancer whose love of dancing had been cramped by my complete lack of terpsichorean talent. I started to escape to the kitchen when a plump, pretty blonde woman deserted her bald husband and grabbed my arm. Ever since reading my book, she said, she had wanted to dance with the man in the gray flannel suit. Telling her that it was going to be a fearful disappointment, I broke into Miss Darlington's fox trot and steered her onto the floor. The blonde lady, it turned out, must have been one of those who trained in a taxi dance hall. A boatswain's mate aboard the *Nogak* once told me toward the end of a long arctic watch off the coast of Greenland that he knew a dime-a-dance girl in Boston who could bring him to full sexual climax without leaving the ballroom floor. The blonde woman must have studied under this paragon. There was so much contact gyrating that my durable fox trot ground to a halt. There was breathy whispering in my ear, punctuated by the quick flick of a tongue. No doubt I would have enjoyed all this enormously if it weren't for the fact that the blonde's bald husband was staring at us, polishing his glasses, and staring at us again while my wife looked daggers at me over the shoulder of a man who was trying to whisper in her ear.

These were the days before group sex was a common topic for drawing room conversation. My first thought was that sin might very well be delightful, but like sailing a ship, it ought to be done right or not at all. What perversion would cause anyone to want to seduce a woman while her husband stood as spectator? If a man wanted a mistress, why on earth would he choose the wife of a neighbor? With New York so close, why should anyone use his home town as a sexual hunting ground?

After everyone had finally gone home, I asked my wife some of these questions. She laughed and said that I was taking the events of the evening much too seriously. Everyone was just kidding around, trying to unwind and have a good time. Why not let it go at that?

Remembering how she had glared at me while I was dancing with the blonde, I wondered why she had grown so sophisticated so fast. Was she enjoying her glimpse of new horizons?

Soon after we moved to Pound Ridge, I drove the few miles to Stamford to see Dick Simon. He seemed happy to know that we were living in a house nearby, but he did not look well, and his big expressive face had lost some of the zest which had kept me going for so long. Sitting on a terrace near his swimming pool, which was now deserted, Dick talked about some of his problems. Always before he had concentrated so on helping me solve mine that he had never mentioned his own.

As I came to understand the situation, Dick's problems stemmed mostly from the fact that he and Max Schuster had sold the publishing firm which they had founded and run for years. After the war it had seemed sensible to follow the advice of lawyers who pointed out that a large capital gain could be realized if the company was bought by some large corporation. The expectation was that Dick and Max Schuster could remain with almost any title they chose and continue to run the company.

The sale had been made and with part of the money Dick had bought the big place in Stamford. For a while Dick's work at the office had gone as smoothly as ever. Then gradually Dick had begun to learn that he was not really the captain of his ship any more. For the first time he was answerable to a board of directors. Some of his decisions were countermanded. Men he did not like were employed and a few whom he detested were promoted. Worst of all, the words "Published by Simon and Schuster" were printed on several books which Dick Simon personally loathed.

He was a big eagle of a man, but now he felt pecked to death by sparrows, and the pain of the situation was made no easier by the realization that he had brought it upon himself.

I doubt whether anyone ever accused Dick Simon of being blind to the advantages of money. He had two houses which seemed to me almost palaces. Much of the time that I knew him, he had a French chef or a French couple who produced memorable meals. His majestic hospitality, his open-handedness with writers, both were buttressed by his phenomenal ability to make money. There were those who thought of him as a man primarily concerned with money, but his torment at the close of his career was not caused by a lack of funds, which he did not suffer. No, his trouble was that he no longer had the freedom to publish what he wanted and to reject what he disliked. Publishing, not money, had been the real passion of his life all along.

Now on the terrace by his swimming pool, he talked about the possibility of starting all over again in his mid-fifties and organizing a new publishing company. Max Schuster seemed more interested in retiring, but Dick was anxious to be back in an editor's chair. While he talked, he kept snapping the fingers of his big hands, an excited kind of clicking that apparently helped him to think. If he started a new publishing company, he asked, would I give him the manuscript of my new book?

Of course I said yes, but I was worried. His face looked gray and the whole idea of Dick Simon of Simon and Schuster going off to found a new publishing company at an age when many executives retire sounded bizarre. He followed me to my car in his driveway. For some reason he was walking a little stiffly, a fact which exaggerated his age. For a few seconds he stared at my Buick station wagon, which was still relatively new.

"I remember that when you first came here, you were driving a beat-up Jeep."

"That's right."

He smiled, as I would have in his position. With reason he could feel that he had waved a magic wand over poverty and turned it into prosperity.

"How are your wife and kids?" he asked.

"Fine. How are yours?"

"They're staying in Bronxville. I just came out here to be by myself for a while. How is your wife taking the big apple?"

"The big apple?"

He made a wry grimace. "Your success."

"She seems to be taking it all right. She sure was glad to get out of Buffalo."

"Well, watch it," he said. "I'd like to see you two lead the kind of sensible, happy life that the authors of best sellers hardly ever seem able to manage."

29

Not long after seeing Dick, I got the glimmering of an idea for a novel. Perhaps I could write a story based on my memories of getting married when I was very young, and perhaps the action could take place on Lake George, where I had spent so many summers of my youth. Before talking to anyone about it, I wanted to write about a hundred pages. The guest house on the other side of the pond, which I had been using as a study, we had recently rented to a friend, Dr. Matthew Rosenchein, who was in the middle of a divorce and needed bachelor quarters. Somehow our big house offered me no private space which could be used as a study except a small, glassed-in porch with a portable electric heater. Reflecting that my work had always gone best in the most humble quarters, I set my typewriter on a sturdy cardtable and began working there late at night after my labors at the *Herald Tribune* and *Parents' Magazine*. I was getting even less sleep than I had during the final stages of my book in Buffalo, but now my crazy schedule was entirely self-imposed. I wasn't sure why I kept the two part-time jobs in New York. In ways that I could not explain, they seemed to offer order and safety, day-to-day accomplishment instead of the long deferred accomplishment which a book represents.

After about a month of working on a rough draft of my new book, I thought I had enough to show Dick Simon. While I was retyping the manuscript, Andrea called to say that Dick was in the hospital. Apparently he had suffered a mild stroke. The doctor, she said, had given me permission to visit. As quickly as I could, I drove to the hospital in New York. Dick was reclining in a room which seemed almost smothered in flowers. Because he had always appeared so tall, so strong and so vital, the sight of him lying on a bed, where I had to look down at him, was shocking. Seen so close, his features looked enormous, almost the face of a giant. The brightly colored jackets of many books littered his bed and the table beside it. His eyes were closed when I came in.

"Hello, Dick," I said.

His eyes opened. For an instant I was not sure that he recognized me. Then he smiled, a little lopsidedly.

"Isn't this a hell of a note?" he asked.

"They say you're getting better."

"Maybe. What are you doing these days?"

I thought that it would please him to hear that I was making some progress on a new book, but I was horrified to find that he became agitated.

"Good, but don't know when . . . Have to get myself in shape. Lots to do. You want an advance now?"

No, I said, and I felt as though I had touched the whip to an eager thoroughbred with a broken leg. There could be no talk of publishing my book for a long while, I said. Gradually Dick subsided. For a few moments he stared at me intently.

"Are you all right?" he asked suddenly. "You look shot."

"I'm just a little tired."

"Pace yourself. You can be a great writer. All you have to do is to learn a little self-confidence. Will it help you to know that all writers without exception are scared to death? Some simply hide it better than others."

For about five minutes he said everything he could to make me feel good. Even when he was almost fatally stricken, he worried that somehow I might need more propping up.

Dick's illness soon turned out to be a professional as well as a personal blow for me. Always he had acted as my agent as well as my publisher, and when people came to me with business deals, I simply sent them to him. Now this was no longer possible, but the news that I was working on a new book to follow *The Man in the Gray Flannel Suit* spread from my friends in Pound Ridge to several publishers in New York and quite a few agents in Hollywood. The publishers I disdained, for they seemed to me to be vultures who were too eager to wait for the old lion's death. One of the Hollywood agents, however, fascinated me with an unusual proposal for a movie: Sid Caesar, he said, was soon to retire from television, and was interested in producing and perhaps directing movies. Would I like to meet Caesar and talk over a few possibilities?

Ever since I had had to pay my way in to see the film of *The Man in the Gray Flannel Suit* in Washington, I had dreamed of making a movie with a director who would at least let me express my ideas. Happily I allowed the agent to take steps to introduce me to Caesar in New York, where Sid maintained an office. On the appointed day, I met the agent at the Harvard Club, where he informed me that he was a graduate of the Harvard Law School.

"If it seems possible that you and Sid can work something out, I hope I can represent you," he said as we walked across town.

"I'll certainly think it over," I said, wishing that Dick Simon was there to give me his advice. The agent did not look as though he had graduated from the Harvard Law School. He was handsome in a way that to me seemed sinister, as polished and overdressed as a Mafia bridegroom.

Sid Caesar's office was small, compared to the executive suites at Time, Inc., and Simon and Schuster. Sid himself was anything but small, however. He towered above me and at the time was so fat that he appeared to fill most of the room. There was of course none of the clowning which I had seen Caesar do on the television screen, but like many great comedians, he could rarely stop being a comic person. Sitting down behind a large desk in the corner, he took two of the biggest cigars I had ever seen from a drawer and handed one to me. On closer view mine had a decidedly green tinge. Caesar lit his with a lighter, sat back in his revolving chair and took a big puff, which almost filled the room. After lighting mine, I puffed back at him, and soon the room was so full of smoke that we could barely see each other. I gave him a brief account of my novel about youthful marriage. Leaping to his feet, Caesar said that he and his wife had been married while still in their teens. Youthful marriage was a subject which always had fascinated him.

The more I told Caesar about the book I was trying to write, the more enthusiastic he got. Soon we were both pacing around his desk, disappearing into wreathes of smoke like destroyers entering a bank of fog. Naturally, I would write the screenplay myself, Caesar said. He would direct it, and his business people would take care of the details of production. Naturally we would not have to worry about money. With his name and my name on the film, the major studios would rush to finance it. He agreed with me that even the best screenplay can be ruined by inappropriate casting. If we could not find actors and actresses suitable for our story, we would conduct a nationwide search for unknowns.

One important thing Caesar emphasized: we would not let the business-men who rule most Hollywood productions command us. Ours would be one movie where the artists would be kings and the businessmen servants. We knew that the public wanted something sensitive and true, not the garish commercial nonsense which the moguls of Hollywood kept serving up. After we had created one movie which showed the world what unfet-tered artists could do, we would go on to produce more and more movies, a whole new wave of free cinema.

For a man who had always been interested in movies, this was heady talk indeed. Best of all was the enthusiasm with which Sid had talked of my ideas for a new book. Say what one will about inspiration and tech-nique, the enthusiasm of people a writer respects is what builds the self-confidence that is necessary for the long job of finishing a book. If I talked long enough with Sid, I thought I could finish a library.

Coughing to get the smoke out of my lungs and rubbing my reddened eyes, I promised Sid that I would have "my agent" get together with his for drawing up the proper papers. The talk of agents made him shrug, a gesture which seemed to me to say, "Who are agents compared to two great artists like us?"

Bidding Caesar a fond farewell and honestly thinking that I had made a friend for life, I met my Harvard Law School, Mafia-bridegroom agent at the Harvard Club. He was glad to see that I was elated after meeting Sid and said he would see about "the details."

In due time some papers were presented to me which were written in a kind of legal and show-business jargon which I found impossible to un-derstand. Sure that Sid Caesar would never cheat me, I signed. When a check for about three thousand dollars arrived as a sort of binder, I used the money to buy a twenty-four-foot racing sloop I had been admiring. My two jobs and the work on the book had put me into my usual state of exhaustion, and as usual, my final solution to that problem was a boat.

For a long time I had been disapproving of Elise's parties, but one of them, at least, served a useful purpose. Fresh from a sail on Long Island Sound, I boasted to a publisher who came to the party about a contract I had just signed with Sid Caesar.

"Could I see it?" he asked.

He was a fairly good friend at the time, and I got the contract from my office. To study the brief document he sat down at my typewriter. The few words appeared to take a great deal of his time. Finally he sighed and looked up at me.

"You've been had," he said.

Panic and rampant paranoia which seemed justified, blotted out what little common sense I had left. For reasons I have never been able to understand, this business of signing a poor contract frightened me more than arctic gales and Japanese torpedo planes had during the war. Somehow I imagined myself and my family ragged and destitute simply because I did not have the wit to conduct my own business properly without Dick Simon. There was also a rising fury at what seemed to me to be the victimization of a writer. Despite my recent good fortune, writers always seemed to me to be one of the most persecuted minorities in the world. In America young would-be writers were widely suspected of hopeless egotism and neurosis. If a writer became commercially successful, college professors and critics sneered at him. If he did not become commercially successful, his wife and children were apt to complain, no matter how much critical acclaim he received. And at all times, of course, writers, who were known to be unworldly, were a mark for publishers and agents who lived off them while patronizing them. As a final tour de force as a loser, I had succeeded in being cheated by a baggy-pants comedian whom I had admired for years.

Actually, of course, I had suffered few if any indignities as a writer, and by any standard had made a great deal of money with less effort than would have been required in most professions, but at times of high emotion like that, the facts cannot be allowed to obscure the truth of emotions. I felt cheated. I was blind angry with that special intensity which can come only when one is badly frightened.

"I won't be fucked lying down!" I said, and when that sentence sounded rather strange even by coast guard standards, I added, "I mean I won't take this lying down. No one can cheat a writer. If the contract is lousy, I'll make sure that the script Caesar gets is equally lousy. I'll bring in a battery of secretaries and dictate it in one night!"

Taken aback by my reaction, which included a lot of pacing and a certain amount of chair-kicking, as well as yelling, the publisher, who appeared to be a mild little man, said that in his opinion, Sid Caesar had not cheated me. Like most performers, he had probably relied totally on a business manager or agent. This man had apparently done battle with my agent and had won hands down.

My opinion of the Harvard Law School plummeted, and it continued to sink as the publisher said that the written agreement could be interpreted in various ways, but that according to one interpretation, Caesar's company could buy the movie rights to my next book for almost nothing. Since almost any novel which followed *The Man in the Gray Flannel Suit* would be of unusual interest to Hollywood, this could be a serious matter. Instead of rushing to hand in a meaningless manuscript which would be bad for my reputation, the publisher suggested that I hire a good lawyer to reach some sort of settlement with Caesar's company. He named a solicitor who specialized in show business and literary law.

I retained the services of this man. Soon the Harvard Law School agent appeared at my house. Why was I contesting the marvelous agreement which he had drawn up with Caesar's company? Didn't I know that the publisher who had said that the contract was no good was simply trying to get control of my manuscript himself?

Not long ago there had been times when no one wanted to see my manuscripts, but now, apparently, I was a wounded deer being fought over by wolves. Since it was obviously necessary to trust somebody, I put my faith in the lawyer I had just hired. In due time he called to say that Sid Caesar had agreed to let me go for only a nominal payment to cover their costs. Despite this good news, the whole affair left me with a bad taste in my mouth. Sid Caesar had in truth convinced me that he would be a sensitive director and an enthusiastic partner in any creative enterprise. The thought that all the haggling about contracts had prevented us from making the movie we had discussed was infuriating.

The continuing illness of Dick Simon and my disappointment about the contract with Caesar combined with the exhaustion of too much work to make me taut-nerved and irritable. Somehow the differences between me and my wife started to grow. In a sense she had the opposite problem from mine: while I was absurdly busy, she had less to do than she had had in Buffalo. Now all the children were in school and it was possible to hire people to keep the house clean. Our home, like many in rural Pound Ridge, was too isolated for much interchange with neighbors, and there were few of the committee activities which occupied so many women in bigger suburbs. She got out her easel and did more painting that she had in years, talked of starting an antique shop, and for the first time since we had been married, built up a wardrobe comparable to that which she had had during her debutante days in Boston. Understandably enough, she was often bored by the time the weekends rolled around and welcomed the inevitable rounds of parties. Perhaps she was right when she complained that I disapproved of these festivities simply because I was a misanthrope. Visually the parties were often impressive, I had to agree. Several of our friends had long, serpentine driveways which they lined with candles in glass globes when they were entertaining. Almost every house in Pound Ridge, it seemed to me, was built near a small pond—something about the terrain made it easy to dig ponds with a bulldozer or dragbucket. Flares were often put on poles in the lawns, where their orange flames were reflected in the dark water. Tables were set with fine crystal which sparkled in candlelight, and the women dressed more elaborately than I had ever seen women dress in the country. Several of our friends were professional musicians who often sat down to a piano or picked up a guitar as the evening wore on. The conversation was far more animated than it had been in Boston, Providence or Buffalo. Everyone, it seemed, was writing or investing in a new play, starting a new advertising agency, or directing a new series on television. My mother had sometimes referred to the nouveaux riches with a touch of scorn, but these people were proud of being self-made and they savored the new opportunities brought by money with much more zest than more seasoned aristocrats could imagine. The trips they took abroad always had to be to some special place which no one else had "discovered," their sports cars were the fastest and most recently designed and the artists they admired were those who were just about to become fashionable.

They bored me. But then, perhaps, I was eternally bored in those years by anyone except myself and my work. Glass in hand, I often found a chair in a corner and dreamed of buying a comfortable ketch which I could sail around the world. If my new book was successful, there would be no financial barrier, but of course Elise and the kids would hate the whole idea, an attitude which was probably sensible enough. Lone voyaging had never appealed to me much. Perhaps there was a young woman somewhere who would like to devote about three years of her life to exploring the South Seas with a coast-guardsman-turned-writer. In my mind's eye I could see this woman clearly. She had dark brown hair and was warmly interested in everything I said, like the lady I had met at the state conference on education.

One party I remember all too well. It took place a few nights before Christmas in a huge modern house which was nowhere near big enough, for the host and hostess had apparently invited everyone they had ever met during their long, gregarious lives. Every room was so crowded that I felt as though we had all been jammed into some enormous elevator. As the night wore on, many guests left and enough space was found in the finished basement for dancing. Elise appeared to be having the time of her life as she glided about with young men, most of whom I had never seen before. Beset by my usual combination of sullen jealousy and boredom, I refilled my glass and retreated to a corner near the bar. There our hostess found me. She was, I suppose, about 45 years old. At the time I was about 37, and she seemed disconcertingly old for the role she was playing, which was that of a temptress. The woman had been drinking too much, and her make-up had melted. For some reason she was wearing a low-cut gown which made it all too clear that she should stick to high-necked gowns. At first she wanted to discuss literature. She was under the impression that I had written *South Pacific* and wanted to congratulate me for it. Figuring that James Michener wouldn't mind, I wearily accepted all credit, whereupon the woman insisted that I dance with her. Figuring that James Michener could take the blame this time for Miss Darlington's foxtrot, I maneuvered my hostess onto the floor. Either because she was too drunk to stand or because she had been stunned by meeting the creator of *South Pacific*, she clung to me so tightly that I was unable to manage more than an uneasy shuffle. She was humming in my ear and gradually I came to realize that she was going through the melodies of the musical comedy which had been made from *South Pacific*. After a while she began to try to add the words, most of which she couldn't remember. Exhausting her repertoire, she said she had a beach cottage in Florida. Sometimes she went down there alone, she whispered in my ear. Would I care to join her for a few days sometime after the holidays?

I have always felt honored—as well as surprised—by any kind of sexual proposition, but I didn't know how to get out of this one without hurting the lady. Maybe I should say yes on the grounds that she probably wouldn't remember me in the morning. What would James Michener do? On a television show I had once met Mr. Michener, and he had looked like a banker. Probably he would have had the sense to stop this curious seduction before the lady had had a chance to commit herself. Apparently the stiffness of my body and my whole attitude were all the reply that my suddenly receptive partner needed.

"You're not interested, are you?" she asked harshly.

"Well, I hardly ever go to Florida in the winter," I replied.

She gave a snort of derision.

"That's the trouble with you writers," she said, "you're *all mind*, aren't you?"

Leaving me in the middle of the dance floor, she fled the room. Glancing at my wristwatch, I saw that it was about two o'clock in the morning. My wife was dancing with a tall young man whose looks I did not like at all. Breaking in on them, I asked when she wanted to go home.

"Not for ages," she said with a laugh. "I'm having a marvelous time."

After getting a fresh glass of Scotch and water at the bar, I walked upstairs. Most of the people had gone, but Johnny Mehegan, a fine musician, was improvising "Satin Doll" on a piano. A buxom red-haired woman was standing by a glass wall, looking out at the pond, where morning mists were beginning to gather. I asked if she wanted a drink, and when she requested Scotch, I gave her my glass while I went to get another. The basement bar was out of ice.

"Try the refrigerator upstairs," someone called.

The big modern kitchen was empty and pleasingly quiet. While I emptied an ice tray, the red-haired woman came in. We sat on a counter drinking Scotch and when our glasses were empty I brought a bottle up from the bar. She had just been divorced and was trying to raise three children in Pound Ridge. What with one thing and another, it was not a town which she much admired.

"It's not a good place for marriages," she said sadly. "The men all go in to New York and carve out all these great careers, while the women stay home and are nothing but babysitters. I think my husband just got bored with me, and who can blame him? Why should a big-time lawyer stay married to a babysitter all his life?"

I tried to console her. We drank more Scotch and I kept telling her how *attractive* she was. We exchanged a few kisses and were startled when somebody came in to make coffee. A clock on the wall said it was almost four in the morning. Soon Elise came in with her coat already on, and said she wanted to go home. Because I obviously had been drinking too much, she drove.

The next morning I slept late. When I finally came into the kitchen for breakfast, Elise looked stony-faced. Later she told me that some gossip had telephoned to tell her of my escapade with the red-haired woman the night before. I tried to laugh it off, but apparently she could not see any humor in the situation.

"What would you do if I did that sort of thing?" she asked. "Do you think it can't happen?"

As I wrote the first draft of my new book I felt a great need to show it to Dick Simon. Although I was dimly aware that a really talented professional writer should be able to finish a book without infusions of praise, encouragement and advice from a publisher, I still had no confidence in, and oddly no knowledge of, the pages I had written. When I was occasionally asked to review a book by somebody else, I felt able to give a fairly accurate estimate of its worth, but the pages which rolled from my typewriter were a mystery to me. Sometimes when I read them my excited mind and imagination built each scene up to heroic proportions. When my emotions were too finely drawn, I would find myself moved to tears by any passage that was remotely sad, and to boisterous laughter by any sentences which had a hint of humor. When I was depressed, however, my whole manuscript seemed leaden, devoid of emotion and meaning of any kind, unreadable even with the greatest attempt at concentration. Where on the sliding scale of my emotions did I have, approximately at least, the viewpoint of a reader who had never before seen my pages?

There was a growing suspicion, a sort of sinking feeling that the manuscript was no good and should be buried before anyone could make fun of it, but there were occasional flights of wildest hope that this was a book whch would last forever. Always an extremist, I felt sure that the novel was going to be the greatest triumph or the worst disgrace, without any possibility of anything in between.

In my opinion Dick Simon was the only person I could trust to read the manuscript. If he disliked it, he would not crush me, and if he liked it, he would know how to help me to improve it as much as possible. The only problem was that Dick's illness grew worse instead of improving. Often I visited him at his home in Stamford. There were no glittering guests there now, only a trusted nurse and Andrea, who kept running between the house in Bronxville and the Stamford place to meet the needs of her husband and four children. Once I saw a sight so heart-breaking that like my father's last heart attack, I could never remember it in detail. Dick was standing by his swimming pool. I do not remember what he was wearing. I think the sky was blue. I was sitting in a chair and looking up at him. He was a very tall man, of course, and from my perspective, he looked even taller. Suddenly he began to fall. I cannot remember any outcry. Instead of crumpling to his knees, he appeared to fall like a great oak tree, crashing full-length upon the ground. I do not remember what happened after that. Presumably I shouted and people came running. Soon he regained consciousness. My mind wanted to believe that the fall had never happened, and sometimes I found myself forgetting it. After making a partial recovery, Dick lay in bed downstairs in his big house, or sat propped in an armchair. An excess of light bothered him and many curtains were drawn. The house was kept more quiet than a hospital. Sometimes Dick wrote a few pages of a memoir he was planning. When I called upon him, he asked me to read them and I found the reversal of our roles disturbing. He was almost as anxious for my approval of his work as I had been for his of mine. Although I of course did not say it, I was surprised to see that he was as much a novice at writing as I would be at publishing. He was too modest to take himself seriously as the protagonist of a story and so discreet that he could say nothing but good about the many famous people he had known. Remembering how he had treated me when I sent him a bad section of my book, I told him that his work was coming great, and that we would discuss it in detail when more was done.

Undoubtedly it would be wrong to give a manuscript of a novel to Dick while he was so weak. Especially because he might want to start his own company to publish it, the strain might be dangerous. On the other hand, I was sure that Dick would be hurt and angry if he read in the newspaper that I had given my book to some other publisher. After the enormous amount of help he had given me, he would have every right to be disgusted.

This was a dilemma to which I saw no solution. As a result, I delayed and delayed, until finally my manuscript was as good as I could make it. Sensing my situation, several publishers offered me some attractive deals. In desperation I had a talk with Andrea, who referred me to Dick's doctor. The physician saw no dilemma at all. Under no circumstances, he said, should I give Dick a manuscript which would tempt or oblige him to go back to work. The news that I was going to get another publisher because of his illness might hurt for a while, but Dick was a realist who had always taken such events in stride.

The next day I made up my mind to visit Dick and tell him my decision. At a big round table in our living room, I finished a late breakfast. A curious thing happened then, the only example I have had, before or since, of the subconscious affecting my body uncontrollably. When I started to stand up to go to Dick's house, my legs would not work. Furthermore, my hands, which I had doubled into fists, would not leave the table. Three or four times I strained to stand up and simply could not.

"What's the matter?" my wife asked.

I was sweating. I could feel the sweat trickling down my back, but I still could not lift my hands from the table.

"I don't think I can see Dick now," I said. "I know what the doctor said, but I just can't—"

"But you have to! You don't want him to read it all in the papers."

She was right. I was negotiating with another publisher, a fact which some columnist might pick up.

"Can you go?" I asked finally. "It might be easier for him to take it from you. You can tell him the truth, that I'm very upset and embarrassed." I didn't add that it would be easier on me, too—that was obvious.

In the end, she did it. Dick obviously was hurt by the news, but he took it with good grace. For several days after that, my wife seemed more than usually distant. Once she asked me how I could possibly manage to be so strong and at the same time, so weak. Has anybody ever invented a satisfactory answer to a question like that?

A *Summer Place*, as I called my new book, was an enormous success before publication, and a great failure after it. Before anyone outside the book trade read it, we sold the movie, magazine and soft-cover book rights for a total of about $700,000 with some profit-sharing in the Warner Bros. contract which brought the take close to a million dollars. As soon as the book was published, however, the reviewers apparently competed with each other to see who could clobber it the worst. I was accused of being simple-minded, a slick panderer to the public taste, and a salesman of soap opera. My old friends at *Time* did not know whether to admire me for getting rich, or to curse me for not being complicated enough to deserve the scrutiny of some of their better brains. At various times they called me a "Typewriter Tycoon" and "The Man with the Golden Typewriter" before going on to say that what I wrote really wasn't worth much. Reading my bank statements and all the derisive criticism, I felt as though someone were trying to make love to me and hit me over the head with a hammer at the same time.

In reacting to all this, my wife and I seemed driven to act out every known cliché about sudden success. We had a champagne party and took the children to Europe aboard the *Queen Mary*. At that time of the year (the fall), the first-class section of the great ship was deserted, except for the crew. My memories of the voyage consist mostly of endless walks down empty corridors, many of which had mirrored walls which showed clearly that at thirty-eight, I had grown too fat. Much of the time the children were seasick and stayed in their bunks while Elise read to them. The only asset of the ship which helped me to survive was a young Cockney bartender, to whom I explained a great deal about literature and the fact that money can't buy happiness. After completing his education for the day, I went on deck and leaning on a rail, stared into the fog which dogged us as we crossed the North Atlantic. How many days and nights aboard the *Nogak* had I spent gazing into such murk? Why, in some ways, had I been so much happier then? The teak rail of the old Cunarder was beaded with moisture and felt slippery under my hands. I remembered that Hart Crane, the poet, had committed suicide by jumping overboard from an ocean liner. Suddenly I had an image of myself vaulting over this rail; I could almost feel the clutch of the cold sea which I had evaded for so many years, and I could almost see the lights of the *Queen Mary* haloed by fog as she drew away from me. The intensity of this vision was such that I stepped back from the rail. Why on earth would I suffer such a strange temptation? Didn't I have everything in the world for which to live?

Because I had been too busy to make arrangements, Elise had left the details of our European tour to a German travel agent who was a friend of a friend. All travel and hotel accommodations had been efficiently made, but there was one major difficulty: we had to follow a precise schedule to arrive at all the places where we were booked at the proper times. If we liked a place where we were supposed to stay one day enough to spend a week, nothing could be done about it, and if we loathed a hotel where we were supposed to stay a week, we still had to pay for the week, even if we walked out after an hour. Officious guides met us every time we got off a plane or train to make sure that we stayed on schedule. The children developed colds and in the finest restaurants kept demanding such delicacies as hamburgers and American ice cream. In Holland we chartered a cruiser to explore a few canals. The craft came with a captain who kept assuring us that we were perfectly safe. When I tried to help him handle the lines, he told me sharply that passengers were supposed to remain in the cockpit. For no good reason this made me furious, and I sat drinking from a prettily decorated jug of Dutch gin which I had thoughtfully brought with me. When Elise said I was drinking too much, I got mad at her.

In Venice Elise said that the elevator operator in our hotel was extremely handsome. She also said that the gondolier we employed was beautiful in a dark, Italian kind of way. When we passed a couple engaged in a hearty embrace on a bridge, I said, "Whatever caused us to let passion like that go out of our lives?"

"Well, he's young and very handsome," she replied.

I knew at that instant that our marriage was over. There was no immediate reason for such a drastic decision—there was just a sort of emotion conclusion. Apparently I did not employ reason much when it came time to make important decisions. After years of working for Roy Larsen, I had made up my mind to quit when I had had to ask another young fellow if I could hold my man's hat down on Canal Street. Perhaps my pride was too touchy to be fair to people. If I felt sufficiently humiliated, there was some sort of flash reaction, and I quit.

Of course I did not say anything to Elise at the time. We kept on our schedule, like some demented train speeding along twisting rails. In Germany we rented a minibus and toured the Black Forest, from which some of Elise's ancestors had come. My daughters argued about the number of marks their allowance should bring them, a debate which was climaxed by David's vomiting in my lap. Apparently the whole trip was affecting him with acute nausea, a condition with which I could readily sympathize.

In Paris I very nearly seduced a chambermaid who came to make up our room while the rest of the family was out sightseeing. She was not even a particularly good-looking chambermaid, but I had as clear an image of tumbling her on the bed as I had of jumping off the *Queen Mary*. We stared at each other intently for a few seconds. Brushing back her hair with her hand, she gave me a timid smile and sat down rather suddenly on the edge of the bed. Suddenly I was disgusted with myself, gave her a handful of francs from my wallet, and bolted for the bar in the lobby.

On the way home aboard the *Queen Mary*, I spent most of my time in a deckchair, staring into the fog and trying to figure out what had gone wrong with me and my marriage. Did all the sudden money have much to do with it?

In a way, I thought. When we were struggling to bring up three children on a small salary, I had always thought that everything would be all right if I could only write a successful book. Much of the time we had been easily as unhappy as we apparently were now. The memory of that made it impossible for me to believe that in poverty there is bliss, while the rich are always miserable. There had, however, been one advantage in striving for wealth: our misery had never seemed to us to be a permanent condition. Soon I would be able to afford to work less punishing hours. Soon we would get a better house and a car which did not excite the pity of my daughters' friends. Always there was that gold pot at the end of the rainbow which would supply solutions to most of our problems.

But what did one do after one had grabbed the pot and found that it actually solved few of the questions which had been churning inside us for so long?

Perhaps the difficulty really lay with youthful marriage. When we both had been in our teens, we had had, superficially at least, a good deal in common. Then I had gone to war, and as Elise often said, I was an entirely different man when I came back. The remark had annoyed me, because how could anyone expect a war to leave a man unmarked? It was the same for most men I knew who'd been away in the war for any period of time. I *had* been changed by the war, and later I had been changed by my years as a junior executive in New York, and still later I had been changed by the rather fantastic experience of writing two best-selling novels. Elise, I was sure, had also changed, though her experiences were less obviously traumatic than mine. To my astonishment I found that I could not accurately describe her any more. In my youth I had thought of her mostly in terms of her extreme beauty, her sweetness and her loyalty. Now I didn't know what she was. Flamboyant interior decorator, devoted mother, amateur painter, ardent party-goer and participant in dance-floor flirtations, hater of boats, rapid-fire smoker of cigarettes, believer in prayer—all those things she was, but they certainly did not add up to the portrait of a woman. Although I had been married to her seventeen years, I still could not get her into focus. Perhaps that was *my* trouble. She often said I did not understand her.

Tired of trying to answer the riddle of my wife, I attempted to see if I could get myself into focus now, at the age of thirty-eight. Thirty-eight might not seem old to many people, but it was close to forty, the beginning of middle-age. My youth was gone, like money spent. What did I have to show for it?

Three fine children and a wife whom I could not quite see. A widespread reputation which I could not understand because I knew it was not true. My books might turn out to read like soap opera, but they certainly were not designed to pander to the public. Why did so many people, from the chancellor of the University of Buffalo to the editors of

Time seem to think that I was clever enough to know what the public wanted and base enough to write less well than I could to supply the demand? As far as I knew, in my field, the better I could write, the more books I would sell. Still, if I was going to be tagged as the man with the golden typewriter, I'd have to live with it. There was no way I could change the way other people thought of me, and plenty of men had gone through life with worse reputations to live down.

I also had traded my youth for money, which was not so bad when I considered the fact that most people are obliged to trade it for nothing but a wrinkled face. My last two books had made a rather fantastic amount of money. Just how much I could keep, I could not know until the tax men argued with my lawyers and until I saw how the "tax-sheltered" investments my lawyer was making for me worked out. It was rather strange to reflect that I had no idea how much money I would have until the dust settled, but presumably there would be enough to support Elise and me in almost any style we wanted for quite a few years, even if we got divorced.

What kind of life did I want for myself? To put it bluntly I wanted a woman who did not think me too old for passion and who in general could admire whatever I was. Whether such a woman should be a mistress or wife, I had no idea. I also wanted a sailing vessel capable of going anywhere in the world. Why ships so fascinated me still, I also had no idea. If I wanted to be sentimental, I could point out that my grandfather had been an arctic explorer and that I was descended from a long line of fishermen, whalers and sailors of many kinds extending back to the Vikings, my mother said. A more likely explanation of my recurring desire to go back to sea was that I felt far more competent there than on the land. A ship was governed by the known rules of nature. The men aboard her lived according to regulations and customs which had been codified over the centuries. People might say that I did not know how to write a book or to manage large sums of money properly, but on the deck of almost any small vessel I felt that I was a seaman who had paid my dues and knew what I was about.

When the *Queen Mary* landed in New York we returned to Pound Ridge. There was a party to celebrate our return, and Elise seemed radiantly happy. The next day I had a hangover and could not bring myself to tell her of my momentous decision, which was still nothing that could easily be explained with words. In time, of course, I did tell her, then appalled by the prospect of creating such havoc, agreed that we should both try to cure whatever was wrong with us. It was not long before she got disgusted one day and herself broached the idea of divorce. Worried about the children and perhaps more scared than I had thought by the prospect of starting life over again more or less alone, *I* talked *her* out of it. Our tensions continued to build and we had arguments so bitter that I can still hardly believe them. Somehow the blindness of love had turned into blind hate. Just as lovers can see nothing wrong with each other, we reached a point where we could see nothing good in each other. Just as lovers usually try to avoid inflicting pain, we searched for words with the sharpest barbs. Realizing that there was something more than a little insane about all this, we both sought the help of psychoanalysts. Absorbed in the study of ourselves, we went through months of talking to each other hardly at all.

My daughters reacted to this debacle in the house in their own different ways. Lisa, who was about thirteen when the trouble became obvious, became stiffly independent. Every morning she dressed herself perfectly, met the school bus on time, and spent much of her afternoons playing with friends or doing her homework. Oddly, she changed from a good student to an excellent one.

Rebecca, a year younger, appeared overcome by anger at the whole world. She didn't want to get dressed in the morning, often refused to go to school and occasionally told me that she hated me.

"What's the matter with Becky?" people used to say.

Since her mother and I were both going to psychoanalysts, we found a third doctor for her. The logistics of our cures were difficult. My doctor was in Scarsdale, Becky's was in White Plains and her mother's was in Ridgefield, Connecticut. Often we seemed to spend most of the day just driving around in search of sanity.

For quite a while my family's doctors' bills were $150 a day. Fortunately, my lawyer said that they were deductible, and were therefore not costing me much. The economics of my situation were often contradictory.

All this went on for two years. We had many brief reconciliations followed by more outbursts. In the hope that we might find peace if we could avoid the parties and the circle of friends we had made in Pound Ridge, we sold the house which we had elaborately renovated there, and bought a house in Bedford Village which had to be redecorated. I bought a thoroughbred horse to ride on the neighboring bridle trails. A large dapple-gray, it was as neurotic as I was, which inspired a certain understanding between us. The frightened animal shied at almost anything that moved and often bolted for no apparent reason. Finally it almost killed both of us by jumping halfway over a barbed-wire fence. As I extricated the struggling beast from the coils of jagged wire, I was as badly frightened as I had ever been, and sold him at the first opportunity.

Elise pointed out that the kind of riding I had been doing was almost suicidal. This worried me, for I had been mysteriously driven to take reckless sails in my twenty-four-foot sloop. Although I was usually overcautious at sea, I sailed that centerboard racing machine from Falmouth to Martha's Vineyard and back alone while small craft warnings were flying. When the wind started to gust up to thirty miles an hour, I took down the mainsail and rigged the jib as a storm trysail. The boat handled perfectly that way, and there was a great sense of elation in bringing her into harbor under full control while the wind kept larger yachts in port.

Unfortunately my recklessness extended to my driving. Always I had prided myself on my careful driving, but in a period of a few months I was stopped so often for speeding that I was only one point from suspension of my license. Also, I had escaped a conviction for drunken driving on the Merritt Parkway only by the strangest kind of luck. The cop who had been writing the ticket had been suddenly called away on an emergency, leaving me to creep home by back roads, where I was not observed.

I did not need my psychiatrist to tell me that a man who really wanted to live would not behave in the way I was acting. Trying to calm down, I accompanied my son on fishing trips. Ever since his triumph on the island of Captiva, he had spent every spare moment exploring the larger ponds of Pound Ridge. Although I had done quite a lot of ocean fishing, I was not used to tiny lakes full of branches that snagged my line when I did not tangle it in the trees overhead as I cast. My nerves were tight and these minor catastrophes caused me to swear in such a fashion that David tactfully assured me that he was quite capable of fishing alone. At night we often played chess. It was hard for me to concentrate and, at the age of eleven, David started to beat me regularly. Not long after that he told me solemnly that he would like to go to boarding school. From friends he had learned the name of a good institution for very young students near Lake Placid in the Adirondacks. Upset by the thought of sending my son to boarding school at the age of eleven, I asked him why he wanted to go.

"Well, dad, put it this way," he said gravely. "I figure I'm a ten-acre kid in a one-acre lot." I thought I got the message. In any case, we sent him to the boarding school, where he seemed to be happy and spent much of his time fishing the streams of the Adirondacks.

Elise had the kitchen in the Bedford Village house painted black— floor, walls and ceiling. After a bitter argument about something or other with me in that kitchen, she tore out of our driveway in our Volkswagen camper. A few minutes later the state police called to say that she had had a serious accident. Hit by another car, she had lost control and had charged through the wall of a large roadside restaurant. She had been thrown clear, and as far as the police were able to make out, she had suffered no more than a broken leg. At the moment she was in an ambulance on the way to the hospital.

I beat the ambulance to the hospital and was waiting as they carried her stretcher in. When I greeted her, she said nothing. I thought she was suffering from shock, but when they moved her into her room after examination, she still would not talk to me. She was not suffering from shock, the doctor explained to me. She simply was very angry at me.

I assumed that her accident had been caused by the recklessness of anger, which can be as bad as alcohol. When the case was finally judged, it was decided that the driver of the car which had started the whole thing by hitting her from behind had been in error, and Elise was awarded a settlement.

"Why did you assume I was wrong?" she asked.

There were more reconciliations and more murderous arguments. I felt like a wire that was being bent back and forth until it broke, and I'm quite sure that she felt the same way, although I never was really sure how she felt. On several occasions I moved out of the house to the Harvard Club, which made me feel like a stock character in an old-fashioned short story. The bar at the Harvard Club was full of men who had been forced, temporarily or permanently, to leave home.

While this was all going on I had an affair with a kind woman about my own age who was a translator of books and business documents. She had been brought up in Austria, where, as Jews, she and her family had been persecuted. In 1939, she had escaped to France, where she hid from the Germans and worked with the underground. She was the first woman I had ever met who understood the nature of war. As a matter of fact, she understood the nature of almost everything important. She had been married several times. Sometimes it seemed to me that she told me about a new husband every time I visited her. When she didn't tell me about husbands, she told me about lovers, some of whom were distinguished men. I cursed my Puritan ancestors for making me jealous of her past.

It was lucky that this lady had considerable experience with men. She recognized me as a typically distraught wretch on the brink of divorce. Asking nothing of me, she comforted me through many bad nights. Even when I awoke in the morning full of nameless guilts and insisted on calling my home (presumably from the Club), to see if my children were all right, she understood. On weekends when I was in exile from Bedford Village, she provided rich spreads of good German and Russian food, the variety and subtlety of which I had never suspected. She built me up, complimenting me on my appearance and the marvelous way in which I made love. She had translated one of my books and read them all. Because she was a supremely literate person, I treasured her compliments, which were never excessive enough to be unbelievable. Under her kind gaze, I felt as though I were stretching in the sun.

The main thing that she taught me was that there was such a thing as life after divorce. It also was possible for me to experience hours of high elation and days of quiet peace with a woman. Life did not necessarily have to degenerate into the desperation which my wife and I seemed unable to escape.

I broke off the affair when Elise and I made one more college try at a reconciliation for the sake of the children. My friend, the translator, did not make my departure difficult. She said that she had expected it all along. For a long while I tried to tell her how much she had helped me. Finally I stopped. She said very little, but from that wise face of hers I suddenly realized that of course she knew.

That reconciliation with my wife lasted only another few months. Most of the time I wrote. Somehow, during all those months of turmoil, I had written another book, *A Sense of Values*. It was about a man and wife working out a permanent reconciliation after infidelity. Before it was finished, I knew it was not good, for I was under some compulsion to write about life as I wanted it to be, not as it was.

I do not remember the immediate chain of events which precipitated the final break-up of our marriage. The last scene, however, remains clear. We were standing in the big living room of the big house in Bedford Village. Elise said, "I want a divorce," and somehow there was a ring to the words which we both knew was final. I packed two footlockers with clothes and books. There was a rather undignified struggle as I got them into the Volkswagen phaeton which I decided to take because Elise would need our bigger car for the children. There were no dramatic farewells. After more than twenty years of marriage, all our love and furies had been spent. There remained only an almost casual good-by.

During the drive into New York and countless nights afterward, I tried to understand why our long marriage had ended, despite so many years of earnest effort to make it work. I rehashed our being people who married young and then were abruptly separated for four years during the war. When I came back I was a beat-up sailor and an ambitious young writer with no real interest in the ordinary amenities of her middle-class life, although I attempted to ride with them. As the years went by I drank too much and my emotions were erratic.

Had I been entirely at fault? Of course not. In moments of anger I ascribed the most undesirable qualities to my wife, and some of the time I might have had some justification. I was also aware that no man is really capable of painting a fair portrait of his former wife. Rarely do men understand their former wives—if they did, the word "former" might have remained unnecessary. Men who paint their former wives as terrible bitches make their listeners wonder why they married such a woman in the first place. Disappointed husbands who complain that their former wives did not love them enough, or were "frigid," must occasionally wonder whether they are lovable enough to deserve passion from any woman. If I chose to believe that Elise was horrible, how could I explain to myself the fact that I had remained married to her more than twenty years, and had three fine children with her? And if she wasn't horrible, how could I explain my willingness to go through this agony of divorce now?

Now there was a riddle! Yet perhaps there was a simple answer. Between the ages of twenty and forty, two good people can grow up in different ways without becoming monsters. We were getting divorced because we had become too different to stay together amicably. All over the United States similar tragedies were being acted out, and some of the participants were able to go on to better things. If I had had the guts to survive the Greenland Patrol, I ought to be able to handle this new kind of adversity. At least divorce didn't make a man seasick.

30

I went to a hotel near the United Nations building which had been recommended by my psychoanalyst on the grounds that apartments were available by the week, month or year. For people who did not know what they wanted to do next, that was an advantage. My room with the two footlockers in the middle of the floor was so quiet that my ears seemed to buzz with loneliness. For a few minutes I considered calling the translator who had treated me so well, but some instinct told me that it is wrong to reopen a well-concluded affair. At any rate, I had not seen her for several months, and I doubted that she had remained alone so long. This was not a time when I felt in the mood for any sort of rivalry. In all probability I should not go rushing to any woman the instant I left my home. For a few weeks, at least, I should live alone and think.

But why was the hotel room so quiet? The concrete walls screened out most of the sounds of traffic far below. Silence had always been conspicuously lacking in my homes. Usually Elise or one of the children was practicing on the piano, and someone always had the big stereophonic phonograph or television set turned up full blast. Often I had yelled that

I needed quiet for my work. Never had I imagined anything like the death-like silence of this room.

Suddenly I became acutely homesick. My children and my wife, or "former wife" as I would have to learn to think of her, still could not be thought about, but I missed my familiar desk, with the drawers which offered everything I needed for my work. I missed my shelves of books, even my closet and bureau, where I could always find appropriate clothes. I missed the big willow trees which I had trimmed, and became agitated over the question of who would mow the lawn. The big lawn-mower which I had brought from Pound Ridge had several idiosyncrasies which would have to be explained to any yard man who was hired. It was easier to worry about this than the children, who had not yet been told about my final departure. As Elise had said, they would not think my absence odd for a few days.

Restlessly I went down to the bar. A lot of men who seemed to me to be homosexuals occupied about half the room. Fashionably dressed, animated and loud, they filled the place with nervous laughter. In comparison to them and almost anyone, I felt leaden and glum. After a few drinks, I headed for the elevator. It was empty except for a gray-appearing man who was carrying a stack of soft-cover books by James T. Farrell. His face was haggard but vaguely familiar. Since boyhood I had read and studied *Studs Lonigan* and many other books by James T. Farrell, who like Hemingway and Faulkner had been one of my father's household gods. The face before me in the elevator was an older version of one I had seen on dozens of bookjackets.

"Are you Mr. Farrell?" I asked.

"Yes," he said.

I introduced myself and said that I had long admired his books. Before he could reply we came to his floor.

"Come on," he said as he got out, and I followed him down a hall. When he got to his room, he put the books down and fumbled with his key. His room was small and the walls were entirely covered with bookshelves which contained, among other volumes, the forty or so novels which he had written in all their many editions and translations. He was surrounded by a library which he had created entirely by himself.

Farrell stood by a desk in the center of the room, and holding his stomach rocked back and forth as though he were in pain. His face seemed grayer than ever.

"Are you all right?" I asked on impulse.

"Sure! Had an operation a while ago and there's a little pain, but I'm all right. How the hell are you?"

"I'm all right."

"How the hell old are you?"

"About forty-one. Why?"

"You look like hell for that age. I hate to see a writer go down the drain. I know your stuff. I'm tough and you're sentimental, but we're both real writers. There are not many of us left."

I could not have been more pleased if I had been awarded the Nobel Prize.

"Now why do you walk around looking so down-at-the-mouth?" he asked.

"I'm in the middle of a divorce."

"Oh, that. I've been through two or three. After a while you begin to lose count."

"I guess I haven't begun to get the knack of it yet."

"You're a writer, aren't you? Haven't you learned anything yet? Women will go to you because of your intensity. They will leave you for the same reason. You will always have a woman but it will never be the same one for long."

That prediction sounded probable, but it also sounded lonely. I wished I was as tough as Jim Farrell.

"Do you have a typewriter?" he asked suddenly.

"Yes."

"Do you have a girl?"

"Not at the moment."

"Well, get one! A typewriter and a girl are all a writer is ever going to have in the long run, and they are all he's ever going to need."

That too sounded probable.

"Do you drink?" Farrell continued.

"Yes. Too much, I'm afraid."

"Try to stop before you burn the house down."

"What?"

"I drank until I went to sleep with a cigar and burned the house down. You might as well quit before a thing like that happens instead of after."

"I see your point," I said.

"Don't let anything happen to your vitality," he said. "I've hung onto mine. You know, when I went into that hospital for my operation, a lot of people figured that I had cancer. All my former wives and agents got in touch with my lawyer to make sure that I had written a will. I have trunks full of manuscripts for posthumous publication and everyone wanted a share. Do you know what I did?"

"What?"

"I told my lawyer to tell them I had written no damn will because I had no intention of dying. I went into the hospital, let them cut me open, and four days later I laid the night nurse!"

"That's vitality," I said.

"It's a writer's stock in trade, boy. They all think it's brains, but it's vitality."

In a few minutes I went back to my room. Jim Farrell had taught me more than he knew. Far older than I, sick, reduced to one tiny apartment in a hotel which was not known for its luxury, alone and momentarily, at least, out of literary fashion, he still worked at his typewriter almost every waking hour and viewed the world with the courage of a lion at bay. Although I thought that he was treated shabbily by a fickle public and certain editors in the book trade who thought only of tomorrow's sales without regard for the vast accomplishments of Farrell's past, he never showed a trace of self-pity, and always had time to cheer me up.

"Do you have trouble sleeping?" he asked me once when I looked a little red-eyed.

"Sometimes."

"I used to until I decided to give it up. Just stop trying to sleep. Work instead. It will get you a lot farther."

Perhaps under the influence of Farrell, I did start working again. The only things I really liked to do, I decided, were to sail a boat, drink, work or make love to a woman. A boat I was trying to design, roughing out sketches for a rugged ketch, but I didn't think that I should attempt to build such a craft until the dust of divorce had settled down. The drink I was trying to control before I burned the house down. A woman I wanted, but the intensity of my need frightened me. There was danger of grabbing the first reasonably presentable female who came along, as plenty of men in my position had done. Loneliness had become such a torture to me that I was liable to propose marriage to the first woman who invited me into her apartment for a night. Clearly a man in my situation should give his emotions time to settle down.

To my surprise, life continued. The children did not seem surprised when I told them about the divorce. They were not stupid, and had seen it coming for a long time. Their lives went on without much change, except they visited me on weekends to make the tour of the museums and the Bronx Zoo with the children of other confused-looking fathers.

For some reason I was depressed by reading that the children of divorced parents are not chosen for service aboard nuclear submarines. There went my children's career beneath the seas.

The book came along fast. For some reason I had chosen as a subject the love of a middle-class college administrator for a seventeen-year-old girl. Was this the expression of some sort of subconscious wish? The few girls that age whom I had known had attracted me little, despite the beauty of youth, because they clearly had thought me no more than mildly amusing at best, and talked in a language which I could barely understand. When I had talked about the war at a party, one of my young listeners had said my tales were interesting, though of course she had not even been born in those days. Realizing that she thought of World War II much as I thought of the Civil War, I felt older than I ever had in my life.

No, young girls in reality did not attract me, but in the world of fantasy I was apparently hooked. The novel about a teenager who proved more mature than her middle-aged lover almost wrote itself.

Then I had no more work to do, except a class in writing which I had agreed to teach on two evenings a week at New York University. The students were adults. Most of them were women, and a few were unusually attractive. Somewhat to my chagrin, I found myself becoming a practiced seducer of my own students. This was against the written or unwritten law of every university, I was well aware, but already times were beginning to change. My victims or co-conspirators were close to my own age, and many had taken the course to fill the empty evenings which followed a divorce.

It both embarrassed and pleased me to find that the routine of a teacher of writing lent itself easily to seduction. For some reason pretty women seemed to me to write unusually well. Their work called for conferences which often led to a few drinks in a bar. If one thing led properly to another, an affair could start and continue smoothly until one or both participants got bored. Despite the guilt that I continued to suffer after any sexual activity, I was surprised to find that these brief affairs offered a great deal of excitement and pleasure without any noticeable pain for anyone. From what my father had told me, I think that that descendant of countless generations of Puritans honestly believed that a man who undertook a love affair was almost certain to be sued or blackmailed if he had any money. In addition he was likely to contract at least one venereal disease. The girl was almost certain to get pregnant. If she had the child, the man would have to support it for life, and if she sought an abortion, she was likely either to die on the illicit operating table or commit suicide in remorse.

With the help of modern science, however, the age of sin without painful consequences apparently was coming into full flower. Of course, I was lucky in that the partners I chose, mostly on the basis of their appearance, turned out to be uniformly tolerant and kind. They were interesting people, too. One of them had gone from being an airline hostess to a designer, manufacturer and salesman of uniforms for airlines and military personnel. The owner of a fairly large business, she had no interest in getting married because she still had memories of the torturous marriage her parents had suffered. Much of the time she was lonely, however, and feared men who might take advantage of her wealth. Her schedule was busy, and she had no time for an ordinary social life. Sometimes she felt that she wanted to make other arrangements which in those days were usually considered a prerogative of the male. Smilingly she asked me whether I would like to be her mistress. At first I said that sounded great, but it also made me feel a little queasy. When she started sending me cufflinks and other bits of jewelry, I bowed out. The memory of making love to her after hours in her display room, where we were surrounded by mannequins wearing the uniforms of naval officers, chaplains and policemen, remain, along with a mental picture almost as clear as a photograph of a resourceful, curiously wounded forty-year-old woman fighting for life and money in New York.

Another of my favorite students was a woman who called herself black, despite the fact that her color was a creamy light tan. When I was stupid enough to mention to her the fact that the word "black" was not an accurate description of her, she replied that "white" hardly described a man like me, who appeared to combine various shades of pink, gray, and tan. A brilliant woman, she was a successful lawyer, as well as a writer whose work had been published in some of the literary magazines. Her background, which she loved to discuss, fascinated me. Since before the Civil War, the women in her family had kept records of births, both legitimate and illegitimate. These women had usually been good-looking, as she was. As a result, a governor, a general and two senators had contributed their genes to her blood. The knowledge that she was more than half white, more than half Southern slaveholder, had come close to giving her a split personality when she was growing up. Finally she had decided that regardless of light color, she was fundamentally black. The ancestors she felt loyalty and love for were the ones who had come straight from Africa.

She had never had an affair with a white man and I had never had an affair with a black woman. It was impossible to dodge the fact that our relationship was based in part on racial curiosity. Before going to bed she accused me of expecting a black woman to be more passionate than whites.

"No, I expect you to be colder," I replied.

"Why?"

"You're upper-class black. Upper-class black women often rebel against the stereotype and become as inhibited as Boston Puritans used to be."

She laughed.

273

"Now, damn it, I don't know what to do."

After a strenuous session of love-making, she said, "Well, was that all nigger?"

"I don't know whether you want me to say yes or no."

"What do you think?"

"Was I all whitey?"

"Yes," she said, and stuck her tongue out at me.

She had a cultivated voice with no trace of what used to be called a Negro accent, or Southern accent of any kind, although she had been raised in Atlanta. When I asked her how she had lost her accent, she snapped, "That's a disease which can be cured."

The fact that her voice over the telephone was indistinguishable from that of a so-called cultivated white person gave her great pleasure.

"On the telephone I have no color," she said. "Sometimes when I kid around with white lawyers, they try to make dates with me. Can you imagine how their faces would look if they saw me?"

"Some would be pleased. You're a fine-looking woman."

"Ha! They'd have a fucking heart attack!"

Her frequent use of profanity was apparently an attempt to re-establish a bond with those who used street talk, or to show me that she really was not as white as she looked and sounded. By turns she tried to be white and black. One evening she read Shakespeare aloud to me for two hours and discussed each scene with a perspicacity which obviously came from years of study.

"The hell with this shit," she finally concluded, put some soul music on her hi-fi set, pulled a huge drum from a closet and insisted that I beat it while she took off her clothes and danced until her skin was wet with perspiration. A little later she got mad at me when as a natural expression of wonder I admired the delicate shadings of color on her body. Somehow I had always thought that people came in uniform colors, but the tops of her breasts were almost golden, while the outsides of her thighs had been brushed delicately with black ink.

"You make me sound ugly," she said. "Anyway, you can be damned sure that I'm all black inside."

After a few weeks she began introducing me to her black friends, most of whom were men. This was a test I abjectly failed. Most of the men appeared intensely hostile to me. At these get-togethers in her apartment, she made a point of serving soul food and what she referred to as "black booze," which turned out to be wine and mixed drinks which struck me as being very sweet. Although I felt it was my own fault, I could not make conversation with anyone in the room. Abandoning me to my social fate, my pupil sat on the lap of a large black man to whom she seemed to be telling humorous anecdotes about me, for they frequently glanced my way and laughed. I left early. When I called her the next day, she said that she was busy, but that she was grateful to me for being a good teacher. I thanked her. I never saw her again, and I never did figure out what she thought I had taught her.

31

When my course at the University ended for the year, I took my daughter Lisa to Mexico. Long ago I had promised her such a trip because she had taken my advice to study Spanish instead of Latin in school. Now she spoke Spanish fluently. At sixteen, she was a lithe young beauty who looked much the way her mother had looked when I first met her. A superior student, Lisa startled me with her carefully considered views on Melville, J. D. Salinger and Tennessee Williams. She also had read all my books, which she was loyal enough to praise, though in the company of Melville, Salinger and Williams, superlatives were difficult. On our first day together she was wearing a severely-cut traveling outfit of blue linen. Her blonde hair was cut shorter than I had ever seen it, exposing her graceful neck. As we waited for our plane at Idlewild Airport, men of all ages glanced approvingly at her. She had good legs, I noticed for the first time. She conducted herself with such poise that she could easily have been taken as several years older. It was curious to think that this was the infant which old Dr. Clark in his bloody coat had handed to me only sixteen years before. The time had passed so fast that suddenly it appeared to me that she had grown up right in my arms as I stood holding her and looking out the hospital window, dreaming of her future.

We flew to Mexico City. Eating with my daughter in restaurants and walking the streets to see the sights, I discovered that for the first time in ages I was completely free of loneliness. The desire to meet a woman who might be interested in an affair had vanished. My daughter and I shared more untarnished memories than I could discuss with anyone else.

"Remember the time ... ?" was a great way to start sentences. Lisa gave me my past back again. Her very existence proved that my marriage, disaster though it had turned out to be, had still served to create three new and promising human beings, even if they never would be allowed to serve in nuclear submarines.

"Remember the time you took me out in the boat on Lake George, and the big wind hit?" she asked.

The racing sloop had been new, I recalled, and I had been anxious to try her out, even though the wind was much too strong. The boat was supposed to carry three men as crew, but only Lisa had volunteered. Like me, she had savored the excitement. Soon after we had cast off, a gust hit us, and we went planing across the lake, drenched by spray. As I rounded into the wind, the boat nearly capsized, but we got her under control and took her flying back to the dock.

"That was *fun!*" Lisa said.

"Remember the time we learned scuba diving?" she asked now.

This too had been during a summer on Lake George. I had hired a young diver to instruct the whole family, myself included. Of us all, Lisa was the one who took off like a fish after a few lessons. Afraid to enter the depths which she wanted to explore, I paid the professional diver to follow her. They found a grappling hook which probably dated from the French and Indian War. She gave it to me, and it was one of the things I had left behind in the house in Bedford Village. Could I ask my lawyer to demand my grappling hook when he drew up the property settlement which had to precede a divorce?

"Remember the church dance?" she asked.

Soon after moving to Bedford Village, I had been asked to chaperone a dance for high school students in the Presbyterian church near our house.

"Don't do it, daddy," Lisa said.

"Why on earth not?"

"They're a rough bunch," she said. "They get into fights with guys from other towns. They drink a lot. You never can tell what's going to happen."

"You think I can't handle a bunch of Presbyterians?" I demanded indignantly. "During the war I was often shore-patrol officer in convoy ports. If I can keep order in a town where the crews of a hundred ships go on their last liberty before sailing, I think I can handle a dance at the Presbyterian church."

Not long afterward I showed up on time for the church dance. Quite a crowd of young men had already gathered. They looked bigger and older than I had expected high school students to be, and quite a few were ducking frequently into a cloakroom, where they apparently had hidden a bottle. The thought occurred to me that if I tried to discipline these youths, I would probably prove powerless. It was true, as I had told Lisa, that I had been shore-patrol officer occasionally while serving aboard the *Tampa*, but on those brief tours of duty I had been backed up by a small army of about fifty boatswain's mates which had been recruited from the other ships. I had been protected by my uniform, the shore-patrol armband and a .45 automatic, as well as the most useful tool of all, a whistle which brought all those boatswain's mates running. With such support it was not hard to be a figure of authority. Here in the Presbyterian church I had nothing but what I hoped was a commanding presence.

A few at a time the girls came in, wearing pretty evening gowns. They appeared much better dressed than the boys, most of whom lounged on the sidelines even after a high school quartet began to play rock and roll music. A thin perspiring minister brought in a bowl of orange punch. While he returned to the kitchen three of the young men screened a fourth who poured a bottle of gin in the bowl. Probably I should confiscate the punch and berate the spikers, but they did not look as though they were susceptible to berating, and I remembered too many dances of my youth which were enlivened by the thrilling news or rumor that somebody had spiked the punch. Sinking down in a chair which had been placed near a pay telephone, I lit my pipe and tried to relax.

The trouble started with such suddenness that there was time to do nothing. Through the front door burst a crowd of maybe twenty burly young men. Later I learned that they had come from Stamford to crash the dance, but when I first saw them I had the odd feeling that they had dropped from Mars. The Bedford Village boys gathered in a group and warily walked to meet them. There was the crack of a fist on flesh, oaths and a general flailing of arms. On one upraised fist I caught a glint of metal. Several of those schoolboys were fighting with brass knuckles.

The minister did a despairing little dance around the mele. "No, no, no!" he kept saying.

Obviously this was the situation which I was supposed to control. Without a moment's hesitation or hint of fear, I put a dime in the pay telephone and called the state police. Then I stood well back from the flying beer cans and bottles. Through long habit I continued to smoke my pipe, which impressed the minister, who later congratulated me warmly on my ability to stay cool. Actually, of course, it is easy to stay cool when one is not encountering any danger. If I stayed in a certain corner, the bottles and beer cans all missed me by several feet.

The barracks of the state police were not far away. Soon after I called, three police cars arrived with shrieking sirens and flashing red lights. Six state troopers, who somehow contrived to make themselves look like a whole company of marines, came charging in, night sticks at the ready. The warring knot of adolescents broke, and youngsters tried to jump out of every door and window of the old church building. The few the troopers managed to collar writhed in their hands like fresh-caught bullfrogs, protesting shrilly that they were innocent bystanders. After they had been taken off for questioning, the minister and I tried to answer the questions of the biggest of the troopers. Apparently he knew more about the cause of the battle than we did. The Stamford boys long had felt that the Bedford Village group was snooting them. As a result, a kind of high-class, suburban gang warfare was developing.

When I got home, Lisa—who had heard about the fight from friends who had telephoned her—was worried about me.

"Are you all right?" she asked.

"Of course," I replied.

"What did you do?"

"For a man who headed the shore patrol in convoy ports, there was no problem. A few tough kids were fighting, so I just handled them, that's all."

"*How* did you handle them?"

"I assumed a commanding presence and spoke in a voice of authority. You learn that in the coast guard, you know."

"I thought the state police had to come in."

"Oh, I called them in after it was all over. After all, I can't possibly make arrests."

She was, of course, only half-believing, and I soon told her the real story, but not before I had a lot of fun demonstrating to her my commanding presence and my voice of authority. Many times she had demanded repetitions of this heroic stance and voice. Now, only two years later in a restaurant in Mexico City, she broke up when I gave her a new and improved version which had all the waiters staring at us in some alarm.

In Acapulco I dreamed of chartering a sailboat with my daughter, and when we tired of that we might go after a sailfish. I had not been so happy for years. When I went to bed at night I needed no alcohol to put me to sleep. At eight in the morning she met me by the swimming pool, a slender figure in a white bikini with a strawberry design. After exhausting ourselves in the water, we ate a hearty breakfast on the terrace, beginning with that great basket of tropical fruit which most hotels in Acapulco offer to their guests. Over breakfast we would plan the day. First of all Lisa wanted to try scuba diving. Explaining that a doctor had told me not to dive because I once had had chronic bronchitis and asthma, and that I also suffered from chronic fear, I begged off, but offered to hire a professional to accompany her. When she agreed, we made an arrangement with a diver whom the hotel recommended. He had a thirty-foot boat which took us to a place in the bay where, he said, they had an underwater statue of the Virgin. Lisa said that she would prefer to see fish. Shocked, the diver said there would be plenty of fish, too. The water was so warm, he added, that there would be no need for wet suits. After helping Lisa to strap on her air tank, he somersaulted overboard and, without hesitation, she followed. I was left standing in the cockpit of the boat with the deckhand, an ancient Mexican who kept going forward to let out

278

more anchorline, despite the fact that there was no wind or current. The only evidence of my daughter was bubbles. For some reason I had neglected to ask the depth of the water here. There was no chart and the deckhand could not understand me. In a few minutes a large glass-bottom boat crowded with tourists came out to see the Virgin. It was soon followed by two more that were owned by the same company. There was a pleased outcry and someone said in English, "a real mermaid." Lisa, I imagined, looked good under water with her white bikini and her golden hair shimmering in the sun. Before long a launch-sized glass-bottom boat came out and started circling over the concrete Virgin and my daughter. Nervously I glanced at my watch. Lisa had been down about half an hour. Before long she would have to come up. Suddenly it occurred to me that the four boats which were slashing the water with their sharp propellers directly over my daughter's head could constitute a real danger to her. If she came up with very little air left, she could not go around the vessels on the surface. If she was exhausted, she might not be able to dodge the bows of the heavy craft, and the wake they made might trouble a struggling swimmer.

In some corner of my mind where common sense resides, I knew that Lisa could come up under our boat, where a boarding ladder awaited her. If she panicked or grew too tired for that, the professional diver was there to help her. Yet here all reason suddenly took flight from me. That professional diver was a *Mexican*. What the hell do Mexicans know about the sea? The fellow's weathered face had seemed fairly villainous to me. Probably he was *raping* my Lisa down there in the shadow of the concrete Virgin.

I was sweating, and tried to talk sense into myself. With scuba gear, sexual intercourse was possible underwater, but rape would be highly risky. It would be all too easy for the victim to pull off her attacker's mask. What got me to thinking such weird thoughts anyway?

Danger. I seemed to smell it in the diesel exhaust from the circling fleet of glass-bottom boats and see it in the hard glitter of the sun on the turquoise sea. That is the way the air had smelled and the sea had looked when the Japanese torpedo plane had seemed to rise out of the waves only a few hundred yards away from us. I knew the stink of danger, didn't I?

I am being absurd, I thought, the way a man might observe that he was falling as he tumbled from the top of a skyscraper. There is no danger. My daughter is diving with a competent professional.

My watch indicated that it was almost time for Lisa to come up. Crazy fears I might have, but there was nothing imaginary about insane boatmen who liked to keep circling over divers. In my mind I had a horrible picture of Lisa coming up with one leg cut off by a propeller. In my arms I held her while she bled to death. What was this overpowering sense of loss which came from the perfectly normal hazard of circling boats? Lisa had eyes, didn't she, which could see?

Perhaps not if she was exhausted. Getting up on the cabin of the little cruiser, I started to yell at the glass-bottom boats and wave my arms to motion them away. Undoubtedly they did not understand my English, even if they could hear it, and an American waving his arms apparently did not seem unusual to them. Noticing a red flag on our bow with the diagonal white stripe which means that a diver is down, I grabbed it and waved it in big arcs. None of the glass-bottom boats paid any attention to me.

"Clear the area!" I thundered as loudly as I could. "Divers coming up, divers coming up! You crazy Mexican bastards! Do you know what you're doing?"

There was no answer but the imperturbable chortle of the diesel engines of the big glass-bottom boats. Weakly I sat down.

"Hi!" Lisa suddenly called from a point somewhere forward of the bow. I rushed forward. With her mask pushed back on her head, she was hanging on to our anchor line. The professional diver was facing her, his hand also on the line. Both were smiling broadly.

"I had a wonderful time," she said enthusiastically. "Pedro here was great. We saw a small shark. I think I would have died if he hadn't chased it away."

I immediately loved Pedro and all Mexicans. Lisa and her guide swam aft to the ladder, and the deckhand took her tank before she climbed up.

"The Virgin is lovely," she said. "It's oddly moving to see her staring through schools of fish."

"Did the glass-bottom boats bother you?"

"A little. The idea that I had an audience kept bringing the ham out in me. I wanted to go up and knock on the glass, but of course I was afraid of the propellers."

"You had no trouble coming up?"

"Of course not. We just came up the anchorline. He has so much out that we came up very gradually."

So my nightmare of loss had had absolutely no rational cause. The thought that I was capable of such an acute anxiety attack was sobering. So was the following self-inquiry whether a strong feeling of love would always for me come mixed with an acute fear of loss.

On the way back to shore the diver offered me a drink from a bottle of tequila, and it was so good that I had more on the terrace of our hotel. Tired from the diving, Lisa was upstairs taking a nap. It was good to sit in the sun knowing that she was safe in bed.

✲   ✲   ✲

That night Lisa and I had another marvelously pleasant dinner. Afterward an orchestra played and we danced, with Lisa making my Miss Darlington foxtrot seem graceful, as only a really good dancer can. We sat down and I ordered Scotch on the rocks. From nowhere, it seemed to me, a nice-appearing young American man of athletic build came up to our table.

"Lisa," he said, "would you like to dance?"

That, in effect, was the last I saw of my daughter during our vacation in Acapulco. Her friend was the captain of the football team in South Bend, Indiana. He was good at scuba diving, swimming, dancing, and almost everything in the world except talking or reading, Lisa reported.

"I guess you could say he's sort of boring, Daddy, unless he's doing something strenuous, but of course here we can do something strenuous almost all the time. And in a way I think of as old-fashioned, or maybe mid-western, he is straightforward and very nice. I think maybe I knew too many terribly intelligent people in Bedford Village. It's kind of a relief to meet someone who doesn't know all the answers to all the problems, even if mostly he just sort of smiles and throws balls around—"

"Where did you meet this brainless wonder?"

"Now, don't be nasty. I met him in the swimming pool when I took a dip one night after you'd gone to sleep. I need someone my own age, daddy. What's a trip to Acapulco without a few dances in the moonlight?"

I had no ready answer to that question. Lisa now disappeared from the hotel for most of the day, and often called me to say she was in her room only when it was very late at night. I worried about her, but obviously there was little I could do to protect her. In view of the fact that there were no acceptable alternatives, my general plan for raising daughters had been, for a long time, to trust in God and hope for the best.

After one day of sitting by the pool alone, my need to meet women returned. There were few women in the hotel except dowagers and girls close to Lisa's age, who were beautiful but probably unobtainable. One widow a little older than I struck up a conversation with me at the bar by commenting on the beauty of "the young blonde" she had seen with me in the dining room most nights.

"Thank you," I replied. "I of course am very proud of her. She's my oldest child."

"Then I win a bet," she said with a mischievous smile. "I have a cynical friend who was sure the girl was your mistress."

"Your friend is not only cynical but sick," I retorted with more heat than the situation required.

"Don't be too critical. A lot of men travel with young girls down here. A woman of my age can expect to attract nothing but beach boys. Most of them want payment in advance, which kind of ruins the romantic mood, and you have to be careful that they don't take your jewel box with them on the way out."

In a rather rueful way, she was an interesting woman. When she learned my name, she said she was the widow of the owner of a fairly-large well-known publishing company. Before marrying her husband, she had been his assistant, and she knew a lot about the business of books.

"You were with Simon and Schuster, weren't you?" she asked.

"Yes."

"You were a friend of Dick Simon. What happened to him? I heard he had a stroke."

"He died," I said.

"When? I've been down here for three years. I go for months without reading any papers and you never can catch up."

My mind seemed to block. Dick's death must have been after 1958, because he told me that the publication of *A Summer Place* had set me back ten years, no matter how much money the book made. If he had published it, I at least probably would have improved it before rushing to the printers.

"I'm not much at remembering death dates," I replied.

I had been up in the Adirondacks visiting my mother, so it must have been summer. For some reason my wife did not go to the funeral—perhaps she felt that she had to take care of the children. At any rate, I drove to New York alone. It seemed a terribly long drive, as though it were all uphill. The memorial service for him was at Campbell's Funeral Home. They had a string trio play music he had loved, and there were formal eulogies by people who had known him well. While the string trio played, I kept remembering that he had told me once that he had started out to be a concert pianist, but had decided that he lacked the talent. I never knew how seriously he took his real talent, which was bringing out talent in other people who lacked the strength and courage to go it alone. I personally know at least a half dozen writers who would never have been writers without him. The thing that bothered me most was that very few of all the writers whom he had helped over the years showed up for his funeral. The services were conducted in part by old business colleagues or rivals, some of them men whose policies he had fought tooth and nail during the last years of his life.

I finished my glass of tequila. Dick Simon was dead, my wife was getting divorced from me, and my daughter Lisa had disappeared somewhere into the Acapulco night. I needed quite a few more drinks to get to sleep.

The next day the widow of the publisher asked me to visit her in a cottage she owned on a cliff high above the hotel. The view of the sea was rivaled only by that from airplanes. The house was small but luxuriously appointed with a terrace surrounding a swimming pool. All afternoon and all evening we talked. She drank as I thought only men could, matching me glass for glass without getting visibly or audibly drunk. What she knew best were the distribution and sales aspects of publishing, parts of the business which I knew least. She also was an astute manager of money. Her inheritance from her husband she had doubled in four years.

"It leaves me in a rather comfortable position," she said. "I never thought I'd be a millionaire."

I did not really know—or care—how much to believe her. I saw a lot of her during the last days of the vacation while Lisa was still cavorting with the Mindless Wonder, as I insisted on thinking of him. The widow, it occurred to me, was as lonely as I was, and longed to get married. Despairing of attracting men in any other way, she had fallen into the habit of flaunting her wealth, real or exaggerated, the way a peacock parades his feathers. There would, I thought, be advantages in marrying such a woman. As far as I could see, she was good, kind and astute. Once she asked me whether I would be interested in forming a publishing company with her. If I did that, I would be in control of everything about my books from the first rough draft to the copies for sale in the bookstores. We might even branch out, she said, lying back on a chaise longue under the Mexican sky. Why not start a small movie company and control the films which were made from my books? The movie of *A Summer Place*, which the critics had damned, was doing phenomenally well at the box office, and the musical score from it was still frequently heard even in Mexico. Why sell the movie rights to a book like that for peanuts.

"It wasn't exactly peanuts," I replied.

"How much did you get for it?"

"A half million plus a quarter of the profits."

"Peanuts," she said with a snap of her fingers. "The picture will make ten million easy, and it was all your idea in the first place."

It seemed to me that I was getting into pretty big business. Still, it was nice to imagine life as a movie and publishing tycoon . . . this little villa in Acapulco would be suitable for an occasional holiday, perhaps I could buy about a hundred-foot schooner which we could anchor anywhere in the world we wanted while we conducted our far-flung enterprises by radio-telephone. . . .

Whether she was a phony or not, I admired the lady. I like direct people who go directly for what they want, and she was fighting for escape from loneliness, as I was. Only one thing stopped me from further examining the possibility of a future together: she looked *old*. Why this should bother me so much I didn't really know. Or rather I couldn't really justify it. After all, I too was middle-aged, only a year or two younger than she. I too was overweight. Even so, I just did not think myself capable of making love to a woman whose figure was so alarmingly similar to my own. Superficial, I suppose, but also rather basic.

Actually I think I felt more than a little in common with this lady, whose face was attractive, with big, dark eyes under bangs of silvered hair. She was apparently just stuck in life, as maybe I was, lusting for kinds of love which she could not get, as maybe I also could not. After constantly advertising her wealth, she complained that all men wanted from her was money. In moments of anger after drinking, she said that all men were prostitutes, the whole lot of us. Yet when I declined her various offers of mammoth financial deals, she was furious. The women with whom I had had affairs had always said good-by to me graciously. This woman in Mexico, whom I had never even kissed, cursed at me so viciously that I walked out of her house without waiting for her to give me a ride back to my hotel. The night was dark and the hill was steep, but it was better to walk than to linger with someone who was such unpleasant evidence that loneliness was perhaps the hardest disease of all to cure.

I did not see much of Lisa until her Mindless Wonder brought her back to the hotel from the beach just in time for us to go to the airport and catch our plane home. I distrusted his bland, innocent face because when I had a bland, innocent face I was mostly thinking about how to get girls in bed. I wanted to ask my daughter whether anything, well, indelicate, had happened on her sojourns with this football player, but of course she would have become indignant and would have laughed at me. Although she was only sixteen, she was already an inscrutable woman. I took refuge in the hope that her intelligence would help her to get through life with less pain than I had experienced recently, and attempted to keep the conversation on the plane light. Trying to help, Lisa told me about her plans for school and college.

"What do you want to do after you get out of college?" I asked.

"I might want to write," she replied shyly.

This answer rather staggered me. I was touched by what seemed to be a compliment by implication. On the other hand, like almost all writers, I hated to see any child of mine go into such a traditionally risky, heartbreaking profession. This I tried to explain to her.

"I didn't know it had been so hard on you," she said. "You've been so marvelously successful."

"Have you enjoyed the success much?" I asked.

"Of course the thing with you and mother isn't much fun. Do you think that would have happened even if we had stayed in Buffalo?"

"No."

"Then success is the whole cause of it?"

"We couldn't have been divorced in Buffalo because we wouldn't have been able to afford it. That doesn't mean we would have been happy. I have often wondered what would have happened if my book had failed and we found we were just stuck where we were."

"What do you think would have happened?"

"We would have been under severe stress, and stress can kill. In one way or another, I think we would have cracked up. For more reasons than I understand, your mother and I just can't make a life together. We couldn't face it, but actually things weren't going right for a very long time. Maybe we never were right for each other, and kept avoiding *that* over twenty years."

"I know," Lisa said. "I always felt it. In some ways the divorce is a relief."

32

When she got back to New York, I drove Lisa back to the house in Bedford Village. The lawn needed cutting. On impulse I got the big mower from the barn, started it up and did the job. When I had finished, Elise came out onto the porch to thank me. She looked thinner, a worn but still attractive woman. I could not tell what I felt as I climbed back into the little Volkswagen phaeton. There was less hostility toward her than in a long time, but I had no temptation to try for a reconciliation. The past was dead, and like anything dead, could only be mourned.

New York also seemed to me to be dead that summer. It was hot and the air-conditioner in my room hummed disconcertingly. My manuscript about the middle-aged professor and the teen-age girl had gone to the publisher, who said he didn't like it much, but would do the best he could. I should have taken it away from him and looked for someone more enthusiastic but I had lost confidence in the work and was in a mood to let events take their course.

Deciding to visit my mother at Rogers Rock, her place on Lake George, I grew more depressed. Since the death of my father, my mother had lived alone. She had a servant and a wide circle of friends, but no one was really close to her, not even her grown children. Now seventy-five years old, she was mentally and physically spry. Only a few years before she had visited Africa. The black Nigerian giant who had lived with us in Buffalo had told her to look him up if she ever got to Lagos, and, by God, she did. The man who had once imperturbably worn my old uniforms and suits, despite the fact that they were much too small for him, had been a senator in his native land, and had entertained her royally in his compound.

Did mother ever get lonely on these solitary travels, or sitting in the big living room of her cottage while the whippoorwills called and the light died on the mountains which surrounded the lake? Of course she must. Or had she found some cure which had bad side-effects, such as the way her features settled into a look of stone? Overcome by compassion for her, I gave her a hug. Her body resisted me as though I were making an improper advance.

"Oh, Sloan," she said, "don't do that. You'll mess my hair all up."

I went back to New York and on impulse I flew to the Caribbean, which I had always wanted to visit. Perhaps I had been seduced by the travel folders which showed beautiful girls on the beaches of all the islands. The travel folders lied. Of course I was traveling off-season, but the only pretty girls I saw were brides on a honeymoon. Morosely I stared at the black beaches of Martinique, where I happened to see the motion picture actress, Claudette Colbert, step from a small yacht to a pier. My image of her had been retained from the winsome young heroine in the movie of the Thirties, *It Happened One Night*, and it was a shock to see that she had become an old lady, her heart-shaped face still familiar, but her frail body twisted by something, perhaps arthritis. Seeing her beauty go, as it were, before my eyes, as though she had just walked from Shangri La, I became intensely conscious of the mortality of my own flesh. I was forty-one years old and still felt young, but how long would it be before I had to totter off a boat on the arm of a servant?

The thing to do in Martinique was to tour the area which had been wiped out by a volcano shortly before the first world war. The trip was expensive and guests from my hotel commonly shared a taxi. My companion for the day was a stewardess from Air France, a tall pale girl with a big nose who to my fevered mind looked like the kind of daughter Charles de Gaulle would be likely to have. She spoke little English, and though I had studied French for seven years at the best preparatory schools and at Harvard, I could manage very little more than *oui* or *non*. The main thing that impressed me about the village which had been wiped out by the volcano was a dungeon where a prisoner was said to have become the only man to live through the holocaust. I wondered whether the prisoner had ever blessed the crime which had caused him to be put underground. What kind of a world was it where only the wicked survived?

"*Seulement les mauvais...*" I stammered to my companion. Looking mildly amused, she lit a cigarette without reply.

That night I took the lady to dinner and after a great deal of wine, I was desperate enough to try to make love to her. Disproving all clichés about French women and airline stewardesses, she seemed cold as an exhausted wife. Although she did not resist me, her hands felt so clammy that I found myself rubbing them as though she were suffering from frostbite. Giving up, I gave her a fond farewell kiss on her pale forehead and whispered thanks for the day. She made no reply and it occurred to me that she might have been asleep or even dead from the moment I had first kissed her. Chilled by this thought, I hurried from her room and had a drink at the bar.

From Martinique I flew to St. Kitts. It had an ancient fort designed by the same Frenchman who had designed Fort Ticonderoga, which was near my mother's place on Lake George. An old guide pointed out to me the massive blocks of stone with which the fortress was built.

"You couldn't build a fort like this any more," he said. "This place was constructed by slaves. You can't get men to work that hard in this climate without a whip."

My trip was lonely but it certainly was educational, I thought. So far I had learned that an actress who had been one of the loves of my youth now looked like my grandmother. God had let only a man who had been convicted of some dreadful crime survive the eruption of a volcano. At least one French woman tended to go to sleep when kissed, and if you want to build a fort in the tropics, you better have a whip. Obviously travel was better than college any time.

I went to the island of Nevis, where Napoleon's Josephine had been born. There I stayed at a luxurious inn which had been built in an abandoned sugar mill high on a mountain. My room had a glass wall overlooking the western sea, where the sunsets were as spectacular and as tinged with green as they had been in the South Pacific. My bed and bathtub were huge. Obviously the room had been built for love, and it was a hell of a place to sit alone. Hurrying to the bar, I found that it was full of elderly people who had flown in from the States on a tour. For some reason they were wearing Hawaiian leis made of brightly colored cellophane, garish sports shirts or dresses and enormous straw hats. After dinner they organized lively square dances, which they asked me to join.

"I don't know how," I said.

"We'll teach you!"

There was no graceful way out. Soon I found myself twirling ancient ladies whose painted faces appeared to me to look like my mother gone mad. They had one game during which everyone joined hands and danced in a circle around me and my partner, who could have been Claudette Colbert's maiden aunt. Suffering a fit of claustrophobia at the thought of being trapped by these panting old folks, I fought back an impulse to lower my head and charge to freedom. Pleading my inability to keep up with them athletically, I retreated to my room with a bottle of rum as soon as possible. A full moon was painting a broad silver path across the darkened sea. A bomber's moon they had called it ashore, but at sea it was a submariner's moon. The reason why was clearly apparent now as a big yawl tacked across the silver path, her white hull and sails as clearly visible as though she were under a spotlight.

Would I feel less lonely if I were sailing my own boat through the Caribbean?

Probably. At least I would have more to keep me busy.

That night I returned to plans to buy or build a little ketch. Her name, I decided, would be *Farewell*. For some reason the melancholy self-pitying ring of that name pleased me. The purpose of my voyage, I decided, would be to sail beyond the edge of the world. Perhaps in the Marquesas Islands, where Melville had found his Fayaway, I too would find a brown girl shimmering in the sun as she stood beneath a waterfall. Whatever else it was, this was a good vision with which to put myself to sleep.

The last stop on my tour of the Caribbean was Antigua. There steel bands seemed to be drumming away everywhere. "The music of romance," one travel folder proclaimed them. Their soft, insinuating rhythms echoed from little night clubs high in the hills. A big steel band on the terrace by the swimming pool of my hotel set the glasses jiggling on the racks behind the bar. When I turned on the radio to get the news, all I received was more of the music of romance. How the hell did the natives stand it?

I was becoming crabby, old and irritable, I realized as I glanced in the mirror behind the bar. From too much sun or too much rum, my face had turned to an alarming shade of brick red. Bleached by the tropics, my hair had turned from its normal shade of light brown to the blonde of my youth, or was it already turning white? Whatever it was, I looked old. Because I squinted on the beach, thin white lines spread from my eyes where the wrinkles had protected the skin. When I raised a drink to my lips in the morning, I was shocked to see my hand shake.

Many of my fellow guests at the hotel were even older than my dancing friends at Nevis. Calling the airport, I tried to cut my visit short, but I was told that "Princess Rose" was flying in or through, and all reservations were being cancelled until the airline ascertained what facilities were required by royalty. For about three days I and the other guests were stuck at the hotel while the music of romance continued to fill the air.

Most of this period I sat morosely hunched over the bar. A thin little old woman who was wearing a bikini made for a much more youthful figure and her husband, a man so fat that he had an almost feminine figure, for some reason tried almost to adopt me. They asked me to have dinner, to take a tour to Nelson's Harbor (which I did), and to play shuffleboard, Ping Pong and bridge, for which I was in no mood. For some reason this pair of old people had a knack of making me feel as guilty as I had felt under the eyes of my parents during my boyhood. The woman seemed to me to be counting every drink I bought, while the man clearly disapproved of my feeble attempts to banter with a pretty waitress who was the only attractive woman in the hotel.

For a while I could not understand why this elderly couple would not let me alone. Glancing at them when they did not know I was nearby, I suddenly figured out that they were probably as bored and lonely as I was. They did not fight in public, but they also never spoke to each other. Slumped in beach chairs by the pool, they were as silent as melting wax dummies. After they had given up on me as a source of companionship, I noticed that they set little traps for an angular young schoolteacher. There was the offer of dinner, and though they had already seen Nelson's Harbor, they took their new friend on a trip there. Soon the teacher was joining them for luncheon by the pool every day. They all talked animatedly, but when the teacher left for only a few minutes, the old husband and wife fell morosely silent.

When finally the airline resumed its flights, the old couple approached me in the lobby of the hotel to say good-by. Feeling guilty about avoiding them, as well as about all those drinks I had had, I asked the wife where they were going next.

"Arizona, I think," she said, "then maybe Mexico."

"It must be nice to follow the sun like that."

The old woman sighed and put her hand on her glum husband's arm. "Yes," she said, "it's nice. Dad here worked his whole life so we could live like this."

I felt a shiver. How many years did I have to build something which could reasonably be called a life?

33

Although I had worked in New York City a large part of my life, I had surprisingly few close friends there. Jim Farrell made me feel guilty because he kept typing day and night, while I somehow had lost interest in my work. As far as writing more or less for the sake of writing went, I seemed to know less and less about life as I grew older, and a writer needs to have at least the illusion of wisdom. How can a self-confessed fool begin a book unless he is to attempt low comedy?

Even my desire for transient love affairs was ebbing. Apparently I had hit the point of diminishing returns. Suddenly the routine of mutual seduction by two practiced, middle-aged people seemed mechanical. Sex, of course, was almost always good, but when I discovered that it did not necessarily provide more than a few moments of release from loneliness, it no longer appeared to offer some magical answer to all the problems in the world. I spent a lot of time at the Harvard Club bar. For a while I thought that all the members of the Harvard Club were as depressed and mixed up as I was, but then it occurred to me that only the few men who spent most of the day at the bar with me shared my problems.

Late one night in my hotel room, drunk, I telephoned Elise and begged to come home. Since my words were so slurred that she could barely understand me, she was not outstandingly eager to accept me. After telling me that we had long ago passed the point of no return, she suggested that I see my psychiatrist with as little delay as possible.

I did this the next day, driving out the Bronx River Parkway. The psychiatrist to whom my friend, Dr. Rosenchein, had directed me was a man who took a few adult patients but who specialized in children. Since my wife had often accused me of being immature, it rather startled me to find myself sitting in the waiting room with ten-year-olds and walking into the treatment room as a nine-year-old with a red beanie walked out. I always expected to see a child's bed near the doctor's chair, but his standard psychoanalyst's couch was seven feet long.

"How have you been?" the doctor asked me.

"Dandy," I replied with a wry face, and began to try to free associate. Although I had concentrated in psychology at Harvard, I never understood how this really helped. It was supposed to take a great deal of time,

I knew. Fundamentally the treatment had to be taken on faith. Since I at the moment had little faith in anything else, I didn't feel as though I had much choice.

Not long afterward my evening course at New York University began. I had always enjoyed teaching at New York University but had guilt feelings about the possibility that some of the ladies with whom I had had a brief affair would return as students. Why this should affect me so strongly, I had no idea, but it did. Before long this mysterious guilt seemed to transform itself into a peculiar kind of fear. During most of my two-hour classes I talked or read papers aloud. What would happen if my throat tightened up and my voice gave out? At the University of Buffalo I had occasionally suffered that fear when I was on the brink of exhaustion, but now it returned in a form that was far more intense. How long could I stand behind my desk dumbly staring at my students? How could I explain it if I suddenly bolted from the room?

These thoughts made my face flush. Marking some passages in a book which I could give any student to read aloud, I decided that I would plead a slightly sore throat and ask the pupils to do the work. If the condition persisted too long, I would simply have to quit the university job. The thought of that saddened me, for aside from the ready availability of intelligent women, the university offered me the only steady connection to humanity that I had at the moment outside of barrooms.

Long ago I had discovered that I am calmest immediately after a good meal. Before meeting my first class of the semester at New York University, I went to a Chinese restaurant named the Jade Cockatoo near Washington Square. Allowing myself two martinis, no more and no less, I enjoyed a platter of lobster egg foo yong. A few minutes before six, when the class was to begin, I stepped into the big elevator of the nearby building of classrooms. To my chagrin, one of my former friends was standing there, hugging an armful of books. She smiled and said hello as though nothing had happened. Of course, nothing much really had happened, in the opinion of most sophisticated people. The trouble was that I never had been very sophisticated. My old friend with the books preceded me into my classroom. There, to my consternation, was another of my more casual partners. She too greeted me with friendly warmth. My God, I thought, maybe there's going to be a whole room full of them! Who can lecture about literature, love and life before an audience made up entirely of former mistresses? Do women get together and talk over their sexual experiences, as men do in the forecastles of ships? Were they comparing notes on my conduct in bed? Were they arranging some sort of practical joke for me?

This line of thought was ridiculous, I told myself. Actually, I should be complimented that these ladies wanted to return to my class. Fucking was apparently a great way to insure a loyal following of students.

Many more students were filing into the hall. I had told the dean that I liked big classes because they gave a greater possibility of discovering talent. Now almost forty men and women had filed into the hall. Only two of the faces were familiar, and these two women sat near the back of the room. Clearing my throat, I began my introductory lecture.

Long ago I had discovered that I could not read a lecture nor even consult many notes. I fumbled my way through the familiar territory of my address as best I could. Tonight my audience seemed kind of dead, I quickly realized. When I made a few remarks which I thought were humorous, there was scarcely a laugh. Relying on a trick which I had often found helpful, I glanced up, sweeping my eyes over the audience to find a responsive face to which I could, in effect, deliver the lecture. One responsive face, even in a huge audience, can do a world of good for a speaker's confidence and for his sense of timing.

Now my eye traveled only to the first seat in the fifth row. A young woman sat there, leaning forward a little to concentrate on what I was trying to say. She had large brown eyes and looked intensely interested. When I went on to attempt one of my rather bookish jokes, she gave a low, musical laugh. I had found a focal point for my lecture, and it soon started to go well.

Only twinges of the fear of being unable to talk returned to plague me, and I managed to fight them down without trouble. From time to time I continued to glance at the woman with the expressive face. She was younger than thirty, I guessed, but how much younger? One reason her face was so expressive was that the blandness of early youth had been erased by thin lines around her eyes and mouth which might be the tracks of a good deal of both sadness and mirth. She had dark brown hair straight to her shoulders, and she wore a blue linen dress of elegant simplicity. When she stood up after the class, I saw that she had a delicately formed figure almost exactly like that of my daughter Lisa. The resemblance was so strong that I was sure she could wear one of the size 7/8 dresses which I had bought for my daughter in Mexico.

The idea of a woman with the face of maturity and the body of a graceful teenager was enormously attractive to me. Shuffling papers at my desk, I watched her while she put on a white raincoat. Dismissing all my vows to refrain from any further personal relationships with my students, I found myself fantasizing a, well, a more lasting kind of friendship with this person who had the curious ability to combine the best of youth and a certain age. Perhaps when she handed in her first paper, I could respond to it with special warmth, if it was any good, and invite her to an especially good restaurant to celebrate the discovery of her talent. Cynical though that sounded, this time, I promised myself, I would not stoop to trying to involve a sensitive-appearing young woman like this in just a steamy, short-lived affair. At the very least I would like to ask such a woman to take a leisurely trip around the world aboard the boat I was planning, or a liner. It was good to have some happy fantasies to use instead of sleeping pills.

These pleasant dreams were dashed when a tall young man appeared, and with his arm around the tiny waist of the woman with the expressive face, steered her out of the room toward the crowded elevator. A woman like that obviously was not a bored divorcée who was trying to fill empty evenings by taking a course in English composition. Of all things, she might actually have entered my class in the hope of learning how to write! Certainly she would be justifiably affronted if her middle-aged professor made some kind of pitch. A girl with all that grace and style was the prerogative of men as young as she was, even if her face was somehow wiser than her years. Packing my papers in my briefcase, I walked all the way uptown to my hotel. Having nothing else to do, I decided to go through some mail from my publishers which had been accumulating for some time. There were two packets of readers' letters, one from the publishers of *The Man in the Gray Flannel Suit* and the other from the publisher of *A Summer Place*. The movies and foreign translations of both books continued to bring me a good deal of mail. Some of it was disturbing. There was a steady stream of letters from teenage girls who, like the heroine of *A Summer Place*, had become pregnant. One of them said that I was the only person who understood her. Neither the father of her child nor her own father showed any sympathy for her. Another woman criticized the note of optimism on which my books ended. She had read them aloud to her husband, who was permanently paralyzed and had bed sores as big as his hands.

Most of the letters, I was pleased to note, were from people who apparently had enjoyed my books and wanted to say so. Those I really appreciated, especially when they added that they did not require a reply. One long letter, which was written in pencil on yellow paper, was from a man who wanted to kill me. Several times before he had threatened me. His reason was that he had written all my books. I had stolen the manuscripts from his house and had had them published for my own profit, without giving him a cent. When, after the first threat, I had telephoned the police in the small Massachusetts town where he lived, they said he was a former mental patient who had a long record of making threats but who never had hurt anyone. After thinking the matter over I had decided not to press charges. His yellow letters were coming more frequently now. As a matter of fact, my would-be murderer wrote me more often than did my own kids.

There were several letters of serious literary criticism which were great for crumpling into balls for target practice with the wastepaper basket, and, best of all, there were two love letters, one from Iceland and one from Japan. Both were from teenage girls who would probably have screamed if I'd ever shown up in person. Although Iceland and Japan might appear to have little in common, the letters were much alike. In halting English which had more charm than the straight stuff, these bright, perceptive girls attested to the greatness of my wit, wisdom and kindness. The girl from Japan enclosed a photograph. Wearing a dress of Western style, she looked at me from the picture with that wonderful mixture of shyness and boldness which is part of the equipment of almost any sixteen-year-old girl the world around.

I typed out replies to the girls in Japan and Iceland. I told them that I loved them too, for I loved all pretty girls who wrote authors to tell them that they loved not just the books but the authors themselves. I thought that the girls showed good judgment, because if there weren't any authors, there wouldn't be any books except schoolbooks, which as everybody knows are written by machines. The admiration of pretty girls, I ended somewhat rakishly, was my favorite royalty earning, and I hoped that they would keep up the good work.

Finally I went to bed. For a long while I could not sleep, but when I did, I dreamed of the lady with the expressive face and youthful figure. In my dream she was in Japanese costume, and she kept insisting that she had written all my books, and that I had stolen them from her. When I proved to her that I had written the books by showing her the calluses on my typing fingers, she changed her mind and said she loved me very much.

That was a lonely winter. The many friends who had attended all those parties in our houses in Pound Ridge and Bedford Village dropped me completely. I thought they probably were being loyal to Elise, but she told me later that they had dropped her too. Perhaps those hard-driving couples of Westchester County feared that divorce was a disease that might be catching, or maybe my former wife and I had destroyed an image of cheerful success when we parted. At any rate, I was stricken off a great many Christmas card lists. For reasons I did not quite understand, this hurt. My reaction was absurd because all those people with the big houses were associated with painful memories, and I had no desire to see them again.

One bright point in my life was the visits of my children. My lawyer told me that Elise had agreed to giving me joint custody of them, a fact which did not change living arrangements, but which made me feel less of an exile. For some reason I got to know Rebecca better on brief visits than I had in our various homes. In some ways Becky was more like me than any of my children. Physically she resembled me more than the others did. My features were more those of my mother, and Becky looked almost precisely like photographs of my mother as a young girl when she was unusually pretty. Like me Becky had a weight problem, which she soon brought under control. In those years she was always on some crazy diet which required her to eat nothing but apples and cheese or fish and special cuts of meat. Like me, Becky had chaotic emotions. At the age of fifteen, she began to develop a vocabulary which would make a boatswain's mate blush. Her anger at me when I drank too much or inferred the slightest criticism of her mother would have burned through steel, but when she hugged me, I felt that she gave me almost enough love to last for a week.

Becky's enthusiasm for life was gargantuan. She loved dogs. One time when she had about a dozen of them, she heard of a collie that needed a home, and provided her room for him. She loved horses, and though it is difficult for a person with a weight problem to ride well, she insisted on jumping and continued, even after she fell and broke her shoulder. She loved friends and acquired them in all shapes and sizes. A grotesquely fat girl, a thin boy with acne who stuttered and a very pretty girl with a freckled nose who rarely said much, all were among Becky's large circle of friends.

Often Becky was not in the mood for conversation as I toured the museums of New York with her, but after returning to Bedford Village, she wrote me the most remarkable letters I had ever received from a child. Funny and affectionate, the letters meant to give comfort and succeeded brilliantly.

Becky had an instinctive knowledge of suffering which is not ordinarily associated with youth. Clearly she did not really expect life, either in the present or future, to be easy for her, me or anyone else. Yet her highly developed sense of humor saved her from being gloomy. When I asked her what she thought of the teachers at her school, she said, "They are highly trained experts in the science of education. They are sensitive, dedicated and devout. Of course, a good many of them are sadists, but you can't have everything."

After a weekend with Becky, I sometimes drove up to Lake Placid to see my son, David. Because I had disliked boarding school so much, I worried about him up there in the snow-covered mountains, essentially alone at the age of twelve. Never quite sure of how big a child should be at any given age, I worried because he seemed short and painfully thin. He had, however, a strange kind of calm and self-assurance. When I asked him how he liked the school, he said, "The whole place is great. They don't try to make the studies difficult. They let me go fishing and hiking by myself, and the teachers take us on some great camping trips. The only thing I don't like is riding horses. I'm not strong enough yet to control them. To tell the truth, I'd rather go down to the farm and ride the pigs. It's more exciting and I don't have so far to fall."

Remembering that the boys I had known at Exeter had talked about little but sex, and that the conversations had amounted to little more than an exchange of ignorance, I asked David whether he wanted to discuss that subject.

"Sure, dad," he piped. "What does this word 'fuck' mean?"

We were dining at the Lake Placid Club. His voice carried widely and several of the people at the table nearest to us looked at us with interest.

"Let's talk about that," I said. "I think there's an open fire in the library."

"Good. I tried to look the word up in the dictionary, but it isn't there. I know that the primary meaning of the word is screw, but when people say 'Fuck you,' they mean to hell with you. How can one word have opposite meanings?"

There was no fire in the library, but the cavernous room was deserted. We sat on a couch, the leather covering of which was beginning to crack.

"I have heard that the word 'fuck' originally was an Anglo-Saxon word meaning 'to plant,'" I began warily. "I'm not sure that's accurate, but it's the kind of thing which should be true, even if it isn't."

He agreed.

"How the word became an essentially derogatory word, or demeaning word for sexual intercourse, I have no idea. How the same word also became an expression of strong hostility, as in 'Fuck you,' I also don't really understand. Maybe the confusion about this one small word reflects the bewilderment of countless generations about the whole subject of sexuality."

"I thought it was supposed to be simple. It is in biology, The sperm goes in, the egg is fertilized, and the young are born."

"For our ancestors it wasn't always that simple. Men generally have a strong urge to mate. If they do so legally, they have to get married, and in the days before birth control they often had a dozen or so children who could turn life into a madhouse if there was not enough money to support them, as there usually was not. In even the recent past, a man who wanted to mate outside of marriage ran the risk of venereal diseases, illegitimate children, and loss of reputation. Changes in custom and the advances of medicine have removed most of the hazards which used to be associated with sexuality, but perhaps we should not be surprised that the word 'fuck' still echoes the frustration and the resulting angers of our uncomfortable forefathers."

"It sure is a complicated little word," he said. "How do queers get queer?"

"I know you're going to think me stupid, but I don't know. Even the psychiatrists seem to disagree."

We talked for about an hour in that big room as the shadows of late afternoon filled it. He questioned me about every aspect of sexuality which had ever occurred to me, many of which made me feel as though I was being examined on a subject which I had not studied at all well. Why had I gone around cutting classes and leaving so many books unread?

"How," he concluded, "can you tell whether a girl wants to go to bed with you?"

I laughed. "There are some things that you are going to have to find out for yourself."

"Can you just ask her?"

"That works sometimes, but if you make a career of it, you're going to hear a lot of indignant *no's*."

"Do women say no a lot of the time?"

"Wouldn't that depend on the woman and the man? Among other things, after all, sex is hopefully a way to express affection, at least, and admiration. If the man does not deserve those, he may get turned down a lot."

"Do you believe all that stuff about bells ringing and great passions that change people's whole lives?"

"Only a few people are capable of great passions. The rest just have to do as best they can. I'll tell you one thing. As a writer I know that bad sex or even ordinary sex is easily described, easily made believable to the reader. Great sex, which by my definition would have to involve the expression of great love, really is impossible to describe, even by the greatest poets. Maybe that's why a lot of cynical people don't believe it exists."

"If it can't be described, how can anyone who hasn't experienced it be sure that it exists?"

"If I ask you to describe a tin-pan alley tune, you can hum it, but can you describe a symphony?"

"I could show you the score. Anyone who can read music can understand a symphony without hearing it."

"I'm getting over my head. What I'm trying to say is that sex can include a great many emotions: release from loneliness, the joy of being loved, the joy of loving, intense desire, the appreciation of the incredible beauty which some women possess ... None of these words can say the unsayable. You know, in spite of birth control and all the rest, it's possible that people still can feel during sex that special exultation which seems understandable for a man and woman engaged in the extraordinary act of creating a brand new human being. Why shouldn't I have felt great pleasure at the moment I helped to create you?"

He giggled. "Boy, dad," he said, "you sure know a lot about fucking. You ought to give a course on it at school!"

A little while later I dropped David off at his dormitory, and drove down icy mountain roads toward New York. Somehow the long discussion of sexuality with my son had disturbed me. There might be some special exultation in initiating the process of birth, but who really remembered the moment when a child was conceived? Usually the miracle happened to tired couples hoping for some modest release after a hard day's work. Why hadn't I admitted to my intelligent son the simple fact that somehow I had reached the age of forty-one with more hope than knowledge about all the sweet or not-so-sweet mysteries of life?

34

New York always seemed lonelier than ever after visiting the children. The only immediate relief was my class at New York University, which met at six every Tuesday and Thursday night. The woman with the expressive face and youthful figure continued to sit in the fifth row, but she never handed in any papers. There was no way I could learn her name, short of asking her for no apparent reason in front of many people, and my plan for striking up an acquaintanceship with her by discussing her literary efforts obviously was not going to work.

It is strange how much a lonely man or boy can become absorbed in the contemplation of a woman he has never met. Before I was into my teens I fell in love with a young waitress at the Rogers Rock Hotel, and looked forward eagerly to seeing her each summer. Forty-one seemed a little old for that sort of thing, but now I looked forward to seeing my good-looking pupil each time the class met, and when she was late my mood and my lecture suffered. Before long I found myself playing a sort of detective game, trying to deduce as much information about her as I could. Because her clothes appeared so expensively tasteful, I at first concluded that she was rich, but gradually I noticed that she had only about five of these elegant outfits. Tweed skirts and cashmere sweaters became her usual garb as winter deepened. She wore no jewelry of any kind and no furs. When the weather was cold, she wore a surplus parka much like the one I had worn in Greenland long ago.

Most of the time she did not speak enough to give any idea of what kind of accent she had. Then one night, when I was discussing "The Night of the Iguana," which was then on Broadway, my memory failed me in the middle of a passage which I thought I knew by heart, for I loved the play and had studied it thoroughly. While I fumbled for some notes in my pocket, the woman in the fifth row started where I had left off, and from memory completed the passage. She did it naturally, almost unconsciously, leaning back in her seat with her eyes closed. She quoted beautifully, without theatrical over-emphasis but in tones which suited the essential tragedy of the play. I was astounded. How many people are there who from memory can complete a passage from Tennessee Williams?

"Thank you," I said.

She made a smile a perfectly adequate reply. While I completed the lecture, my mind kept trying to analyze her voice. I had always prided myself on my ability to learn much about a person's background from his or her speech, but this woman's voice defied rational examination. There was no echo of national or regional point of origin, except for the fact that the woman was obviously American. There was no hint of economic class in her diction, except for the fact that precision of pronunciation is usually the result of considerable education.

What does a voice so scrubbed of defects mean? Usually such diction is possessed only by television announcers, radio announcers, or actors— people who have taken a lot of voice training. Did she know Tennessee Williams because she was an actress?

This possibility saddened me. I had known few actresses in my life, but from the small experience I had had with them, I judged that falling in love with an actress could be both exciting and self-defeating. Already in fantasy I was having a great affair with the woman with the expressive face and the astonishing knowledge of Tennessee Williams. The last thing I wanted was to see her disappear into Hollywood.

When the class was over for the night, a slender, dark-haired young man who usually sat in the third row got up and walked to the woman with the expressive face. I could not hear what he was saying, but he was talking very fast, and I guessed that he was introducing himself, making a pitch. After a few moments they left the room together. The man was about twenty-five years old. What could I expect?

When the next class began, the dark-haired young man was chummily sitting next to the woman with the expressive face. He had bad teeth, I noted with satisfaction, and he was thin, rather than pleasingly slender. If I had a fight with him, I could probably take him with one hand, even if I was almost twenty years older. I could write better than he could, make more money than he could. Why would a woman prefer him to me?

Why would I probably prefer a woman twenty-five years old to one my own age? And why did I have to keep asking myself these damn-fool questions?

Sometimes it was hard to concentrate on my lecture. When the next class began, I was happy to see that the dark-haired young man was back in the third row, where he belonged. The woman with the expressive face seemed to be taking everything I said down in a spiral notebook. It was curious to be in such close communication with a woman whose name I had not yet been able to learn.

If she was an actress, I found myself speculating, she must be unemployed. If she had been unemployed all fall and winter, how did she support herself? The unwelcome thought that she might be somebody's mistress crossed my mind. Someone had told me that the mistresses of rich men frequent the campuses of colleges in New York because time hangs heavy on their hands. Naturally, I knew perfectly well that one cannot determine from a woman's appearance whether she is a mistress, wife or spinster, but I felt confident that the lady with the expressive face would not be so disloyal to my fantasies. Could she be a model? No, models were usually thinner and much taller. This woman could not be much more than five feet three.

From what country had the forebears of this woman with the expressive face come? Her diminutive size and mobile features suggested some sort of Latin origin to me, but her skin was conspicuously white and was liberally seasoned with freckles, I observed as I passed her in the aisle. Somehow I did not associate freckles with the Latin style. Her clothes were subdued in color and design, either New England or British in their simplicity. There was no way I could guess her ancestry.

Toward the end of the school year, I longed to meet the woman with the expressive face, if only to answer all the riddles she had posed for me. Of course I knew I could simply go up and talk to her, either before or after class, but my rather precarious dignity as a lecturer seemed at stake. More than that, I felt quite sure that she would be genuinely disgusted when I began to change roles from the teacher whose words she carefully recorded to the middle-aged man with an obvious glint in his somewhat reddened eye.

If I approached her in the classroom, she would of course assume that I wanted to discuss Tennessee Williams or some of the other authors I had quoted. Her suspicions would begin when I asked her to have a drink with me. Giving me the benefit of the doubt, she might accompany me to a bar in search of literary conversation. I would of course provide that for a while. But as I tried to see her more and more frequently, my mask would slip, revealing, perhaps, the face of a satyr. Then she would give me her firm farewell, probably as kindly as possible. And I would stand transfixed, my guts in shock.

Why did I imagine that the process of rejection would have to be so agonizing for a grown man? Couldn't I just shrug and start looking for another girl?

For some reason I didn't think so. I had never been turned down by a woman, *not* because of any superior attractions but because I never asked the important question until no question was necessary.

The truth was that I was suffering from an excess of vanity, not sensitivity, I told myself, but I still could not force myself to walk into the center of that crowded classroom for the simple purpose of talking to a young woman I admired, despite the fact that she had filled my fantasy life for months. Why hadn't she handed in a paper? If she simply did that, we could converse naturally without forcing on me any strange crisis of nerves.

For the first time I realized that she must know that the best way to strike up a conversation with me would be to hand in a paper. The fact that she had not done so proved that she did not want to get any closer to me than the fifth row. Wasn't that good reason for trying to forget her?

I was aware that most of my thoughts were ridiculous. An unassuming young woman just came to sit in on a series of lectures and was not to blame if her crazed professor insisted on making her a fantasy subject for juvenile romances. What the whole business really proved was that I was going soft in the head from idleness and should head out to sea as soon as possible. Sailing a small ketch around the world would at least keep my mind occupied with reality.

Always before my plans for buying a ketch had progressed little beyond the fantasy. Now I got in touch with yacht brokers. After going over many photographs and designs I arranged to drive to the little town of Catskill, on the Hudson River, where a staunch little vessel called the *Sea Wind* was being built. I scheduled the trip for a Sunday late in April, two days after my last lecture for the semester was scheduled at New York University.

The last lecture was kept short to leave me time for discussion of some of the last papers which had been handed in. It was a warm spring evening, and the girl with the expressive face was wearing a summer dress of jade-green silk, very pretty. By chance the first paper I picked up was by one of the women I had known the previous year. It was a short story about a sensitive young girl who had been loved and left by a brutish professor. It was miserably written, but I had started to read it aloud to the class, as I did most of the work by the students, and I had to finish. Without pausing for comments, I plunged into a pleasant story which an old man had written about his boyhood. I thought the class would go on forever.

Finally the bell rang. A few students came up to thank me for my efforts and more stood chatting with friends they had made in the class-room. The girl in the jade-green dress was talking to several young men. In a group they moved toward the door and with a curiously intense sense of loss, I realized that I would never see her again. Although I had no idea what kind of person she was, it occurred to me that she must possess some highly unusual quality to keep me admiring her from afar for so long. While I was thinking all this, I found myself trotting from my desk to the door, which I reached just before the woman in the green dress and her circle of friends did.

"Hello," I said to her. "I just wanted to ask you, how come you never handed in any papers?"

"I was just auditing the course," she said. "You taught me enough about writing to make me realize that I can't do it. I mean that as a com-pliment. I despise teachers who try to make any art look easy."

"Perhaps I discourage people too much."

"A great many young writers need discouragement," she said with a wry smile.

I laughed.

"What are you going to do, now that the class is over?" she asked.

"I don't know," I replied. "I'm thinking of buying a little ketch and sail-ing around the world." I felt like an idiot.

"Alone?"

"Yes."

"If you get lonely, let me know. I've always dreamed of taking a trip like that."

I felt like proposing marriage to her right there, but of course she had spoken lightly, keeping her suggestion nine-tenths a joke. There was a pause during which I was too confused to say anything. Quite a few people in the room were now staring at us. The woman whom I had known the year before was holding the story I had returned to her against her breast. I was afraid she was going to cut in on our conversa-tion, but she stalked out the door. If short stories could kill, I was obviously dead.

"I know you like the theater," the woman in the green dress continued. "If you'd like free tickets, I always have plenty of them. Just give me a call."

"I'm afraid I don't know your name," I said. "That's the trouble with not handing in any papers."

"Betty Stephens," she replied. "I'm a theatrical press agent, or an apprentice theatrical press agent to be exact. Here, I'll give you my home and business numbers."

Taking a pen from a brown leather bag slung from her shoulder, she jotted a few lines in her spiral notebook and tore out the page. "I have to run," she said, handing it to me. "Call me any time you want tickets. They won't cost you a cent."

The group of people around us all seemed to explode toward the door, carrying Betty Stephens with them. The piece of paper which I held said in a clear firm hand: "Theater Tickets. Call Betty Stephens." Two telephone numbers which I judged to be at midtown addresses followed. The paper was a pale green, only a little lighter than the color of her dress. Folding it carefully, I put it in my wallet and walked to my hotel.

That night I had trouble sleeping. Over and over I kept trying to clarify my situation. After all, very little had happened. I had met an attractive young woman who offered theater tickets. Why was I filled with a conviction that I was about to have an affair which, unlike the others, was going to have some enormous effect on my life? I liked to think that it would be a long, sunny affair, but I feared otherwise. The girl obviously was too young and pretty for a man forty-one years old. Such affairs often end with the girl going off with a man her own age— that, of course, is a phenomenon which is almost to be expected. This particular woman seemed to me to be full of a lot of barely contained energy and a kind of secret excitement which was one of the things which animated her face. How could I keep up with her?

The old movie *Blue Angel*, in which a middle-aged professor is horribly humiliated after acquiring a passion for a young show girl, flashed in my mind. The scene in which the old man is taught to earn his living on the stage was still vivid. There the old fool was flapping his arms and crowing like a rooster while eggs were broken on his bald pate. What better way to dramatize the folly of loving Marlene Dietrich?

But this Betty Stephens did not resemble Marlene Dietrich. She had appeared so open and friendly that I couldn't make out whether her offer of theater tickets was part of a flirtation or simply evidence of generosity. Or perhaps it was part of a press agent's job to give away tickets which were not selling to anyone who would show up.

I wanted to see her again as soon as possible. Figuring that a press agent's office would not be open until ten, I called at 10:30 the next morning. Betty had just got in.

"Is it too early to take you up on your offer of theater tickets?" I asked after identifying myself.

"Of course not. It's a *beautiful* day, isn't it?"

I had not yet raised the shades of my hotel window, but I agreed, wondering if anyone could possibly be as happy as she sounded.

"What play do you want to see?" she asked.

"Is there anything you haven't seen? I've had a secret hope that I might persuade you to go with me."

"Oh," she replied, sounding surprised, disappointed. My mask had been dropped, I realized. The friendly middle-aged lecturer with a wife, (as far as Betty knew) and three children whom I had occasionally mentioned in class, this paragon of virtue was now obviously on the make.

"I didn't think you'd turn out like all the rest," she said, keeping her voice light.

"I'm *not* like all the rest," I continued. "For one thing, I'm older than most of the people you know. That sets me apart."

"I didn't mean to sound quite the way I did. You see, part of my work is to give away theater tickets when it's necessary to paper the house. You'd think it would be easy to give away tickets, wouldn't you? Not at all. Two out of three men grin and say, 'I'll go if you go with me.'"

"And I thought I had hit upon an entirely original gambit!"

She laughed and there was an awkward pause.

"Are you really interested in boats?" I asked.

"They've always fascinated me, but I've never been on anything smaller than a liner. Are you really going to sail around the world?"

"During the war I was a coast guard officer. The idea of taking some kind of a long voyage aboard a small vessel has always been in the back of my mind. Sunday I'm going to take a drive to see a little ketch that's in the Hudson River at Catskill. Do you want to go?"

"Sure! What time do you want to start?"

"Is 10:30 in the morning too early for you?"

She said no and gave me the address of her apartment building, which was on 56th Street, directly across from the back of Carnegie Hall. After hanging up, I found that I had been sweating profusely all through the call. The outcome of it left me with unreasonably strong and directly conflicting emotions. I was both jubilant and scared. An anxiety attack much like the one which I had suffered when Lisa went diving in Mexico hit me. I was well on the way to making some kind of monumental fool of myself. Probably this Betty Stephens would get cold feet and not show up anyway. That would probably be the best thing that could happen in the long run, but how was I supposed to handle this obsession which seemed to be intensifying every day? Somehow I had never expected to be drowned in such a sea of adolescent emotions at the age of forty-one.

At ten Sunday morning I drove my car to a parking lot near Carnegie

Hall. Pacing back and forth on 56th Street until my watch read exactly 10:30, I entered her building. Most of the women I had met since leaving Bedford Village had lived in Greenwich Village apartments which could be reached only by climbing several flights of stairs. Here there was a neat if simply appointed lobby, and an elderly elevator operator in a plum-colored uniform asked me what floor I wanted. When I said the seventh, he asked me in a pronounced Irish brogue whom I wanted to see up there.

"Miss Betty Stephens," I said.

"And who shall I say is here?"

When I gave him my name, he went to a house telephone on the wall. Did he announce every visitor, or was there something especially suspicious about me? To inspect the little ketch, I was wearing white sneakers, khaki trousers, a faded khaki shirt left over from my coast guard days and a tweed sports jacket. My hair had just been cut relatively short. Suddenly I remembered that the great photographer, David Duncan, who as a favor had taken my picture for a dust jacket, had said, after studying my face, that I looked like a Russian general. Since he had just returned from Russia, his opinion had shaken me. Was the elevator operator now saying to Betty, "A guy down here who looks like a Russian general wants to see you"?

"Let's go," the operator now said as he entered the elevator. I followed him. The door shut with a sharp bang, like that of a trap. During the slow ascent, the operator appeared to be studying me suspiciously. I looked at the metal ceiling of the machine, which needed paint.

"Seven," the operator said finally.

I got out of the elevator.

"Over there," he said, pointing to the left.

Apartment 702 was only three doors from the elevator. There was a button for a bell. When there was no immediate answer, I knocked. My fear that Betty Stephens would think better of meeting me rose again, but hadn't she answered the telephone when the elevator operator called?

The door opened. Without immediately saying anything, she darted from the doorway to the center of the room. She was wearing a summer dress, a Paisley print of blue on a wine-red background. It was low-cut with spaghetti straps, revealing a figure which looked to me like youth incarnate. Before I had moved from the door, she gracefully dropped into a deep ballerina's curtsy.

"Welcome to my house," she said.

Part 6
"My House Is Your House"

35

After her memorable curtsy, Betty went to a tiny kitchenette. She had one of those glass coffee-makers which are shaped like an hourglass warming on the stove. While she poured the coffee, I glanced around, looking for clues which might explain the character of the occupant. It seemed like the apartment of a college girl. There were a lot of books, including one of my own, on shelves and in paper cartons. Most of the furniture was of a sturdy maple, except for an armless studio couch which reminded me of one I'd had at Harvard a few hundred years ago. In a second room, of which I could see only a little through a partly open door, there was a bed with a ruffled skirt. There were no pictures on the walls and no rugs.

"I'm just moving into this place," she said as she handed me a cup of coffee. "I haven't had a chance to fix it up yet, but the location is marvelous for any show business type, don't you think?"

I agreed. She offered me a box of rich little crackers or cakes which were unfamiliar to me. When I asked her what they were, she said, "Scottish shortbread. Do you like it?"

"Very much. Are you Scottish?"

"Half. My mother was Scottish. My father is Irish. Not Irish-American. They are completely different. My father is a Dubliner."

She spoke with pride.

"In that classroom I kept trying to guess your background," I said. "Somehow there seemed something strongly Latin about you."

She laughed. "Most of the Spanish Armada was wrecked on the coasts of Ireland, and in the old days Ireland traded a lot with Spain. Quite a few Irish women look Spanish. Maybe that's where the expression 'black Irish' came from."

Going into the bedroom, she took her white raincoat from a closet and returned. It was spotlessly clean, as it had been the first time I had seen it in the classroom. Being a natural slob, I took notice of things like that.

We rang for the elevator. The face of the operator, which had seemed so glum to me, broke into smiles when he saw Betty. Lapsing into an even broader Irish brogue than I had noticed, he began to deliver himself of what seemed to me to be an excess of blarney.

"Ah, but you are lovelier than ever on this dreary day," he began. "Sure, but you are more welcome than the sun itself!"

"Ah, Bobbie, what would I do without your compliments to start each day?" she asked, surprising me by using a musical brogue, no hint of which was usually in her voice. "You send me out into the world each morning with my chin up, feeling like a queen!"

We reached the ground floor and headed for the street.

"I didn't know you could talk Irish," I said as we headed for the car.

"I have several brands of English. Irish I picked up when we were living in Dublin. Scottish my mother and grandmother taught me. Brooklynese I of course picked up in Brooklyn, where we lived when we weren't in Dublin."

"But how about your regular voice. Where did you learn that?"

"I hired a voice teacher. I didn't want to sound like a combination of all the voices you hear in a Brooklyn bar."

About the voice teacher, at least, I had guessed right. Arriving at the car, I opened the door for her. Noticing at last that it looked like rain, I asked whether she wanted me to put the top up.

"We can always do that if we have to," she said. "I love an open car, and I hardly ever get a chance to ride in one."

Practically every woman I had ever met wanted the top put up to protect her hair. I got into the car and drove to the Hudson River Parkway, dodging trucks and buses which loomed over us.

"You drive well," she observed after a few minutes. "Usually I'm nervous on the road, but I feel safe with you."

Practically every woman I had ever met told me that I drove too fast, too slowly or too jerkily.

"That's a great looking coat," Betty said a little while later, timidly touching the cuff of my sleeve. "I always love tweed. They make wonderful tweed in Ireland."

Because I had never been a neat man and was shaped in a way that defied the art of most tailors, few women had ever complimented me on my clothes. I felt like a boy running home with gold stars all over his report card.

But where was home?

Here in the little car with this young woman whom I hardly knew at all, it suddenly seemed. She had been complimenting me so much that I wanted to return the favor.

"Do you want to know the first thing that attracted me to you when the class began last fall?" I asked.

"Yes." She smiled.

"You have a very expressive face. When I'm lecturing I often look for someone in the audience who looks like someone I'd like to know. You helped me a lot."

"And that makes me feel very good," she replied, hesitated, then said, "To be honest, I noticed that you weren't exactly ignoring me. Not at the first lecture, but soon after. Then you began talking about your children. You mentioned them quite often in your lectures and I figured that any interest I had in your world would have to stay strictly academic."

"My wife and I are separated. The lawyers are supposed to be working out the divorce."

"How long has that been going on?"

"About six months."

"That must be hard," she said.

"It has been, but it's almost over. I feel like a man coming up for air."

"Now I know why you looked so miserable all winter," she said. "I often wondered how a man who had been so successful could look so damn forlorn."

I felt myself encouraged to talk about myself as I never had in my life. It was as though I thought I could explain everything that had happened to me in forty-one years if I only talked fast enough. A light rain started but we were driving fast enough for it to be swept over our windshield without wetting us. The miracle of driving in the rain without getting wet struck me as somehow symbolic. With the heater warming our legs we were comfortable. She sat with her face intent on mine, as she often had in the lecture hall. Seen close up, her face appeared even more distinctive than it had in the distance. She had remarkably high cheekbones. In that way her face a little resembled Claudette Colbert's, the actress whose aging had so pained me on the island of Martinique. I could not imagine Betty growing old. Twenty-eight, she had said she was, but she seemed to wear youth like a permanent possession.

When the rain came down harder, I stopped under a bridge to put up the top. The car warmed up, and Betty took off her white raincoat. The wind from a window I had left slightly open ruffled the light material of her dress. The temptation to sit behind the wheel like a lecherous adolescent, sneaking peeks at her bosom was painfully strong. What is it about the curves of well-formed breasts half glimpsed through cotton and silk that can make even a middle-aged man dream of building empires?

Suddenly I thought of the last book I'd written, which was still awaiting publication after numerous rewrites. In many ways Betty resembled the seventeen-year-old dancer whom the middle-aged protagonist loved. Charlotte, as my character was named, had long dark hair. Both the imaginary character and the real one had large brown eyes, and both had this particular kind of figure—dainty, lyrical, yet sensual. Both were little more than five feet tall.

"There's a character in my next book who reminds me of you," I said to Betty. "She's a young dancer about seventeen years old."

"I'm a little old for the part," Betty said, "but I am a dancer. I just decided to try press agentry a few months ago."

So, in many ways, she was Charlotte miraculously come to life from my pages, like a movie expertly produced. Before long people would say that I had based the character on Betty, I correctly suspected. The truth was more interesting: first I imagined a woman and then I apparently went forth to look for her.

"What kind of a dancer are you?" I asked.

"I started at the Latin Quarter when I was only fourteen years old. I can do most of the nightclub stuff."

"I know someone else who started to dance in nightclubs when she was about that age . . . Margo, Eddie Albert's wife, a fine actress and a great person."

"Yes, I've heard of her. . . . Nightclubs are tough schools, as I'm sure she'd agree. Of course, I got into it for the money. My mother was sick and dad was having trouble finding work."

There was a pause during which the rain on the canvas roof of the car seemed loud. I tried to picture her at half her present age dressed in whatever adolescent girls wore at the Latin Quarter.

"I was a pony for a long while," Betty continued.

"A pony?"

"That's what they call a very small show girl. I had a few good jobs. When I was sixteen I danced very briefly in *Guys and Dolls* on Broadway, and I had a stint at the old Hawaiian Room at the Lexington Hotel. I was one of the hula-hula girls."

By chance I had often seen advertisements of the Hawaiian Room in *The New Yorker*, with pictures of the girls. It was easy to imagine that I had seen a photograph of Betty at sixteen, that this was why her face looked vaguely familiar.

"Well, that's about the end of my great career," she went on. "I've danced in nightclubs. When I got sick of that, I became a pretty good secretary. For a while I was manager of a photography studio. And I've done a little modeling, not the glamorous stuff. Mostly hand modeling. The modeling agencies sort of passed me out piece by piece, like a chicken. Hands were my specialty."

"How does a hand model work?"

"All I had to do was to fix my nails carefully and hold a plate of cake or whatever for the photographer. You can see me on cake-mix boxes and in dozens of recipe books; there's always this big hand holding out a platter."

She held out her hand, which was as delicately formed as the rest of her, and acted as though she were holding out a platter.

"I was even a breast model once," she said. "An agency for the White Rock people spotted me . . . them. I had to kneel on this fake rock and hold a kind of semi-transparent piece of cloth in front of me. My breasts seemed to please them, but they cut off my head and substituted one from some other girl. We both felt badly about it. You can see why after a while I decided to try out as a press agent."

I laughed, and she laughed with me.

"One other thing," she said, "I went to Brooklyn College. I studied Home Economics, but it rarely did me any good. Most of the time I didn't have much of a home, and how can you have any economics if you don't have any money?"

"You sound as though you've had a fairly rough time and managed to enjoy a lot of it along the way."

"In a way, you're right. The best part, I think, was when I lived in Ireland. My mother didn't much like it over there and had a good job here. Dad usually had some kind of a business going in Dublin. It was a fairly mixed-up situation, but wonderful for me. The homes most familiar to me were the Cunard liners."

To me all this was fascinating but not quite real. Most of the girls I'd known in my youth, God help me, had gone to Vassar or Wellesley. Soon after that they'd married one of the men in gray flannel suits which I had written about, and moved to New Canaan or one of the hundreds of suburbs like it. They were pleasant enough, I guess, but they seemed kind of dull compared to a "pony," a dancer from *Guys and Dolls*, a hula-hula girl, a model with hands for selling cakes and the breasts of Psyche on the bottle of White Rock soda water.

"I think that the rain is letting up," she said, and she was right. The rain stopped just before we got to Catskill, which proved to be a small village near a picturesque yacht harbor. Signs pointed the way to the yard where the Sea Wind ketches were being built. A salesman showed the path to one of the little vessels which was on a cradle. Sleekly designed and stoutly built, the white topsides and red bottom gleamed as the sun finally came out from behind the clouds. A somewhat shaky ladder led from a mud puddle about twelve feet up to the deck. I held it for Betty to climb, expecting her to creep timorously upward as most women I knew would. When the salesman appeared to give me the cabin keys, I glanced at him. When I looked back at Betty, she was standing on the deck as though she had flown there.

"Come on up," she called. "It's a wonderful little ship."

The *Sea Wind* was expertly constructed—I was not surprised when not too long later I heard that several yachts of this model had sailed around the world. Still, she was about the same size as my old sloop, *The Yankee Trader*. As in almost any twenty-eight footer, the cabin was small, with narrow bunks and a tiny galley. Imagining how this boat, like any her size, would roll before a following sea, I inadvertently steadied myself on a hand rail. Was there any woman in the world who would really enjoy sailing a small vessel in the open sea for long?

Betty was happily inspecting the galley cabinets when the salesman called from the bottom of the ladder. Clambering down to see what he wanted, I found him standing with a stout man whom he introduced as his boss. If I was seriously interested in buying the boat soon, the stout man said, he could make me a good price. Taking a pad of paper from his pocket, he scribbled a figure on it and handed it to me. It was $14,000, which even in that day, was an extremely good price for a little yacht of that quality.

"For that I can let you have her with life rails, ready for sea," he said, lighting a cigar. "Handled properly she can go anywhere and back. I'm sure you know that."

"Yes," I said, and stood back a few paces to get a better look at the boat. The hatch slid open and Betty stepped from the cabin to the deck. After waving at me, she stood steadying herself with one hand on the shroud while she looked up the tall aluminum mast. I know it sounds like a clichéd image, but the wind blew back her skirt and hair as though she were standing in the prow of a ship, a figurehead. Outlined against the newly blue sky, she looked infinitely delicate, fragile as a china figurine. Sometimes life can be too good to believe. Betty Stephens was the kind of person who made it seem that way.

"Do you want her?" the stout man asked.

"The price is more than fair," I said, "but I have a few things I have to decide first."

Slowly I climbed the ladder. I was trying to figure out just what it would be like to buy this boat and put to sea alone. Anchored or underway, I would be uncomfortable and intolerably lonely. The idea of finding some beautiful girl in the South Seas might tease me on, but that was a childish fantasy. Where in the South Seas or anywhere else in the world was I likely to find a woman more interesting than the one who was standing on the deck of the boat now?

"Are you going to buy the boat?" Betty asked, enthusiastically.

"No," I said, sitting down in the cockpit. When she joined me, the place was so cramped that our knees touched.

"Is something the matter with her?"

"No."

There was a pause during which she looked at me quizzically.

"There has to be some value in getting older," I said. "I hope I have begun to know reality from fantasy. And I'm sure the reality is that I'd be hopelessly lonely aboard this boat alone, and that few women would really enjoy life aboard a small boat at sea once they learned what it was like."

"What is it like?"

"It would make you seasick for days, weeks, maybe months."

"I never get seasick."

"This is no Cunard liner. You also would be wet much of the time. Hatches and vents always leak. You would be cold. No adequate cabin heater has yet been invented for small sailing craft. You would be exhausted, and most of all you would be terrified. Before long you would hate the man who got you into such a mess."

"You're pretty convincing. Why did you ever want to get such a boat?"

"In the mood I was in, I didn't see many alternatives."

After luncheon in a restaurant overlooking a harbor that was almost landlocked, we got back in the car. I forgot what we talked about, but I was so confused and bemused by the time we reached the Thruway that I headed in the wrong direction. About an hour later I was astonished to see the towers of Albany looming ahead. She laughed good-naturedly and I was glad to have the extra time with her. I still hadn't been able to figure out what I was going to do when I stopped at her apartment to let her out and watch her disappear into the elevator with her adoring old Irish operator.

It's strange how scraps of a day's conversation will stick in the mind like pieces of torn clippings in a scrapbook. On the way back to New York, she said, "I'm afraid I misled you about something."

"What?"

"I said I went to Brooklyn College, but I only finished two years."

"In that case, I never want to see you again. I only go out with college graduates."

"For some reason it's a serious matter with me," she said. "All the time my mother was sick, she wanted me to finish college. I was dancing almost all night and I slept through most of the lectures, but I did my best. Sometimes I pretended to mom that I was sort of just on the brink of graduation because it made her feel so good. Often I lied to personnel men when I applied for a job, because they never check with colleges on things like that anyway, and the bastards treat you much better if you say you're a college graduate. With friends, though, I don't like to fake it."

"Neither do I," I replied, "but honesty is sometimes a dangerous policy."

315

"How?"

"If I say you're so beautiful that I'm almost afraid to look at you, you'll think that I'm making it up as part of a clumsy seduction game."

"No," she said, but her big eyes looked startled.

"If I say that everything you have told me about yourself brings me closer to that supposedly dangerous moment when I feel driven to say, 'I love you,' you will think me completely nuts."

"On our first day together?" she asked, her eyes laughing. "I'm afraid you're right: I would think you *more* than a little nuts."

I felt hurt. Her tone hardly sounded encouraging, and she was, of course, laughing at me. I had made a fool of myself at what appeared to be exactly the wrong time.

"What's the matter?" she asked.

"I don't know why I have to write such lousy dialogue for myself. I do much better for imaginary characters. Even if you didn't graduate from Brooklyn College, you have every right to give me lousy reviews."

Leaning across the car, she gave me a quick kiss on the cheek. "I love your dialogue," she said. "I just don't know how to answer it. You forgot to write any lines for me."

The old lines from Leigh Hunt sprang to mind. I recited them:

> Jenny kissed me.
> Say that health and wealth have missed me.
> Say I'm growing old, but add,
> Jenny kissed me.

"I've always loved that poem," Betty said, "and I've always wondered who Jenny was and what happened."

"I think she was Thomas Carlyle's wife. She was just a good friend of Leigh Hunt, and I'm afraid that nothing really happened."

"That's terrible," Betty said. "That must be just about the most famous kiss in literature, and it all went for nothing."

Our chatter continued. All of it seemed unforgettable at the time, but most of it was forgotten almost immediately. Actually, the words were not important. They were only an almost vain effort to express the rising excitement I think we both were feeling, excitement mixed with hope that in spite of all the odds, which always favored disappointment, this day might possibly lead to more like it, and just possibly end by changing our lives.

We reached New York a little before six in the evening. I asked her to have dinner with me and she accepted. Since she was dressed for a good restaurant, but I was not, I parked by my hotel.

316

"Do you want to come up with me while I change, or do you want to wait here?" I asked. "Or you could have a drink in the bar if you like."

"I'll go with you," she said.

I loved the way she walked. Chin up, shoulders back, she walked the way they used to try to teach rich girls to walk in finishing schools, usually with little success.

"Do you walk that way because you're a dancer?" I asked.

"Dancers usually walk like this," she replied, and caricatured the way a person who is totally tired might walk, rubber legs and all.

We both laughed.

Returning to her normal graceful gait, she said, "If I'm walking well, it's because I've been happy all day, and I'm looking forward to a good evening. You have yourself to thank for that."

Reaching the hotel, she preceded me through the revolving door. In the lobby Jim Farrell was buying a Sunday paper. His appreciative eye lighted up the moment he saw Betty, so much so that he didn't notice me.

"That's James T. Farrell," I whispered to her. "Would you like to meet him?"

"Yes!"

"Jim," I said, steering her toward him, "I have a friend here who would like to meet you. Betty Stephens, this is James T. Farrell."

"Good evening, young lady," Farrell said, literally beaming.

"Mr. Farrell, I hope you won't think me naïve, but you're the first real literary giant I've ever met."

Jim's beam became, if possible, more enthusiastic.

"I'm afraid I'm a little short for that role, but I'll try to grow up to it. Sloan, you're very fortunate. I'm glad that you finally wised up."

"What?" I asked, startled.

"You've been wandering around this dump like Little Eva looking for an ice cake. I'm glad you've finally found a girl who can make you stand up straight."

Glancing at his watch, he concluded, "I've got to run. Admiring your girl is fine, but I'm off to meet one of my own!"

So saying, he trotted out the front door, a short, stocky man who must be, at the very least, twenty-five years older than I, but still driven by that indomitable vitality of which he was so justly proud.

"Somehow he makes me want to cry," Betty said as we entered an elevator.

"Why?"

"I don't know. He should be living in a castle. So should you, for that matter. What are you two doing in a place like this?"

"We're just lucky, I guess."

Betty gave a somewhat pained laugh. When the elevator stopped at my floor, I led the way to my room. Since I had not been expecting visitors, the place reflected the chaos in which I had been living. Magazines, newspapers and books surrounded the armchair like a small sea. Blueprints for the Sea Wind ketch we had just seen covered the bed. More coats and ties were on the straight chairs than in the closet. In the kitchen the breakfast dishes were still on the table where I usually worked, while my typewriter and briefcase were on the floor.

"Oh!" she exclaimed, as though she had just seen an automobile accident. "Is it as bad as all that?"

"Don't they have any maid service?"

"I cut it out. I never could find anything I wanted after she came."

Taking a blue suit and a clean white shirt from the closet, I headed toward the bathroom to change.

"Can I clean up a little?" she asked. "I promise not to touch any papers."

"Sure, go ahead if you want, but don't feel you have to. I'm used to living in a mess. That's one thing I learned, living aboard a small ship. Everything usually ended up on the deck."

I dressed as quickly as I could, knotting my Harvard tie carefully. I owned a lot of Harvard ties, not because I really liked them, but because I kept forgetting that you had to have a tie to enter the Harvard Club. When I appeared with an open shirt, there was nothing to do but buy a Harvard tie in the lobby, the only kind they sold. If Betty looked in my closet, she would think I was the most corny loyal Harvard man of all time.

When I came out of the bathroom I had to crawl around on my hands and knees to locate my black shoes, which were under the bed. In the kitchen I could hear water splashing. Betty had already hung the odds and ends of clothes in the closet, and now she was doing the dishes. In an incredibly short amount of time, my rooms looked neat.

"Do you mind if I look at this?" Betty asked, going to a photograph of my three children that stood in a leather frame on a night stand near my bed.

"Of course not."

She picked it up and studied it intently. The photograph had been taken the previous Christmas in Bedford Village by their mother, who was giving a lot of time to photography. It was a good picture which dramatized the different personality of each child. In it, Lisa looked almost adult, a sleek little beauty, Westchester County to the hilt in appearance, although I knew she was more than that. Becky was smiling with all the poignance and intensity which sometimes made me want to cry when I thought of her. A Golden Retriever was resting its head on her lap, and she was stroking it. Between his two sisters, David stood in a new blue blazer and gray flannel slacks. He looked like, well, David—nobody else looked like him. Rail-thin, his features much less regular than those of the girls, he stood almost at attention, but his face was dreaming. David was not there at all—he had gone fishing or was climbing a mountain peak.

"They're beautiful children," Betty said. "Do you still see them much?"

"I have joint custody." That fact was a great comfort to me. "I see them quite a lot on weekends. When I get settled somewhere, I hope I can see them more."

"Your girls are real beauties," Betty said, continuing to study the photograph. "Your wife must be beautiful, too."

"My former wife," I said. "I've already begun to think of her as that."

"Is she as beautiful as your daughters?"

"When she was their age, she was."

Somehow I felt nervous. Getting up, I poured myself a Scotch and offered Betty one. She shook her head.

"Can I get you something else? I have the makings for a martini."

"I don't drink."

"Can I get you a cigarette?"

"I don't smoke."

"Are you a Presbyterian or something?" I asked with a laugh.

She smiled and shook her head. "Dancers have to stay in shape. It gets to be a habit. Or a curse."

Sipping my drink, I glanced at her, trying not to stare. Among other things, she was extraordinarily relaxed. Most young women who came to my apartment alone would be tensely waiting to see if I was going to make a pass at them. Apparently Betty was confident that I had better timing than that. We had known each other only about eight hours. The day's drive had tired us, we were hungry, and beyond that the inspection of the photograph of the children had somehow depressed us. My mood felt leaden as I led the way to the door.

"Beat you to the elevator!" she suddenly said, and went dancing down the hall ahead of me. Not knowing what was going on, I followed her as fast as I could. Panting, I caught her just as she rang the bell. She was laughing and suddenly I felt like laughing too.

"What was that all about?" I asked.

"Do you bet me a dollar I can't get to your room and back before the elevator comes?"

"It's a bet."

Down the hall she dashed, waving her arms as though she were flying. Her face flushed, she returned just as the elevator door opened. We were both laughing as we got in.

"You win," I said, taking out my wallet and giving her a dollar.

"It was just a game," she said, refusing to take it. "When I was a child I used to run whenever I felt bad. It still works for me, and sometimes I can make it work for other people."

"It worked for me. I feel great again." Curiously, this was true. She had run my blues away.

We walked to a good restaurant, and I ordered a celebratory dinner to match my mood. I had all sorts of complicated French dishes. She had a grilled steak and a green salad without dressing. She ate no potatoes, no bread and no dessert.

"Why on earth do you have to diet?" I asked.

She smiled. "So people will ask me why on earth I have to diet. They don't ask fat people that."

"How long have you been on your diet?"

"As long as I can remember. Like I told you, diet and exercise and staying in shape just sort of became a way of life for me. Besides—I realize this may sound conceited—I *like* my body, my living machine. I like it enough to try to take care of it."

"Well, the truth is, I like your living machine too," I said, and actually found myself blushing like a fifteen-year-old boy.

36

When dinner was over, we walked back to the car. It was only about nine o'clock, and I dreaded the thought of the evening being over.

"Do you know any nightclubs that are open on Sunday night?" I asked.

"I'm afraid I'm not much for nightclubs. After you've worked in them a few years, the very smell of them is sickening."

"I hate the idea of taking you home and saying good night."

She laughed. "Come on up to my place, if you want. I can give you coffee, and I might even find a few bottles of booze somebody gave me. When you give out a lot of theater tickets, you get the damndest presents from strangers for Christmas."

After parking near the back of Carnegie Hall, we walked slowly to the lobby of her apartment building. Already it seemed natural and good to hold hands. A different elevator operator was on duty. A gaunt, disinterested man, he took us to the seventh floor without comment. She walked ahead of me to her apartment and unlocked the door. The room with the studio couch and maple table looked startlingly familiar, as though I had lived there half my life. While she hung up her white coat, I felt as nervous as a boy taking a girl home from a high school dance.

"Do you want Scotch or coffee?" she asked, going to the kitchenette.

"I should have the coffee, but I'm afraid I want the Scotch."

The door of her refrigerator slammed. In the silence that followed, there was an odd cooing sound.

"Do you hear that curious cooing?" I asked.

"It's pigeons. Millions of them live in the airshaft. Some roost right on the sills of my windows. I like them. Do they bother you?"

"No. It's a rather contented sound."

"They all snuggle up together," she said, handing me a glass of Scotch on the rocks. "They have each other, they don't have to work and they can fly like angels. Why wouldn't they be happy?"

I laughed, but the feeling of tension increased as she sat on the edge of her studio couch. Feeling awkward even for me, I kissed her. It was a good kiss, the kind that answers many questions.

"Do you mind if I talk seriously a minute?" I finally asked her.

"Not if it isn't unpleasant," she said wryly.

"I don't think it's unpleasant, not all of it, anyway. Look, I'm forty-one years old. That's too old to fool myself and too old to try to fool you."

Getting up from my chair, and still somehow feeling like a character in a play, I started to pace in front of the couch, where she sat.

"Like a lot of men in the process of getting a divorce, I'm not very reliable," I continued. "I've had some affairs which started off with great excitement, but didn't last long. I can't really trust my emotions any more, and maybe nobody else should trust them too much."

"A lot of people are in that boat, even if they haven't been divorced."

"But you're a lot younger. You have time to experiment. What I am trying to do is to feel my way toward some kind of reality. Today I made progress. For one thing, I realized that buying a boat for some kind of world cruise is crazy. I still have responsibility for my children. I still think I should write books. And no woman I know would be happy for long on that little ketch we saw today. It's important for me to realize that because I can't be happy for as much as one week without a woman. I don't say that because I'm pretending to be some kind of a sexual athlete. It's just that life to me is completely meaningless if I'm alone."

"Me, too," she said.

She sounded very serious, matching my tone. I no longer felt we were in a play. I glanced at my watch.

"It's nine forty-one on the evening of April 22, 1962. Right now I can say with complete sincerity that I love you. Sure, it's quick, but so are most kinds of explosion. To tell you the truth, after one day of driving to

Albany and back, I have to bite my tongue to stop myself from asking you to marry me, and one thing I was sure I'd never want was to get married again. I've admired you for a year in a classroom and for one day we've talked a lot, but I'm just sane enough to realize that I really know very little about you. I wouldn't buy a boat without knowing more about her than I know about you, but whether it's crazy or not, I trust my intuitions, my subconscious, whatever, and all their signals are very much go. Am I boring the hell out of you? Do you think I'm crazy?"

She laughed. "Not exactly."

I kissed her. On a scale of one to ten, the kiss seemed to me to rate about fifteen. Clearly I was losing my head, something I hadn't done in more than twenty years. The last time had led to an unhappy marriage, I reminded myself. But now I had more sense, didn't I?

"I don't think you're exactly playing fair," she said.

"Why not?"

"There are or should be certain rules for the whole game of seduction. One thing it's not fair to do is to mention marriage, however lightly. With eighteen-year-olds, that may be acceptable, but with women my age, who are dying to get married, no matter what they say, offering marriage is like sitting by a watering hole during a drought to shoot deer."

"You're not going to convince me that you're finding it so difficult to get married."

"Oh, I get proposed to all the time. Boy, do I get proposed to! A nice old doctor old enough to be my father wants to marry me. Of course he's bald and fat, but he makes something like two hundred thousand a year, he keeps telling me. Then several bright young men who are just starting up life's ladder want to marry me. I think they want to take me to a nice house out in Levittown, give me three children and slouch by the television set drinking beer every Sunday while I chase the kids around the back yard. You see, I'm not really a very nice girl, at least not in the usual sense. I don't want a dull rich old man, and I don't want a dull poor man. I want an exciting man who can help make me feel alive. Is excitement a childish thing for a woman twenty-eight years old to want?"

"Hardly. I've wanted it all my life. Maybe that's why in spite of everything, I think I really loved the war. Maybe that's at least partly why I broke my back writing all night. Instinctively it was a way of getting where the action is."

"Where is it?"

"For me, right now, it's right here with you."

So saying, I startled myself by yawning. She laughed easily.

"Do you want to spend the night here?" she asked.

"If I do, you may never get rid of me. You'll have to have the cops come and pull me out."

"I'll take my chances," she said.

"All right, but from now on I'm not responsible for anything I say. One of our rules ought to forbid promises when we're on the verge of going to bed."

Still talking, we went into the bedroom. One reason that I kept chattering so was that for the first time in my life I was suddenly plagued by real fear of sexual inadequacy, maybe even impotency. Her carefully dieted and exercised compact body all aglow with youth seemed so superior to my bearlike form that it seemed wrong to put the two together. The more I saw of her physical delicacy, the more she reminded me of my daughters, and perhaps she activated all the brakes I had created to stop any sexual feelings for them. Whatever the reason, I approached her bed like a damn frightened virgin. Changing her clothes in the bathroom, she came out wearing a white cotton nightgown of knee length. Most of the women I had known recently seemed to favor black lace or transparent cloth of various colors. Betty's schoolgirl nightgown was totally charming, but it almost did me in—I felt all the more as though I was about to make love to a child.

Lighting a candle in a brass candlestick, she put it on a small table beside the bed. Lying down to wait for her, I had one of those terrifying attacks of acute anxiety. Much as I had been tempted to jump from the *Queen Mary*, I had a sudden vision of myself leaping through the windows at the foot of the bed and falling seven floors to the bottom of the airshaft. This time my motivation did not seem so mysterious: I would do it after proving myself impotent with this woman I most wanted.

"What's the matter?" Betty asked when she got into bed.

"Sometimes I go a little crazy," I said, and for the first time in my life I talked to a person who was not a psychiatrist about imagining impotency, though it had never happened to me, and also imagining suicide as a result.

"If there's anything that could drive a woman away, it's this kind of confession," I concluded miserably.

If she had made fun of me, or if she had been only nominally sympathetic, I have no idea what would have happened to me. Except for the candle, the room was dark, and somewhere she had left a phonograph playing Debussy. The warmth of her small body against my own, nearly twice her size, brought a wonderful sense of relief from fear, a delicious comfort. She rubbed my back and shoulders, which were hunched tight.

"Some romantic lover am I," I groaned.

"You're going to be fine."

Soon, miraculously, I was, so much so that I worried that I was being too rough, but her delicate little body seemed to be made of warm steel. When, afterward, I thanked her, she smiled sleepily and said, "The pleasure was mutual. I always heard that writers are good in bed. You're a dandy representative of your profession."

I felt knighted.

"Marry me now," I said. "To hell with common sense."

"I'm too sleepy. I love you, though."

"And I love you."

We had not yet said these words to each other. They sounded natural, comforting and good.

I was so keyed up that I got up and had a few drinks before going back to bed. When I awoke, it was almost noon. Betty had gone, but she had left a note on her pillow. It said, "I had to go to work. Coffee is made. Orange juice and other breakfast stuff are in the refrigerator. Stay as long as you want. I'll be back about five-thirty. If you are willing to risk my cooking tonight, I plan to serve an Irish special—corned beef or something horrible like that. Thanks for yesterday and last night. Even if you soon disappear in a puff of black smoke, you have made me feel better than I have in years. I have never felt so at home with any man, and it's damn good to be home at last. Much love, Betty."

On impulse I called her up at her office.

"Are you going to stay for dinner?" she asked.

"I told you that you'd never get rid of me. The camel's nose has now entered your tent. Do you mind if I bring my shaving stuff and a few clothes over from my apartment?"

"That's against my policy, but for you . . . Of course bring over your stuff. My house is your house."

"That's a nice line. I could fall in love with a girl like you, even over the telephone."

"Do it. Listen, do you want me to do the proper thing and keep our relationship, or whatever it is, a deep dark secret?"

"I guess so, until my divorce is final."

"Oh, the people up here know better than to put it in the papers. I'm sorry, but I just felt I was bursting this morning, and I did a little boasting about you to some of the girls in the office. I didn't say we had talked about marriage. I just said that you took me to see a boat."

"Nothing wrong in that . . . Oh, hell, say anything you want."

"I'll be discreet, but I do love to boast. Betty Stephens, consort of great writers—I also told them I'd met Jim Farrell. Can you believe that some of the girls had never heard of him?"

After having Betty's good breakfast, I drove to my hotel to pack a change of clothes, some pajamas and toilet articles to take to Betty's place. Before leaving, I looked at those two rooms where I had been so lonely and miserable. It occurred to me that there was a chance, maybe even a good one, that I would never have to endure living alone again.

37

We were sensible enough to make ourselves wait six months before getting married. Because Betty said she had promised her father that she would never marry a man he had not met, we flew to Dublin in September.

The Aer Lingus plane was trimmed with green. The hostess was a charming round-faced girl with pink cheeks. She of course spoke with a strong brogue and wore a green uniform. Since the plane was almost empty when we boarded it in New York, we had our choice of seats. Shortly after we had taken off, the girl smilingly brought us a complimentary bottle of cold champagne.

"I hear you're going to be married in Ireland," she said. "One of our chaps saw it in the newspapers."

"Marry a press agent and see what you get," Betty said as I pulled out the cork with a satisfying pop. For this occasion she broke her rule against drinking, and we sipped the wine from plastic glasses.

Since we had met in April we had suffered only two bad days. Those had occurred in July when Betty had insisted that she have a few days alone to think before finally committing herself to marriage. Piqued by such caution, which I worried preceded rejection, I had gone to Grossinger's in the Catskills, which I had always wanted to visit. There I had met Lisa Lane, who had been a national and world chess champion of various sorts. An attractive young woman, she too was in love with someone who was not there. We sat by the pool consoling each other until Betty finally called me home. Apparently Betty had resolved whatever doubts were in her mind, for her sunny disposition had, if possible, improved.

"What did you do up at Grossinger's?" she asked.

"I learned how not to play chess."

"How did you manage that?"

"I met a woman who can play thirty guests at Grossinger's at the same time without losing a single game. The way not to play chess with her is to talk about love instead."

Soon after that, Betty happened to see a picture of Lisa Lane in a newspaper. Surprised that a chess champion looked like a model, she was briefly furious. And I was pleased.

"It's been a long time since anyone cared enough about me to be jealous," I said. "I've never been more flattered."

"Two days, two lousy days and you're talking about love with a woman who has a figure like Marilyn Monroe and a goddamn brain like Einstein's. Don't talk to me about this writer bit. It's the biggest come-on that anyone ever invented. What in hell would you be doing if you left me for a whole week?"

When I laughed, she stopped, looked and joined me.

"Do you really want to marry me?" she asked suddenly.

"I will if you don't keep throwing me out."

"I had to think. A few things have been worrying me for a long time."

"Like what?"

"I'm afraid that you expect me to make you happy, and I don't honestly think that marriage can make anybody happy for very long. And maybe you'll be disappointed if you find that you're not making me ecstatic all the time. I don't think I could stand the strain of trying to be happy, happy, happy all the time."

"Often we'll probably be miserable, but I'd rather be miserable with you than alone."

"Will you be able to stand my moods? I'm only half black Irish, you know, but sometimes I can be one hundred percent bitch. I can't control it."

"Let's just take it as it comes."

"When we do get married, or if we do, would you mind a church wedding if my family wants it?"

"Wouldn't there be religious difficulties?"

"I've always sort of assumed that you're a Protestant."

"A back-slid Episcopalian, to be exact. I always sort of assumed that you are some sort of retired Catholic."

"Don't say that where my father can hear! You're liable to get hit by a chair. Like everybody else in my family, dad and I are Protestants. In Ireland that's not something you take lightly."

"Then a church wedding will be fine if they can work it out."

So now the big plane was heading east, effortlessly flying above a hard fall gale. Betty was sleeping with her head on my shoulder, and her left hand on my knee. In the dimly lit cabin, the engagement ring I had given her glistened on her finger. Over the tip of the plane's wing, I could see one bright star or planet, probably Venus. Two nuns in seats near us sat with their heads bowed, as though in prayer. When the stewardess offered me an Irish whiskey, I took it, succeeding in letting Betty continue to sleep. Never before had I sampled Irish whiskey. The brand was Bush-mill. To me it tasted strong, a little harsh, smoky, a drink as violent and complex as Irish history itself.

Betty had told me that her father was going to meet us at the Dublin airport. I don't know what kind of a man I expected. Without knowing it, I may have molded my stereotype of an Irishman from the image of the old actor, Barry Fitzgerald, a gnarled little fellow with a clay pipe. Betty's father, Robert Stephens, was hardly this sort. A big man who looked strong despite his ample girth, he had a highly-colored complexion. His bushy eyebrows and full head of hair had turned silvery white, which he insisted on calling blond. At the time he was about sixty years old.

Seeing Betty, he waved enthusiastically. She ran to him and they hugged with the intensity of lovers. When she introduced me, he extended to me a hand like that of a clean blacksmith. Stepping back, he looked at me as intently as someday I would probably examine men my daughters wanted to marry.

"You're the same size!" Betty exclaimed. "Dad, what size coat do you wear now?"

As it turned out, we were precisely the same size. Recalling that Betty was the same size and had the same coloring of my mother, I felt peculiar. Are the marital choices of most people so influenced by their parents?

"I'm sorry I can't help you with your baggage," Bob said in a Dublin accent, which seemed to me to be a much more precise and musical version of the ordinary Irish brogue. "My heart has been acting up a little lately."

As I gathered the baggage, the task seemed familiar. As a boy, that had been my job when my father's heart condition worsened.

Bob led the way to his Austin sedan, which he had parked near the door to the airport. Betty and I sat in the back, where she hooked her arm into mine companionably. From the brief glimpses I got of it, the city of Dublin looked much like Boston, or Boston as it had once been. There were few tall buildings. Cobblestone streets were not uncommon, and there were a good many brewers' wagons drawn by horses which looked like Percherons. The traffic policemen looked more like marine cadets than cops. The cars were mostly old and tiny, while most of the people walking on the sidewalks were drably dressed and tired appearing. Despite all I had heard about the beauty of Irish women, there were few pretty girls in the crowd even when we went through fashionable sections, where the looks of the buildings and cars improved.

"Poor old Dublin always looks so poor when I first see it," Betty said.

"Ah, things are improving now," Bob said. "We're not New York yet, thank God, but then again, we're not the poor farm. The Japanese, the Germans and all sorts of people are pumping capital in."

A few minutes later he stopped at a small but comfortable appearing hotel. Thinking that he had been driving toward the homes of Betty's aunts, whom she had told me about, I was surprised.

"I made a reservation for you here," Bob said. "It's not quite as grand as some of the others, but the food is good and it's much less expensive."

After taking our bags from the trunk of the car, I opened the door for Betty.

"Ah, she's not getting out here," Bob said. "Until she's married, she'll be staying with my sister, Lottie."

Chaperonage! Irish chaperonage! That was something I had not foreseen. After giving me a demure kiss, Betty was whisked away in her father's car. Amused by my own discomfort, I went into the elegantly appointed little hotel. The bar was paneled with highly finished mahogany, and was almost as elegant as that of the Ritz in Boston. The spigots for draft beer and ale had handles of polished wood two feet long. To sample the wine of the country, so to speak, I ordered Guinness stout. Almost black, it had creamy foam and a faint flavor of licorice that must be an acquired taste. After I had registered, a bellboy showed the way to a small but comfortable room with a lace bedspread. There was nothing wrong with it, except that to me it felt clammy-cold.

"Is there any way I can get some heat up here?" I asked.

"Of course!" the bellboy said. "In just a minute."

After I had tipped him, he disappeared. Soon to my astonishment he returned, carrying a brass bed warmer shaped like a big banjo. The round part of it, which presumably contained red-hot coals, had been wrapped with strips of a blanket. The whole thing looked like some of the antiques my mother collected. After putting the contrivance under my blankets, the bellboy asked, "Will that be all right, sir?"

"I guess that will be fine," I replied. Why hadn't Betty warned me that a trip to Ireland in 1962 was like a return to the eighteenth century?

By six o'clock that night my amusement was turning to intense irritation. I was lonely and I was bored. Most of the subjects with which the Irish *Times* concerned itself appeared to be Irish politics, and the equally arcane Irish sports. Nothing else to read appeared available in the hotel lobby or nearby stores. Since her father had given me no address, I did not know how to get in touch with Betty. Was I being placed in some sort of ceremonial isolation, or were her relatives simply trying to get rid of me? Was this treatment the reason why I had never really heard of any great Irish tradition of hospitality? As far as I could see, this whole operation was beginning to look like a landing on an enemy beach.

Finally Betty telephoned. She apologized. Somehow she had not realized that there would be so many complications. Although we were both Protestants, there would be some religious difficulties. To get married in an Irish church, it was necessary to attend one for several weeks. Beyond that some clergymen did not like to officiate at a ceremony which involved a divorced man, and the civil authorities demanded to see a copy of my divorce papers to determine if they were authentic. Also, banns would have to be posted and printed in the newspapers for several weeks. Until all these problems had been solved, her aunts were determined to keep Betty safely away from me. In New York, all kinds of things probably went on, one of the ladies had said, but in Dublin they still knew right from wrong.

Repeating this information to me, Betty giggled.

"God damn it, you're *enjoying* this nonsense!" I said.

"I am not! I miss you as much as you miss me, but this whole thing is kind of funny. Have you ever been chaperoned before?"

"Not since I was fifteen. How long is this nonsense going to go on?"

"At least a month, I'm afraid."

"You mean I'm going to be stuck alone in a damp cold hotel for a whole month in this God-forsaken country?"

"Hush! Ireland is anything but God-forsaken. And cheer up. Aunt Lottie wants you to come to tea tomorrow at about four. Dad will pick you up at the Royal Hibernian."

The next afternoon Bob drove his Austin cheerfully without saying much. Apparently the kidnapping of my fiancée and the incarceration of myself in a medieval hotel seemed perfectly normal to him. Twenty-four hours alone had been enough to cause me to think in somewhat exaggerated terms, I knew, but I still felt as though I deserved an apology.

Betty's aunt lived in a modest brick house surrounded by gardens which were so well kept that the lawns and flowers did not seem quite real. A dozen or so relatives were there for the tea. My first impression was of plump, dignified women dressed in grays and blacks, much like the guests at one of my mother's teas. The men tended to be thin and tweedy, more distinctively Irish in appearance than their wives. The tea was held in a room of modest size in which a peat fire glowed in a tiny, tiled fireplace. Everything about this room and the whole house was scrupulously clean. A big table in front of the fireplace was covered with snowy Irish linen. The baskets which held candy and cookies were made of the famous

Waterford cut glass and the tea service was delicate Belleek china, colored ivory and green.

Looking around the room, I could not find Betty. Where were these pleasant people keeping her, anyhow? While Bob introduced me to relative after relative, I resented the fact that he presented me simply as a friend. There was no talk of a wedding. From the kitchen several women carried platters of different kinds of home-baked bread which smelled good. These, with plates of ham sandwiches, cookies of a dozen kinds and an enormous angel cake, filled the table. As Aunt Lottie sat down to pour the tea, Betty appeared on the stairs in the next room. She was wearing a simple dress of white wool which I had not seen. Around her neck she had put a string of cultured pearls which had been one of my presents to her, and her dark brown hair had been brushed to a glossy sheen. To me she looked so much like an eighteen-year-old bride that I held my breath. Conversation stopped as she entered the room, gave me a quick hug and a kiss on the cheek.

"How are you holding up?" she whispered in my ear.

Before I could answer, she turned to the relatives she had not seen recently. Some of them had such thick Irish accents that I could not understand them when they talked fast. Several of them had a great deal to say to Betty, and I soon realized that at this party I was not going to have much of a chance to see her. A tall man about seventy-five years old, with a hooked briar pipe, beckoned to me and asked if I would like a drink. Grateful, I accepted a glass of Irish whiskey with very little water. Remembering that I had left my pipe in my overcoat, which had been put in a large hall closet, I went to retrieve it. There were a great many London Fog trench coats like mine hanging from hooks, and I had to investigate quite a few to locate my own. While I was doing this, Betty came looking for me. As she passed the door of the closet, I had an idea. Feeling as though I were an actor in a horror movie, I reached out my hand, grabbed her arm and pulled her into the closet.

"What's going on?" she asked in astonishment.

I shut the door, which automatically put out the light. The closet smelled of cedar shavings, moth balls and damp tweed, a combination which suddenly was exciting. I kissed her and was comforted to feel her put her arm around my neck.

"When you came down those stairs you were so beautiful," I began.

There was the reassuring sound of her soft laugh and more kisses.

"Put your coat in here," a woman said to some new arrival, and tried to open the door.

Quickly I grabbed the knob and held it shut. She was a strong, determined woman, and for a moment there we had quite a tussle.

"It must be the damp weather," she said finally. "It's fast stuck. I'll have Bob fix it. Meanwhile, put your coat on the chair."

There were receding footsteps. Before Betty's father came with hammer and chisel, she and I escaped. Smoothing her hair with her right hand, she led the way back to the living room.

During the next few days Betty and I found various ways to steal a few minutes alone. The basement stairs were a welcome refuge, and so was the big bathroom on the second floor, where we had to look through the keyhole to make sure that no one was coming as we walked out together. It's a terrible thing to chaperone a twenty-eight-year-old apprentice theatrical press agent and a forty-two-year-old writer, but it taught me that the days of all those restrictions must have offered secret delights which most people nowadays cannot begin to imagine. A kiss in a closet may not sound like a very great thing, but the few I enjoyed I shall never forget, not if I live to be a hundred.

38

Because arrangements for a church ceremony were so complex, we settled for a civil ceremony, but even that could not be hurried. Betty had a brilliant idea. She prevailed upon her father to take us on a tour of Ireland. He planned to take a woman whom he had known for a long while with him. His thought was that Betty and I could chaperone him and his friend while they chaperoned us. This appeared to me to be a peculiarly Irish concept, but it worked all too well for a few days.

Bob's friend was a gentle lady of perhaps fifty years whose family owned a large store in Dublin. When she was only about twenty, Bob told me, she had married a man who left her after only a few months. A Roman Catholic, she petitioned the Pope for an annulment but was refused. For almost thirty years she had lived the life of a spinster.

This woman was tall, slender, rather gaunt-faced and white-haired. She sat in the front seat of Bob's Austin with him while we toured; Betty sat in the back with me. My regression to adolescence had continued to the point where there were all kinds of excitement in putting my arm around Betty, or having her shoulder pressed against me when the car rounded a curve. If I took too much advantage of these little accidents, Bob, who kept close contact with us in the rear-view mirror, cleared his throat alarmingly. He was too sophisticated to be prudish, he had told me, but his friend had delicate sensibilities that had to be protected.

On our first night we stopped at Wexford. We stayed at a big "guest house," the sort of place which in America used to be called a tourist home. I hoped that somehow Betty and I could get some privacy there, but found immediate disappointment. A room on the ground floor had been reserved for Betty and the woman who was accompanying her father. A room on the third floor was ready for Bob and me. It had only one three-quarter bed. The handles had been taken off the faucets of the bathtub and sink to prevent anyone from using hot water. As in many Irish hotels of the time, there was no heat. Dressed in his underpants because he did not want to unpack all the bags, Bob slept slantwise across the bed. Soon after I put out the lights and started clinging to the edge of the mattress, he began to snore. Aboard a small ship one becomes aware of the snoring habits of others, but I had never heard such a virtuoso snorer as he. Sometimes he sounded like a tuba being played while it was about a quarter full of water. Sometimes there was a fine reedy note, like a moose call. Beset, perhaps by bad dreams, he lurched about, and for self-defense I lurched back. Each of us weighed close to two-hundred pounds. The bed creaked, the single blanket would not cover both of us. I got up, put on my clothes, and sneaked downstairs. When I tapped on Betty's door, she came to talk to me through the crack.

"Will your father be hurt," I asked, "if I insist on having my own room?"

"He'll think most of the money. A double room is cheaper than two singles."

"I'll pay the difference if necessary. I have trouble with insomnia anyway. Your father is a charming man, but sleeping with him is like bedding down with a water buffalo."

She laughed.

"I should have warned you. Let me know how you make out."

The proprietress of the establishment apparently had heard me walk down her creaking stairs, and afraid that immorality was afoot she was waiting in a long flannel bathrobe on the landing of the second floor.

"Madame ..." I began.

"Young man, don't madame me. I have always kept daycent lodgings here for daycent folk. Now what are you doing wandering around this time of night?"

When I asked if she had a single room available, she said, "Will you pay extra?"

"How much?"

"It will cost you a pound."

The room turned out to be on the first floor, not far from that of Betty

332

and the woman with the sad history. After the landlady had returned to her quarters, I tip-toed to Betty's room, and again tapped. When I whispered my new room number, she replied in a barely audible voice that she would be there as soon as she could. In only about half an hour she appeared.

"My jailer is asleep," she whispered as she closed our door and locked it. "I don't think she'll wake up soon."

Moonlight was streaming through our room's only window. A glass pitcher that stood in a big glass bowl on a nightstand gleamed as though it had been carved from ice. The smell of the sea was in the air, not surprisingly in view of the fact that our guest house stood near Wexford Harbor, but I had not noticed it before. A frosted mirror above an old chest of drawers reflected moonlight and the moving shadows of the curtains. Betty kissed me and I thought that Ireland was the most beautiful place in the world.

For about two weeks we continued our tour, covering most of the south of Ireland. I was so bemused by my own emotions and those of Betty that I paid scant attention to the beauties of the famous scenery which we passed. Leafy glens, lush valleys, the serpentine course of narrow rivers through luxuriant grass, all these were vaguely reminiscent of Vermont somehow grown to a bigger and more dramatic scale. Villages where almost all the streets were cobblestoned, the silhouettes of hilltop castles which did not look ruined until one approached closely and the ubiquitous use of horses reinforced my first impression of entering the past. The musical Irish place names such as Killarney, Glendaloch, Shannon and Tipperary (an ancient town which in my imagination, at least, still echoed the sadness of the old World War I song) fell sweetly upon the ear. Once when an enormous flock of sheep stopped our progress on the road and surrounded our car, I felt as oddly impatient as I had in New York traffic jams. The gentle pace of rural Ireland took a few weeks to learn.

The deeper we progressed into the country, the more it seemed to me to be a never-never land in which both landscapes and people were bewitched. In the frequent mists distances were hard to judge, and the size of everything was distorted. A tall man on a big white horse shrank before my eyes to a boy on a donkey as they emerged from a patch of fog. After speeding for hours on the twisting narrow roads of shining macadam, we found we had covered a grand total of nineteen miles.

Once we witnessed an accident which appeared to me to be peculiarly Irish. An Austin sedan of ancient vintage rounded a curve at high speed as it approached us and flipped to its side, sliding into the grass. Trying to remember the first aid that I had been taught in the coast guard, I jumped from our car as soon as Bob stopped and raced to it. A tall, thin man climbed from a window and stood brushing his pants with his hand.

"Are you hurt?" I asked breathlessly.

"Hurt? Of course not. Can you give me a hand righting the old thing?"

A man who had been riding a handsome bay mare in the neighboring field cantered up, and a farmer drove up on a tractor. With the help of a bus-load of tourists who arrived, we tipped the little car back on its wheels. After making sure that it started without trouble, the tall, thin man gave us all a hearty wave and sped away into the mist.

To me it seemed like a day in which nothing could go wrong. The inn where we stopped that night was luxurious for rural Ireland and there was a pub down the street which attracted Bob and his friend. Although it was a cold September afternoon the giant marigolds and other flowers which grew outside the windows of my room were untouched by frost. When, at my request, a bellboy kindled some chunks of peat in the small brick fireplace which was the chief ornament of my room, a gentle warmth suffused the whole place. Betty was wearing a dress of green linen which I had often admired in class before I even knew her name, and I realized that all those handsome linen dresses of hers of course came from Ireland. Her mood was as ebullient as mine. As darkness fell, the peat fire filled the room with a rosy glow. After making love, we sat on the floor by the hearth and stared into the graying embers.

"I'll always remember this," I said.

"Me too, but I'm getting scared."

"Why?"

"I've never ridden a high like this for so long. I'm afraid it's going to be hell when we come down."

"Maybe we can stay up."

"What goes up . . ."

"I'll catch you," I said, and we both laughed.

We still felt good when we returned to Dublin about a week later. There we found that the legal arrangements had been completed for our marriage in the Registry, the equivalent of an American city hall. In the astringent economy of most Dubliners at the time, there was no talk of a reception of any sort. Although Betty had not mentioned the matter before, she said to me now that getting married should be different from licensing a dog.

We both found awaiting us great packets of letters from America. My children discussed their resumption of school, movies they had seen and books they had read. They hoped that I was having a good time in Ireland and gave their best to Betty, whom they had briefly met, but made no mention of my approaching marriage, for which they had congratulated me with odd formality when I had first told them about my plans. Although I did not think they meant to display it, their letters were obviously full of pain, a kind of pain which I could do nothing about, but which churned my guts.

There were also several letters from my former wife, Elise. Shortly after leaving her, I had worried about her a great deal, but a friend had told me that she seemed happier than she had in years, and was living an active social life. Now she told me that she planned to sell the house in Bedford Village and buy one in New Canaan, a move which indicated to me that she had not found Westchester County too hospitable. She was turning more and more from painting to photography, and a dark room which I had built for her in the cellar was proving handy. That dark room, she said, was the one thing she did not want to sell.

There were several other letters from Elise. They were all pleasant, occasionally nostalgic and undemanding. Always, she said, she had wanted to see Ireland, and she envied me the opportunity. She too sent her regards to Betty, whom she had met briefly while dropping the children off at our apartment in New York.

"Give my regards to your beautiful Irish girl," she said. "What a wonderful guide she must be to that lovely country!"

Somehow all that good cheer didn't seem quite real.

When Betty came into my hotel room, she saw me sitting on the bed surrounded by letters. Elise's distinctive handwriting she recognized, I knew. My former wife had often sent bills incurred by the children to me in New York.

"Letters from home?" Betty now asked, a little wryly.

Ever since I had met Betty, I had made a point of proving I had no secrets by showing her my mail. After skimming the pages rapidly, she sighed and said, "It's inevitable. She wants you back."

"There is nothing whatsoever in there to indicate that. And anyway—"

"It's not what she says, it's the fact that all of a sudden she has taken to writing you letters again. All you used to get was bills."

"Perhaps she's feeling just a little homesick for the past. Isn't that natural at a time like this?"

"Apparently," Betty said. "I got a letter today too."

She handed me an envelope of airmail tissue. The letter was from a man she told me about, a childhood friend to whom she had been informally engaged off and on over the years. His words were friendly, perhaps a little rueful, and left the clear implication that if she wanted to change her mind about getting married in Dublin, he would be waiting when she returned to New York.

"Look," I said, "no sane man would ever expect people like you and me to come to the marriage altar without a past. So your guy wants you back, and my former wife is feeling a little nostalgic about me. We're not in bondage. We still have lives of our own—"

"You always are going to feel torn between your children and me—"

"Nonsense. And they can spend time with us when we get a big enough place—"

"I still keep wondering whether any real happiness can come out of so much trouble. Think how happy they'd all be if you went back!"

"Elise and I were married for twenty years. Don't you think we gave it enough of a try?"

She didn't answer that, but she also did not look happy, and when I kissed her she gave no response at all.

The day before our marriage was scheduled in the Registry, Betty was in my hotel room helping me to pack some new tweed coats I had bought. At a little before noon, the telephone rang. Thinking that it was one of her relatives, Betty answered it.

"It's the overseas operator," she said, paling. "It's Elise."

I picked up the receiver and the pain of the conversation which followed was at least dulled a little by the sensation of being swept entirely away from reality into a nightmare from which I must soon awake.

Elise's voice was deceptively calm. "Sloan," she said, "I'm sorry to mess up your plans, but you have to come home."

"Why?"

"There's a man here who is threatening to kill the children."

"There's a *what*?

"A man is threatening to kill the children. He has an enormous knife—"

"Can you slow down a little and tell me this from the start?"

"He's a perfectly nice appearing man. An agent brought him. He said he wanted to buy the house and he kept coming back to be shown through it again. When he asked me why I was selling the place, I said that I had just been divorced. The next day he made a pass at me, and when I turned him down, he said he was going to kill the kids. Under his raincoat he had an enormous hunting knife which he showed me."

"Have you called the police?"

"Of course! As soon as he left! They took his description and all that, but they don't have enough men to station one here at the house all the time. That's why you have to come home!"

"Have you heard from him again?"

"Of course! That's why I'm so worried! He keeps calling on the telephone. He says that if I don't treat him better, he's going to come after the kids. Really, if you have any sense of responsibility, you have to come home!"

"I'll call you back in a few minutes," I said, and hung up. My face was drenched with sweat.

"What's happening?" Betty asked in a voice gone dead.

Briefly I described the situation.

"Jesus!" Betty said in disgust. "What a ploy! If she loves you this much, why did she let you go in the first place?"

"There are three possibilities," I said. "If it's a ploy, that's the least worry. If there really is a man with a knife, I can easily handle it from here."

"How?"

"If the police can't help, I'll station private detectives at the house. The thing that really worries me is the thought that Elise is having some sort of a crack-up."

"Won't you have to fly back to find out?"

"Let me see what I can do by telephone."

Grabbing the receiver, I called the analyst I had been seeing. Describing my situation, I asked him to call the psychiatrist that Elise had been visiting.

"Doctors will talk more to doctors than to relatives or former relatives of a patient," I said. "Can you find out whether Elise has imagined this whole nightmare?"

My doctor said he would call me back.

"My *God*," I said to Betty, "I've added another possibility for my doctor. Maybe he'll think *I'm* the one who is crazy!"

Betty did not laugh.

"Let me say something," she began. "No matter what the explanation of all this is, I think you should go home. Your children must be scared to death. Go home, and if you want to, stay there. Don't worry about me. I've made my own living since I was fourteen years old, and no one has had to worry about me *ever*."

She was crying. I was stroking her face with a damp washcloth when the telephone rang again. It was my doctor. In his dry, precise voice, he said, "I talked to Mrs. Wilson's doctor at some length. Your former wife, in his opinion, is making a good adjustment to the divorce, and certainly does not seem capable of delusions. She had told him about the incident involving the man with the knife, and he has done a little checking up on his own. Apparently a state hospital where he is a consultant recently released a patient with the behavior pattern your former wife described. He threatens, but doesn't kill. The information has been turned over to the police. Is there anything else I can do to help you?"

"No. I can't thank you enough."

"How are you getting on?"

"I'm fine. Never felt better in my life."

"How's Betty?"

I had brought Betty in to see the doctor because she had seemed curious about this man I visited so often.

"She's fine," I said now. "We're going to be married tomorrow if I can handle this crazy crisis about the man with the knife."

"As I remember, you told me about a man somewhere in Massachusetts who keeps writing threatening letters to you."

"Yes."

"Such things happen quite often, especially to people who for some reason excite envy. Take every precaution, of course, but I don't think that the fellow who threatened your wife is enough reason to delay all your plans."

"Thank you," I said.

"And give Betty my best. When you brought her into my office, I thought that she was a delightful young woman. It must be pleasant in Ireland this time of year. To tell you the truth. I think I envy you."

With a short laugh (the first I had ever heard that astringent appearing doctor give), he said good-by and hung up.

"What was all that about?" she asked.

"My psychoanalyst says that you're a delightful young woman and that he envies me. Now I can never leave you. It would be bad for my mental health."

"But what did he say?"

"Elise is sane. The man with the knife is real, though probably he does no more than threaten. It's time for phase two of this little war."

On the telephone I got Mort Leavy, the lawyer who had attempted to steer me through the labyrinth of the divorce courts with as little pain as possible. He also helped me with the evasive maneuvers which were deemed necessary to avoid the tax men who considered writers to be unusually tasty morsels, and all in all seemed to me to be a fellow who could handle almost any conceivable problem. The task of protecting children and a former wife against a man with a hunting knife apparently seemed to him to be just another detail in the normal run of his daily work. He immediately assured me that he would send Pinkerton detectives to stand guard in Elise's house around the clock. This would be expensive, he assured me cheerily, but perhaps their cost would be considered deductible.

"How's Betty?" he asked.

"This thing has kind of shaken us, but she's fine. The wedding takes place tomorrow."

"Congratulations," he said, "and don't worry about Elise and the children. I'll see that they are protected if I have to mount a machine gun on your front porch myself."

Only one more call was necessary, and that was to Elise. She seemed relieved to hear about the Pinkerton detectives.

"They can protect you better than I can," I said. "I'm not even licensed to carry a gun."

"I found your old rifle, but I don't know how to load it," she replied. "Anyway, thanks a lot."

The brevity of the conversation appeared to be a reproach. Suddenly it appeared to me that I had been reproached by women all my life. Only Betty almost never disapproved.

"The whole thing is settled now," I said to Betty after describing the solution. "Now we can *forget* it."

"No," she said with a smile. "That's going to be one thing you and I are never going to be able to do."

39

The Registry in Dublin was a cavernous building that looked like a cross between a railroad station and a morgue. The man who officiated at our wedding resembled photographs of Neville Chamberlain in his last years and was dressed rather like an undertaker who had prepared himself for the funeral of an important man. After glancing at the papers I showed him, he looked at us both with marked distaste. Probably he was a good Catholic, I concluded, and did not like helping a divorced man to get married, even in a civil ceremony. Perhaps I imagined it, but he actually seemed to sniff, as though judging the ripeness of dead fish.

"Are you Sloan Wilson?" he asked me.

"Yes."

"Are you Betty Joan Stephens?"

"Yes," she replied.

"Sign your names here."

We penned our signatures in a large notebook on a table.

"You're married," he said.

"Is that all?" I asked.

"No need for any more," he replied, slapping the book shut.

In the Gorham Hotel I arranged to have a reception. Betty's relatives came, but this was not the bang-up Irish wedding party that I had expected. People sat sipping whiskey while a young man played the accordion alone in a corner. Betty herself looked dejected, and I complicated matters by getting much too drunk. At the end of the evening, the manager of the hotel refused to take my check or honor my credit cards, despite the fact that I thought I had established credit.

"You've got to remember," Betty's father said. "In Dublin they won't give a writer credit if he leaves his kidney in a glass."

The only way that I could pay for the reception and for several nights which I had spent in the hotel was to use the traveler's checks which I had saved for further travels.

"It would be really much more convenient if you could honor my American Express card the way most first-class hotels do," I said icily to the manager, who also seemed to look like Neville Chamberlain.

"I'm sorry if you Americans do not always like Irish customs," he haughtily returned.

"Do you like American money?" I asked, trying to keep my words from slurring. Tearing a traveler's check of small denomination from my book, I tossed it on the floor.

It was a lousy drunken trick, but I sure drew an audience as I continued to toss traveler's checks on the floor. Most of them were for ten or twenty dollars. Since I owed the hotel something like $1500, quite a pile of paper mounted around the manager's feet. Apparently the sight of such disrespect shown to himself and to money pained the old man terribly. Each time I ripped a check from the book and sent it sailing he shook his head. Finally the sight of so many dollars on the rug was more than he could stand. Kneeling, he began to pick them up.

At this point, Betty, who had been changing her clothes, pushed through the crowd which had surrounded us. Seeing the old man on his knees, she said to me, "What happened?"

"He wouldn't take a check or a credit card. He wanted his money in traveler's checks and I just gave it to him."

"Oh, *Christ!*" she replied, and kneeling down, helped the manager to pick up the checks. Trying to be gallant, I helped her.

"Don't get in the way," she said. "I don't know what's the matter with me. Why would I marry a lousy drunk?"

340

We had an argument and missed the boat to London on which we had reservations. When I told the taxi driver to take us to another hotel, Betty was dangerously quiet.

"To tell the truth, I don't know why I got married at all," she said when we reached our room. "How do you think I got to the age of twenty-eight without getting married? Plenty of men asked me, plenty of *good* men, but I had too much sense. How many people do you know who are happily married? Well *you* should know, you've been through the whole crazy business. I feel sorry for Elise. No wonder she's crazy. My God, if she spent twenty years with you, she must have been crazy from the start!"

I'd never heard her carry on like that. I felt sunk.

"Now don't look so hurt," she said as she hung up her dress. "I *told* you that I am a terrible bitch, didn't I?"

Somehow the night came to an end. The next morning we flew to London. We stayed at the Grosvenor House, where I telephoned the company which published my books in England. The man I knew there was out, and the others seemed vague when I asked if they could help me to establish credit at a bank. My sense of importance injured, I glanced at Betty, but obviously she still loathed me. Even before we unpacked our bags, we had a terrible fight which ended with me shouting at her as cruelly as I had shouted at my first wife. She was terrifyingly good at quick comebacks. Over a period of about half an hour we destroyed each other and kicked the corpses into the gutter, where we kicked them again. At the conclusion of this mortal combat, Betty stood up and looking as calm as though she had never heard an angry word in her life, announced that she was going out to visit some relatives. I didn't even know that she had any relatives in London. As I watched her small, erect form walk down the hall to the elevator, I felt sure I would never see her again.

When Betty came back two hours later I was in bed, feeling awful. After feeling my forehead, Betty called a house physician, who said that I had bronchitis.

"You see what happens when you mistreat me," I said, and for the first time in what seemed like a long while Betty laughed.

The malaise which we had been suffering ever since all those letters had come from America disappeared as quickly as it had come. Perhaps it had taught me something, I reflected as I recovered from the bronchitis. When would I learn that it is not necessary to make a sharp reply just because a woman makes one? With a grin I remembered some advice a friend had given me out in the South Pacific during the war: "Never argue with a pretty girl. If she makes you angry, just imagine the way she looks nek-kid. No man can argue long with a nek-kid girl."

Sexist though it may be, the funny part about this advice was that it worked. The only trouble was that I was fool enough to tell Betty about my new method.

"Now, damn it," she said, "every time you agree with me about anything, I'll know that you're just sitting there stripping me. Like that *New Yorker* cartoon. I'm no lady in a cartoon. Keep that in mind."

I assured her I would. And I did.

Soon I came to love the Grosvenor House. Room service spread lavish meals on our bed and picked them up without bothering me for more than a few minutes while I recovered from bronchitis. Downstairs, I found—to my gratitude—my credit cards were honored by the man at the front desk, by a travel agency, and by a store which sold women's clothes. Before we were married, Betty had never let me buy expensive clothes for her because she said she had always had a rule against accepting such gifts and prided herself on following it until she actually went to the altar. Now it pleased me to surprise her with a traveling suit and a fur coat, which was not quite mink but which would be warm in the fall weather. Carrying two bulky boxes, I went to her room.

One thing I loved about her was that she always received a present as though it were the first which had ever been offered to her. With unfeigned enthusiasm she started by admiring the way in which the box was wrapped. When she saw the fur coat, she held it against her cheek.

"It's not really mink," I said. "I think it's muskrat."

"Who cares? It's warm and lovely and beautiful!"

Putting it on, she turned up the high collar and twirled by the mirror.

"I shall never be cold!" she said. "I'm protected. In spite of everything I've said, that's what I love about being married!"

"Is that all?"

"No, it's not all, but the rest is harder to say."

Eagerly she opened the box of dresses, exclaiming as she held them up. "How did you know my size so soon?" she asked.

"Size 7/8, the same as my daughter Lisa. It's also the size they put on mannequins. It's a size a great many women like to think of themselves as being."

"How do you know all this?" she asked with a laugh.

"You'd be surprised at the number of little nuggets of information a man can pick up during a lifetime of chasing women."

She threw a pillow at me and went into the bathroom to try on one of her new dresses. Folding her fur coat on her arm, she stared into the mirror on the back of the closet door.

"My name is Betty Wilson," she said. "I am looking at Mrs. Sloan Wilson. That doesn't sound like me, and the woman in the glass doesn't look like me. But she's not a bad-looking broad, and she's beautifully dressed. What does a rich bitch like that do when her husband brings her beautiful presents?"

Her hugs were often so intense that there was something poignant about them, as though she were driven by more emotion than could be expressed. Sometimes when I kissed her I half-felt as though I were consoling her, and often there was compassion as well as passion in the way she made love to me.

"You know something?" she asked.

"What?"

"I really feel married now. It's not strange any more."

"How come?"

"I'm getting all repressed in bed. Isn't that what wives are supposed to do?"

"You didn't seem to me to be notably repressed."

"I was faking it. I mean, don't you think I'm getting the hang of wife-hood awfully fast?"

I swatted her one on her petite rear end.

Part 7
"A Christmas Tree as Big as the World"

40

A few days later we flew to Majorca to continue our honeymoon. At Formentor we saw a young actress who was so startlingly beautiful in the style of Elizabeth Taylor that, she said, she had been fired from the set of Cleopatra, the film which was currently being shot in Italy, because the director did not want a younger version of his star to attract the attention of his audiences.

"Do you believe that stuff?" Betty asked me as the young beauty, dressed in the briefest of bikinis, walked on the beach.

"I suppose it could happen."

"You think she's incredibly beautiful, don't you?"

"I think she's a good-looking woman. Who wouldn't?"

"Isn't that the way it goes? All my life, practically, I've been proud of my figure. I've exercised and I've dieted and taken care of it every way I could. At almost any party, I've got the best figure in the room, even compared to women who are much younger. Then finally I get married, go on my honeymoon, and what do I find? Some goddamn actress who got fired because she's more beautiful than Elizabeth Taylor and who parades around the beach in a bikini that shows all too clearly that she has a figure which makes me look like an old bag!"

"Do you think I love you just for your figure?" I asked.

"Well, if you love me for my mind, you're nuts."

"I love your mind too—"

"You mean you think I've got a lousy figure? One look at this goddamn female who's more beautiful than the most famous movie star in the world, and you're practically saying, 'Good old Betty. Her body's a mess, but thank God she's no dummy . . .' "

When she started hitting me with a damp towel, I ran into the sea, where she followed me. Laughing, we swam into the azure waves while the girl who was more beautiful than Elizabeth Taylor continued to stroll alone on the beach.

In Spain we rented a car and drove through the hot, red countryside from Barcelona to Madrid. Grapes were being harvested, and when we got out of our car, a man threw Betty a bunch from the top of a high old cart. When, in her almost nonexistent Spanish, she thanked him, he blew her a kiss, grinned and drove off.

When we got to Madrid, I took Betty to a restaurant there where, I had read, Hemingway liked to eat roast suckling pig. The dish cost a lot, and we had to wait nearly an hour to get it. For some reason the hind end was presented to Betty. On the sizzling platter it looked like an infant ready to have its diaper changed. Putting her napkin to her mouth, Betty left the table and nothing could induce her to return to finish her meal.

"I don't give a damn if Hemingway likes that stuff or not," she said. "If he does, he must be a regular cannibal. Even if a man writes all the books in the world, he doesn't have a right to get away with that!"

By the time we got to France it was October, and the automobile show was causing a great shortage of hotel rooms in Paris. The room we finally located at Le Bristol was $175 a night. Despite the fact that I had resigned myself to enduring this expensive luxury for a few days at least, Betty said the price was immoral.

"I couldn't sleep in a room costing that much," she said.

"Then what are you going to do? Leave Paris?"

"I have some friends near here. We could stay with them."

"This is our honeymoon! I don't want to sleep on a couch in somebody's living room."

"Let's give it a try," she said, going to the telephone.

Her friends were a man and a woman who owned a drugstore in a suburb of Paris named Antony, Seine. They greeted Betty with open arms and I gathered from all the talk than an American uncle of hers had helped someone close to them to settle in the United States. Now they ushered us into a big, beautifully appointed bedroom on the second floor of their house and invited us to stay there as long as we possible could. When I happened to go downstairs early the next morning, I found my host and hostess attempting to sleep on a narrow couch bed.

"We can't impose on these people like this," I said to Betty. "We have to go."

"No, we don't," she retorted. "My Uncle Robbie sponsored one of their best friends in the States. We gave to them. Don't you know that sometimes people enjoy giving back? Beyond that, they like us and are curious about what kind of a man you are."

Apparently Betty was right, for in a week of being displaced, these kind people gave no sign of protest. They had a Spanish cook, and the food they served in the courtyard behind their house was superb. Perhaps it was my state of mind, but the fresh-baked bread, the cheeses, the delicately flavored poultry and fish all tasted better than anything I had eaten even in a four-star restaurant.

In Italy we rented a car to drive from Rome to Venice. On the two occasions I had visited Italy in the past I had, for various reasons, been miserable, but Betty had never been there and wanted to see it. Uninterested in antiquities or our fellow tourists, we kept our little Fiat moving until we got to Siena. There we came on a hotel so old that it looked as though Caesar himself might have stayed there. The room we were shown was modest, clean and cheap, with a window overlooking a shopping area that made the cobblestoned streets of Ireland look modern. The rough schedule I had made up called for us to hurry on to Florence, Pisa and Venice, but we were so happy where we were that we let more than a week slip by. That October the public rooms and halls of the ancient hotel were deserted. Many curtains had been drawn and few lights were turned on. Most of the time, there was not a sound to be heard. To me, and I think to Betty, the effect was soothing, not gloomy. The food was excellent, and at dinnertime we were served by three waiters. In our bathroom there was a memorable marble tub, almost the size of a double bed, with a brass lion's head from the mouth of which water spouted. The towels were the biggest I had ever seen, and were piled on a shelf where a steam pipe kept them warm.

Lying in bed one night after Betty had gone to sleep, I found myself worrying about my children, and also about my new book, *Georgie Winthrop*, which should be published soon. Unlike my other books, poor Georgie had stirred no advance-publication movie talk or expressions of interest from book clubs. Maybe I was washed up at the age of forty-two, as plenty of writers had been after a successful book. Now that I had a new wife, three children and a former wife to support, what would I do if the money ran out?

Involuntarily I rolled over in the bed rather suddenly.

"What's the matter?" Betty asked.

As I did all the time now, I told her.

"Let's go home," she said. "For me, too, it's just about time . . . By the way, I've always heard people make fun of honeymoons, but this one worked, for me, anyhow."

"I've had a marvelous time. What's it done for you?"

There was a pause before she said, "I've learned to feel like a wife. I'm your wife. You're my husband. In sickness or in health, for richer or poorer. I guess I'll always be sorry that no one said those words for us, but we can say them for ourselves, can't we?"

"We can mean them and we can live them, which is more than a lot of people can do."

"That's right."

"When we go back to New York, I want to move right back into my apartment until we're sure that we have plenty of money. Then do you know what I want to do?"

"What?"

"I want to have a baby. You said you wouldn't mind."

We had not discussed the matter much. Now the idea both pleased and scared me. I told her that.

"Don't worry," she said. "If I have to, I can make good money as a press agent. But I'll tell you something strange. All my life I thought I was peculiar because I didn't really want a baby. Now I can hardly think of anything else. Why do you think I've been so turned on about sex lately? Partly you, of course, but partly because I hope there will be an accident. Ever since London, I've been forgetting to take the pill, something I've never forgotten before. I never knew that I could change so much."

"Does it bother you to take the pill?"

"Sometimes I almost gag on it. Neither of us is exactly too young to have a family and I start thinking, what are we waiting for? My mind goes 'round and 'round. What right do I have to ask you to have a child? You've already got three to send to college."

"Let me give you a piece of advice," I said.

"What?"

"A woman like you should have a child!"

"I'll be pregnant within about one hour!"

"I've never been afraid of a pregnant woman in my life."

Laughing, she gave me a hug. When we flew home a few days later, she seemed to glow like one of those fires of Irish peat which can warm a whole room without a single flame being visible.

Soon after we returned to Betty's small apartment in New York, *Georgie Winthrop* was published. Although there were a few good reviews, the majority ranged from bad to vitriolic. For some reason these attacks hurt me more than the bad notices I had received in the past. It was difficult for me to talk about the book, and on a Merv Griffin television program I suffered such stage fright when asked to summarize my story that I could barely stammer out a few words. Luckily the comedian, Milt Kamen, came to my rescue with a flood of jokes which required me to do nothing but laugh. Afterward friends who had seen the program said that I had started out fine, but that terrible Kamen had managed to steal the show. Maybe so, but never was a victim more grateful to a thief.

More blows soon came. In discussing my financial situation, Mort Leavy pointed out that certain tax-sheltered investments which I had made while under the guidance of another lawyer were brilliantly successful as a way to avoid taxes, but not very helpful as a means of providing sustenance. The truth was that the money put into the tax-sheltered investments was lost and would never provide worrisome tax problems again. My talk with Mort also helped me to realize that Hollywood was fast changing. Regardless of the quality of my work, I probably could not soon expect to sell movie rights for big sums of money.

Most of my savings, Mort continued, were earmarked for the support and education of my children and to meet the other stipulations of the divorce disagreement. Enough money was left for Betty and me *if* we lived modestly and *if* my general pattern of writing profitable books continued. I still had some income from the movie of *A Summer Place*, and in general there was no reason to panic.

When anyone tells me that there is no reason for panic, the first thing I always do is panic. After all, people don't go around saying that there is no reason for panic unless a perfectly good one exists. The only time I ever told the men aboard the *Nogak* during the war that there was no reason for panic was when we were in the middle of a full-fledged hurricane which was driving us into the dark arctic seas at a speed which I couldn't even begin to guess.

My financial position was harder to fix than a position at sea. My income was based essentially on a share of the profits which several books and a movie *might* make. The bite of the government was always unforeseeable even by lawyers. This was allowed, and that was disallowed after months of haggling. A cattle deal I'd entered with some actors on the advice of a lawyer was disapproved in California and approved in New York. The situation was a mess. The thrifty rules of my New England forebears were reversed. It was bad to save money because the government would take it, but good to spend because no one could take away the memories of, say, a trip to Europe, and in some circumstances, travel costs could be deductible. But "deductible" only worked if you had something to deduct from. Thinking about all this always made me hurry to the nearest bar for a double martini.

To earn myself some peace of mind and revenge myself against the reviewers who had been so unkind to *Georgie Winthrop*, I decided to write another book. Since our tiny apartment on 56th Street did not have a place for me to work, I rented a cheap room in a nearby hotel. It had spotted green walls and looked like a place where traveling salesmen came to die. The thought of the prior occupants of the room often disturbed me as I sat crouched over my typewriter. This was probably a place where many an unloved man had taken some poor, slack-faced prostitute who hoped to earn enough money for her night's supply of drugs. High on a closet shelf I found two empty vodka bottles. What intensity of guilt would make a man hide his drinking even from a hotel chambermaid?

Maybe it was these ghosts in the room which made it impossible for me to think of anything to write. Even the big wastepaper basket which I had brought with me remained empty, for I couldn't think of anything good enough to write and throw away. Telling myself that this kind of block had happened to me before, I paced up and down my tiny room. With a sense of shock I noticed that a path had been worn in the center of the rug. What had bedevilled the people who had paced here before?

To pretend, at least, that I was working, I forced myself to remain in my "office" until five each afternoon. Lugging my heavy old briefcase more or less from habit, I started walking the few blocks home to 56th Street. Once when I was feeling particularly frustrated, a sportscar charged at me while I was crossing Seventh Avenue in the middle of the block. Despite the fact that there was little traffic, the driver blared his horn and came to a skidding stop a few inches from my feet, where he continued to blow his horn. As if that was not enough, he proceeded to yell at me. Ordinarily I would have walked on, ignoring him as best I could, but on this evening my nerves were so tight from days of fruitless work that I exploded. Before I really knew what I was doing, I lifted my heavy briefcase high in the air and brought it down on the hood of the sportscar with all my strength. They don't make these sportscars as well as they used to, I observed; my briefcase left a substantial dent. There was a moment when the incredulous driver apparently refused to believe what had happened to him. He sat there behind the wheel, white-faced for perhaps five seconds before jumping out of his little cockpit, ignoring the door. Thinking that he was about to attack me, I was pleased to see that he was quite a small man about my own age. Instead of attempting to teach me a lesson, he began rubbing the dent in his hood with as much shocked disbelief as a soldier might display while exploring some ghastly wound. The light changed in my favor, and picking up my briefcase, I got lost in the crowd. Only then did I begin to wonder what would have happened if a policeman had witnessed my crime. Would he have booked me for assault with a deadly weapon against a car?

When I got home, I tried to remember that Betty was having her own frustrations. Although she had exuberantly expected to get pregnant within an hour when she decided to have a baby, two months had gone by without success. She of course understood that this is hardly unusual, but some concept which she had of herself was injured.

"I told you, all my life I've made practically a religion out of taking good care of my body," she said. "What's the point if the damn thing doesn't even work?"

"I wish you didn't have three children," she added a few minutes later.

"Why?"

"Because then I could blame this whole damn thing on you."

"Maybe I'm getting old."

"No. It's just that my machinery doesn't work. I got so mad at it today that I started talking to it. 'Come on, uterus! Come on, Fallopian tubes! Come on, ova! It's time to do your thing!' "

She was sitting on her studio couch, which was strewn with some new curtains she was making.

"Everybody hates wives who greet their husbands with a long list of their troubles," she said. "I told you mine, let's hear yours."

I told her about attacking the sportscar.

"That's beautiful," she said, her eyes lighting up. "Why don't you roam the city, the secret avenger of all the poor pedestrians? How many cars do you think you could net in a day? Do you mind if I paint the silhouette of a little sportscar on your briefcase the way fighter pilots in the movies put a little Jap flag on their plane every time they shot an enemy down?"

She was silent for a while, fiddling with the curtain material. Finally she said, "Want to hear something funny?"

"Sure."

"They want me to be a society girl."

"What?"

"Some very high-toned ladies have been calling. I think they think I'm your first wife. Why can't I be Mrs. Sloan Wilson the Second? Anyway, they want me to be a sponsor for some damn ball at the Waldorf. What does a sponsor do, anyway?"

"I've never been sure."

"Then *another* woman called. 'Is Mrs. Sloan Wilson there?' she asked as though I were the maid. I told her to wait a minute while I looked under the bed."

"What did she say?"

"I think she thought she hadn't heard it. Anyway, I put on a very high-toned voice when I came back to the phone and she sounded happy. It seems that she wants me to be in charge of the blood bank at the Red Cross."

"Do you want to do it?"

"Well, it's the kind of thing which the idle wives of rich men do, isn't it? Can you imagine me having a problem with idleness?"

"Do you?"

"I get a little lonely, sitting around here all day. For a while there I thought of going back to work, but I don't really think that your wife should be an apprentice press agent. I got word that an old friend of mine who is putting together a nightclub act has a spot for me as a dancer, but you'd go through the roof if I did that, wouldn't you?"

"The right thing to say is no, but the truth is that I'd have to think about it a little while to see how I would feel."

"I don't think I want you to want me to do those things. Why go back to my old life when I'm starting a new one?"

A few days later Betty asked me to buy a Christmas tree. I was used to buying trees for large country houses. In a parking lot where there was a good variety of fir, spruce and pine, I chose a tree which appeared to be well-shaped and arranged to have it delivered. When it arrived only a few hours later, I was dismayed to discover that it was much too high for the ceiling of our apartment, and filled almost half the living room.

"It was crazy of me to buy it," I said. "I'll take it back."

"*No*," Betty said. "A Christmas tree as big as the world! If you can get a saw, we can create a whole new kind of Christmas scene up here."

All the next day she worked on the tree. When I returned from my "office," the fully decorated tree dwarfed everything else in the living room. Branches which she had cut from the top and bottom decorated every window. The whole apartment was filled with the fragrance of pine.

"It's like a child's dream," she said. "The room is all tree!"

"It's beautiful," I said, as indeed it was.

"When I was a kid we didn't have much room and I always dreamed of having a real tree," she said. "Of course, I had no idea that it would smell so good!"

Because we were trying to save money, she asked me to get her nothing expensive that Christmas.

"All I want is some demitasse cups," she said. "Six would be enough, and there are plenty you can get for a couple of dollars apiece."

It's not much fun to buy a cheap present for one's bride, and I delayed the purchase until the last minute. On the day before Christmas I went to Tiffany's, and as I had expected I found a huge variety of demitasse cups, some of which were surprisingly cheap. After admiring rows of cups which cost a hundred and more dollars apiece, I settled on some which were made of Italian pottery. Too thick to be graceful or pleasant on the lips, they nonetheless were prettily colored and six of them cost less than twenty dollars. While waiting for my purchase to be packed in the pale blue box which helps to make almost any gift from Tiffany's exciting, I looked at cups of solid gold, English bone china cups with gold rims, cups of translucent porcelain—who could imagine so many kinds of costly cups?

When my package didn't appear, I went to the wrapping room, which on the day before Christmas was as crowded and confused as the headquarters of a general during a massive attack. My saleslady spotted me there and handed me my elaborately wrapped gift. Picking my way through holiday crowds, I walked home and hid the pale blue box in a closet.

That night Betty and I sat up late on the studio couch, which had been pushed into a corner to make way for the tree. At about ten I went out for a barbecued chicken and a bottle of wine. It was beginning to rain slightly and a cold wind was blowing. When I returned, Betty said, "What's the weather like?"

Before I could answer, she added, "No, don't tell me. I like our air-shaft. As long as you stay here, you can imagine any kind of weather you like. I have chosen a cold clear night with a full moon and spotless snow everywhere. It's a great night for miracles, just the way it's supposed to be."

In some ways it did appear to be a miraculous evening. We talked little and we played no music, but we both felt a sense of contentment which was almost religious in its intensity. A little after midnight Betty said, "It's Christmas. I'm dying to give you my gift. Do we have to wait?"

She gave me a briar pipe of a kind which I had often admired, but had never been self-indulgent enough to buy for myself. Also a humidor for tobacco which was of English manufacture, and which could easily have been designed to hold the crown jewels. She gave me books which she had heard me admire, and a bottle of the best Irish whiskey, and some beautiful tweeds which she had shipped from Ireland.

"I thought that we were going to economize," I said.

"Ha!" she replied in triumph. "None of this cost you anything. I still had a few bucks from my own savings account!"

Now it was time to present my rotten little gift of Italian pottery, all eighteen dollars worth of it. As I carried the blue box from the closet, I found myself first wishing that I had bought something better and then praying that somehow those cups of clay could somehow transform themselves into gold.

"I'm afraid this isn't much," I said lamely as I handed the box to her.

"Tiffany's!" she said. "Am I shameless? I always love to get boxes from Tiffany's!"

Speedily she undid the paper and took the lid from the box. From the tissue paper she lifted a demitasse of English bone china with a band of solid gold around the rim.

"Oh!" she exclaimed with a sharp intake of breath. "God, what taste you have! And how did you know that I've admired English bone china ever since my grandmother showed me a cup she brought from Scotland?"

For one of the few times in my life, I was absolutely speechless. My immediate fear was that the remaining cups in the box would turn out to be Italian pottery. But no, all the cups were English bone china ringed with gold. And there were twelve, not six, of them. Remembering that the cups of this kind which I had seen at Tiffany's were at the most expensive end of the counter, I figured that the cups were worth about a hundred dollars apiece.

"It takes a real man," Betty said, "to know that a woman who asks for inexpensive Christmas presents doesn't mean a word she says."

"I cannot let our life be a living lie," I began melodramatically.

"What do you mean?"

Wretchedly I explained the fact that I had bought cheap pottery. "There must have been some mistake in the wrapping room," I said. "Somebody, somewhere is being given hell by his wife because he gave her cheap cups."

"No," Betty said. "I prefer to believe that it's a miracle. And if Tiffany's tries to take their cups back, I'll switch off the elevators and fight on every stair landing!"

The prospect of this battle apparently terrorized Tiffany's. After a pleasant exchange of letters, they acknowledged their error, agreed with me that no man could take a Tiffany cup away from his wife, and ended up by presenting the cups to us as a gift. Long afterward, they also told me that they never heard from the person who had bought English bone china and got Italian pottery.

"I *told* you the whole thing is a miracle," Betty said.

41

The day after Christmas the children came in from Bedford Village to visit us. Because I had been unable to get any clear idea of what they wanted for Christmas over the telephone, we had delayed major purchases. Now Lisa said she wanted clothes and Betty prepared to take her on a tour of the expensive dress houses where she still received enormous discounts in return for theater tickets she had given in the past. Becky wanted a certain kind of guitar which was made in Spain. After a few telephone calls, Betty managed to find a store which offered to sell her such an instrument at cost because one of Betty's former bosses had done a lot of business there.

"How do you arrange these things?" Lisa asked in astonishment.

"I'm a city girl," Betty replied. "In Brooklyn, where I grew up when I wasn't in Ireland, my Scotch grandmother never bought *anything* without spending at least a day on the telephone to see if she could get it at a discount. When she was in her seventies she still went to every grocery store on her bus route to make sure she got the best price."

"She must have been quite a woman," Lisa said.

"She still is quite a woman. She and my gramps raised seven children and kept the house together all through the depression. My mother and I lived there too when my father was in Ireland . . . Now what got me started on all this?"

My children were interested and begged her to go on with stories about her family. Watching their intent faces, I realized that enough time had gone by to enable them to think of Betty as an individual, not just the dancer and apprentice press agent which the newspapers had reported to be my second wife.

Before long Betty and my daughters began their shopping tour. As they waited for the elevator I noticed that the three of them were much the same size, laughing and talking like three schoolgirls off on a fling.

I was left alone in the apartment with my son, who stoutly maintained that he did not want any more Christmas presents. Everyone in the family knew he liked fishing, he said, and he'd already gotten enough tackle to clean out the oceans of the world.

"Maybe you'll see something in the stores that you'll like," I said, and we started to stroll toward Fifth Avenue. At fourteen, he was growing so fast that the cuffs of his trousers were always much too short. Still lean, and strong as a whip, he stalked along on his long legs so fast that I had difficulty in keeping up with him. His personality appeared to be maturing even faster than his body. There was an air of polite reserve about him which would have pleased his Boston ancestors. As a matter of fact, I reflected, David at the age of fourteen had somehow contrived to make himself more of a Harvard man than I had ever managed to be. His lean narrow face and prominent nose were far more aristocratic than anything in my family album. Despite the bad years he'd suffered as a result of the divorce, he appeared to be enjoying a kind of serenity and inner confidence I'd never managed.

"Would you like a chess set?" I asked as we passed a store which specialized in them.

"No thanks. I have one, and anyway, I don't play chess much any more."

"Why?"

"At school everybody is much better or worse. Anyway, it's a waste of time with all the reading I have to do."

"Does the school really work you that hard?"

"I'm not talking about assigned reading. There's a whole library of books I should have read before now if I ever expect to get anywhere."

"Just where do you expect to get?"

"Well, fundamentally I'm a naturalist," he said. "Of course nowadays that's a little more complicated than it was in Thoreau's time. I'm not sure whether I want to be a biologist, a zoologist, a botanist, or maybe a marine biologist. Then of course there's this umbrella word 'ecologist,' which kind of means everything and nothing. Whatever I do, I've got to be good at some fairly advanced mathematics. Math has always been my weak point, but I'm learning to overcome that. Any scientist of course has to learn to express ideas mathematically."

In the back of my mind I had been wondering whether I should take him to F.A.O. Schwarz, the toy store which in his early youth had fascinated him so much, but now that did not seem like a very appropriate idea. Where does one take a fourteen-going-on-forty-year-old scientist in New York? What had interested me when I was fourteen? Girls and boats.

"Do you have any interest in boats?" I asked David.

"Not really. I think I'm a little scared of them."

Would he like a rifle? When I was fourteen, I liked to hunt rabbits, but a rifle did not seem an appropriate gift for a young naturalist.

"Don't worry about buying me something, dad," he finally said. "I'm pretty deep into Thoreau these days. I find that it's really true: a man doesn't need a lot of *things*."

"Have you found the great fallacy in Thoreau yet?"

"Is there one?"

"Wasn't his whole way of life at Walden Pond great for a bachelor like Thoreau but impossible for anyone else?"

"Well, Thoreau only spent a few weeks at the pond. I think his work there is a metaphor, like the Bible. Its truth and poetry go all to pieces if you start to take them literally."

I nodded. What the hell else could I do in the face of such wisdom?

Finding ourselves in the neighborhood of the Harvard Club, we went in. Many of my old friends were at the bar, and I enjoyed introducing them to my lean intellectual son.

"Well, David," a loyal Harvard alumnus and real "old boy" said, "you'll be coming to Cambridge with the class of sixty-eight, won't you?"

"I'm not quite sure about that," David replied.

"What do you mean, you're not sure? If those bastards running the admissions office give you any trouble, just tell your father to tell me."

"That's very kind of you, sir," David said, "but to tell you the truth, I doubt that I will be going to Harvard."

The loyal alumnus looked shocked. "Why not?" he demanded.

"I'm not looking for the best university," David said. "I'm looking for the best biology department, and that doesn't necessarily mean Harvard. I understand that biology departments can change pretty drastically from year to year."

"Why, we have a very strong biology department," the loyal alumnus thundered. "It has a brand new building as I remember. You mark my words . . ."

"Yes, sir," David said with a smile, "you can be sure I will."

Noticing that it was about twelve-thirty, we went to the club's cavernous dining room. Fortunately an elaborate buffet lunch was being offered, and I found an aspect of my son which remained adolescent. Heaping his plate with everything from a cold lobster to cranberry jelly, he emptied it in less than five minutes, and, in all, returned four times for more.

"Did you really like Harvard?" he asked me suddenly.

"I wouldn't have missed it for the world. How else would I get to join the Harvard Club?"

"I mean, did you *really* like it?"

"Between the time I was eighteen and twenty-two, I lost my father, fell in love with your mother, and went to World war II. Somehow I wasn't in a mood for studying much."

"I hope all that doesn't happen to me," he said.

"To relieve your mind on one score, I can say that I'm feeling fairly durable and have no immediate plans for dying. Wars I can't predict. As for falling in love while you still are very young, I can say only that I shall pity you if you do and pity you more if you don't."

He laughed. On the way home he allowed me to buy him a pair of trousers which were long enough to strike up a temporary acquaintance, at least, with the tops of his shoes.

When we got home, Betty and the girls were waiting for us, all decked out in the elegantly simple kind of clothes Betty usually wore. Sitting in the only corner of the room available because of the enormous Christmas tree, they were sipping coffee from the Tiffany demitasse cups and laughing as Betty told the story of how we had acquired them.

Finally Lisa announced that it was time for them to be going to the station to catch their train back to Westchester. Thinking, perhaps, that I wanted to be alone with them, Betty cleaned up the dishes while I rode down in the elevator with the children to help them catch a taxi.

"Betty is kind of everything," Lisa said as we stepped from the elevator.

"What does that mean?"

"Well, she's Scotch and she's Dublin Irish and she's a Brooklyn girl. She's a press agent and a dancer. She's only about ten years older than I am, but she's been working for fourteen years and seems to have an incredible amount of information about the theater, clothes, and God knows what else. I take it she wasn't raised in circumstances that were exactly plush, but she says she can't remember how many times she's been to Europe because her parents kept going back and forth from the time she was born. I think she's fascinating. Somehow I never expected to have a stepmother like that."

"Do you like her?" I asked.

"Well, I can easily see why you love her. 'Like' isn't a very good word to describe this step-relationship. After all, I really want my old man back and she's got him. When I get over that, I'll love her. Meanwhile, I admire her and I'm grateful to her, daddy, because I know you're in good hands."

This little speech of hers left me embarrassingly close to tears. When a taxi stopped near us in traffic, I ran to open the door. Hugging her new guitar, Becky came running, kissed me on the cheek and smiled.

"*Love!*" she said, giving that one word an intensity and poignancy which seemed to express her whole soul, and disappeared into the cab. Lisa and David followed. Suddenly I was alone on 56th Street and grateful that I did not have to stay alone for long.

"Did you have any trouble getting a cab?" Betty called from the kitchenette, where she was drying each Tiffany cup as though it were the last one in the world.

"No trouble," I said, my throat still oddly constricted.

"It's not fair for you to have kids like that," she said. "Why can't you have stupid, snotty-nosed brats like everyone else does? You've given me a hard act to follow. What am I going to do if my kid looks like an Irish gnome?"

"Does that really worry you?"

She put the cup she was drying on a carefully folded towel.

"The thought crossed my mind, but my instinct tells me that my daughter is going to be just like my mother, and my mother was among other things a saint. Even Norman Vincent Peale thought so."

"Norman Vincent Peale thought your mother was a saint?"

"They went abroad together."

"Under what, uh, circumstances?"

"Oh, it was all very respectable. I don't remember the details . . . I don't think I was even born yet . . . but it was some sort of church-organized trip. Anyway, he always said she was a saint and a lot of other people did too."

"And this means that you're hoping to have a saint for a daughter?"

"A nice, funny kind of saint, which is what mother was. During the days when she was so terribly sick in the hospital and we knew that the thing was terminal as they call it, I had this kind of conviction that someday I'd have a daughter just like her, that I'd *replace* her, so to speak. I know that sounds terrible, but for me it took a lot of the sting out of her death."

"Will you be upset if you have a son?"

"I won't have a son. You know, there are some things I just *know*. I promised my mother that I would name a daughter after her. That was the last thing I said that she understood. Probably I should ask you if you mind having a daughter named Jessie, but now that I've told you this story, how could you object?"

"Jessie is a pretty name. Why didn't you tell me all this before?"

"Just because I haven't been psychoanalyzed doesn't mean that I'm not repressed. Anyway, until I get pregnant, what's the point?"

She dried another cup before adding, "Do you mind if I tell you something silly?"

"How silly?"

"Maybe you'll think it's pretty bad. You know, in the hospital they bring these book carts around. My mother read all the time, especially when she was very sick. Now, I don't know whether I remember or imagine it, but I think she was reading your book, *Gray Flannel*, just before she died. It came out in the spring of 1955, didn't it? She died just before Christmas that year. She read most of the best sellers. With all the publicity you got, it kind of figures that she read it. Either in my imagination or in memory, I can hear her telling me that she liked it. I know this is kind of crazy, but the idea of that sort of puts my whole world together. The father of the new Jessie will be an author the dying Jessie loved. There, I've said it. If I'm sentimental once in a while, you'll just have to blame it on my Irish blood."

When we went to bed that nght, Betty had another surprise for me.

"I'm going to ask you to do something which may sound ridiculous," she said, "but I want to give it a try."

"What's that?"

"I happened to meet a girl I used to know at the office," she said. "This girl, Joan Goodman, read a book that says that the magnetism of the earth affects human fertility. Doctors say that the theory hasn't been proved, but Joan has a friend out on Long Island who'd been trying for years to have a baby. She tried this new method and it *worked*."

"How does one go about trying this new method?" I asked warily.

"When we make love, we have to have our heads pointing due north. If that doesn't work, we try due east. . . ."

"We sort of box the compass, eh?"

"Please don't make fun of it! It won't cost us anything to try. Joan even borrowed the compass her friend used."

From her bag, Betty took a boy scout compass, and handed it to me.

"Am I heading due north?" she asked, stretching out diagonally across the bed.

"Well, that poses a problem. You see, you've got a magnetic compass here. A magnetic compass is subject to variation, which is always marked on charts, and deviation, which is caused by the magnetism in the steel of a ship, or in a building."

"The people out on Long Island didn't fuss with all that junk. They just lined up according to that compass."

"In all probability they enjoyed some very inaccurate screwing."

"But it worked. How is Jessie going to get born if you keep laughing at me?"

"The best children are conceived during laughter. Now, if this northerly heading doesn't work, can we come right slowly to zero five zero degrees with both engines full ahead?"

She threw a pillow at me. She had tied a Christmas ribbon around her hair and her breath smelled of the after-dinner mints someone had given us. A tall, new Christmas candle burned on the dresser. Outside our window the pigeons sounded content with some bread Betty had fed them. On a distant street a siren wailed, probably an ambulance, I thought, a sudden reminder that life would not always be so sweet.

"Is it really true that the best children are conceived in laughter?" she asked.

"Only if the parents are on a heading of south south east a half east. And don't worry about conceiving. If things don't work out tonight, I'm going to bring a gyroscopic compass in here. We won't have any errors with that baby."

The ambulance was coming nearer, and for a moment I was afraid it would be drawing up before our apartment house. . . . Gripping Betty's warm shoulders, I hurried to make love.

42

It took Betty about a year to conceive. When she was sure that the great event had actually occurred, she immediately telephoned all her relatives in Ireland and the girls in the office where she had worked.

"I feel absolutely great," I heard her say. "Just the way the books say, it's a spiritual experience. Of course I have to throw up all the time, but I feel spiritual anyway."

Our building on 56th Street was inhabited mostly by theatrical people and had long been a sort of haven for retired musicians. One woman who had been in the building for more than thirty years said that to the best of her knowledge no baby had ever been born there or brought there from the hospital. For this reason Betty's condition inspired a lot of talk on the elevator as it became obvious. A slender actress of about forty years, whom I shall call Jeannie Jansen, was the least inhibited of Betty's admirers.

"A baby!" she said, placing her hand on Betty's swelling stomach. "A living, breathing baby! Can I touch for good luck?"

"Sure."

"It's all a miracle, of course, isn't it? Are you married?"

"Yes."

"Say what they will, that makes it all much more convenient. Can I visit you sometimes? I see you often in the elevator, and I know you live on the seventh floor."

"Apartment 702," Betty replied. "Drop in any time."

On occasion we regretted that invitation, for Jeannie soon almost began to live with us. By the armful she brought in books on natural childbirth, the desirability of breast feeding, and any number of books on how to raise a child without psychic disaster. Most of these she read before giving them to us and quoted liberally.

"Do you know that most women are not mammals?" Jeannie asked Betty.

"What are they?"

"I don't know. Maybe reptiles. Anyway, most women do not nurse their young, and that's the definition of a mammal."

"Maybe I won't be able to nurse," Betty said.

"If you don't nurse our baby, I'll never speak to you again."

When Jeannie was not giving us maternal advice, she entertained us with stories about her spectacular sex life. Jeannie's hobby, it seemed, was bedding down with as many celebrities as possible, with the thrill in direct proportion to the celebrity's current fame. The joy of these brief liaisons was prolonged by talking about them for years. Rarely did Jeannie lack an audience. She was a good raconteur and had an encyclopedic memory for the sexual tastes and peculiarities of almost everybody in *Who's Who*.

Since she was a good-looking woman and a fairly well-known actress, Jeannie had no trouble finding material in the show business world, but —according to her, anyway—she had soon exhausted the possibilities offered by even the most haughty stars. Seeking new worlds to conquer, she had swept through Wall Street, but was distressed to find that no one knew the name of even the richest bankers, a fact which made it difficult to boast about making them her conquests. Finally Jeannie went to Washington and hit pay dirt. When she dropped the name of a senator or cabinet member with whom she had allegedly spent the night, everyone in the room came to attention, and when she dropped delicate hints about one president or another, people got that look in their eyes which they acquire when they are under the impression that they are a witness to history in the making.

To while away the hours when she was not feeling good, Betty made up a little skit which was supposed to give the essence of Jeannie. Coming into our living room snapping her fingers and swinging her shoulders as Jeannie often did, Betty said to me, "Hi there! You'll never guess what a *fantastic* time I had last night. It was George again. George who? What other George is there? George *Washington* of course, cherry tree, ax and all. Only that's a lot of hooey. He never did chop down any goddamn cherry tree, and like any other goddamn politician he lies at least half the time. His P.R. men just make him carry this ax and cardboard cherry tree around. After all, it's a hell of an image, isn't it?

"What kind of a night did I have with him? Well, it started out as a madhouse. The Secret Service insisted that he tie up that big damn white horse of his way over by the Waldorf so people would think he was sleeping there. Then that wife of his, Martha, pulled a zoo when she heard he was going out, and all hell broke loose. One thing I can tell you, though, is that you can't fault George Washington on macho. No woman can push him around. After telling the Secret Service to sit on Martha, he came right over here to see me.

"So you are surprised that George Washington was right in our very own building? Well you might be. He came up the backstairs, of course. It's bad enough to be a president, but when you're the father of your country, you have to be very discreet.

"Anyway, we lay around for a while at my place listening to records. George particularly digs Ray Charles. He smokes a funny little clay pipe and drinks rum, of all things, neat. Of course George is not as young as he used to be and I guess the Revolution took a lot out of him. Don't quote me, but whatever the reason, I think George is getting kind of close to the edge of being a lush. Now, if you breathe a word of that to anyone I hope God strikes you dead. After all, I'm the last one in the world to start rumors. The truth is, I probably exaggerated the amount he drank. He was pretty sleepy, but we'd been smoking pot all night. That's the stuff he really laps up!

"How was George Washington in the sack department? Well, if you're turned on by wooden false teeth, he's the man for you. To sum up, I'd say he was the best father this country ever had, but in the sack, baby, *forget* it!" . . .

It was Jeannie who finally talked us into trying natural childbirth. Betty and I had read a couple of books about it, but we had made no decision. Then Jeannie started talking about how Betty should greet the climactic experience of giving birth with joy instead of allowing a doctor to dull her sensations with drugs. And why, Jeannie demanded, should the father be walled off from the miracle he started? Were men to remain emotionally ignorant of the origins of life forever?

Betty's obstetrician was a tall, melancholy man who looked as though he had become somewhat matter-of-fact about the great miracle of birth which Betty was getting ready to perform. When he learned that we wanted natural childbirth, he said, "Do you tell the dentist not to use Novocain when he pulls a tooth?"

"Childbirth is not a disease," Betty said. "It's a perfectly natural function."

"Then why do you want a doctor at all?"

"Just in case something goes wrong," I replied.

"Do you want to stay in the delivery room?" he asked me.

"Yes."

"Have you ever seen a child delivered?"

"No."

The doctor sighed and looked miserably out of the window. To me he seemed like a man who truly hated his job, especially when people like Betty and I complicated it. All he needed was Jeannie to tell him about the miracle of life.

In the evenings, regardless of the doctor's distinct lack of enthusiasm, Betty and I attended lessons in natural childbirth. Miracle or no miracle, the lessons were pretty comic. During some of them the women lay on the floor rubbing their bellies and panting very hard, while the men counted in stentorian tones. All this, I was told, was "to take the woman's mind off her contractions." When a few minutes later I used the word "pain," the instructor quickly corrected me. The key word was "contractions."

As the great day approached, I became more and more scared. Although I like to think of myself as a rugged, war-hardened fellow, I had been spared the sight of blood in the battles I had fought. A movie showing the miracle of childbirth had almost forced me to leave the room. What if I fainted in the delivery room? What if I died of a heart attack at the moment my child was entering the world?

Betty was so elated over the prospect of having a daughter to name after her beloved mother that I feared that she would be genuinely shocked by the arrival of a boy, never mind one of the tragic accidents of nature which sometimes greet eager parents. What would I do if God chose me, as they say, to be one of those special parents to love and care for a retarded child?

When we got back to our apartment after our last class in natural childbirth, Betty packed a suitcase for going to the hospital. Soon Jeannie came in, carrying a box of dainty garments which she had made for the baby.

365

"You're a Catholic, aren't you, Betty?" she asked.

"Half Irish but Protestant," Betty replied.

"Good. I want Catholic, Protestant and Jewish prayers for you. I'm Jewish, but we'll have to find a Catholic. I think the super is one. He's been dying to get to know me a little better, as they say. If I wink at him he'll pray all day."

It was a little after eight in the morning of January 23, 1964, that Betty felt her first strong contractions. Taking a taxi to the Lenox Hill hospital, we drove through streets already crowded by people hurrying to work. It was a cold clear day with a bite in the air which reminded me a little of Greenland. Gradually we progressed from a waiting room to a labor room to a delivery room, where the doctor often left us alone between contractions. Betty was lying on an operating table with an over-size sheet draped loosely over her. Every once in a while the doctor would peer under this sheet. Sometimes he told me to stand in the corner facing the wall while he did more complicated things. This made me feel ridiculous, but still, I was not a bit sure that I wanted to watch him do more complicated things. There was a little blood on the sheet now. Betty was panting and rubbing her belly as she had been taught and I did a little counting to help her time the contractions, but her face was bathed in sweat and the doctor did not avoid the word "pain."

"If the pain gets too bad, let me give you something," he said. "Natural childbirth can be a matter of degree. It's not a religion."

She shook her head vehemently. Her whole body was shaken now with major contractions. She grabbed my hand and her long nails sank into my palm. What surprised me was the fact that the labor dragged on so long. Anyone can stand pain for a few minutes, but this went on for eight hours! Finally Betty became so weak that she could hardly raise her head for a drink of water.

"I'm going to knock you out, young lady," the doctor said. "You've had enough pain for today. Any objections?"

"No," Betty said weakly.

After giving her an injection, the doctor turned to me.

"Your wife is unconscious," he said. "If you've been staying here for her sake, you can now go."

Dazed, I went to the waiting room like a sleepwalker. To my relief, I found Jeannie there.

"How is she?"

"No danger, I guess, but a lot of pain. The miracle of life is no picnic."

"Will this help?"

From her big handbag, Jeannie took a pint of vodka and two paper cups. With shaking hand, I poured.

"To Jessie," Jeannie said. "To a happy arrival."

The vodka tasted good and made the time pass faster. An hour went by, maybe two. At one point Jeannie went out for sandwiches and cold beer. The waiting room smelled of ether and strong cleaning solutions, that indefinable hospital smell. Thinking of the time my first wife had delivered a stillborn baby while I was in Greenland, I felt sorry for her all over again. Was Betty taking so long to deliver because something was seriously wrong?

Finally a nurse came to the waiting room.

"Mr. Wilson? I just want to tell you that your wife is all right. She is out of sedation and she insists on showing you the baby herself. It will be a few minutes."

"Is the baby all right?"

"Eight pounds, four ounces, and not a mark on her, even with the forceps—oh, damn! I promised your wife I wouldn't tell you it's a girl."

"I won't let on," I said, and realized that tears of relief must be showing. Jeannie, well-stocked as always, handed me, in order, a Kleenex and a drink.

Perhaps another hour went by before I was called to Betty's room. She was sitting up in a new pink bedjacket that Jeannie had given to her. Cradled in her arms was a baby with surprisingly thick hair, just the color of her mother's.

"Come meet Jessie," Betty said. "In one way, at least, she's already like my mother. Mom was almost always late."

Part 8
"If You Don't Get on the Dock, I'm Going to Throw You in the Water"

43

When, a few days later, we brought Jessie back to our apartment on 56th Street, everyone from the elevator operator to a seventy-year-old lady who lived on the top floor with a twenty-six-year-old lover wanted to see the new baby. A non-stop party developed in our tiny living room, where people waited to visit the bedroom. I worried about the effect of germs on the baby, but Betty serenely replied that the child was in no danger.

"As long as I nurse Jessie, she gets my immunities," she explained. "It's in all the books."

She was very proud of her ability to nurse. In the hospital, she said, a nurse had laughingly told her that she could probably feed the whole baby ward if she wanted to.

"I never had any trouble nursing at all," Betty said wonderingly to Jeannie. "No pain, not the slightest discomfort, and even at first Jessie got all she wanted. They haven't got her on supplements or anything."

"What does it feel like?" Jeannie asked.

"Gentle, warm, nice. I can't describe it. Who can describe making love?"

Many people in the building, some of whom we had never seen, brought food to our door during the week that followed our return with the new baby. Our modest refrigerator was bursting with casseroles, hams, and all sorts of fancy dishes. Some of the people to whom Betty had given theater tickets sent bottles of booze, which came in handy at the parties in our living room often swelled by my friends from the Harvard Club and the Carnegie Tavern across the street.

"Sloan, this party has been going on for six weeks!" Betty said at last. "And I think it's getting worse. The doorbell and the phone never stop."

It was a cold March morning when I walked to a travel bureau to find a quiet place in the sun where the three of us could recuperate for a few weeks. Four days later we were sitting on a beach on the island of Eleuthera in the Bahamas. That part of Eleuthera had at that time escaped the tourist boom and our beach was deserted. Under a thatched beach umbrella, a topless Betty sat nursing her daughter and staring at the brilliantly colored Bahamian waters. Rounding a headland was the island mail boat, which, I had discovered, was named the *Ego*, a startlingly precise name for most small ships. The blue waves which hit her high bow were exploding into white spray which gleamed in the sun.

"Could you run a boat like that?" Betty asked suddenly.

"Sure."

"You've always dreamed of living on a boat, haven't you?"

"I'm afraid that the idea isn't too practical right now."

"Ever since Jessie was born, I've been trying to make plans. Our apartment is way too small for us now. Where do we go?"

"Not to sea with a new-born baby. It's been done, but it's not my kind of operation."

"I wouldn't want to go now, of course, but if we wait too long, Jessie will have to be in school. Could we handle a three-year-old on some sort of houseboat?"

"Probably, if we stuck to sheltered waters."

"Then we might have three years before we had to settle down. Do you like the idea of living on a boat?"

"I would if we could afford it and if you really liked the idea instead of just doing it for me."

"I've been a gypsy all my life and I love these islands. Could we live down here for a couple of years?"

"If I can finish another book."

"When we get home, let's get a place with a proper study for you and a room for Jessie. Ever since Jessie's been born I've been planning . . . Gosh, that sounds nice!"

"What?"

"Dad and I were always starting sentences with the phrase, 'Ever since Jessie died . . .' Now I'm saying, 'Ever since Jessie was born.' You have no idea how good *that* sounds."

Our stay on Eleuthera was long, lazy and restful. One of the teachers in the local school asked me to give a lecture to his students, not about books, but about ice, rivers, and mountains, none of which they had ever seen. On Current Island, which was easily reached with a Boston Whaler, an ancient woman wove us a basket just large enough for carrying Jessie. Skin-diving in shallow water, I caught many varieties of brightly colored small fish which Jessie was already old enough to stare at with apparent interest.

"It isn't often that I find a place I want to go back to," Betty said. "When I'm sitting on that beach with Jessie and you, I honestly feel that I have everything I could ever want in the world."

Apparently there always has to be a serpent in paradise. In my case it was alcohol. There is a temptation to say that the idleness of a beach resort, plus my usual worries about money and my apparent inability to write another book created tensions which alcohol helped me to soothe, but I knew enough now to realize that not even the physicians who specialize in alcoholism really understand why a man drinks. Perhaps there are invisible wounds of the psyche, and perhaps there are chemical needs which cannot yet be understood. Perhaps alcoholism, like some other of our major and yet unsolved diseases, can only be described but not explained.

I was not, I hoped, a repulsive drinker. I didn't hit people in bars, insult them, wreck automobiles, or yell at my wife. All I did was sit sipping martinis until the tension went out of my arms and legs. Then with great care I wove my way back to our room to go to sleep. With infinite wisdom, I think, Betty never berated me for this almost nightly performance, but her eyes were dark with worry every time she leaned over me to loosen my tie and take off my shoes.

"Are you feeling well enough for a serious discussion?" she asked me one morning as I sat on the beach blinking in the sun.

"Sure," I said, wishing for a Bloody Mary.

"We've got a big problem. Agree?"

"Problem with my booze?"

"Will you hate me if I say what I feel?"

"Shoot."

"I think the stuff is killing you and I don't like to see the man I love killed."

"I've been a drinker all my life, but I guess it's been getting worse lately, hasn't it?"

"It will always get worse until you find some way to handle it. I've been through this with my father and about half of my friends in New York. You know, they have doctors who specialize in alcoholism . . . it really *is* a disease, you know."

"I know . . . but the trouble with doctors who specialize in alcoholism is that they generally want their patients to stop drinking. That can be a hard road to walk."

"It's better than the last mile."

She didn't smile when she said it.

"I'm damned if I know how all this happened," I said. "I used to be a hearty drinker and a connoisseur of fine wines . . . now, all of a sudden, I'm an alcoholic. I don't feel like an alcoholic! Somebody told me that alcoholics never have hangovers, and I have a terrible one!"

For a few minutes we lay quiet, watching the waves come crashing in to die on the beach.

"I'll see a doctor as soon as I get home," I said. "Still I have to live until I get there. Do you mind if I have a Bloody Mary?"

She was walking away as I said it.

373

*   *   *

The psychoanalyst whom I had been seeing agreed that I should see a specialist in alcoholism and recommended a famous one, Dr. Ruth Fox, who had an office in her midtown apartment. When I applied for an appointment a girl told me that Dr. Fox was on vacation and recommended another physician, whom I shall here call Dr. Clean.

Dr. Clean's office was in a richly-appointed apartment in the East Sixties. He was a dapper man of perhaps thirty-five years who wore well-cut jackets in pastel colors—sky-blue when I first met him. His face was deeply tanned and he wore dark glasses, even indoors. Somewhere I'd heard that people who habitually wear dark glasses indoors are apt to be suffering from a severe neurosis of some sort (if not eye trouble), but I'd also heard that patients who quickly find fault with a psychiatrist are not trying to be cured. The doctor led me to his office, which looked much like that of a network vice-president, subdued in color, rich in texture, modern in design. Sitting in a high-backed swivel chair, he motioned me to an armchair in front of his desk and asked me how much I drank.

"That's hard to answer," I replied. "I think that's secret information which I hide even from myself. You see, I have all these bottles at home for parties and—"

"Is it a quart a day or more?"

"Oh, I don't drink anywhere near that much!"

"Judging from your appearance, I'd say you do."

"My appearance?"

"After dealing with alcoholics for a good many years, I can tell quite a lot from skin-tone—the eyes, the degree of slovenliness—"

"The degree of what?"

"Slovenliness. When was that suit of yours last pressed?"

"Well, actually, we just flew in from the Bahamas. Eleuthera Island. They have no cleaners out there. Will my health improve when I get it pressed?"

No smile.

"I always begin with a little discussion of alcoholism," he said, sitting back and jingling a key chain which he took from a desk drawer. "It's a psychosis. Unless arrested, it is of course, a progressive disease. Without treatment you can expect only to get rapidly worse. How old are you?"

"Forty-four."

"Do you have a normal sex life?"

"I've never been quite sure what 'normal' is."

"Oh, for a man your age, say a couple of times a week."

"I'm not normal. Of course, my wife just had a baby and that slowed us down a little, but usually we're a good bit above normal, I'd say."

"You sound a little smug about that. Are you sure that your wife is as happy about the situation as you are?"

"Why do you ask that?"

"Because alcoholics often live under the illusion that they are God's answer to the women, when in point of fact, there's not a woman in the world who wants to go to bed with one. Does your wife drink?"

"No."

"Do you have any idea what you've been putting her through?"

On and on his attack went. Of course, it must be designed to produce fear of drinking, I thought, and in that Dr. Clean was successful. Toward the end of the hour he taught me that probably I had only shreds of a liver and kidney left, and started on my rapidly deteriorating brain.

"Do you know how many brain cells are destroyed by a single shot of gin?" he was thundering as a bell which he had set to mark the end of the hour rang. "Do you know how many shots of booze you have had in your entire life? If you can figure that out, I can tell you what fraction of a brain you have left!" . . .

When I got to the street, I was shaking so that I felt compelled to shoot a few more brain cells on a drink, just to get home.

"How did it go?" Betty asked.

"I feel that I'm a mere remnant of a man. Do you hate making love to me? He says that every woman in the world hates making love to a drunk."

"That probably's true. And I *have* appreciated the fact that you hardly ever ask me when you're drunk. You just go to sleep."

"Well, at least I have some sense. Why do you suppose this Dr. Clean specializes in alcoholism if he hates drunks?"

During the next few weeks I continued to visit Dr. Clean and each time he painted a more lurid picture of the effects of alcoholism. I was not trying to make a joke of him or myself, but he upset me so that I soon found myself drinking more than ever in order to forget the terrible future in store for me. When Dr. Fox finally returned from her vacation, I took my business, so to speak, to her. She was a calm, gray-haired motherly woman who tried to build the ego of alcoholics, rather than destroy it.

After attending Dr. Fox's "drunk class," as I tended to call her group therapy sessions, for several weeks, I worked my way up to a class for advanced drunks. There, to my astonishment, I found Dr. Clean. He was even wearing his sky-blue jacket again. For a moment I thought that he was there as some sort of medical consultant, but no, he was there as a patient. After a startled glance at me, he took a notebook from his pocket and studied it furiously. When, twenty minutes later, his turn to address the group came, he said, "Something I have dreaded for years has happened tonight. One of my former patients is here. For a doctor to reveal himself before a patient as an alcoholic is painful enough. To explain that my alcoholism is complicated by the fact that I am a homosexual is more difficult. What my former patient believes is important only to himself. What I have to do is to find a way to live with something better than self-loathing."

"Jesus Christ," I thought.

When the session was over, the doctor fell in beside me as I entered the elevator. He said nothing until we reached the street.

"I'm sorry . . . did I help you at all? I told you all the things I wanted to tell myself."

"Maybe you ought to take it a little easy on us drunks, including yourself."

"Have a drink with me. I know it's crazy, but I don't often get a shock like I got tonight. I expected you'd probably sock me."

"Why should I do that?"

"I took money from you under false pretenses, didn't I? And I gave you a terrible battering, almost as though I were trying to break you down—which really was only because I was trying to break myself down. You couldn't have known that, of course. Maybe I *wanted* you to sock me . . ."

He then urged me to go to his apartment for a drink, but I quickly told him that I had promised Betty to hurry home. Late that night, or early the next morning, the telephone by our bed rang. Sleepily I answered. It was the unfortunate Dr. Clean, sounding so drunk that I could hardly understand him.

"Will you go?" he kept asking. "Will you go?"

"Go where?"

"To Greece. Friend has cottage. Beautiful view. You'd love Greece. I can really show you how to enjoy it."

"I can't leave my wife and child," I said. "Have fun, and take it easy on the booze."

"Who was that?" Betty asked as I put down the receiver.

"My doctor."

"You're telling Dr. Fox to take it easy on the booze?"

"My other doctor, the one who's an alcoholic homosexual."

"What a mess . . . sometimes it seems to me that everybody is fighting a damned war, except who's the enemy? What enemy shot down that poor damn doctor? What makes you drink? . . ."

44

Alcoholism, of course, is not an enemy which one can vanquish for sure forever, but Dr. Fox, whose husband had succumbed to it, was a wily and dedicated fighter. After a few months of attendance at her drunk classes, I found myself able to stay on the wagon most of the time. In the roomy apartment we'd found near 90th Street on Central Park West, Betty fixed up the dining room to be my study. It was a fine place for pacing while I tried to think of a book.

At just about this time Lisa telephoned to say that her mother was about to marry a physician named Sawnie Gaston, whom she had met at David's school, which one of his two daughters attended.

"I've met him several times, and he's really very nice, daddy," Lisa said. "He was divorced, too, but his ex-wife is an invalid and his daughters are with him most of the time. We're going to have quite a household!"

This news definitely filled me with what I believe are called mixed emotions. First there was the perhaps crass relief at finding that I did not have to support my former wife financially for the rest of her life. There was also relief from a worry which had surfaced when the man with the knife had threatened the children, the dread that my former wife, like so many recently divorced women, would go a little crazy and not be able to cope either with her own problems or those of the children. The thought of my children acquiring a second father, a stepfather, made me plain angry.

"We're going to have quite a household," Lisa had happily said, and of course my son and two daughters would be spending a lot of their time with their mother and this man, whom I had never met. Probably this doctor wouldn't drink at all, would be marvelous at casting flies on suburban ponds and would show David everything in the world about biology.

The fear that I would lose my children was ridiculous, I told myself. The truth was that by getting remarried Elise would be completing the whole process of a constructive divorce. When she and I had been married, our children had been able to draw support only from two people who were tired, frustrated and hovering on the brink of nervous collapse much of the time. Now, by the alchemy of divorce, the children had two parents and two step-people. If Dr. Gaston was anywhere near as stable and cheerful as Betty, the children had certainly improved their situation.

That's what I kept telling myself.

When I wasn't vainly trying to write a book or playing with Jessie, who soon developed into an alert, inquisitive baby, I was dreaming of the idea Betty had mentioned in the Bahamas, my old plan for living aboard a boat. Our big apartment was so expensive, I realized, that a boat might save us money. Besides, I now no longer had to pay alimony. The vague sense of guilt I'd felt at the thought of sailing away from the children was lessened by the realization that the children rarely visited us much now that Lisa was beginning college and the others were in boarding school. And, if we went no farther than the Bahamas, I thought, they might visit us during their vacations more frequently than in New York, a city they said they disliked.

Two problems still stumped me. Although I did not think that it would be any more expensive to live aboard a boat than in our apartment, I was not quite sure how I could lay hands on the fairly large sum of money which would be needed for the initial purchase of a vessel capable of cruising safely to the Bahamas. Secondly, I wanted to make sure that my drinking habits were under enough control to justify my becoming the captain of a boat with a crew consisting of only a woman and a small child. Regardless of his own problems, Dr. Clean had succeeded in scaring me about mine.

Although for some reason it took a bit of courage, I decided to have a complete physical examination. Since Dr. Matthew Rosenchein out in Pound Ridge had struck me as the most thorough doctor I'd ever met, Betty and I drove out to see him on a bright day in June. It was a Saturday, a day when Mattie did not normally see patients, but he had asked us to have lunch with him and his new wife before going to his office.

When we drove up in front of his house, Mattie was mowing the lawn. With his shirt off he looked like a weightlifter and I asked if he did that to keep in shape.

"I never exercise," he said with a grin. "I must have had muscular forefathers. Come in and meet my bride. She's Irish. You two girls ought to have something in common."

After a pleasant luncheon Mattie took me to his office, where he spent about two hours going over my sadly unmuscular body. Although he couldn't be definite about the results until he heard from the hospital laboratory to which he would send samples of my various fluids, he said that I seemed to him to be in fine shape.

"You mean, I haven't been ruined by the booze already?" I asked.

"Well, I haven't counted every brain cell," he said with a laugh, "but I'd say you're fine for another forty years or so if you can cut out the drink. So far your body has stood up to it surprisingly well."

After shaking my hand, he turned to walk the short distance to his home. Anxious to get there and full of good animal spirits, this man who claimed that he never exercised was soon sprinting. Jumping over a hedge, he gave me a wave and disappeared.

At the time I had no intimation that that would be the last time I was ever to see Mattie Rosenchein. Not too long afterward a bee stung this great, strong man, and he was found dead in his office. Could anyone write a novel about a fine physician who was cut down in mid-career by a bee? Would anybody believe it? Ridiculous. Terrible.

I'm glad that I didn't know about Mattie's short future when I left him in Pound Ridge to drive up to the Adirondacks. Betty and I were in good spirits as we arrived at my mother's house on Lake George near Ticonderoga. At the front door Chester Miller, a cheerful man who had worked for my mother for twenty years, ushered us into the shadowy, high-ceilinged living room which long had seemed to me to be an echoing cave of memories. Mother was in the garden picking flowers, he said, but would soon be back. When Betty asked him for a place where Jessie could sleep, Chester led her to my boyhood room, where an iron crib that had been used for me and all my children still stood. After putting Jessie in the crib, Betty sat beside it and softly sang the old popular songs which she preferred to "Rock-a-bye, Baby." Pacing in front of a huge stone fireplace which my father had designed, I found myself remembering the night a quarter of a century ago when I brought Elise here to introduce her to my parents. Younger than our daughter Lisa was now, Elise had looked forward to a happy summer weekend. When my father died on the night of our arrival, I think youth ended for both of us.

Despite the giant fireplace and the fine view of the lake from the big front windows, I'd rarely been happy in this fairly spectacular room. Whether my mother's nature or mine was responsible, I always somehow felt called to account when I visited her here in what I irreverently used to call "the throne room." Sitting in the high-backed Boston rocker which she preferred to upholstered chairs, mother would ask how my marks were going at college, when my next promotion in the coast guard was due, and later, when my next book was to be published. Because there had never been a divorce in the family, I needed all the courage I could find to tell her that Elise and I were ending our marriage. After digesting this fact for a moment, mother said, "That must be awfully hard on both of you, dear. And won't it be terribly expensive?"

When I had first brought Betty here to meet mother shortly before we were married, I'd warned her to expect a good many questions about her forebears and her education.

"I don't mind the forebears stuff," Betty had replied. "Dad always says we're descended from Irish kings, and there were so many of them that practically every Irishman must have a touch of royal blood. The education thing may be hard, though. How's she going to go for two years of Brooklyn College?"

"Tell her you worked your way through. Dad worked his way through the University of Virginia, and mother was always impressed."

When we'd visited mother on that momentous day here in this shadowy living room, Betty had worn one of her pretty summer dresses of Irish linen, and she'd put a yellow daisy in her shiny dark hair. A half century older than Betty, mother had sat in her Boston rocker, a regal figure with her white hair swept back in a fashion of her youth and a dress of light blue silk.

"Mother, I want you to meet Betty Stephens," I'd said. "We're planning to get married next month."

"Where?"

"In Ireland," Betty had told her. "My father lives in Dublin."

"Her people are all Protestants," I'd added hastily.

"We have some Irish ancestors," mother had said, and went on to explain their peregrinations.

Never had I heard her speak of Irish ancestors. English, German, Danish and French, yes, but the Irish ancestors she seemed to be inventing on the spot. Out of courtesy, I wondered?

In a short while Betty had excused herself and gone to the bedroom we'd been assigned to repair her makeup.

"Do we really have Irish ancestors?" I'd asked my mother.

"Well, they stayed in Ireland for a few generations on their way from England to America."

"What do you think of Betty?"

For the first time in my memory, I saw a twinkle in the eye of my sternly puritanical mother.

"The girl is obviously a charmer," she'd said, "and she has a very pretty figure."

If mother had described Betty with a long, low whistle, I could not have been more astonished. Never in my life had I heard her mention a person's *figure*.

After that, Betty and my mother had got on together fine. Realizing that Betty had never heard any of the family history and lore, mother embarked on a sort of lecture series.

"I'm sorry to talk so much," she often said. "It's just that I am alone so much ..."

Never had I really understood how much she hated being alone. In the quarter century since my father had died, she had spent most of every summer sitting in the old Boston rocker and staring at the lake. Her winters in New York were not much better. How could I, who could not stand to be alone for more than a day, fail to sense her loneliness? ...

Now I heard my mother walk up the steep steps to the front door. She was carrying a flat basket of marigolds which she had picked, and she was wearing a wide-brimmed hat of finely woven straw. Her hug was always fugitive, as though we might be interrupted in our embrace by a policeman who was sure to put us both in jail, but her greeting was warm. While Chester prepared dinner, I built a fire in the fireplace, laying the logs on the old Hessian andirons.

"Our ancestors made Hessian andirons because they liked to spit on the Hessians," my father had once explained. "Up Connecticut and Massachusetts way, the Hessians weren't as popular as they might be. Mercenaries rarely are."

As a boy I had tried spitting at our Hessian andirons, but it was a messy business. When I was ten or eleven, it was impossible for me to imagine how one could hate enough to want to spit on a little iron soldier.

"Well, what are you doing these days?" mother asked, moving her Boston rocker closer to the fire.

I told her that I was working on a new book which was not coming along very well and added that I was toying with the idea of buying a boat for a home and for cruising the Bahamas.

Her eyes gleamed. A stiff old lady my mother might be in some circumstances, but when boats were mentioned she once again became the little girl who'd been born at the Naval Academy, the daughter and sister of regular naval officers.

"What kind of a boat?" she asked.

"Power probably. I still love sail, but a sailing vessel that was big enough to be a permanent home for us would be too big for me to handle alone."

"How big?"

"In the neighborhood of fifty feet, I guess. We'll need room for the whole family on vacations and a place for me to work."

"How much will it cost?"

"Well, that will depend on a lot of things. I'll want twin diesels, everything in top shape. I'm guessing at a price of $50,000, unless I luck onto a good old boat that hasn't been allowed to go to hell."

"Do you have $50,000?"

"Right now I don't have fifty thousand dollars, or anything like it. Furthermore I'm still in tax trouble, and the government is liable to grab whatever I have in the savings bank. However, the tax trouble should be over sooner or later, I keep thinking, and I do have a new book under way ..."

"My finances are a terrible tangle, too," mother said. "Somehow everything keeps costing more and more while my income gets less and less. Still, if you need help when you buy a boat, I'd do all I could manage—"

"Thank you," I said, remembering the time she had helped me to buy the *Yankee Trader*. When it came to boats, nobody ever had a more generous mother.

"This isn't a condition, mind you," mother continued, "but if you do get a boat, could I take a cruise with you sometimes?"

"Of course."

"I hated that cruise I took with your father when we got caught in a storm off Atlantic City, but that's the only time I ever got seasick. From the winter when I went south on the *Drone*, when I was just a little girl, to the summer when you took me out on the *Yankee Trader*, I have enjoyed every time I have set foot aboard a boat of any kind. I'd love to take one more cruise before I get too old."

When we left Lake George a few days later, we had talked about a boat for the Bahamas so much that she already seemed a reality. When we returned to New York it was something of a comedown to realize that I still had a book to write, and that we would wait until Jessie was a couple of years older. The dream of the boat proved a good influence on me, however. To make sure that I wouldn't have a drinking problem when I set out on our cruise, I continued to see Dr. Fox and tried my best to drink no alcohol at all, as she was unreasonable enough to demand. I also worked hard, and turning dreams into reality of a sort, began to write *Janus Island*, a novel about the Florida keys, boats, and a search for sunken gold. With our eyes intent on the future, two years passed fast.

45

"I think I have the boat you want," the yacht broker said.

For weeks I had been driving up and down the coast looking at boats which might be suitable for our new life, as we had begun to think of it. All were too expensive, too rotten, too small or too big.

"Tell me about her."

"This one I just want to show you. Can you spare a day?"

Having finished *Janus Island*, I had plenty of time. "Where are we going?" I asked.

"Oxford, Maryland. Chesapeake Bay."

For a few months I'd been stationed aboard a buoy tender in Chesapeake Bay during the war before going to the *Nogak*. The gentle, fertile lands which surround it had made a strong impression on me after Greenland, and I'd always wanted to go back.

"Want to go look at another boat?" I asked Betty.

"If you don't mind, no," she said. "Jessie has a cold and, according to this dream I've had in my head, you take me to see a boat after you've found a marvelous one."

In the agent's car we began the long drive to Oxford.

"What's the name of this boat?" I asked.

"The *Irish Mist*. Right now she's painted green."

Somehow that was odd, I thought. It sounded like a pleasant co-incidence, but Betty disliked professional Irishmen and would want to change it.

"Why do you think this boat is so good?" I asked.

"Just take a look at her. That's all I ask."

It was October, my favorite month. When we reached Maryland the fields were golden in the sunshine and everywhere there was the excited gabbling of wild geese. Oxford was a town which looked as though it were still awaiting news of Washington's armies, and still uncertain whether to support or oppose anything so uncouth as a revolution. The agent turned into the driveway of a private estate, rounded a clump of oak trees and stopped.

"There she is," he said.

The green vessel lay moored to a private wharf. In the bright sunshine the jade-colored paint, the mahogany rails and the chromium steering wheel and binnacle all shone as though they were brand new, but the design was old—in fact, it was based on that of a World War I subchaser, long and narrow as a barracuda. Whatever her age, her topsides were seamless, expertly joined wood as smooth as steel. Her decks were teak, I could see as I walked nearer. The louvers in the mahogany door of the after cabin were fitted together like the parts of a fine violin. Around the cockpit was a combing of skillfully bent mahogany an inch thick with an elegant cap rail.

"Nevins," I said suddenly to the agent as I stepped aboard.

"How did you know that?"

"How would you recognize an old Packard?"

"Nevins has been out of business for years," the agent said. "The name doesn't mean much to most people nowadays."

"Nevins, Lawley, Herreshoff," I said, showing off a bit. "In their way they were real old masters and they're all gone. Well, I've got to be careful not to be carried away. Let's see how practical this old beauty is for us."

In the after cabin there were two bunks and a table which would be just about right for my typewriter. Next came the engineroom, with two 4-71 diesels and a diesel generator, all very shipshape. Next was the deckhouse, with two couches and little else except space for making it better. Further forward were another double cabin, a cramped, old-fashioned galley and a narrow V-shaped forecastle which contained two pipe berths meant for a professional crew.

"Of course she could be made much more comfortable," the agent said. "The present owner has kept everything simple. He has a whole bunch of kids. Those couches make into beds."

Without saying anything, I went back to the wharf, where I could see the old vessel in some perspective. With that narrow beam she would punch into a head sea in fine style, and probably she would run well, but with the wind on her beam she would roll her crew's eyes out. That beautiful door on her after cabin was not watertight, and her big cockpit would fill the first time she got a taste of green water. But, compared to most modern motor yachts her size, I considered her seaworthy or at least seaworthy enough for the sheltered and semi-sheltered waters I intended to cruise. The main drawback of the old vessel, as far as I was concerned, was the damnable beauty of that finely drawn bow and delicately contoured stern. It was nearly as hard to be objective about such a boat as it would to be about a breathtakingly attractive woman one had just met.

"Want to know the price?"

"What is it?"

"Only $18,500. The owner wants to sell and not everybody wants an old boat, no matter how sound she is."

384

From my point of view the price was marvelous—I'd been trying to gear myself up somehow to scratch up more than twice as much for a suitable boat. With some of the money saved, I could make this lovely old vessel decently comfortable for Betty, Jessie and my mother, all of whom would be happiest and safest if kept far away from anything remotely resembling an Atlantic gale. Abandoning all effort to make the boat "salty," I'd install a spinet piano which Betty loved so much in the deck house, where one of the couches was now standing. There would still be room there for an open fireplace. Adequate heating and air-conditioning would also be installed. If this boat was to be a home, my ladies weren't to feel they were camping out.

Near the property where the boat was moored there was an elegant old inn that served crab cakes as a specialty. From a telephone booth there I called Betty.

"Did you find one?" she asked eagerly.

"I can't tell yet. I've fallen in love with one, though. We'll have to pay experts who don't love her to survey her and tell us what she is."

"Why do you love her?" Betty asked with a laugh.

"Why do I love her? Let me count the ways. She's old and narrow and uncomfortable."

"Why do you want her, then?"

"She's beautiful, probably sound, built by men who were artists, and she's cheap."

"We're going to buy her, aren't we?" Betty asked with a sharp intake of breath. "I mean, this whole thing is starting now, isn't it?"

"Probably."

"What's the name of the boat?"

"The *Irish Mist*! She's all-over green."

"Oh, *no*! Here I've spent most of my life trying to get away from all the blather about Ireland—"

"We can change the name."

"What to?"

"How about the *Scotch Fog*?"

"Why don't you name it after some place your people come from?"

"We'd end up with something like the *European Mixture Moisture*."

"Forget it. When can I see it?"

"Come right now. But remember when you see it that I'm going to put your piano and a fireplace in the deckhouse. There'll be heat and air-conditioning—"

"Wow! Just what I've always wanted . . . a man who really knows how to rough it."

❖   ❖   ❖

For the first time in Jessica's life, Betty left her with a friend and flew to Washington, where the agent and I met her. It was a rainy day, a bad time to show anyone a boat. Betty was wearing a red-and-white raincoat, the first gift I'd bought her in preparation for a life afloat. As we drove to Oxford, I wondered what I'd do if she said that she hated the old boat. Naturally I'd give up the idea of buying it, but then we'd both be depressed and there was the possibility that it might take months or even more to find a craft we both liked that we could afford.

"Any boat looks bad in the rain," I said to Betty as we turned into the driveway of the estate where the *Irish Mist* lay.

Leaning ahead to see better, she said nothing. As the car stopped, she jumped out and stood in the rain, looking at the ancient boat, which despite the weather, still seemed to gleam on the leaden water.

"She *is* beautiful," Betty said. "She looks fast. Is she?"

"She used to be. When she had gasoline engines, maybe she did thirty knots, or close to it. With diesels, she's much slower, safer and cheaper to run."

"Can we go aboard?"

The agent led the way. By chance we all stepped from the wharf to the deck at the same time. Responding to the weight of three people, two of them heavy men, the narrow old yacht rolled, spilling buckets of water from an awning that covered her cockpit. Some of this drenched Betty and she ducked into the deckhouse, where she wiped her face with a handkerchief I gave her.

"Here is where your piano will go," I said quickly. "The fireplace will be just about where you're standing."

Without saying anything, she went below. To avoid making the stateroom seem crowded, the agent and I didn't follow. When she came up she said, "The galley is hardly a dream kitchen, but I could fix it up. Are there other cabins?"

I showed her the after stateroom, with the big table and an adjoining shower.

"This is it?"

"I'm afraid so."

"But there will only be three of us most of the time. I think there's plenty of room. And the joinery, as you said, deserves a place in a museum."

"Then it's all right with you if we buy her?"

"*Yes.* I don't know anything about boats, but she is so graceful..."

"Think again. She's going to be our home for three years at least, if we buy her."

"I still say yes."

I kissed her, hugely delighted and exhilarated.

"Does buying a boat always make you feel like that?"

"No, mostly it's just that like most pretty girls you look your prettiest when you're saying yes."

She even let me get away with that . . .

Betty hurried back to Jessie and New York as soon as she could while I remained at the inn to conclude the details of the sale. When the old vessel became legally ours, she had to be documented with her old name or a new one if I wanted a change. After thinking the matter over, I named the graceful old cruiser the *Pretty Betty*.

The agent said, "You sure know how to get your wife to like a boat! I wish more of my clients had your technique."

"She already liked the boat," I told him.

The next time Betty visited the boat in Oxford, the new name was painted in large gold letters on the stern and on life-rings by the gangway, all very nautical.

"Good God!" she said, and for a moment I thought that she was going to cry.

"I love it," she explained after a few moments. "It's crazy and it's wonderful and it's the biggest compliment I ever had in my life, but every minute I spend aboard this boat I'm going to have to dress to the hilt and keep my hair in perfect condition! If I don't at least do that I'll be known as the horrible hag of the *Pretty Betty*."

The children also seemed happy about the purchase of the boat. Lisa at twenty was a junior at the University of Pennsylvania and Becky was a sophomore at Boston University. David was starting at the University of Rochester, and all hoped to join us for Christmas or Easter vacations in Florida. My mother I'd promised to have aboard as soon as we had finished a shake-down cruise south—to make certain that all the machinery was working properly.

"I'll go on standby," she said cheerfully. "My bag's packed and I can leave New York on about one hour's notice!"

It was early November before the work on the *Pretty Betty* was done in a small boatyard in Oxford. At three, Jessie was able to hop nimbly aboard. With some odds and ends of wood from the yard's workshop, I started a fire in the tiny fireplace, which had been installed. On deck a cold fall wind bulged the canvas "dodger" with which I had lined the usual liferail to make sure that Jessie couldn't fall overboard, but below we were snug and the burning scraps of mahogany smelled good.

"When do we head south?" Betty asked.

"When we get a good weather report," I said. "What I'm planning here is a chicken cruise. At the slightest hint of a gale I head for port and I never leave port without a good weather report. My confidence in my own chicken-heartedness is such that I promise you a cruise without a single taste of bad weather."

"Is that really possible?" she asked with a laugh.

"Well, the inland water route is mostly protected and should offer an alert chicken little trouble. The Bahamas will be more tricky, but you can visit just about every island without being more than twenty-five or thirty miles from port if you have a shallow-draft vessel like this one. If a chicken is scared enough, he ought to be able to foretell the weather three or four hours ahead. So unless I make the mistake of getting brave, you ought to have a very quiet cruise."

"That's exactly what Jessie and I want," she said, and sitting down to her piano, began to play "Deep Purple," which I've liked since my college days.

To be a chicken of the sea, I found right there in the beginning, takes more discipline than bravery. For two weeks the weather was foul on Chesapeake Bay. A more courageous man would have lost patience and left the quiet port of Oxford. After all, winter was coming on and it was possible for a vessel to get stuck in Chesapeake Bay until spring.

But I remained steadfastly frightened of what a fall gale on the bay could do to my little boat, my wife and daughter. Only after two weeks of waiting in Oxford did I hear reports about improving weather, blue skies and quiet waters. Even then I was so scared of my own inability to repair diesel engines that I hired a mechanic to accompany us the first day.

Rewarded for our patience, we found that first leg of our voyage, from Oxford, Maryland, to Norfolk, Virginia, an unmarred delight. The weather was like early June, a little chilly, but clear and almost completely windless. The broad expanse of Chesapeake Bay, which can get almost as brutal as the open sea, was so still that it reflected the cloudless sky above. The *Pretty Betty* sliced through these quiet waters at a steady speed of twelve knots and used so little fuel that I thought the gauges must be wrong. Because they had not been used much recently, the engines proved that they needed some new seals or gaskets, but our mechanic showed me how to make those repairs. We'd promised to pay him twenty-five dollars for the single day we'd retained him, but he had such a good time singing and playing the piano that he offered to go all the way to Florida without pay. It was that kind of a day when everything turned out much better than anyone would have a right to expect.

The next morning the fall gales started, but all we had to do was nip across the head of Norfolk Harbor and duck into the Dismal Swamp Canal, which was as straight, dark and unruffled as it was when George

Washington (who I still like to think of as Jeannie's lover) first surveyed it.

In Daytona Beach, Florida, our engineer returned to his family in Oxford and Betty's father, Bob Stephens, came aboard. He'd never been aboard a boat like this and was enthusiastically astonished by everything he saw. As we sped through the glittering waters of the Indian River, porpoises started to jump as high as our rail, so close that Jessie reached out her hand to try to touch them. Big, shiny beauties about six feet long, they splashed back into the river, showering our decks with spray.

Every time we stopped for the night in port, Bob repaired to the local bars, where by some phenomenon which I never understood, he was immediately surrounded by hordes of laughing Irishmen. After all, I reasoned, when I go into bars I can sit alone all night. Did Bob carry some powder in his pocket which, when mixed with whiskey, produced instant Irishmen?

Many of these friends Bob brought back to the boat for a drink or a midnight snack. One of his favorites, I remember, was a big man who said he owned a big Ferris wheel at Coney Island.

"Every time that wheel turns," this man said with delight, "I make a hundred dollars. It turns and it turns, and that's why the drinks are on me when we go back to the bar."

By the time we got to Eau Gallie on the Indian River, I was exhausted, and felt a little sick. What if I became so sick I couldn't operate my vessel while we were in some remote part of the Bahamas? On our small-scale chart of the islands I marked the location of physicians whose names were given in reference books.

Having done that, I almost immediately felt great again. In the bright winter sunshine we continued south from Kennedy Space Center to Palm Beach, where Becky and Mort Leavy, my lawyer and friend, were to meet us for a Christmas cruise before we picked up my mother for a quiet voyage through the canals to Lake Okeechobee, which she said she'd always wanted to see.

Becky arrived with a rock and roll guitar player. She'd told me that she was bringing a friend, but had not elaborated on his profession. He was a large, rather portly, long-haired man who looked curiously middle-aged, despite the fact that he was in his early twenties. Most of the time he spent dozing in the sun. Even when the rest of us were getting in lines or holding fenders, he sat there sipping beer and moving his right hand to silent rhythms.

I hated him. It was not reasonable to hate him, I knew, but I was overcome by a desire to jerk his deck chair out from under him.

"What do you think of Bo?" Becky asked.

"They say hating isn't healthy," I said. "I hate people who make me hate them."

"Why do you hate him?" Becky asked with a mysterious smile.

"Why the hell are you smiling like that? Makes you look like a sort of diabolic angel."

"I figured you'd hate him. You're not exactly the same type."

"Is that why you brought him down here? So I'd ruin my digestion by hating him?"

"Don't worry about it. He hates you too."

"I suppose that makes him an ideal shipmate."

"I just hope that in time you'll get to like one another."

"What do you mean, in time? Are you planning to marry this beached whale?"

"No, but he's a good friend. You'd find out why if you talked to him."

"How can I talk to him? He shows no knowledge of the English language. Everything is either 'far out' or 'right on, man.' There are chimpanzees that have been taught a vocabulary bigger than his."

"He makes fun of your nautical language. 'Take in the starboard anchor, back the port engine, drop the scupper,' and all the rest."

"That man wouldn't last two days in the coast guard. I'd like to see him on the Greenland Patrol—"

"You wouldn't last two days with a rock and roll band."

"You mean, I couldn't learn to beat a guitar like a drum and howl?"

Becky laughed and the days of her vacation passed without any confrontation between me and her musician. When they had gone, Betty said to me, "I think you're in a little bit of trouble."

"Why?"

"Because that young man is really quite pleasant. He's working his way through college by playing with a band. There's really nothing about him for you to hate except the fact that he's with your daughter. If you're going to hate any man your daughters like, it won't be long before you don't have any daughters. I know. I went through that with my father."

"Your father liked *me*, didn't he?"

"Not much, not until he got to know you. He hated all my guys, and that's one reason why I didn't see him very often."

"At least I'm not a rock and roll guitar player," I said, and moodily went to study my charts, where everything was clear and precise.

A few days after Bob left the *Pretty Betty* to return to Ireland, we picked up my mother. I had worried about this cruise, for any eighty-year-old woman can take dangerous falls aboard a small yacht, even if the vessel is kept in protected waters. Beyond that, my mother's only apparent weakness was non-stop talking. Although it was understandable that a person who lived alone most of the time gloried in communication, I worried that my mother would drive my wife crazy. When we visited her at Lake George, she followed Betty from living room to kitchen to bedroom, pressing home one more chapter of the family history. Even when other people were around, Betty was my mother's favorite target because she never interrupted, or looked as though she weren't listening. For a weekend such punishment was perhaps tolerable, but penned with mother in the narrow confines of a fifty-two-foot boat for two weeks, Betty might well become completely exhausted.

"There's no way to mention it without hurting her feelings," Betty said as we drove to meet my mother at the West Palm Beach airport. "Let me handle it."

Down the ramp of the plane mother hurried, her gate as spry as a woman's half her age. She was a small, fragile appearing woman, I saw with a sense of shock. In my youth she had been stout, and perhaps I retained a child's image of a towering mother. A salty lady, she was wearing shoes with rope soles, and her single bag was of soft canvas which could fold easily under a bunk.

"So good to see you!" she said, holding her straw hat on her head with one hand.

She and I exchanged our quick, almost embarrassed hug. Betty shamed me when she gave mother the bear squeeze she reserves for all relatives she likes, and the old lady responded to it, gently patting Betty's shoulder and smiling. Jessie, who'd been holding her mother's hand, hung back.

"Why, there you are, Jessie!" mother said, unwittingly making her voice as stern as I remembered from my own childhood.

Jessie, who had just turned four, put her thumb in her mouth.

"You are sucking your thumb," my mother sternly observed.

"It doesn't hurt," Betty gently said.

"Of course not. Sloan sucked his thumb practically until it was time for him to go to Harvard."

"I did not!"

"Anyway, you have a very pretty daughter here. Every time I see her, she looks more like her mother."

"She looks like my mother," Betty said with a smile. "I like to think it's reincarnation."

"All children are reincarnation," mother said. "Sloan looks the most like me, but we're not really alike. I never could get him to go to church, keep up his French, or take care of a garden."

The *Pretty Betty* lay at the end of a wharf that was much higher than her decks. The problem of how we were going to get my mother aboard had been bothering me for two days. Before going to the airport, I'd rigged a complicated boarding ladder.

"Is that for my sake?" my mother asked, glancing at it. "You don't have to go to all that trouble for me. I'm old, but I guess I can still skin aboard just the way I used to on the *Drone*."

Disdaining the boarding ladder, she leaned forward to catch one of the awning supports, and stepped lightly to the rail. "What a beautiful boat," she exclaimed.

On that note of endorsement, we cast off and headed north to the canal which leads to Lake Okeechobee. As mother kept Betty involved in interminable conversation on the deck abaft the wheel, Jessie felt neglected and began to cry. As I tried to find my way through a maze of channels, the sound of voices so close to my ear distracted me, and I got an idea.

"Mother," I said, "on naval and coast guard vessels, there's always a rule and usually a sign calling for silence on the bridge. The reason is that it's really hard to concentrate on navigation when people are talking. On small boats people aren't so formal, but it's still a good idea for everyone to keep fairly quiet on the bridge."

"There's no real bridge here," mother said.

"Well, I consider this whole area near the helm the bridge. The important thing is to avoid distracting the helmsman."

"That sounds very sensible," she said, and suddenly shut up. In the silence that followed, the engines appeared to throb loudly.

"What's that?" Jessie asked, pointing to a floating log.

"Silence on the bridge, dear," mother said. "The helmsman must concentrate."

Throughout the cruise mother never talked on the bridge. Below she was still a Niagara Falls of words, but when Betty got tired of it, she could always take Jessie to the bridge to sun. For a while I thought mother had been fooled by my attempts to quiet her tactfully, but a few days later she said, "I'm doing pretty well, aren't I? Even below decks I'm trying to control my talking, and on deck I say nothing at all. Next time I come aboard, you won't even have to bother about all that stuff about the bridge." Pretty smart old lady.

The cruise through the canals and Florida's enormous lake was a fine one, with the water calm and the sky fair. When we steamed close to the banks of the canals, mother loved to sit with the binoculars, studying the herons, the egrets, the cranes and the terns. The plant life was an equal delight to her. Somehow she appeared to know the name of all the varieties of tree, flower and fern.

When we took her to an airport at the end of the cruise, she said, "Did I prove myself seaworthy?"

"You certainly did."

"Then how about taking me to the Bahamas next time?"

I promised to arrange it, but the Bahamas were already beginning to scare me. A vast collection of badly charted islands, with few doctors, no coast guard, and large uninhabited areas seemed a poor place for me and Betty to cruise with an eighty-year-old woman and a four-year-old child aboard a narrow old yacht.

46

All in all, Betty, Jessica and I spent five years aboard the *Pretty Betty*—from 1966 to 1971. That length of time now seems incredible; in memory it all compresses itself into a period little longer than a month's vacation. Still, I wrote two of what I think of as my best books (*Away from It All* and *All the Best People*) in the after cabin of that old vessel. Despite my fears of the Bahamas, we cruised much of them, often with my son David or a native guide to help us.

The most difficult cruise we took to the Bahamas was also the last one, and I remember it as an example of the best and worst of living aboard a small vessel. In the winter of 1970 my mother telephoned me to ask me urgently to take her to the Bahamas. This she had requested many times, but now she had a special reason. The navy, she had been informed, was going to dedicate a building on the island of Andros to her older brother, the late Sloan Danenhower!

To understand fully what this meant to my mother, one would have had to know even more of the family history than I did. My Uncle Sloan Danenhower had graduated from the Naval Academy soon after the turn of the century, and had been something of a hero in World War I. Soon after that he had dropped out of the navy and had been involved in the research that had enabled him to help to take a World War I submarine, the first *Nautilus*, under the arctic ice. A skilled salvage man, he had tried and failed to raise the *Normandy* when she sank at a New York pier at the beginning of World War II.

Of that much I was fairly sure. Beyond that there was the mysterious fact that I almost never saw my Uncle Sloan at our house when my father was alive, and his name was spoken, if at all, as though it somehow should not be spoken, like a word that had something to do with sex. Since my mother devoted a lot of time to telling me that I should get along with my brother, I couldn't understand why she had dropped hers. Or had he dropped us?

Such questions can obsess a small boy. Was my mother arguing with her brother about money? Once when I went into the library, I heard my father talking about wills and loans. My mother mentioned her brother's name before they realized that I was listening and told me to go away.

Somewhere I also heard that my uncle had had three wives. Imagining him to be married to all three at the same time, I pictured him with a small harem aboard a submarine. Maybe *that* was why my father, who thought that even masturbation was terrible, couldn't get on with him.

When I was in my mid-teens my Uncle Sloan bought a surplus light-ship to serve as his home in the harbor of New London, Connecticut. Some people said he bought *two* lightships, one to be his home and the other to be his office, and that he painted HOME in huge letters on the side of one and OFFICE in equally big letters on the side of the other. His idea, I heard, was to commute from home to office in a rowboat. That was the kind of story I kept hearing about my Uncle Sloan.

The tale about the lightship was partly true, I found. A Sunday news-paper supplement carried the story with a picture of my uncle with his sleeves rolled up sitting at the wheel of what appeared to be a huge ship. Since there were no photographs of him in our house, I really studied it. A rugged, handsome man in his middle years, Sloan Danen-hower had the powerfully muscled arms of a heavyweight fighter. Since no one in my family whom I knew had visible muscles, I regarded this phenomenon with interest. Did my father dislike him because he was afraid of getting beaten up?

As soon as I saw that picture, I wanted to visit my Uncle Sloan, but the whole family discouraged me and made me feel disloyal to our side. Later I heard that his lightship or ships had been sunk in a hurricane. One report was that the bottom fittings of one vessel had corroded, sink-ing her at the wharf. The implication I got was that my uncle's vessels always sank. Maybe that was why my father so obviously thought that his brother-in-law was no good.

During World War II and my first years at work, I forgot about my Uncle Sloan. Then while I was living in New Canaan I was startled by a newspaper story that with banner headlines announced that the old sailor's wife had been found dead in what some regarded as mysterious circumstances. Later bulletins brought the reassuring news that the death had been entirely natural, but my mother had a last word: "Why does he *do* things like that?"

The next I heard of Uncle Sloan, he was an old man in his late seventies. Suffering what appeared to be a lasting depression, he lived in a nursing home in Old Lyme, Connecticut. Finally forgiving her brother for whatever he had done, my mother asked me to drive her to Old Lyme. We found him alone in a small room, a little old man with a stubble of white beard on his sunken cheeks. My mother's hand was shaking as she placed it on his shoulder.

"*Bon jour, mon frère,*" she said. "*Comment allez vous?*"

"*Très bien,*" he said, standing up to kiss her.

For an hour they spoke in French, which they apparently had studied together in their distant childhood. When I finally escorted my mother to the car, she said, "Poor Sloan doesn't look very well, but isn't it marvelous how he's kept up his French?"

After that we visited Sloan Danenhower fairly often. Fundamentally, he seemed to me to be a man of enormous ability who was facing the fact that his accomplishments were far smaller than his dreams had been—not, when you come down to it, so different from most men. Even his real successes were often forgotten. When the nuclear submarine *Nautilus* went under the arctic ice, most newspapers neglected to mention that an old World War I submarine had been the first *Nautilus* to prove that a sub could survive there.

Sloan Danenhower died a short while later, but some of the rumors about him lived on. A distant relative claimed that the navy had shown my uncle few honors at the funeral because his separation from it had been more or less enforced when the old man was found in Times Square waving his sword at the moon.

"... waving his sword at the moon?" I repeated in astonishment.

"When he couldn't raise the *Normandy*, he went a little crazy and started waving his sword at the moon—in Times Square."

That rumor had always sounded unlikely to me, if only because naval officers almost never carried swords in World War II. Still, I liked the picture—to me it was a heroic one, not a slur. A man who waved his sword at the moon because he couldn't salvage a ship had to be my favorite relative. . . .

Now, years after his death, the United States Navy in all its majesty was to name a building at an underseas research center after Sloan Danenhower. The center was on the island of Andros in the Bahamas and my mother was urgently asking me to take her there.

"The boat isn't in very good shape right now," I answered. "Won't the navy send a plane for you?"

"They offered, but I said that we have our own boat. What's the matter with it?"

"It's just that I haven't done much work on her during the past year. My typewriter has been keeping me busy."

"I looked at a map and Andros is practically next to Miami. I should think that somebody who has commanded coast guard vessels—"

"Okay!" I said. "We'll do it."

Going to the bridge, I found a chart which covered the area we were to sail. Mother was right about one thing: the trip from Miami to the research base which the Americans shared with the Bahamians on Andros was only about 180 miles. A tough 180 miles for an eighty-four-year-old lady it might be, however. For starters we would cross the Gulf Stream, which almost never was calm in winter, and which would strike our narrow old vessel on the beam. Then we would have the Great Banks to cross, a lovely area of extremely shallow water where an inaccurate compass could easily send a vessel into reefs, and mine had not been compensated for a year, during which several alterations which might affect it had been made. Next came the Tongue of the Ocean, an extremely deep area which could get rough in bad weather. The last stretch was a sail along the barrier reef of Andros, where there would be no buoys or markers of any kind. If my neglected engines failed during an on-shore wind, there would be hell to pay.

Although I knew that I was exaggerating the hazards of a short cruise, I kept thinking of more dangers. What if I had a heart attack or fell overboard? What would Betty, a seven-year-old child and an eighty-four-year-old woman do out there in the Gulf Stream or on the Great Banks all alone?

Obviously I would be foolish to start without another able-bodied sailor aboard. Since mother wanted to start immediately, I didn't have time to find a really competent professional. Canvassing the people I knew or half knew, I finally found an airline pilot and his wife who agreed to tie up their own cruiser and go with us.

From the start this voyage turned out to be a comedy of errors. As soon as we cleared the wharf, I found that one of my water pumps leaked. When I put back to have it fixed, the pilot, whom I'll call Joe, said the pump could function as it was, and delay would be expensive for him since he'd left his dogs and cats at an animal hospital.

"I don't intend to put to sea with defective equipment because of dogs and cats," I said solemnly.

Both Joe and I were used to having our own way aboard boats and we argued while mother, sitting serenely nearby in a deckchair, read. By the time I got the pump fixed, Joe was angry. Swiftly we crossed Biscayne Bay and entered the Gulf Stream, which was rough. We rolled horribly. Putting the helm on automatic pilot, I took a tour to check on seasick people and loose gear. In the after cabin, mother was in her bunk, where I had advised her to stay in rough weather. In the deckhouse Joe and his wife, whom I'll call Jill, were sitting on the couch drinking

Bloody Marys. Since I'd long had a rule against myself or anyone else drinking aboard my boat at sea, this posed a problem. Should a rule always be enforced or should exceptions be made for a presumably sophisticated airline pilot who owns his own boat? My judgment was influenced by the fact that I'd just had an argument with the man about his damned cats and dogs. I hesitated.

"Will you have a drink?" Jill merrily asked.

"I don't drink at sea," I said, whereupon they both burst into derisive laughter.

In the cockpit I found Betty and Jessie, who had long since acquired strong sea legs, and who were watching a school of dolphin. As our little vessel cleared the land, she began to roll even worse, plunging and dancing as only *Pretty Betty* could in the Gulf Stream. After a few minutes Joe came from the deckhouse and stood clutching the rail, contemplatively watching yellow patches of Sargasso weed bob by.

My able-bodied sailor, it turned out, was wretchedly seasick as he stood there on the windward side of the boat. After he had staggered below, I worked for half an hour to clean up after him.

When I entered the deckhouse, Joe was nowhere to be seen, but Jill was trying to play the piano. Either she didn't know how to play the piano, or she was dead drunk, or both. In the top of her bikini she'd stuck a pack of cigarettes.

"Have a cigarette," she said, pushing at me.

"Don't smoke 'em," I said.

"Don't smoke, don't drink. Do you do anything else?"

The answer to that was a leer, which I didn't much feel like. "Right now I have to run this boat," I said.

"Don't make such a big deal of it. What say we get together tonight . . . there's gotta be a place . . ."

"I think we're off course," I said—not great but better than a leer—and went off to check on the automatic pilot. Finally I sat down wearily in the helmsman's seat. Betty soon joined me.

"Your friend Joe is asleep in your bunk," she said. "He wanted to take a bath. When I told him it was too rough, he said the two of us could handle it together and started chasing me around the forecastle. How can somebody be horny and seasick at the same time?"

"I'm going to kill him," I said.

"He's just another drunk. How's Jill doing?"

"She wants to get together with me tonight. 'There's gotta be a place' . . ."

"You mean right here on this little boat with your wife, your daughter and your old mother, that woman wants you to lay her?"

"Joe is just as bad, isn't he?"

"My God, wife-swapping stalks the *Pretty Betty* ..."

Four hours later we passed Gun Cay and sailed onto the Grand Banks, where the water was vodka-clear over the yellow sand. While I got out my equipment for taking an azimuth of the sun, mother went up to a big seat on the bow to watch the formations of coral and seaweed glide beneath us. Jessie sat with her—the first time I'd seen her voluntarily sit near her grandmother.

"What are you doing, commander?" Joe asked as he perched on a rail near me.

"Checking my compass."

"Why do you have to do all that damn fool stuff? We're not crossing the Pacific."

"Haven't had my compass compensated recently."

"So what? I haven't had mine compensated since I've had my damn boat."

"Do you take her to the Bahamas often?"

"My engines aren't right yet, but if I can navigate a DC-8, I can navigate a little pisspot, don't you think?"

"I don't know."

"What do you mean, you don't know?"

"I don't know if you can navigate a little pisspot."

"I consider that an insult," he said, and went below, presumably for a drink.

Fuck you, I thought, and berated myself silently as I'd done any number of times already for my bad judgment in asking this character aboard, never mind my good intentions.

The Tongue of the Ocean was calm. To the delight of my daughter, wife, and mother, a pod of whales was basking there in the last rays of the sun. At nearby Chubb Cay of the Berry Islands, we moored for the night. While checking the engines, I lifted up the floorboards and saw that the stuffing boxes were leaking badly. I put my hands on the huge monkey wrench which was there for tightening them and went at the task, which was one of those I hated worst. Almost immediately the wrench slipped and I barked my knuckles.

"What are you doing now, commander?"

At the companionway above me Joe was sitting, glass in hand.

"I'm tightening the stuffing boxes."

"You're doing it all wrong, commander. They never did teach you coasties much about engines, did they?"

"What am I doing wrong?"

"Turn them the other way."

"Joe, I've lived aboard this boat more than four years. About once a month I tighten these stuffing boxes. Wouldn't you think I'd have it right by now?"

"I don't know, commander. Some people learn slow."

With a roar of laughter he walked toward the marina's bar. When I went below to wash up, I said to Betty, "Why the hell does he bug me like that? All I'm doing is giving him a free ride to Andros and back."

"You might say he's got multi-level internal conflicts, or you might say he's a natural born son-of-a-bitch."

"I just hope he cuts it out," I said. "I don't want an explosion aboard here, but I can feel myself ticking."

The next day Joe carried on with his campaign. On the run up the coast of Andros he needled me for taking frequent bearings. When I told him I was trying to find an unmarked cut in the reef which in the right place would have a maximum of five feet of water over it, he said, "What's the problem? Run down your distance and turn in. You don't draw any water anyway, do you?"

"Loaded like this, about four feet."

"Then what's your problem, commander? You're going to give yourself and everybody aboard ulcers if you keep on like this ..."

I said nothing. As much as anything, I was annoyed to find myself reacting with such anger to him. That bothered me more than anything he said. . . .

When my bearings showed me that I was outside the unmarked cut, I made my ninety-degree turn and headed in with the fathometer pulsing. The water was so transparent that the reef seemed ready to bite into my keel, but the reading told me that I still had six feet. As that turned to five feet, I was as tense as a man about to fall off a cliff. My instinct was to slow down, but I had a swift current on my beam and wanted to hit the middle of the cut. At half speed we sped over the hungry-looking coral hands.

"What the hell are you doing, man?" Joe suddenly shouted, running from the stern.

"What's the matter?"

"This isn't the right place! You're going to beach her!"

A glance at the fathometer showed me that we were in eight feet of water. The hungry coral was sinking back into the depths. Sure that we were over the bar, I gave myself the luxury of a dramatic gesture. With one hand I pushed both throttles forward. *Pretty Betty* lept ahead at flank speed.

"What are you doing?" he yelled again.

"Heading for the harbor. I happen to think it's the right one—"

"Nobody should enter a harbor like this at full speed—"

He was, of course, right about that. I slowed down.

I moored the *Pretty Betty* at an old wharf which extended into a swift-flowing river. After telephoning the nearby research station, I learned that the captain of the base was expecting everyone aboard our boat to dinner in the building which had been named after mother's brother. We had about two hours to get ready before jeeps would be sent to bring us.

To recover some emotional equilibrium, I took a long hot bath in the tub which we had installed in the forecastle. When Betty offered to wash my back, I said, "I know it's ridiculous, but if that man gets out of line once more, I'm going to throw him overboard. It will happen before I can stop it."

"Just do me a favor," Betty said.

"What?"

"Save his wife for me."

By the time I got dressed and turned over the facilities we still had more than an hour before we were to be picked up. In the after cabin there were ominous sounds of merry-making, and when I knocked on the door I found that Joe and his wife had made no move to get dressed.

"I just want to explain that I don't want to keep my mother waiting for this dinner," I said. "It's kind of a big moment for her."

"Don't worry, commander. My God, we've still got plenty of time. Don't get your ulcers stirred up."

When we had fifteen minutes to go, mother came on deck dressed in a beautiful gown of blue silk, with a crocheted shawl.

"When we were little, my brother once said he liked me in blue," she said. "He wasn't one to give many compliments, but when we went to a cousin's wedding, he said he liked my gown."

The jeeps which were to take us to the base were five minutes early. In one of them the four-striper who commanded the outfit, a surprisingly young-looking man in starched khaki shorts, came to escort mother. They waited for us in the front seat of his car.

"Come on, Joe, the captain's here . . . mother's waiting in the car with him—"

"Hold onto your shirt, commander, we'll be right along."

We all waited for what seemed an eternity. The drivers of the other jeeps paced back and forth as though on sentry duty.

"We're running way late," I called into the after cabin.

"Now, commander, hold your *water*. The ship isn't sinking, is it?"

Then it all happened so fast that I couldn't control myself, just as I'd warned Betty. Bursting into the after cabin I said, "All right, enough. You've thirty seconds to get on the dock, both of you. You've got three choices. Stay at the hotel up there. Get Bahama Airways to fly you home, or sleep on the beach. One thing you're *not* going to do is stay aboard this boat a minute longer."

"Well, what the hell did we do?" Joe asked. He actually sounded indignant.

"Just shut up . . . if you don't get on the dock I'm going to throw you in the river. Which do you prefer?"

Suddenly Betty appeared behind me.

"He said he was going to throw us in the river," Jill sort of moaned, and I realized that she was already more than a little drunk. Her blouse was still unbuttoned. "Would he really *do* a thing like that?" she asked Betty.

"He's going to take your husband and I'm going to take you," Betty said. "So, honey, why don't you just get up on the dock the easy way?"

While clambering up to the wharf, poor Jill broke into tears and Joe kept screaming at me while I threw assorted suitcases, leather boxes for carrying liquor, and what appeared to be tons of cosmetics to him on the wharf. Mother and the base commander regarded all this with astonishment while the drivers of the jeeps ran to their cars for cover. Just before leaving for the hotel, which was only a few hundred yards away, Joe came running up to me as though he were going to tackle me.

"I just want to tell you that no one has ever treated my wife and me like this in our entire lives," he said with considerable dignity.

"Well, I guess we were innovations for each other. Do you have enough money to get home?"

"I'd *swim* before I took it from you," he retorted, did a military about-face and joined his wife, who was waiting by a palm tree, still whimpering. Arm-in-arm they started up a path toward the hotel.

"Damn!" Betty said. "On top of everything else, they leave us feeling guilty and sorry for them. And they don't really know what they did, anyway. With people like that, how can you win?"

Afraid that mother would be badly upset by all the unpleasantness, we rushed to her car as soon as we'd recovered our breath. She gave the whole scene a grand-lady dismissal:

"I know, dear," she said when I tried to explain. "Guests can often be troublesome. Now let's go ahead and see my brother's building."

The building turned out to be the senior officer's mess for the research center, a choice I thought my uncle would probably enjoy, since he was known as a convivial man not averse to the enjoyment of fine viands and spirits. The building was luxuriously appointed, but the thing that impressed me most was a printed brochure which gave the reasons why Sloan Danenhower Hall had been named after my uncle. The list of ships he'd commanded and his successes in salvage and submarine research were greater than I'd heard, but the accomplishment of his I enjoyed reading about most was the blowing up of the city of Nassau on the island of New Providence, only fifty or sixty miles away from Andros. Nassau, it seems, was on fire. Stationed aboard a naval vessel in the harbor, my Uncle Sloan realized that the only way to save half of it was to blow up the other half, thereby putting out the blaze. This he got permission to do legally, and, according to the navy, carried out his mission with bravery and skill. Thinking of my uncle blowing up half an entire city, I somehow began to suspect that that was the high point of his flamboyant life. How could be ever have topped it?

After a festive dinner the commanding officer of the base took mother and the rest of us on a tour of the research center. This mother seemed to enjoy, but on the way back to our boat she stopped once more to admire the plaque which gave the name of Sloan Danenhower Hall. For a long while she stood before it, almost as though she were going to kneel in prayer.

"I wish he could have seen it," she said to me as she turned away. "He never really got any honors while he was alive."

When we got back to our boat, I still felt guilty about the ridiculous fracas I'd had on the wharf with our former passengers and I again apologized for it.

"I know this was an important evening for you," I said. "I really regret starting it out all wrong."

"Well, I didn't really like those people much myself," mother replied with a smile. "Fights like that I don't really understand, but I'll tell you one thing: if anybody would understand, it's your Uncle Sloan. If he'd been sailing with us, I'm sure he would have felt right at home."

The next morning everybody aboard our boat was besieged by "doctor flies," a green insect about three times the size of a horse fly which can sting so hard that it can draw blood and leave permanent scars. Hastily casting off our lines, we hurried to sea, where a brisk breeze blew the insects away.

"That's what I like about a boat," Betty said. "If you don't like something, you can just leave."

"But I would have liked to see more of Andros," mother said. "I hear that the jungle areas are like Africa. How far could you take this boat up the rivers?"

"I've never seen any charts of the rivers. I don't know that any exist."

"Couldn't you make some?"

"Not with a crew that looks like a girl's seminary."

"I think that's very unkind of you," she replied. "The feminists, or women's lib, will be getting after you and well they should."

It was a beautiful day with just enough of a swell to set waves breaking on the barrier reef, making it look like a long skirting of lace on the indigo sea. Although I had dreaded cruising the coast of Andros with only my aged mother, my wife and small daughter for crew, the landmarks I'd passed the day before were familiar to me and the sky was a robin's egg blue without a cloud. When we passed the Tongue of the Ocean, the same or a new pod of whales was there, including a mammoth mother with a baby at her side. Jessie begged me to go close to them, but I'd heard too many stories of whales sinking small boats and hurried onto the Great Banks.

"They wouldn't sink us," Jessica said indignantly. "They're *nice!*"

"Nice creatures can often hurt, dear," mother said. "Think of what people have done to whales. I don't blame them if they do sink yachts."

The water over the Great Banks was, if possible, even clearer than it had been when we had come. On the sandy bottom we could see starfish, horseshoe crabs and schools of small fish which scattered ahead of us. Every once in a while the sun-dappled sand gave way to miniature castles of coral, some of which were all but hidden in the midst of forests of waving green grass. Jessie climbed out to a pulpit of stainless steel which we had built over the bow and stood with her face alight with wonder as new delights raced toward the briskly moving boat.

"Can I go out there?" mother suddenly asked.

"Sometimes it's hard to hang on."

"If a child can do it, I can. Anyway, if an old lady like me falls in, what's there to lose?"

I finally persuaded Jessie to give up her post, and mother edged up to the bow. With the wind blowing her hair and dress back, she looked like an ancient figurehead which had mysteriously aged as a person, not as a statue of wood. For perhaps an hour she stood there, moving hardly at all, her eyes glued to the water, where the colors kept changing with the varied texture of the bottom.

"I'm tired," she said at last.

As I helped her in, she added, "I think that is the most beautiful sight I have ever seen. No one's art can even touch it."

When the sun set that night, the water changed from rose to a brilliant orange, like a sea of fire. As that color died, I dropped anchor only about a mile from Gun Cay. Soon the fading light revealed a half-moon rising over the Great Banks and a spangle of stars as bright as any I had ever seen. The *Pretty Betty* lay completely quiet, her generator stilled by the beauty of the night. On a seat in the cockpit near the stern, mother sat with a blanket over her knees.

"I hate to think that this is the last time I shall ever be on a boat," she said suddenly.

"Why does that have to be?" I asked.

"Because I'm eighty-four years old."

There was a short silence during which we heard the current chortling under the stern.

"When I was a girl on my grandfather's boat, I always thought my father was in the sea because I had been told that he had drowned. Somehow that thought didn't scare me. The sea seemed friendly. It was his home. . . . A morbid thought, I suppose. . . . What are you and Betty going to do next?"

"Well, maybe this is our last night at sea, too. We're thinking of selling the boat."

"Why?"

"We only intended to stay aboard three years, and now it's almost five. A boat just doesn't make much sense now that we have to stay tied up nine months of the year so Jessie can go to school. And the cost of maintaining a boat like this goes up all the time."

"What are you going to do?"

"We've thought of living in Ireland or trying London. To tell you the truth, I don't know."

"I wish you'd just stay here aboard the *Pretty Betty*! Why does everything change all the time, just as soon as I learn to like it?"

Late that night I got up to check the anchor and found mother halflying on an upholstered bench in the cockpit. She was in such an awkward position that my heart jumped to my throat.

"Mother!" I said, touching her shoulder. "Are you all right?"

"Where am I?" she asked, straightening up.

"With me aboard the *Pretty Betty*."

"Sloan?"

"Yes?"

"Do you know they've named a building after you?"

"I'm your son, mother. They named a building after your brother."

"Of course, I'm sorry. Isn't it a shame that he never knew?"

When I had helped her into her bunk in the after cabin, she said, "The moonlight through the porthole. Look how it dances. When I was a girl it danced like that. At least the moonlight never changes. . . ."

We took only a few more cruises aboard the *Pretty Betty*. Lisa got married and a short time afterward came with her young husband for a tour of the Florida keys with us. Since attending their wedding in New York, Betty and I hadn't seen them at all, and had not had time to get to know our son-in-law very well. A strikingly handsome young man who looked like an athlete, Peter Strick was preparing to be a physioneurologist, which meant a person engaged in brain research. A humorous, unpretentious man who proved mighty handy with the dock lines, he was immensely likable despite the fact that my daughter was showering an outrageous amount of affection on him, to the nearly total exclusion of me.

"I'm supposed to be enough for you," Betty said when I explained my feelings. "Besides, you've still got Jessie. It will be eight or ten years before she finds someone she likes better than she does you."

Soon after Peter and Lisa had returned to their home in Philadelphia, my son David arrived with a pretty girl who looked a little as his mother had at her age. At twenty-one David was a bit taller than I, thin and muscular. His work at the University of Rochester had entitled him to be taken seriously as a marine biologist. He wanted to go to Bimini for skindiving. Immediately after landing there, he got so interested in a beach full of snails that he hardly entered the water.

"What's so interesting about snails?" I asked him.

"Look at them! They're not just a jumble. There's a band of one species along the low water mark and rows of about six different species go right up to the high water mark. Each row consists of one species without any intruders."

"Doesn't that just mean that snails of a feather flock together?"

"I think that's anthropomorphizing, the greatest sin for a biologist. Snails don't get together for the same reasons people do. I can't be sure yet, but my theory is that they're trying to avoid competition with another species for food and living space. You see, those guys who are awash even at low tide lead an entirely different life from the ones who hardly are touched by water, even at high tide. I can't tell much with my pocket microscope, but it looks to me as though each row eats entirely different things."

Back on the boat, David's girl was less than fascinated.

"This is the first time I ever lost a guy to a snail," she said to Betty.

Feeling that my son was going to have a hard life, I headed back for Miami as soon as he garnered his last bucket of carefully labeled snails. On the way across the Gulf Stream we got into a terrible argument about how he was going to handle his draft board when he graduated from college. Since draft boards were taking graduate students unless they were in medical school, the fact that he planned to take his doctor's degree in biology wouldn't help him.

In a way our argument was a strange one. Before it had started, we both had agreed that the war in Vietnam was a tragic mistake, as he called it, or a typically idiotic government foul-up, as I termed it. His idea was that his only course was to declare himself opposed to the war on moral grounds and take the consequences, which would probably be jail. Since he belonged to no church, he would not try to appeal to religious beliefs, and since he would gladly fight if his country were invaded, he could not say that he was opposed to all wars. This would make his conviction to a two-year prison term almost inevitable.

My idea was cynical but, I thought, much more efficient. What was the point of trying to fight honorably with a government which had already proved itself crazy enough to waste the lives of tens of thousands of men? Why allow oneself to be thrown into prison? All David had to do was have himself examined by a good doctor. As a child he had had asthma. Mattie Rosenchein would have his records and would see if the asthma still persisted.

"Dr. Rosenchein is dead," David said, and that was the first time I learned that my strong young friend had been killed by a *bee*. The news not only saddened me, it infuriated me. Somehow even the bees were fighting for our crazy government war policy. In a world where a damn bee could kill a fine physician, who could hope for any escape from lunacy?

"I'll find another doctor," I said.

"To hell with that," David said. "I prefer to declare myself and take my lumps. If everybody did that, the war would have to stop."

"Do me one favor," I said. "Before you set yourself up as Jesus Christ, ponder the phenomenon of crucifixion. It's not just history or a myth. People who act inflexibly on principle outrage lesser people. One way or another, saints get stoned to death or nailed to the cross—"

"Thanks, dad, but I think that's bullshit." At least he said it with a smile. "Let me take the helm for a while. Maybe the wind will clear my head of foolish scruples."

Soon after we moored in Miami, David told me that he was going up to Ticonderoga, where he'd registered while visiting me at Lake George, and declare himself to the draft board.

"Those people up there will eat you alive," I said. "You're a summer person who obviously should be sent off to war before the native sons. Besides, Ticonderoga is a hotbed of patriots. They still think they're fighting the French and Indian wars, and by God, they're going to win them yet!"

"Stop being such an idealist," he said with a crooked grin. "I'll call you and let you know how I make out."

"Remember, they let you make only one call from jail!"

Helping his girl from the after cabin, David stepped to the wharf. As I watched them walk to the car of a friend who was to drive them to the airport, I had the sinking conviction that David would never be the same again after two years in jail.

During the next two days I had nightmares about my son's probable future. In my imagination I saw him clubbed by prison guards, raped by hordes of giant homosexuals and stabbed when he objected.

On the third day David telephoned.

"Hi, dad," he said cheerfully. "I'm in Ticonderoga."

"What happened? Are you in jail?"

"I'm in a bar. I appeared before the draft board for two hours yesterday and today they asked me questions for another hour. I told them 'the business of a biologist is life not death.'"

"That must have wowed them. What happened?"

"Today I was formally declared a conscientious objector. I may have to do some work for the government, but it can be in my field. I told them that that couldn't include biological warfare, and they agreed. Anyway, I won't be drafted."

"All this happened in *Ticonderoga*?" I asked.

"It's a nice town, Dad. The guys on the draft board are thoughtful, honest people."

"I'll be damned!"

"Keep the faith, dad," David said, and hung up.

Only a short while later Becky called. Would I object if she started in at the Columbia School of Nursing?

"I'm delighted," I said, "but how did this happen?"

"Well, college has never meant much to me, but this would at least be useful. Maybe I'll turn into Florence Nightingale!"

"That's marvelous," I said. "What happened to the rock and roll guy?"

"Oh, he just sort of rocked and rolled out of my orbit. I'm completely friendless at the moment. All I have is you."

"For that I'll send you kisses and money."

"I have a scholarship, thank you. They sort of give you the first year of nursing school free to suck you into a lifetime of white slavery."

After I hung up I sat looking at the silent telephone. With satisfaction I thought that my three older children seemed to be well started in life. Now the only people in our family with any problems were Jessie, Betty and me. The boat needed extensive repairs after five years with little but surface maintenance. Although my last two books had received the best reviews I had ever had, times were apparently changing and sales could not even be compared to my earlier novels. The tax men, who had been circling me like wolves for years, seemed ready to close in. Beyond that, Jessie had started to dislike her strict Episcopal school, and Betty and I had started to be fed up with the high—low?—life on the Miami boat docks. There had been drunken fights, and a seemingly normal friend of ours, the wife of a physician, had taken to stripping in a dockside bar, an action which caused some people to believe she was liberated and others to think she was nuts. Whatever, it seemed a signal to us to pull up anchor.

A few weeks later I received a letter from a man who said he wanted to buy the *Pretty Betty*. He knew her whole history, from her earliest days, when she had been Guy Lombardo's *Tempo IV*. Guy Lombardo had described her lovingly in an autobiography, he said, and he had read my *Away from It All*. A boat that had had two books written about her must be something special, he said. Did I want to sell and if so, how much did I want?

Half hoping that he wouldn't like the boat, I invited him to come and see her. Driving from New York in twenty-four hours, he showed up on our dock almost immediately. After talking to him for an hour or so, I realized that he knew a great deal about repairing and maintaining a boat. He liked working with his hands, and hoped to spend most of his spare time making the old boat good as new.

Obviously he was the ideal person to take my lovely old lady of a boat. He did not quibble about price, and suddenly the *Pretty Betty* was no longer ours.

As was our right, we took the trail boards and the life rings carrying the name *Pretty Betty* with us. After we'd lugged our personal possessions to a second-hand car we'd bought, we returned to the dock to take one last look at the old vessel which had been our home for five years. Rocking slowly at her moorings, she still looked as graceful as a pretty ballerina curtsying after a dance. Breaking into tears, Jessie ran to her mother. With her arm around her daughter, Betty started toward the car.

"Don't look back, honey," she said to Jessie. "Just be glad you're sorry you're leaving her. It's when you're glad to leave that you've been hurt."

Part 9
"You've Done It!
You've Done It!
You've Done It!"

47

In part because we had no place to go, we drove to my mother's house on Lake George. It was early in July, but the two-story living room of her big old summer "cottage" seemed to absorb dampness from the lake and the surrounding forest. Most of the time mother sat staring into the flames of the fire which flickered in the huge fieldstone fireplace my father had designed.

Betty and I were put in the room I'd occupied as a boy, with Jessie in my sister's old room. Here time had stood still. A faded Harvard banner with my class numerals, '42, hung like a tattered battle flag from one wall. On a nearby shelf were some of the loving cups I'd won at sailing regattas, a few with the silver plate peeling off the copper. In a large bookcase there were volumes on boxing, on racing tactics for sailboats, and whole sets of Dickens and Conrad that my father had given me, complete with my own bookplate, a gift from mother, which said *"Ex Libris* Sloan Wilson" and featured an engraving of a tall clipper-bowed schooner. On a wall over the bed mother had hung a formal photograph of me as a coast guard ensign, a fairly priggish young man who looked more like the new English teacher at a boy's school than anyone capable of running a ship.

"I hate this place," Jessie said, shivering. "It's spooky. How long do we have to stay here?"

"Till we get a place of our own," Betty said.

"But where?" Jessie asked.

For a month we tried to answer that question. After conferring with my lawyer, Mort Leavy, I realized that our funds were even more limited than I'd expected. After writing friends in London, we found that it would cost even more to live there than it would in New York. Betty's father wrote that "the troubles" were intensifying in Ireland. Though the fighting was confined largely to the north, the tensions were spreading to the south, where the IRA had many of its roots. Most of the places I knew well, such as New Canaan, Pound Ridge and Bedford Village, had become more outrageously expensive than ever and represented to me a kind of life I just didn't want for my family or myself.

"If I can find a place where I can write one good book, maybe we can go anywhere we want," I said to Betty.

"But where?"

We priced houses in Vermont, but the ones we saw were expensive, either to buy or to rent. As the weather turned unseasonably cool for midsummer, the idea that we had no home that could withstand winter, or even fall, made me feel panicky.

"Maybe mother would let me winterize this place," I said. "At least it would give us a kind of headquarters."

Mother made no objections, but for many reasons it proved technically almost impossible to winterize a summer cottage that my father had successfully designed to stay cool in August.

"You could bunk down in my apartment in New York," mother said.

For that suggestion I was grateful, but her two-bedroom apartment would prove hell for the four of us, and why did I have to go crawling home to mother, anyway, at the age of fifty?

Growing more and more upset, I drove into Ticonderoga to do some marketing and mail some letters. About four doors from the post office I saw an attractive if somewhat tumbledown house. Rambling roses grew on the rail of its sagging front porch. In the front yard there were two ancient larch trees. More roses and wild grape vines grew on trellises in a side yard. The house itself was built of white clapboards, some of which were peeling. I guessed that the place was more than a hundred years old. Despite the fact that it looked as though it had stood deserted for a long time, there remained something sturdy about the old structure that stood ready to defy another century. Fluttering on one of the larch trees was a faded cardboard sign which said "For sale" and gave the number of a real estate agent.

Stopping at the agent's office in the village I asked for information about the old house near the post office. It had, I found, a relatively new oil furnace, one bathroom, a "modern" kitchen with a new washing machine, a fairly large living room, a dining room, and a large bedroom downstairs. Upstairs it had four bedrooms, two of medium size, two small. Beyond this there were various laundry and storage rooms and a woodshed at the back of the house.

"How much is it?" I asked.

"Well, it's a good house and it ain't going cheap, even if it is an estate sale," the agent said.

"What's the asking price?"

"We ain't asking, we're waiting till we get our price. We want $11,500. Of course that includes the furniture, better than a half acre of land, and a pretty good barn with a concrete floor out back."

"I'll go get my wife," I said. "We'd like to be shown through it."

"Eleven thousand five hundred!" Betty said. "For a whole house? But do you really want to live in Ticonderoga?"

"A friend of mine once described it as 'the town that progress never touched,'" I said. "Maybe that would be good for a change. And I've always kind of loved the place, ever since the draft board believed David."

"Do they have schools here?" Jessie asked.

"A brand new elementary school was built just a few years ago."

The agent met us on the front porch of the house. He had difficulty turning the lock of the front door, but finally we walked in. Betty gasped. The rooms were good-sized, but the place was a shambles. An unmade bed filled a small room between the living room and the dining room. Clothes had been scattered almost everywhere. In the center of the living-room a wheelchair holding an ancient Raggedy Ann doll confronted us. On every level surface there were medicine bottles, basins and other sick-room supplies.

"Place don't look like much now," the agent said. "The woman who lived here the last fifty years or so used to keep it immaculate. Then she took sick. She loved this place and she wouldn't let them take her to the hospital till the last minute. Now all her relatives are too old to clean up after her. You'd be surprised at what two or three days of work would do here."

Going over to a wall, he knocked it with his fist.

"Most of the walls here are six or seven inches thick, old oak and pine as good as new. If you don't believe me, ask the electrician who bored holes through it. I can get you his name."

Silently Betty and I walked through the house. It was only a story and a half high, which was why the upstairs was much smaller than the downstairs. Still, after the confined space of our boat, it seemed enormous.

"Why are there no fireplaces?" Betty asked.

"There are three chimneys," the agent said. "This house used to be heated by stoves. It was built around the time when they discovered that cast-iron stoves heat a lot more efficiently than fireplaces. It was some years after that that they decided to build fireplaces as ornaments."

"We can put in a Franklin stove," I said.

In the middle of the living room, Betty stood looking confused. "It could be nice, but it's all such a mess," she said. "Still, for $11,500 ... where else in the world could we buy a furnished house with so much room for that?"

The agent accepted our deposit. As we drove to a grocery store to do our shopping, I looked at the village as though I'd never seen it before. Although it stood in a setting of great natural beauty, on the rushing river that flows from Lake George to Lake Champlain, it had long ago uglified its surroundings. Most of the eastern side of the village was dominated by the gigantic empty buildings of a paper mill that had recently built a new plant five or six miles away.

"I've heard they're going to take those old buildings down soon and replace them with parks," I said.

"That will help," Betty replied. "Why do so many of the stores have false fronts? It looks like a set for a Western movie."

"I don't know," I said. "Anyway, we're just going to stay here until I get a chance to write a new book."

That night neither Betty nor I could sleep. On the one hand, it seemed sensible to buy the house which could be sold when we could afford better or kept as an inexpensive headquarters if we were ever able to spend most of our time traveling. On the other hand, a decrepit old house in a mill town . . .

I think that the desire to have some kind of snug home, any kind that could get us through the winter, influenced us most as the Adirondack nights began to grow cold. Beyond that, I perhaps sensed that no new book was coming together in my head. I wouldn't admit it, but I wanted a place where, if necessary, we could survive on very little money. What better place for that could there be than Ticonderoga? At least we would start with a snug house.

At breakfast the next morning Jessie asked, "Can I have a swing at the new house, daddy?"

A swing was one thing she had missed on the boat.

"I don't know if we'll have a tree with a proper limb," I said. "Do you want to go look?"

With Betty we drove to the old "new house." It looked charming in the morning sun—from the outside. The two larch trees had no branches suitable for a swing, but near our old barn in the back yard there was a magnificent elm which had somehow escaped the Dutch elm disease. The only trouble was that its lowest projecting limb was about thirty-five feet high.

"How would you ever get a rope over that?" Betty asked.

"I don't know, but it would make one hell of a swing. The higher the rope, the wider the arc."

"Could you shoot an arrow with a string over it?" Betty asked.

"Let's do that!" Jessie said, dancing around with delight.

"There're too many leaves and light branches around it," I said. "An arrow with string would get stuck up there."

Remembering that I had seen an old stove in our barn when I'd inspected it the afternoon before, I went in to have another look at it. The barn was in such bad repair that it depressed me. Probably it would have to be torn down at considerable expense. The old stove, however, had a large lid with a smaller one fitted to the center of it for use when a little pan was to be heated. With the center lid taken out, the larger one formed an iron disk about eight inches in diameter with a three-inch hole in the middle of it.

"If I can find a long clothesline to tie to this," I said to Betty, "maybe I can throw the thing over the limb. It's heavy enough to crash through the leaves and twigs."

"But nobody could get it up there," Betty said.

"I want to try. Let's buy a couple of hanks of clothesline."

"I saw some in the laundry room," she said. "I think that old door is unlocked. Let me try to get in."

"Is clothesline good for a swing?" Jessie asked.

"No. But when we get it over the limb, we can attach it to a strong rope and pull it up."

In a few moments Betty came back with a large coil of clothesline. While I attached one end of it to the stove lid, and coiled the remainder of the line, several neighborhood children came to watch.

"He'll never do it," a ten-year-old boy said when Betty explained the situation.

Asking everyone to stand back, I heaved the stove lid as hard as I could. It missed the high limb by at least ten feet. The children laughed.

The next time I missed by only about five feet, and was greeted with cheers. From every direction more children arrived, and quite a few adults. I felt as though I were performing in an Olympic stadium.

My next five or six throws were near misses and each was greeted by gratifying applause. Just as I was starting to get the hang of the art, however, my shoulder started to hurt. Each of the next five or six throws was worse than the last, and each was greeted by boos, catcalls and Bronx cheers.

"Come on, daddy!" Jessie said. "You can do it!"

For her my honor was at stake, I realized. Giving a mighty heave, I succeeded only in hitting the barn and making the ache in my shoulder spread to my back.

"Damn! God damn!"

"Hush!" Betty whispered. "These are our new neighbors."

"Damn the neighbors! My shoulder hurts."

"Well, stop this foolishness! Nobody could get that thing up there. It must be forty feet high. We'll get Jessie one of those little backyard swings on steel posts.'"

"Damn the steel posts!"

I was sweating so hard that I had to wipe my hand on my trousers before I picked up the stove lid, an object which I was beginning to hate. In addition to my shoulder and my back, my head ached and my breath was coming short. Obviously I was getting old. Damn old age! Gripping the sweat-slippery stove lid, I went into a kind of throwing frenzy, picking up the lid the moment it landed and throwing it again. A few of my throws almost reached the limb, but most went wild. Swearing and throwing and half falling with exhaustion, I persisted in making a fool of myself while the new neighbors relapsed into a kind of horrified silence.

"Please!" Betty said, gripping my arm. "Stop it! For a damn swing, you want to kill yourself?"

"One more time!" I panted, crouched low, and then straightened up, heaving the stove lid with all my force. Sweat was stinging my eyes so much that I had to keep blinking, but I saw the black lid shining in the sun as it sailed over the limb, crashed through the leaves, and thudded into the grass, leaving the clothesline doubled over the big branch. If most of my audience had not been on their feet anyway, I think they would have given me a standing ovation. The applause, as they say, was deafening. With Betty and Jessie I walked toward our house like a Shakespearean star after the greatest triumph in his life.

"You've done it!" Jessie said. "You've done it! You've done it! You've done it!"

Throwing a stove lid over the limb of a tree might not be much of a victory for some men. In the dark years that lay ahead, the foreshadows of which I may have already begun to feel, I often remembered that backyard triumph as proof that, after all, there are glorious victories as well as defeats in life. I'd seen some beautiful sights in my half century of life: graceful boats on the Bahamian banks, crisp new books of mine fresh from the printer, my young wife holding our baby to me. The memory of a stove lid sailing over the limb of a tree thirty-five feet high hardly can be ranked, I suppose, with the truly important things in life, but it often has served to comfort me when it seemed as though I had mysteriously lost the ability to succeed at anything.

48

On the afternoon of the day I threw the stove lid over the limb, I called Mort Leavy to ask how I should go about raising $11,500 for a house.

"I'm not so sure you can afford a house right now," he replied.

"Well, how are we going to live? It gets cold up here in the Adirondacks, and we can't exactly hibernate the way the bears can."

"How much is this house you want going to cost?"

"I told you, eleven and a half grand."

"You mean, that's the *total* price?"

"Yep. It includes a half-acre of land, a barn, and a house with five bedrooms, all completely furnished."

"For $11,500? I thought you were talking about a down payment. Do you have any more properties like that up in Ticonderoga?"

While lawyers were making our purchase of the old house final, I spent a good deal of time acting as a sort of lifeguard for my mother and daughter. Though she was in her mid-eighties, mother still liked to swim for at least an hour every summer day. About a quarter of a mile from her house on Lake George there was a small sandy beach. After putting on her favorite blue bathing suit and a white rubber cap that left her deaf, she went boldly striding in, splashing water on her forehead and breasts to give her body a warning of what was coming. Using the side-stroke or the breast stroke, she could paddle along for what seemed to me to be hours, touring the old wharfs that surrounded the swimming beach. The only trouble with this performance was that she tired like a clockwork toy running down. Once I glanced at her just in time to see that she was lying motionless in the water, face down. With the help of a friend, I lifted her to a dock. Almost immediately she came to, and couldn't understand why we were upset.

"I just got a little tired," she said.

Being a lifeguard for Jessie was just as demanding. She had first learned to swim in a Florida pool at the age of three and now, at eight, could do almost anything in the water that a fish or duck could do. Disdaining the beach where her grandmother began her voyages, Jessie dove from anything—the roof of an old boathouse, the pilings of a rotten wharf, even a diving board. She could move like a trout, and if I took my eyes from her a moment, I would finally spot her half a mile away at Windmill Point, or swimming along the shore toward Rogers Slide, a mile in the other direction. Every time she did this sort of thing I lectured her severely, but I simply could not make her believe there was any danger in the water.

"You absolutely terrify me," I said to her finally. "I've been around the water all my life, and you're the kind of person who's most likely to drown—"

"Why?" she asked, eyes widening.

"Because you don't even know enough to be scared. Even the best swimmer in the world is a bad boat. Swimmers can take no rough water at all, and all kinds of things can go wrong with them to sink them even in the calmest water. If you go swimming alone, or get out in the middle of the lake where there's nobody who can help you, you just must want to die."

She stared at me solemnly. "Oh, daddy, why are you so worried about me all the time?"

For that question, I don't think any father has ever had an answer comprehensible to his child. In any case, trying to be a lifeguard for both Jessie and mother at the same time was enough to drive even an old coast guardsman into a nervous breakdown. I could hardly wait for cold weather to come.

When the closing had finally taken place, Betty and I began work on the old house. Because we wanted to take advantage of the good weather we began work on the outside. The dilapidated appearance of the house was caused mostly by troubles easily fixed. In only one day we repaired the sagging gutters and started to scrape the front of the house where the paint had cracked and peeled worst. Finding a pair of clippers in the woodshed, I trimmed the bushes and vines which were choking the front and side porches. While Betty continued with the painting, I attempted to fix the back of the house, where the foundation had crumbled under the laundry room, causing it to sag at a crazy angle. Realizing that I wasn't really up to this kind of repair, I hired a man by the name of Charles Luce. Mr. Luce brought some enormous jacks. With the help of another man he lifted the old log beams of the laundry room floor into position. After bracing them there with more logs, he built a plywood mold for a thick wall under it.

"There," he said, brushing his hands. "I guess that's about it."

"You mean you've finished? But the job's only about half done—"

"You just pour concrete into that mold. Add a few rocks. Anyone can do that. I have a tough job I have to do for an old lady before winter sets in."

"How much do I owe you?"

"Thirty dollars, and I'll leave a couple of jacks in case you have to trim her out again."

In Westchester and Fairfield counties you didn't make repairs to a house for thirty dollars. I paid him and soon found he was right—anyone could finish the job. Of course I didn't know that plywood can sag unless it's properly braced, but I figured that my foundation wall with the beautifully curved sides was stronger than the unimaginative straight-sided kind.

After getting the outside of the house reasonably under control, Betty, Jessie and I began to clean up the fantastic mess inside. This was slow work because every article had to be examined before being thrown out. Mixed with barrels of old newspapers, clothes gone to tatters, and medicine bottles, we found assorted magazines dating back to 1902, a lovely old lace-trimmed slip which Betty liked to wear as a dress, a cast iron bank in the shape of a dog which ate coins, and an enamel brooch with a tiny diamond in the center of it.

The house also had some liabilities we hadn't discovered in our brief inspection tour. The roof over two of the bedrooms upstairs leaked. As a result one of them had crumbling plaster behind the peeling wallpaper. Also, the toilet in the single bathroom moved like a rocking chair whenever anyone sat on it. This novel effect was caused by the fact that the floor under it was rotten, offering the possibility that a heavy person like me might go plunging into the cellar beneath at an awkward moment. The couch in the living room had everything in it broken but the back. The roof over the dining room also leaked. When I finally called in a contractor, he said he could fix the whole place up absolutely fine, including re-wiring, for $10,000. Shades of *Mr. Blandings' Dream House*? Still, a total cost of $21,500 for a house like ours in top shape wouldn't be bad, I thought, but we decided to do as much of the job ourselves as we could. The official reason was that we wanted to save money. That we did, but I also wanted to delay the moment of starting a new novel as long as possible.

While we were working on the house we lived with my mother in her unheated cottage on Lake George. That year she wanted to stay as long as possible at the lake to enjoy the fall foliage "one more time," as she put it. In early September a fall gale sent the temperature down to the low thirties, and no matter how high I piled the logs on the old Hessian andirons, the big fireplace couldn't keep us warm. Finding mother huddled by an electric heater in her bedroom, I said, "Why don't we all move into our house in the village?"

"Is it ready?"

"It's ready to keep us warm."

As soon as we had had breakfast, we drove in to the old house near the post office. This was the first time mother had seen it, and I seemed to be seeing it with her eyes. It was a funny, oddly comfortable little old house without any pretensions whatsoever.

"It's cold here, too," she said.

"Wait till I put up the heat."

Touching the thermostat on the wall, I heard the whir of the furnace in the cellar, a sound the sweetness of which can be appreciated only by people who have lived in unheated cottages. Almost immediately a ribbon tied to one of the hotair registers straightened out like a pennant in a gale.

"It's already getting warm," mother said, holding her hands over the register. "You know, I think you've found a very sweet little place."

Outside our front window a huge maple tree in the perfect shape of a wine glass already blazed with color.

"Why, that's more beautiful than anything I've seen in the mountains," mother said. "I think it might be lovely to live here. I'm not so sure that I want to go back to New York."

"It's obvious that she wants to live with us," Betty said a few minutes later to me in the kitchen.

"For more than a visit?"

"Well, she's almost eighty-five years old. How long do you think a woman that age can expect to keep on living alone in an apartment?"

"Over the long run, we'd all go crazy," I said.

"Well, we have five bedrooms and it wouldn't cost much to put in another bathroom."

"No, but I don't like to think of her alone in New York either."

The conversation wasn't pursued that day, but when Chester drove my mother back to New York, she made a point of asking whether she could visit us on Christmas, so that she could see snow unsoiled by soot.

"Come any time you want," Betty said as she kissed her good by. "And stay as long as you want. We'll always be here."

"How come you're better to my mother than I've ever been?" I asked Betty after mother had left.

"It's easier," she said. "Don't you know anything?" She kissed me when she said it.

A little while later in a junk shop I bought an ornate "Round Oak" stove of cast iron that we installed in the living room and two less antique stoves for other parts of the house. After I'd installed all these we felt that the house looked more or less authentic for its period, and more than that, the stoves would be good insurance if anything happened to the furnace. On the first snowy night I put some chunks of spruce in the ancient "Round Oak." Soon its lid glowed ruby-red and the fragrance of spruce made the room smell like a summer forest. With the lights out, we sat watching the new snow slant by a lantern on our porch while Betty helped Jessie pop corn and roast apples on the stove.

"I like this better than the boat," Jessie said. "When will you teach me how to use a sled?"

Contentment was one thing, but meeting deadlines and making money were another, I reminded myself the next morning. To fill some of the holes in my finances left by the tax men, I'd taken an advance from a publisher for a new novel. The publisher wanted me to finish the job in approximately a year and expected to see a few chapters almost immediately. Carrying a table, a straight chair and an old Morris armchair into one of the small bedrooms upstairs, I declared it my study. Rolling a fresh piece of paper into my battered old typewriter, I started at it.

In the next few hours I wrote twelve outlines for a novel, not one of which had a trace of thought or emotion in it. One thing I did accomplish that day. Out of a handsome old barrel I made what was probably the biggest wastepaper basket in Ticonderoga.

49

I've never been able to figure out whether I get depressed because I can't write or whether I can't write because I get depressed. Whichever, I soon felt lower than I ever had in my life. Although I didn't realize it at the time, depression creates all kinds of reasons to justify itself. I was depressed because I felt myself fast aging, growing white-haired and fat. I was depressed because, once again, I was starting to drink too much. And I was depressed because in view of all the other things that depressed me, I couldn't see how Betty could stand me, and I also couldn't see how I could live as much as three days without her.

Even events which were made to be celebrations depressed me. That fall, in Rochester, New York, David married the pretty girl who hadn't liked the snails of Bimini, or who had not enjoyed losing my son to them for a day. It would be absurd to make much of that, I realized, but Mary looked so startlingly young in her wedding dress that I could think only of my own first wedding, a memory that damn near had me in tears. For Elise and me there had been so many lost years before we'd made the simple discovery that we were completely unsuited to each other. Elise also came to David and Mary's wedding. I looked at her—a well-dressed matron standing beside her second husband, a lively sixty-five-year old physician. Somehow she didn't look like anyone I had ever met, and I felt embarrassed as I kissed her on the cheek in greeting after the ceremony.

Betty wore a long gown of blue and yellow that discreetly hugged her figure and made her look so young and desirable that it scared me. At the reception it seemed to me that all the men were flirting with my wife. Though Betty in all the time that I'd known her would no more think of getting involved in idle flirtations than she would take kindly to the idea of playing with a loaded gun, I felt so jealous every time she exchanged a few words with another man that I felt sure I was going out of my mind. My discomfort grew so intense that I started to get drunk, restraining myself at the last moment when my tall slender son came up to chat with me before he and Mary started their honeymoon.

"Have you kissed the bride?" he asked.

I did so, feeling that I was touching a startled fawn. Then the wedding was over and through a pelting rain we started back to Ticonderoga.

"Thank you for not getting drunk," Betty said.

"Has it reached that point, where I have to be thanked for staying sober?"

"Weddings are tough, I know. My father always had trouble at weddings."

The windshield wipers made a scratching sound.

"I was terribly jealous of you," I said suddenly. "Maybe it's crazy, but I was."

"Did I do anything to set that off?"

"Yes. You looked half my age, a woman I probably don't deserve to keep."

"I've always thought I didn't deserve you. It's nice if we can both feel that way, isn't it?"

For a few minutes I felt reassured. Then I decided that she was still thinking of me as a sailor and a writer. How would she feel when I had obviously ceased to be both?

In February every member of our greater family got together to give mother a party to celebrate her eighty-fifth birthday at the Harvard Club in New York. Cousins and the cousins of cousins were there, along with countless friends. Mother, in a new black dress, sat in the middle of the big room sipping champagne and expounding for one and all the finer points of the family history. Since I'd last seen her she'd lost weight and I was struck by the sight of her near skeletal face and deep-set eyes. My brother, who had worked for years as a librarian in Philadelphia, and my sister, who had married a lawyer and was living in Northport, Long Island, were there. We didn't see each other often, and I sometimes felt a tinge of guilt when we got together. Our father would be angry at us. He'd often said that sisters and brothers should stick together. Now as I told my sister and brother good by, I had the thought that probably the next time we would see each other would be at our mother's funeral.

The last toast drunk that night was to my mother's ninetieth birthday. I proposed it.

"That's very nice of you, dear," mother said, "but I'm not sure that I could stand another party like this."

Back in Ticonderoga Betty set up her sewing machine on the dining-room table and started to make curtains for the whole house. Each day I typed furiously and each night I threw out everything I had written. When a thin young man came to the door to ask me to teach him how to write, I told him that I had known once, but had forgotten. When he refused to believe me, I said that he should try emptying out my wastepaper basket every night.

I felt deeply sorry for myself. How could such a terrible thing happen to a nice guy like me? One morning I got so angry that I brought my fist down on the keys of my typewriter so hard that they stayed down, apparently forever. The only good thing was that a friend regularly stole reams of typewriter paper for me from the huge new paper mill on the outskirts of the village. In that respect, anyway, Ticonderoga was a great place for a writer to live.

After I'd bought a new typewriter in Burlington, I had the illusion of getting off to a new start, but the new keys made no more sense than the old ones had. Trying to escape the frustration every morning, I walked down to get the mail and the *New York Times*. Because it seemed to be snowing almost always that winter, I bought fleece-lined boots that came halfway to my knees. With a red cap that Betty had knitted for me and an old coast guard greatcoat that I treasured even though it was falling apart, I must have made a surprising sight, but the people of Ticonderoga paid no attention to me. In some ways more sophisticated than most city people, they apparently figured that every man should have a chance to dress strangely, if he wants. Only summer people would object to it.

Usually our mailbox held nothing but bills, but sometimes there was a letter from someone who had found one of my out-of-print books in a library. In the old days I had often let reader letters pile up in a closet without being opened. Now I read each one and fired off an immediate answer. On one day when the temperature was plunging to thirty below, I got a letter from a woman in Miami who said that someone had given her an old copy of *A Sense of Values* for her to read in the hospital while her father was undergoing an operation.

"You took my mind off my troubles for three hours," she said. "I guess you've gotten better reviews than that, but I thought you would want to know that one reader, at least, is extremely grateful."

I actually framed that letter and hung it over my desk. Usually, however, there was nothing to do when I got back from the post office except to read the *New York Times*. During those gray days of March I read the *Times* in such detail that I even became an expert on wheat futures and sow bellies.

When Jessie came home from school there was always a welcome interruption. Sometimes Betty and I would take her sliding on an old sled we'd found in our woodshed, and once we built an enormous snow giant in our front yard. Another time I persuaded a friend who knew Lake Champlain well to take us fishing through the ice. In a tiny cabin warmed by a wood stove we snugly sat while a gale howled down the great white canyon of the lake. Jessie caught a fine big pickerel which we immediately cooked on the lid of the stove in aluminum paper.

After we all had helped do the dishes in the evening, Betty often lent Jessie a hand with her homework. Because Jessie was nervous about sleeping alone, especially when the north wind howled under the eaves just outside her room, Betty usually went to bed with her at about nine o'clock. At that hour it was impossible for me to sleep, and I was too tense for either books or television. After an hour of pacing in the living room, I generally put on my greatcoat and walked the short distance to the Roma bar, which apparently was run by an Irish radio operator from the merchant marine named Paul Smith. Sitting there with a double Scotch in my hand, it was comfortable to watch the seemingly eternal snow slant down by the bar's frosted windows, and talk to Paul about the war.

Like me, he'd served aboard a tanker. The other men in the bar were mostly mill workers and people who, for one reason or another, were now on relief. The guys on relief sipped a single beer all evening, while the paper-makers drank fast. Most of us had been in one war or another. War was the one thing we had in common. Occasionally we sang. No one can sing, "It's a long, long way to Tipperary" better than the guys on relief at the Roma bar.

The descent into alcoholism can be deceptively pleasant at first, like the gentle slopes of a mountain which lead a skier to the abyss. The men at the Roma bar soon became my friends. Sometimes after a few double Scotches, washed down by cold beer, I would realize how important paper-makers are in this world. Where would all the writers be without these paper-makers? How could the government operate without paper for paper work?

"You damn right!" the paper-makers said, and offered to buy me another drink.

Above the bar in the Roma there still hung a weathered sign saying, "Remember the *Pueblo*." It was probably the last sign of its kind in the world, but when matters of national honor are at stake, the boys at the Roma never forget. As a former coast guard officer, I was listened to with respect as I described what I would have done had I commanded the *Pueblo*.

"Machinegun 'em!" I thundered. "Let 'em have the depth charges, set at fifty feet!"

"Wait a minute," Paul Smith said from behind the bar. "The *Pueblo* didn't have no depth charges. I know that for a fact."

"Well, that's the trouble! The son-of-a-bitch *should* have carried depth charges. That's where the whole deal got fouled up!"

Many a snowy night the *Pueblo* kept us occupied. Then one evening, as I'd half dreaded, a young master sergeant walked in with ribbons showing he'd served in the Vietnamese war. Inevitably the men started to discuss the merits of *that* conflict, and before long one of them asked for my opinion.

"I've been against our getting into that war from the start," I blurted, wondering whether I was about to be thrown out of the bar.

There was a moment of silence.

"Well, mister," the sergeant said, "you ain't been there. I been there four years, and mister, you don't even know what it means to hate that fucking war. But at least you're against it. Which is more than I can say for most of the fucking civilians I've met. Can I buy you a beer?"

That night we all had such a good time that Paul kept the bar open an hour later than usual. When I walked out into the snow, my boots slipped on a patch of ice and I fell into a bank left by the snowplow. It was soft and I felt curiously comfortable there. A streetlight overhead made the snow sparkle all around me. Oblongs of yellow light from the windows of the Roma lay like abstract designs on the icy sidewalk and street.

"Can I help you up, old-timer?"

It was the young sergeant from Vietnam.

"I'm not an old-timer!" I said. "Jesus Christ, I'm only forty or fifty years old—"

"Even so, you better get your ass out of that snow, unless you want to freeze it for posterity."

He helped me up, but when I got to my feet I found that my legs were surprisingly weak and, to my chagrin, I actually sank to my knees.

"Goddamn it, I can't leave you out here to freeze to death," the sergeant said. "Where do you live?"

I pointed up the hill to my house. Lights still shone in the windows.

"Hell, if it's that close, I'll help you home. Put your left arm around my neck."

The sidewalk was slippery, but we finally made it to my front porch. Before I could thank him, the sergeant gave me an ironic little salute and went off into the night. Once inside our warm living room I found that somehow I didn't feel in the least drunk. Far from feeling sleepy, I was so tense that I knew I couldn't sleep at all. Thinking that one more drink might quiet me down, I found a pint of whiskey I'd had the foresight to slip into a drawer in my study. There my memory stopped.

In the morning I woke up in my bed. I was wearing only my undershorts, and my other clothing lay in a tangle on the floor. My head throbbed, and I gradually realized that I had the great-grandfather of all hangovers. Although I could remember nothing since finding the bottle in my study, I had the foreboding that I'd done something terrible. Quickly I put on fresh clothes but I couldn't find my fleece-lined boots.

Barefoot, I ran downstairs, where Betty was sitting in the kitchen drinking a cup of coffee.

"Betty, are you all right?" I asked.

"I'm fine. How are you?"

"I guess I tied one on last night. It's funny, I can't seem to locate my boots."

"I threw them out," she said.

"You threw out my good boots? Why?"

"You don't remember anything about it?"

"Not a thing."

"Well, sit down, because I don't think this is going to make you very happy."

"What did I do?"

"You came up the stairs at about two in the morning, undressed and collapsed on the bed. At about three you got up, apparently feeling too sick to get to the bathroom. I wish there were some delicate way I could put this."

"What happened?"

"You got sick in your wonderful boots, first one and then the other. Then you went back to sleep."

"I could never do a thing like that—"

"If you need proof, they're out in the woodshed."

All I could say was the obvious. "This time I've hit bottom, but at least I can only go up . . ."

"Do you want to drive over to Burlington to see a doctor? And there's a chapter of AA in Port Henry, I found out. Do you want to give them a call?"

"Look, I can handle this problem myself!"

For a month or so I stayed off the booze completely. Having proved to myself that I could stay on the wagon, I tried to drink like a gentleman, with only a few glasses of wine a day. This stage lasted about two months before I found myself drinking more and more every day. This time I got shocked into sobriety by Jessie, who said frankly that she hated me when I was drunk. For another month I stayed off completely, and so the cycle kept repeating itself for the next two years.

During my sober moments during the end of that winter and spring, I forced myself to write a long novel. The manuscript was rejected by every editor who saw it. Even my very first manuscripts, which had been written in my twenties, had not been rejected. I hated all the editors and most of all, myself. How could a man lose all his talent like a key from his pocket? How were the bills going to get paid? Is it really so wrong to take a drink during a period of extreme stress?

Drunks ask lousy questions.

During this entire time Betty remained unbelievably calm, even affectionate.

"I don't see how you can do anything but hate me," I said to her one morning after falling off the wagon once again.

"Would I hate you if you had infantile paralysis?"

"Maybe the damn thing *is* a form of infantile paralysis," I said wearily. "I certainly am paralyzed, and my behavior couldn't be more infantile."

"You'll get over it. In your own time in your own way, you'll get over it."

"How can you have such faith?"

"My father used to have a bad time with the booze, and he got over it fairly well. Lots of people do. Everybody with booze trouble doesn't have to end up in the gutter. Half the actors I've met are struggling with it and they go on year after year—"

"But you never yell at me or give me advice. Most people would tell a guy like me to go to AA."

"I've mentioned it. I have friends in AA. It can only help those who want to be helped in their way."

"I've always hated the idea of it. Being a drunk is bad enough without having to hang out with drunks all the time."

"Is that why you go to the Roma bar?"

"Ouch. Look, I know that booze is the biggest problem I've got and I'll handle it the best way I can . . ."

Soon after that Betty decided to teach dancing in our house. I worried that she'd given up on my ability to make a living, but she said that any woman in Ticonderoga needed some kind of work to keep her busy. Cleared of furniture, our living room soon was full of children learning ballet or adults hoping to learn the rhumba before taking a Caribbean cruise.

In the spring Betty's father came from Ireland. The big man with the pink face and the snow-white hair looked as powerful as ever, but he said that he felt too old for continuing his business in Ireland and planned to sell it. Since Betty and I had been married, he had singlehandedly built a little factory which manufactured steel furniture, including most of the bus seats used in Ireland. Its sale, he figured, would provide for his retirement, and at the age of seventy, what more did he need?

As soon as he saw our old barn, Bob's eyes really lit up. After inspecting it thoroughly, he pronounced it fundamentally sound. Checking it again the next day, Bob said he had a great idea. If he bought all the materials, would we let him convert the barn into a dance studio for

Betty and a small apartment for himself? Then Betty could put our furniture back into our living room, and he could have a place to stay when he wanted to visit us during his retirement.

His enthusiasm was catching and I saw nothing against it. After we'd gone to bed that night, Betty said, "I'm glad that you like dad's idea, but you know what's happening, don't you?"

"What?"

"Inevitably we're going to have him living here in his old age. I want that, but do you?"

"He wouldn't be much trouble down there in the barn."

"Don't kid yourself. Old people are always a responsibility. Who do you think will be taking care of him when he gets sick?"

"Well, I guess that's life," I replied, feeling rather noble.

"Then what do you think will happen if your mother wants to move in?"

"That may be too much life!"

In the morning I found Bob in the dining room making sketches of the way he was going to make the barn look. That afternoon I helped him order lumber and tools. The next morning he and I were both down there in the dusty old barn setting up temporary supports and dragging away the few rotten timbers he'd found. I also helped him take down the huge old barn doors to make room for new siding in the front of the building. When these tasks had been completed, the old Irishman picked up a hammer and announced that he would complete the rest of the project by himself.

He seemed to have made our decision for us.

While Bob was still working on the barn Rebecca graduated from nursing school. We attended the exercises at the Columbia School of Nursing, where nurses of all ages and sizes stood almost at attention, row on row, like a battalion standing ready to demolish the enemy. Somehow I'd forgotten how tiny Becky was. In all there were only about a hundred and ten pounds of her. With her pale blond hair drawn back and her petite figure prettily accentuated by her brand new uniform, she looked to me like an actress starring in one of the hospital dramas so popular on television.

Becky appeared in good spirits but, if only in my imagination, her candid blue eyes still looked hurt. Alone in our family she remained unmarried and she did not seem to have many close friends. Fresh from Westchester and Fairfield counties, she now proposed to live alone in New York and work in huge hospitals, some of which, I'd been told, made a battlefield seem peaceful in comparison. I worried about her and I was proud of her.

50

Bob went back to Dublin to wind up some business affairs, and not long after that, my sister telephoned from New York to say that she was deeply concerned about our mother. After more than twenty years of looking after her better than anyone else could, Chester had quit to take a job that paid much more. Unable to get along with the new people the employment agency sent to her apartment, mother was trying to live alone and cook for herself. Since she'd never been without help during the eighty-five years of her life, there was something rather gallant about this attempt to be self-sufficient, but she was so absent-minded about leaving pans on the stove that my sister worried she'd start a fire. Beyond that, she apparently had lost her ability to manage her personal finances. Her account at the bank was overdrawn, bills went unpaid and checks from her investment people mysteriously disappeared. Beyond that, mother still ranged all over Manhattan on shopping tours by taxi and afoot, and my sister lived in fear that she would be mugged. Her memory, hearing and vision were almost gone.

We were now faced, I realized, by a classic dilemma. Obviously mother couldn't continue to live alone much longer. She indignantly refused, my sister said, even to consider the idea of going to a "retirement home," a convalescent home, or any sort of institution. Perhaps she would consent to live with one of her children. Since my sister had long been caring for her husband's father, who was now in his nineties, my sister didn't see where she would find the strength or the room for another ancient invalid. My brother didn't have room in his small house for anyone but his wife, his four children, and himself. Apparently I was the only close relative in a position to help.

"If I have to leave New York, I suppose I can," mother said when I talked to her about all this, "but I *don't* want to live with you and Betty. I want a house of my own!"

When I told Betty, she said that she'd noticed a pretty little cottage for sale on land adjacent to the back of our property. I arranged for it and had an electric chair lift installed. In New York my sister had all mother's furniture and personal possessions shipped to Ticonderoga and took care of her until Betty and I had a chance to make the new cottage comfortable for her. Following my sister's advice, we put mother's old living room furniture in her new living room. The interior of the house, in fact, looked much like her apartment in New York when we had finished with it. Her familiar pictures on the walls and curtains contributed to the illusion.

I still am not sure whether the duplication of her apartment was a good idea or not. Apparently she'd suffered a series of strokes, for she was more confused than I had expected when she arrived with my sister. Sometimes she knew that she was in Ticonderoga, and sometimes she asked me to tell the doorman that she wanted a taxi to take her uptown. At still other times she thought it was summer and that she was in her cottage on the shores of Lake George.

"Those darn motorboats have been awfully loud today," she said to me once after some motorcycles had gone by.

We hired companions to take care of her during the days. It was harder to find someone with whom she could feel comfortable at nights. Finally Betty, Jessica and I contrived to sleep in the cottage's single extra bedroom.

My mother's main trouble was that, partly because of her poor vision, she could find nothing to occupy her mind all day and often could not sleep at night. The doctors provided pills and reassurance, but nothing seemed to help much.

I kept telling myself that old age is the natural result of a healthy life and should not be considered a tragedy.

A year went by, marked only by the acceleration of her decline. Usually she would take her electric lift to her bedroom at about seven in the evening, for she slept better early than late. Often she lost track of time an hour after she had gone to bed. Glancing at her clock, she would see that it was only a little after eight. Believing it to be morning, she would get up, take a bath and dress carefully. As she came rumbling down on her electric lift she would twist her thin lips into a smile and say, "Good morning, everybody! Good morning!"

Jessie said she didn't like her and mother asked me to discipline Jessie. They fought over the question of what television program was to be watched. Finally Betty installed a second television set upstairs.

Late one night I heard my mother muttering indistinguishable words in her bedroom. Hurrying there, I found her sitting up in her bed.

"I want to go under the water," she said.

"What do you mean?" I asked, feeling chilled.

Startled to find that I was there, she said, "I want to go under the water, the way my brother did in his submarine. I wish I could have gone under the ice with Sloan. Do you suppose that his submarine had windows?"

Not long after that we could not find mother when we came down to cook breakfast. Just as I was putting on my coat to look for her, she came in the front door looking more pleased than she had in weeks.

"Where have you been?" I asked her.

"Oh, just to see some people and places I loved," she replied with an enigmatic smile.

In the days that followed she talked to me a lot about aspects of the family history that she'd never mentioned before. We discussed her father, a naval officer who had survived the entire *Jeannette* Expedition, probably the most disastrous and torturous arctic expedition of all time, only to shoot himself after returning home.

"Why do you think he did it?" she asked me for the first time.

"Emotional exhaustion, maybe. And the snow had left him nearly blind. Anyway, he did much more in his short life than most people ever do."

"I wish, I wish he hadn't had to do it. Do you know that I can't even remember him? I was only a baby when he died."

For the first time I thought of my mother growing up without a father. She had always seemed so imperious looking that it was hard to imagine *her* in need of affection. Was her own childhood, often lonely, a reason why she had always seemed to me to be so stiff?

When mother wasn't talking with me, she often sat reading one or another of the three books my father had written. She had gone over them so often that now she hardly needed her glasses. Sometimes she would quote one of my father's poems for me and say, "I remember the day he wrote that one." There was a short pause before she added, "Isn't it *stupid* that he should die so young and I should go stumbling on forever?"

Betty brought in some tea and poured it.

"From the start I had a problem with my husband and brother," mother said. "I loved them both, but never in God's world were two men less alike. My brother had the blood of our father. He was an adventurer and an explorer from head to toe, a great, strong man with the fists and voice of the professional sailor he was. My husband, on the other hand, was gentle, a teacher and a poet. Both men were almost unbelievably handsome, in completely different ways. When I first met your father, while the two men were still getting along, I felt like a queen when I walked down Fifth Avenue between them."

"Why did they quarrel?" Betty asked.

"Well, when Sloan came to my wedding, he looked disheveled and he kept referring to my husband as 'that damn schoolteacher.' My husband was gentle, but he wasn't weak. At the reception they had words and Sloan left. Afterward there were arguments about money—my grandmother's finances concerned us both. Sloan kept being more and more rude, and sometimes he asked me to side with him in our various disputes against my husband. It was difficult, but I finally told him never to come to our house again. After all, I was married to my husband, not my brother..."

"I think that took some courage," Betty said.

"Well, I missed my brother and now I miss them both. Courage doesn't help much when you're old."

A few weeks later mother complained that she was all alone in the world. When I reminded her that she had three grown children and nine grandchildren, she said, "I don't care about the facts, I *still* feel all alone in the world."

In October she enjoyed being driven to see the fall foliage.

"I sometimes wish people were like maple leaves," she said. "They are more beautiful when they're dying than when they're young..."

Soon after we returned to our house, she complained that she felt pains all over her body. The next day I took her to the best of the local doctors. Except for minor disorders usual for aged women, he could find nothing wrong, a fact which appeared to disappoint my mother.

"When you're young, the doctors can fix anything," she said on the way home. "When you get old, you find that they can fix nothing, as though they'd forgotten everything they ever knew."

Sometimes she couldn't remember Betty's name or Jessica's, which bothered her less than her inability to retain the name of the minister at her church and of the ladies she met there.

"They'll think me *stupid*," she said. "When I was young I didn't consider myself anywhere near as beautiful as my cousin Ethel, but I knew I was much smarter. Now why is God making me both stupid and ugly at the same time?"

"Without memory, without eyes and without ears, without friends, what is the point of courage?" she asked me.

I should have had the sense to take her to a nursing home then, but once I mentioned the possibility, and she said, "I'd rather die first."

Late in October I got an idea for a novel that I wanted to explore. To work without interruption, I often got up early in the morning to go to my study in our house.

On Saturday mornings, when Jessie had no school, Betty and Jessie often slept late. If mother got up earlier than they, she seemed to enjoy getting herself a cup of coffee and a bowl of cereal in the kitchen.

On the morning of November 2, 1974, I got up at about six to finish an outline of what I hoped would be a new book. Having sat up late for a movie on television, Betty and Jessie slept until about a quarter to nine. Going to the kitchen, Betty could not find my mother, and a quick search of the small house showed that she wasn't there. Betty called me.

"She's probably gone out for another of her walks," I said, and hurried to our car.

I searched every place in Ticonderoga where I thought she might possibly be. The church was locked and the stores were empty at that time in the morning. Finally I consulted the taxi companies to see if she had decided to go somewhere outside of the village. One driver said he had taken her out to her cottage on Lake George on two occasions in the past, but not this morning.

I notified the police that my mother was missing. They asked if it was all right if they put that bulletin on the radio and I said yes.

Then, with a terrible feeling of inevitability, I drove to her summer cottage to see if somehow she had found someone to take her there. It was a cold, gray, windy November day. The big summer cottage was closed, and every door was locked. There was no sign of my mother near it. The gusts from the slate-colored lake felt like Greenland, and I hurried back to the car. At home, Betty said that there were no new developments. At first I thought there was no other place for me to search, but then I remembered the swimming beach near her house.

She was not on the beach. To get a better view of the whole recreational area there, I walked out on an old dock. That's when I saw a body in the water, floating or grounded only a few feet from shore. The body was face-down. It was that of a woman wearing a blue bathing suit and a white rubber cap. Jumping into the icy water, I turned the body over. It was my mother, but the face really was not my mother's face, it was only the grim mask of death. Picking my mother up for the first time in my life, I carried her ashore. When I put her down on a lawn, her body was so relaxed that it seemed to hug each contour of the earth. Never in life had I seen my poor insomniac mother achieve anything like this deep repose. The wind was very cold. Wishing that I had a blanket to cover her, I got in my car and drove off to tell the police.

The police soon found an independent taxi driver who had driven my mother to the swimming beach very early that morning. She had been well dressed and had acted normally as far as the cab driver had been able to see.

"We're going to have a meeting out here today," she had said, indicating one of the old buildings in the recreational area.

"It's a little early, isn't it?" the cab driver had replied before taking his pay and driving off.

The police found her clothes and bag where she had left them, not a hundred yards from the place where I had found her. The police also found her footprints, the only ones on the beach, heading toward the water. Apparently she had waded about fifty feet and had swum not much more than one hundred feet before the icy water closed in on her.

The doctor who had treated her only a few days before examined her now. The final verdict was that she had died of drowning caused by senile dementia.

Much later, when we distributed her personal effects to her children and grandchildren, I found a note in a jewel case that indicated she had planned her death right down to the detail of making sure what ring went to what granddaughter. The vision of her putting on her blue bathing suit in that icy wind and walking down that familiar beach to meet death will never leave me.

After the funeral many of her relatives and friends gathered at our old house. Turkeys, hams, and casseroles were brought by our neighbors, even those who hardly knew any of us. I crowded the dining room table with bottles of liquor. Soon the party became noisier than that which had celebrated my mother's eighty-fifth birthday. A few distant relatives kept pressing for details of her last minutes and my discovery of her. Two people wanted to know when the will would be read. A curious aspect of my mother was that though she had lived on fairly modest means after inflation set in and the excessive caution of her bankers withered her fortune, her manner was such that most people assumed she possessed enormous wealth. Her houses and apartment had such style when she was living in them that I, for one, thought they would do justice to a Morgan or a Rockefeller, but as soon as she died these places suddenly looked ordinary.

At my mother's funeral I got profoundly drunk. When I took my clothes off and sprawled on our bed, Betty rubbed me down as though I were an old boxer who had just finished a tough fight.

51

For three months I seemed to feel myself spinning downward. Reaching some strange, unfamiliar plateau of alcoholism, I found that shots of whiskey now tasted like nothing but warm water. A dozen of them tossed off in quick succession seemed to have no effect on me whatsoever until I tried to walk. Twenty minutes after having a drink, my whole body seemed to scream for another. At night I couldn't sleep for more than an hour.

Never before had I realized the meaning of the word "depression."

Although Betty was treating me with the skill of a loving nurse, I couldn't see how any woman could stand a man in my condition for long. Jessie avoided me whenever she could. My writing obviously was nowhere. With no income how could my family survive? With all the alcohol I was gulping, I didn't think that problems of my long-range financial survival were much to worry about, but the thought of leaving Betty and Jessie with so little was enough to make me take another drink.

Because I couldn't sleep at night, I often napped in the daytime. One afternoon I woke up to find two people standing by my bed. One was Betty and the other was my son.

"Hello, dad," David said in his usual tones of cheer.

"Hello, son."

"How are you feeling?" David asked.

"Not so good."

"What's the trouble?"

"The trouble, goddamn it, is that I have turned into a fucking drunk!"

"Well, let's do something about that. Do you want to take a little drive?"

The horror of being put into some sort of institution took hold of me.

"We'll be home tomorrow," Betty reassured me, "and I'm going to stay with you every inch of the way."

At the time I was so confused I could only follow my wife and son to the car. Later I found out that Betty had been so worried about me that she had called David, who was studying at Michigan State University. Flying home immediately, he had helped Betty to make a plan that started with taking me to the psychiatrist who'd seen me while I was living in Pound Ridge. On his advice I submitted to a complete physical examination and then graduated to a psychiatrist in Burlington, Vermont, who was close enough to Ticonderoga for me to see regularly.

"Lord," I said to the doctor who had helped me when I was in Pound Ridge, "I've been over this roller coaster about a hundred times and I still drink. Can't we try something new? If going to AA will help, I'm sure ready for that too."

"That can't hurt, but I have something that I want you to try first. It's called lithium. It doesn't help everybody, but sometimes the results are quite dramatic."

The doctor in Burlington saw me a few days later. "Well, I see that lithium has been recommended for you," he said, leafing through a sheaf of papers. "And I see that the physical examination shows that you're in fairly good shape for your age."

"Miracle of miracles," I said.

He smiled. He was a tall, thin young man who looked a little like my son.

"What do you know about lithium?" he asked.

"Nothing."

"It works best with people who have the bipolar disease, those who used to be called manic-depressives."

"Am I manic-depressive?"

"We don't use that term, but I would guess from the record that you are bipolar."

"Which is a nice way of saying that yes, I'm manic-depressive?"

"That term is much more scary than necessary. That's why it was dropped. The important thing is that you are the type that may find lithium most helpful."

"So it all boils down to the fact that I'm as lucky as all get-out to be a complete nut because we real bats get much more help from lithium than simple neurotics can—"

"I've never heard it put just that way, but there's some truth in it."

The doctor then went on to explain that lithium is, among other things, dangerous. An overdose can kill as surely as though it were a drug. Frequent blood tests are necessary to make sure dangerous levels aren't reached. When beginning the treatment, there can be dangerous side effects.

"It sounds kind of perilous," I said.

"Nowhere near as perilous as alcohol. Want to try it?"

Quickly he scribbled some notes on a prescription pad. As soon as I left his office, I headed for a drugstore. Lithium, it turned out, came in pills about the size of an aspirin tablet. They were a light gray-green in color and tasted bitter if I didn't swallow them quickly. They produced no high and no low. At first I could see little point in taking them, since they had no immediate effect at all.

"How soon will I know whether the lithium is working?" I asked the doctor.

"Oh, I think we should leave ourselves about eighteen months."

"*That* long?"

"Sometimes it works much quicker."

"How do you tell what's happening?"

"Aren't we mostly concerned with what we want not to happen?"

Since I still felt too shaky to do any writing, I worked around the house, painting walls and cleaning out the cellar. A month went by, then two.

"This damn lithium is stupid," I complained to Betty. "I feel exactly the way I did before I took it."

"Except, you're not drinking."

"No. I've had my share of that. I don't even think of it any more."

"No craving?"

"You know, the thought of the stuff actually nauseates me a little. I can't understand how I ever got hung up on it."

Betty lowered her head.

"What are you doing?" I asked.

"I am praying that this miracle lasts. And if it does, I am going to have a large altar made in this house so we can all bow down and worship lithium."

52

My mother has been dead a year now, and the lithium has helped me to forget about alcohol almost as long. No alcoholic can afford to believe that he has won a permanent victory over his treacherous enemy, but I've learned to be fairly confident I can hold my own with him.

Here in Ticonderoga it has been a beautiful summer. The keys of my typewriter have become unfrozen. What joy to get up in the morning and have so much work to do that I lack the minutes even to glance at the headlines in the *Times*!

The other day Rebecca came to visit us, bringing her new husband, John Moldover. They were married during my mother's last summer. A slender, dark-haired young man, John is a physician, a resident at Strong Memorial Hospital in Rochester, just a half-day's drive from Ticonderoga. They say they hope to stop by often. I don't think they will—both have such heavy schedules at the hospital. It's best to expect married children not to visit, and hope they surprise you once in a while.

Soon after Becky and John left, David stopped by. During the months when I had not been able to keep in close touch with him, he and Mary had been divorced—a case of mutually consenting adults, he said. Now he had his doctor's degree in zoology from Michigan State University, and a marvelous grant that enabled him to do research more or less on his own wherever he chose for two years.

"I thought you were a biologist," I said.

"A zoologist is a biologist who likes animals. That's me."

David had still more news. He'd met a girl, Anne Clark, who was just getting her doctor's degree in zoology from the University of Chicago. She had a grant to do research on primates in South Africa. He hoped to marry her soon and they planned to study the animals of Africa together. He sounded like he was finally on his way.

A few weeks later, Lisa called. She was pregnant! Her great job as an assistant curator at the National Portrait Gallery in Washington now seemed dull, and she could hardly wait, as she said, to do the mother bit.

I had hardly figured out what it was going to mean to me to become a grandfather when Becky called from Rochester. She was pregnant! Her new job with a kidney unit would have to go by the board.

As I had told Lisa, I told Becky that I was glad for her because, in my fifty-five years, nothing had given me such immediate and lasting pleasure as being the father of four children. This of course was true, except for the more intense joys Betty had given me. Those I did not feel called upon to explain to anyone.

Then summer was over and all the summer people went home. The maple trees burst into flame, and the grass, which had been sown where the old paper mill in Ticonderoga had previously stood, turned to gold.

On September 19th, our thirteenth wedding anniversary, Betty, Jessica and I drove to New York. The building where we had spent our first years together, opposite the back of Carnegie Hall, had been turned into an office building. The Harvard Club, however, was much the same, and we had lunch there together. While we were finishing our coffee an old friend in the publishing business stopped by. I asked him if he'd had any recent news about Jim Farrell.

"Somewhere I heard that he married a fine woman and is living in style," the publisher said. "I'm not sure that's true but I hope it is. I run into him at parties every once in a while, but the last time he was so surrounded by admirers I never got close to him."

"If you see him again, will you give him a message from me? Just say that his advice was good, and that I quit drinking before I burned the house down."

The publisher laughed and jotted my words down in a little notebook.

One of my anniversary presents to Betty was a suite of rooms for the night at the Algonquin Hotel, a more expensive hostelry than we had been using for a long time. As a surprise for me, she wore the pretty summer dress with the paisley pattern I had so admired the first day I met her in her apartment and drove her to see a little ketch made for circling the globe. It still fitted her perfectly and to me she still looked like a young girl in it.

"Somehow I've lived twice," I said. "My first life failed with my first marriage, and then you let me start all over again. I almost botched my second life up for fair, but I feel as though you are now letting me start one more time, still with a high school bride."

"Honey, I'm *not* your high school bride," she said. "I've been to graduate school..."

Later that night, she said, "What do you want to do with the rest of your life?"

"Only recently have I begun to believe I had a future."

"You've got to get out of that! You're only fifty-five years old, and I've never seen you look better. What's next? Do you want to keep on living in Ticonderoga?"

"I'm not sure we'll have enough money to do much more than that. Anyway, Ti is a good place to write. Now that they've taken the old mill down, it's a pretty little village. No strikes, no racial battles, no fear of being mugged in the streets—it still has a lot to recommend it."

"Ti is peace. But if you made a lot of money, would you want peace or excitement?"

"Excitement," I replied with a grin. "Where would you like to find it?"

"I'd like to go to Africa and see all the animals," Jessie interjected. "David told me I could visit him."

"Well, that's an idea," Betty replied. "*After* we see all the animals, I'd like to go to London for a while to gorge myself on the theaters. I think I have a friend over there who could get us free tickets. Then I'd like to drive all around Ireland again, following just the route we took before. If we did that, could you learn to say nothing whatsoever about religion?"

"I *never* talk about religion."

"Not here, but in Ireland you and dad often got going on it. I'm afraid the two of you will be bombed by one of our quaint, charming, blarney-talking old members of the IRA."

"Let's not go back to Ireland. A country where a man can't talk about religion is too heathen for even me."

"Where would you like to go, then? The Bahamas?"

"I don't think that you can ever really go back again."

"Where *do* you want to go?" Jessie demanded.

"I don't like traveling as a tourist much. First we should pick a place I might be able to write about. China would be my first choice, or maybe Russia. I've also thought of chartering an adequate vessel someday and going back to the South Sea Islands I saw during the war. Even Greenland still has some strange fascination for me."

"I thought you said you can't go back," Betty said.

"Well, the wartime places weren't filled with any deep personal emotions."

"David said I'd like South America," Jessie said.

439

On a brief field trip David had once visited Costa Rica and some of the countries near it. Having learned of the Pan American Highway system, he'd come back with notions of driving all the way from Ticonderoga to Brazil.

"There might be a book in that," I said, "if we lived through it..."

"How would you like to buy another boat?" Betty asked.

"The kind of boat I'd want would cost a couple of hundred thousand dollars these days," I said. "Even my dreams I try to keep within limits."

"Where would you go if you did have such a boat?" was Betty's next question.

"'A boy's will is the wind's will'—my father used to love that poem. I think about going back to sail again and running where the winds took me. That of course is an absurdly romantic notion, and anyway I'm no longer what you'd call a boy—not even an 'old boy.'"

After a while Betty put Jessica to bed in an adjoining room. When she came back, she lay down on the sofa. She put her head in my lap.

"I can live happily in Ticonderoga, if that's the way things work out," she said, "but I do love to dream of all the exciting places we can go in this world. Remember that old hotel in Siena and all the little shops lit only by lamps?"

I nodded, remembering.

She yawned, patting her lips with those long, delicate fingers which once had graced all those thousands and thousands of recipes and advertisements of cakes.... "When I was a model, they sold me out in parts like a chicken," she'd once said.

"What's your favorite place in the whole world?" she asked me after a pause.

"Here."

"Here?"

"Here is my favorite place and now is my favorite time."

Epilogue

Things I Have Learned in a Half Century of Living

1. Liquid shoe polish doesn't work.
2. A man who wants time to read and write must let the grass grow long.
3. Beware of people who are always well-dressed.
4. The hardest part of raising children is teaching them to ride bicycles. A father can run beside the bicycle or stand yelling directions while the child falls. A shaky child on a bicycle for the first time needs both support and freedom. The realization that this is what the child will always need can hit hard.
5. It's impossible to treat a child too well. Children are spoiled by being ignored too much or by harshness, not by kindness. Rich kids are often spoiled not by their toys and automobiles, but by parents who are too busy to pay much attention to them.
6. It is impossible to treat a woman too well.
7. It is impossible for a woman to treat me too well.
8. The definition of a beautiful woman is one who loves me.
9. Children go away and live their own lives, starting when they are about eighteen. Parents who accept this as a natural part of the order of things will see their grown children surprisingly often.
10. Friends are fun, but they are more dangerous than strangers. Strangers ask for a quarter for a cup of coffee, while friends ask for a thousand dollars, no questions asked if you're a *real* friend. Some friends also have a roving eye for your wife and your daughters.
11. Success in almost any field depends more on energy and drive than it does on intelligence. This explains why we have so many stupid leaders.
12. One way to teach children some hard truths about alcohol is to drink too much. None of my four children drinks and the reason, my eldest daughter reports, is that I taught them to hate the smell of the stuff. No one can say my youth was wasted.
13. The national bird of the United States should be the sparrow. Sparrows are proliferating all over the place, while the eagle is an endangered species. I for one don't want my country symbolized by a fierce loser.

441

14. Despite all the advice about how to achieve connubial bliss, a happy marriage is usually an unearned miracle. The reasons why some people get on so well together are as mysterious as the reasons why other people fight.

15. When things break around the house, call a handyman. No intelligent man is capable of fixing anything, unless he has made home repair his business.

16. It is impossible to lose weight lastingly and all diets are atrocious.

17. Either afloat or ashore, it is normal for everything to go wrong. No one should ever be surprised or unduly upset by foul-ups. They are a basic part of the human condition.

18. Many children should be treated as adults and many adults must be treated as children. Age has very little to do with capabilities.

19. When I was young I was briefly interested in politics, but politics soon bored me. I was interested in business for a long while, but business eventually bored me. Religion I never understood at all. Although it may sound sentimental, the only real meaning I have found in life has been in my wife and children. Without them I would be in more despair than a bankrupt millionaire.

—Sloan Wilson